Taking SIDES

Clashing Views on Controversial Issues in American History Volume I The Colonial Period to Reconstruction

Sixth Edition

Edited, Selected, and with Introductions by

Larry Madaras
Howard Community College
and
James M. SoRelle
Baylor University

The Dushkin Publishing Group, Inc.

To Maggie and Cindy

Photo Acknowledgments

Part 1   Library of Congress
Part 2   Library of Congress
Part 3   Museum of Art, Carnegie Institute, Pittsburgh, Pennsylvania
Part 4   Library of Congress

Cover Art Acknowledgment

Charles Vitelli

Manufactured in the United States of America

Sixth Edition

10   9   8   7   6   5   4   3

Library of Congress Cataloging-in-Publication Data

Main entry under title:
    Taking sides: clashing views on controversial issues in American history, volume 1, the
    colonial period to reconstruction/edited, selected, and with introductions by Larry Madaras
    and James M. SoRelle.—6th ed.
    Includes bibliographical references and index.
    1. United States—History. 2. United States—Historiography. I. Madaras, Larry, *comp*. II.
    SoRelle, James M., *comp*.
       E178.6.T35   973—dc20
       1-56134-326-9   94-48862

Printed on Recycled Paper

The Dushkin Publishing Group, Inc.

PREFACE

The success of the past five editions of *Taking Sides: Clashing Views on Controversial Issues in American History* has encouraged us to remain faithful to its original objectives, methods, and format. Our aim has been to create an effective instrument to enhance classroom learning and to foster critical thinking. Historical facts presented in a vacuum are of little value to the educational process. For students, whose search for historical truth often concentrates on *when* something happened rather than on *why*, and on specific events rather than on the *significance* of those events, *Taking Sides* is designed to offer an interesting and valuable departure. The understanding that the reader arrives at based on the evidence that emerges from the clash of views encourages the reader to view history as an *interpretive* discipline, not one of rote memorization.

As in previous editions, the issues are arranged in chronological order and can be easily incorporated into any American history survey course. Each issue has an issue *introduction*, which sets the stage for the debate that follows in the pro and con selections and provides historical and methodological background to the problem that the issue examines. Each issue concludes with a *postscript*, which ties the readings together, briefly mentions alternative interpretations, and supplies detailed *suggestions for further reading* for the student who wishes to pursue the topics raised in the issue.

Changes to this edition   In this edition we have continued our efforts to move beyond the traditionally ethnocentric and male-oriented focus of American history, both in terms of the issues and the authors selected to represent the clashing viewpoints. This edition depicts a society that benefited from the presence of Native Americans, African Americans, and women of various racial and ethnic origins. With this in mind, we present seven entirely new issues: *Were the English Colonists Guilty of Genocide?* (Issue 2); *Was There a Great Awakening in Mid-Eighteenth-Century America?* (Issue 5); *Was President Jefferson a Political Compromiser?* (Issue 8); *Did the Bank War Cause the Panic of 1837?* (Issue 9); *Was the Mexican War an Exercise in American Imperialism?* (Issue 12); *Have Historians Overemphasized the Slavery Issue as a Cause of the Civil War?* (Issue 14); and *Was Reconstruction a Success?* (Issue 17). Although Issue 12 is new, one reading has been retained from the previous edition because of its effectiveness. In addition, for the issue on Abraham Lincoln (Issue 16), one reading was changed to gain a fresh perspective. In all, there are 14 new selections.

A word to the instructor   An *Instructor's Manual With Test Questions* (multiple-choice and essay) is available through the publisher for the instructor using

Taking Sides in the classroom. Also available is a general guidebook, *Using Taking Sides in the Classroom*, which discusses methods and techniques for integrating the pro-con approach into any classroom setting.

Acknowledgments   Many individuals have contributed to the successful completion of this edition. We appreciate the evaluations submitted to The Dushkin Publishing Group by those who have used *Taking Sides* in the classroom. Special thanks go to those who responded with specific suggestions for this edition:

Bill Allison
Bowling Green State
    University

Joseph F. X. Cunningham
Seton Hall University

Jack Devine
Stockton State College

William P. Dionisio
Sacramento City College

John Whitney Evans
College of Saint Scholastica

James O. Farmer
University of South Carolina,
    Aiken

Maria-Christina García
Texas A & M University

Jeanine L. Grossman
Fullerton College

Richard P. Guidorizzi
Iona College

Ted M. Kluz
Auburn University,
    Montgomery

Joseph R. Mitchell
Howard Community College

Kristine A. Norvell
Moberly Area Community
    College

Elliot Pasternack
Middlesex County College

Kenneth E. Peters
University of South Carolina,
    Columbia

Neil Sapper
Amarillo College

Paul Simon
Xavier University

Michael Smuksta
Viterbo College

H. Micheal Tarver
Bowling Green State
    University

Lisa Thomason
University of North Texas

We are particularly indebted to Maggie Cullen, Cindy SoRelle, Barry A. Crouch, Virginia Kirk, Joseph and Helen Mitchell, and Jean Soto, who shared their ideas for changes, pointed us toward potentially useful historical works, and provided significant editorial assistance. Sandy Rohwein and Miriam Wilson (Howard Community College) performed indispensable typing duties connected with this project. Finally, we are sincerely grateful for the commitment, encouragement, and patience provided over the years by Mimi Egan, publisher for the Taking Sides series, and we appreciate the work of David Dean, administrative editor, David Brackley, copy editor, and the entire staff of The Dushkin Publishing Group.

Larry Madaras
Howard Community College

James M. SoRelle
Baylor University

CONTENTS IN BRIEF

CONTENTS

Professor of history Gary B. Nash argues that colonial American culture emerged from a convergence of three broad cultural traditions, which produced a unique triracial society in the New World. Professor of history David Hackett Fischer contends that the cultural traditions of the United States were transported by migrants from the British Isles.

David E. Stannard, a professor of American studies, insists that the colonists carried out a conscious militaristic policy to exterminate the Native Americans. Steven T. Katz, a professor of Near Eastern studies, contends that the Pequot War was not an instance of premeditated genocide carried out by New Englanders against the Native Americans.

Associate professor of history Carol F. Karlsen contends that the belief that women were evil existed implicitly at the core of Puritan culture, which is why alleged witches were generally seen as women. Professor of sociology Kai T. Erikson argues that the Puritan colonists' efforts to restore a common sense of mission, which they believed had eroded, produced the Salem witchcraft hysteria.

Professor of history Allan Kulikoff claims that Chesapeake slaves developed a distinct indigenous culture in the years between 1740 and 1790. Associate professor of history Jean Butenhoff Lee emphasizes the difficulties that slaves encountered in trying to create a stable community life in eighteenth-century Maryland.

Professor of history Patricia U. Bonomi defines the Great Awakening as a period of intense revivalistic fervor that spawned an age of contentiousness in the British mainland colonies. Professor of American history Jon Butler argues that the colonial revivalistic activities of the eighteenth century had a limited impact on pre-Revolutionary American society—not what can be accurately described as a "Great Awakening."

Pulitzer Prize–winning author Carl N. Degler argues that upper-middle-class colonists led a conservative American Revolution that left untouched the social class structure of an upwardly mobile people. Prize-winning historian Gordon S. Wood argues that the American Revolution was a far-reaching, radical event that produced a unique democratic society.

Political scientist John P. Roche believes that the Founding Fathers were superb democratic politicians who created a Constitution that supported the needs of the nation as well as the rights of the people. Political scientist Michael Parenti argues that the Constitution was framed by financially successful planters, merchants, and creditors in order to protect property rather than individuals.

Professor of history Morton Borden argues that President Thomas Jefferson was a pragmatic politician who placed the nation's best interests above those of the states. Professor of history Lance Banning argues that Jefferson was committed to westward expansion, the elimination of the national debt, and the eradication of the pro-British trade policies incurred by the Federalists.

Professor of history Thomas P. Govan argues that President Andrew Jackson's refusal to recharter the Bank of the United States seriously damaged the U.S. economy. Professor of history Peter Temin believes that international factors were far more important than Jackson's banking policies in determining fluctuations in the American economy in the 1830s.

Professor of history Alice Felt Tyler argues that American reformers in the antebellum period were seeking only to perfect human institutions. Professor of
history David J. Rothman contends that antebellum reformers established orphan asylums and reformatories primarily to enforce strict discipline among
those seeking refuge in these institutions.

Professor of history Albert J. Raboteau claims that the religious activities of
American slaves were characterized by institutional and personal independence. Professor of history John B. Boles asserts that the primary religious
experience of southern slaves occurred within a biracial setting in churches
dominated by whites.

Professor of history Ramón Eduardo Ruiz argues that for the purpose of conquering Mexico's northern territories, the United States waged an aggressive
war against Mexico. Professor of diplomatic history Norman A. Graebner argues that President James Polk pursued an aggressive policy that he believed
would lead to the acquisition of those territories without starting a war.

Professor of history Suzanne Lebsock believes that slaveholding women subverted the institution of slavery by protecting favored bond servants and
even by freeing slaves through their wills. Professor of southern history Elizabeth Fox-Genovese insists that the privileges associated with owning slaves
prevented these women from joining the ranks of the abolitionists.

Professor of history Joel H. Silbey argues that historians have overemphasized the sectional conflict over slavery as the primary event leading to the
Civil War. Professor of history Michael F. Holt maintains that both northern
Republicans and southern Democrats seized the slavery issue to reinvigorate
the loyalty of party voters.

Professor of history Richard E. Beringer and his colleagues believe that the
Confederacy lost the Civil War because it lacked the will to win. Pulitzer
Prize–winning historian James M. McPherson maintains that either side
might have emerged victorious in the Civil War but that three major campaigns won by the Union ultimately led to the Confederacy's defeat.

Professor of history Phillip Shaw Paludan believes that Abraham Lincoln is the greatest of all the American presidents because Lincoln succeeded in preserving the Union and freeing the slaves. Professor of English literature M. E. Bradford characterizes Lincoln as a cynical politician who abused his authority as president and as commander in chief during the Civil War.

Kenneth M. Stampp, a professor emeritus of history, argues that the period of Reconstruction after the Civil War produced many positive economic, political, and social outcomes. Professor of history Eric Foner maintains that radical rule was unsuccessful because it failed to secure civil, political, and economic rights for southern blacks.

INTRODUCTION

The Study of History

Larry Madaras
James M. SoRelle

In a pluralistic society such as ours, the study of history is bound to be a complex process. How an event is interpreted depends not only on the existing evidence but also on the perspective of the interpretor. Consequently, understanding history presupposes the evaluation of information, a task that often leads to conflicting conclusions. An understanding of history, then, requires the acceptance of the idea of historical relativism. Relativism means that redefinition of our past is always possible and desirable. History shifts, changes, and grows with new and different evidence and interpretations. As is the case with the law and even medicine, many beliefs that were unquestioned 100 or 200 years ago have been discredited or discarded since.

Relativism, then, encourages revisionism. There is a maxim that "the past must remain useful to the present." Historian Carl Becker argued that every generation should examine history for itself, thus ensuring constant scrutiny of our collective experience through new perspectives. History, consequently, does not remain static, in part because historians cannot avoid being influenced by the times in which they live. Almost all historians commit themselves to revising the views of other historians, synthesizing theories into macrointerpretations, or revising the revisionists.

SCHOOLS OF THOUGHT

Three predominant schools of thought have emerged in American history since the first graduate seminars in history were given at the Johns Hopkins University in Baltimore in the 1870s. The *progressive* school dominated the professional field in the first half of the twentieth century. Influenced by the reform currents of Populism, Progressivism, and the New Deal, these historians explored the social and economic forces that energized America. The progressive scholars tended to view the past in terms of conflicts between groups, and they sympathized with the underdog.

The post–World War II period witnessed the emergence of a new group of historians who viewed the conflict thesis as overly simplistic. Writing against the backdrop of the cold war, these *neoconservative* or *consensus* historians argued that Americans possess a shared set of values and that the areas of agreement within our nation's basic democratic and capitalistic framework were more important than the areas of disagreement.

In the 1960s, however, the civil rights movement, women's liberation, and the student rebellion (with its condemnation of the war in Vietnam) fragmented the consensus of values upon which historians and social scientists of the 1950s had centered their interpretations. This turmoil set the stage for the emergence of another group of scholars. *New Left* historians began to reinterpret the past once again. They emphasized the significance of conflict in American history, and they resurrected interest in those groups ignored by the consensus school. In addition, New Left historians critiqued the expansionist policies of the United States and emphasized the difficulties confronted by Native Americans, African Americans, women, and urban workers in gaining full citizenship status.

Progressive, consensus, and New Left history is still being written. The most recent generation of scholars, however, has focused upon social history. Their primary concern is to discover what the lives of "ordinary Americans" were really like. These new social historians have employed previously overlooked court and church documents, house deeds and tax records, letters and diaries, photographs, and census data to reconstruct the everyday lives of average Americans. Some have employed new methodologies such as quantification (enhanced by advancing computer technology) and oral history, while others have borrowed from the disciplines of political science, economics, sociology, anthropology, and psychology for their historical investigations.

The proliferation of historical approaches, which are reflected in the issues debated in this book, has had mixed results. On the one hand, historians have become so specialized in their respective time periods and methodological styles that it is difficult to synthesize the recent scholarship into a comprehensive text for the general reader. On the other hand, historians know more about the American past than at any other time in history. They dare to ask new questions or ones that previously were considered to be germane only to scholars in other social sciences. Although there is little agreement about the answers to these questions, the methods employed and issues explored make the "new history" a very exciting field to study.

The topics that follow represent a variety of perspectives and approaches. Each of these controversial issues can be studied for its individual importance to our nation's history. Taken as a group, they interact with one another to illustrate larger historical themes. When grouped thematically, the issues reveal continuing motifs in the development of American history.

NEW SOCIAL HISTORY: RED, WHITE, AND BLACK

Some of the most innovative historical research over the last 20 years has dealt with the colonial period (1607–1763) and reflects the interests of the new social historians. The work of several representatives of this group appear in this volume. For example, in Issue 1, Gary B. Nash sets the tone for the readings on early America when he suggests that colonial society must be studied from the perspective of the cultural convergence of three broad groups in North America—Native Americans, Europeans, and Africans. He takes issue with David Hackett Fischer, who insists that the seeds of American culture were sown solely by migrants from the British Isles.

Issue 2 evaluates the nature of the contact between Native Americans and English colonizers. David E. Stannard charges the colonists with carrying out a policy of wholesale genocide against the Atlantic coastal tribes they encountered over the course of the seventeenth century. Steven T. Katz, however, reexamines the 1636 Pequot War in New England and finds little evidence of a concerted program by the colonists to exterminate the Native Americans.

Two issues explore the field of women's history. In Issue 3, Carol F. Karlsen analyzes the relationship between the Salem witchcraft hysteria of 1692 and Puritan attitudes toward women. The belief that women were inherently evil, Karlsen concludes, operated at the core of Puritan culture. Such attitudes made it easy to blame women for disruptions in New England society. Kai T. Erikson, however, asserts that the witch trials provided a rallying point for Puritan settlers who sought to restore a common sense of mission to their community, which they felt had been seriously eroded.

Issue 13 looks at the alleged role played by southern slaveholding women in the abolition of slavery. Suzanne Lebsock believes that slaveholding women in the antebellum South possessed a value system distinct from their male counterparts, which enabled them to identify more closely with the subordinate status of their chattel servants and to subvert the institution of slavery. Elizabeth Fox-Genovese, however, insists that southern slaveholding women supported the slave system. Their desire for the privileges associated with owning slaves, combined with their own racism, prevented these women from abetting the abolitionist movement.

Within the past three decades, the perception of blacks in American history has changed dramatically. More consideration has been given to African Americans as active participants in the development of America, not simply as "victims" or "problems." In Issue 4, Allan Kulikoff concludes from his analysis of probate inventories, court depositions, and diaries and account books kept by whites that slaves in late eighteenth-century Maryland and Virginia had begun to develop a distinct African American culture. Jean Butenhoff Lee provides a direct rebuttal through her case study of demographic patterns in Charles County, Maryland.

Most scholars have offered generalizations about antebellum slavery based on an examination of the records of large plantation owners in the Deep South. Several have considered the impact of the slave system on the black community, including religious institutions. In Issue 11, Albert J. Raboteau argues that slaves were able to maintain their own systems of religious worship without interference from their masters. John B. Boles, on the other hand, insists that the primary religious activities in which slaves engaged operated in a biracial setting in the churches of their masters.

RELIGION, REVOLUTION, REFORM, RECONSTRUCTION

Beyond suggesting that much of the colonizing experiment in British North America was motivated by a search for religious freedom, many textbooks avoid extended discussions of religion as a force in history. In the last half-century, however, professional historians have assumed that the religious revivals of the mid-eighteenth century, known as the "Great Awakening," sparked intercolonial unity, and some have described this event as a direct precursor to the political upheaval of the American Revolution. In Issue 5, Patricia U. Bonomi offers a traditional view of the Great Awakening as a series of revivals occurring throughout the American colonies from 1739 to 1745 that generated a divisiveness that affected a number of religious, social, and political institutions. Jon Butler denies that any great unified revival movement emerged in the eighteenth century, and he suggests that historians abandon altogether the label "Great Awakening."

The nature of the American Revolution is considered in Issue 6. Carl N. Degler depicts the Revolution as a conservative movement that produced few social or economic changes. Gordon S. Wood, in contrast, views the American Revolution as a truly radical event that led to the adoption of a republican form of government in the newly established nation.

During the 1830s and 1840s, a wave of reformism swept across the United States. Various individuals and groups sought to strengthen the democratic experiment in the nation by ridding the society of its imperfections. Issue 10 explores the motivations behind these antebellum reforms. Alice Felt Tyler insists that humanitarian goals underlay antebellum reform impulses. David J. Rothman notes that by the 1850s institutions such as schools, prisons, and hospitals for the mentally ill were established to control the behavior of the nation's citizens. Rothman sees the emerging poorhouses as an attempt by the middle- and upper-class elite to control the social behavior of the masses and to maintain moral order in the United States.

The Civil War is one of the most frequently studied episodes in American history. In addition to the causes and consequences of the conflict between the North and the South, an enormous literature has emerged that addresses the military decisions and battlefield engagements that composed the war. In Issue 15, Richard E. Beringer et al. argue that a collective guilt over slavery seriously weakened Southern goals. Hence, despite adequate manpower and weaponry, the South lost because of an insufficient will to win. James M. McPherson focuses more directly upon actual military engagements and concludes that either side might have won the war. The ultimate success of the Union, he determines, was contingent upon winning three major campaigns between 1862 and 1864.

Perhaps no period of American history has been subjected to more myths than the era of Reconstruction. Only within the past 30 years has the traditional, pro-southern interpretation been revised in high school and college texts. In Issue 17, Kenneth M. Stampp presents a classic statement of Reconstruction revisionism. While recognizing the shortcomings of Republican rule in the South, Stampp nevertheless concludes that the radicals achieved their key political, economic, and social goals. In response, Eric Foner admits that the positive accomplishments of the era of Reconstruction should not be overlooked, but he reminds his readers that the more idealistic goals of full freedom and equality for the former slaves fell far short of the radicals' intended results.

POLITICS IN AMERICA

The American people gave legitimacy to their revolution through the establishment of a republican form of government. The United States has existed under two constitutions: The first established the short-lived confederation from 1781 to 1789; the second was written in 1787 and remains in effect over 200 years later. In Issue 7, John P. Roche contends that the drafters of the Constitution of the United States were democratic reformers. Michael Parenti, however, argues that the Constitution was an elitist document framed by a group of financially successful planters, merchants, and creditors in order to protect the rights of property over the rights and liberties of persons.

No discussion of American politics is complete without an examination of the lives of some of the key presidents. Two of the greatest (according to historians) were Thomas Jefferson and Abraham Lincoln. Issue 8 examines Jefferson's political ideology and seeks to determine the degree to which he adopted the programs of his Federalist opponents once he entered the White House. Was President Jefferson a political compromiser? Morton Borden characterizes Jefferson as a moderate and practical politician who placed the nation's best interests above those of the states. Lance Banning, on the other hand, portrays the Jeffersonian Republicans as ideologues who were committed to westward expansion and who sought to eliminate the national debt and pro-British trade policies incurred by their Federalist opponents.

Abraham Lincoln is the focus of Issue 16. Phillip Shaw Paludan presents an admiring vignette of the nation's 16th chief executive that defines Lincoln's greatness in terms of his ability to mobilize support for the interrelated goals of preserving the Union and emancipating the slaves of the South. The late M. E. Bradford's hostile analysis presents Lincoln as a cynical politician who precipitated the Civil War, abused executive authority, and feigned commitment to the freedmen.

Most historians have argued that Lincoln became president in 1860 because sectional conflicts over the slavery issue divided the nation and destroyed the second political party system, comprised of Whigs and Democrats, in the late 1850s. Political historians, employing a statistical analysis of election issues, voter behavior, and legislative patterns on the local, state, and national levels, however, have rejected or significantly modified the traditional emphasis on sectionalism in the 1850s. In Issue 14, Joel H. Silbey argues that historians have paid too much attention to the sectional conflict over slavery and have neglected to analyze local ethnocultural issues as keys to the Civil War. Michael F. Holt maintains that both Northern Republicans and Southern Democrats seized the slavery issue to highlight the sharp differences existing between them and thus to reinvigorate the loyalty of their traditional partisans.

ECONOMICS AND DIPLOMACY

As the United States began to develop a complex market economy, more sophisticated means of financing the development of larger agricultural units and factories became necessary. Alexander Hamilton, the nation's first secretary of the treasury, engineered through Congress the controversial First Bank of the United States, chartered in 1791. Allowed to lapse by the Democratic-Republicans on the eve of the War of 1812, the central banking system was revived in 1816 when Congress granted a 20-year charter for the Second Bank of the United States. This bank, of course, became the focal point for the controversy between Jacksonian Democrats and Whigs known as the "Bank War." Issue 9 discusses whether or not this controversy, which led to the demise of the Second Bank of the United States, might also have caused the economic collapse of the late 1830s. Thomas P. Govan argues that President Andrew Jackson's refusal to recharter the Second Bank of the United States, while politically popular, harmed the long-term economic growth of the United States. Peter Temin claims that international factors, such as changes in the monetary policies of the Bank of England, the supply of silver from Mexico, and the price of southern cotton, were far more important than Jackson's assault on the bank in creating serious fluctuations in the American economy during the 1830s.

The discussion of antebellum foreign policy in Issue 12 concerns both U.S. diplomatic relations with the rest of the world and America's self-perception within the community of nations. Did the U.S. government conceive of its power as continental, hemispheric, or worldwide? And what were the consequences of these attitudes? Ramón Eduardo Ruiz argues that the United States waged a racist and imperialistic war against Mexico for the purpose of conquering what became the American Southwest. Norman A. Graebner believes that President James K. Polk pursued an aggressive (but not imperialistic) policy that would force Mexico to recognize the United States' annexation of Texas and to sell New Mexico and California to her northern neighbor without starting a war.

CONCLUSION

The process of historical study should rely more on thinking than on memorizing data. Once the basics (who, what, when, where) are determined, historical thinking shifts to a higher gear. Analysis, comparison and contrast, evaluation, and explanation take command. These skills not only increase our knowledge of the past, but they also provide general tools for the comprehension of all the topics about which human beings think.

The diversity of a pluralistic society, however, creates some obstacles to comprehending the past. The spectrum of differing opinions on any particular subject eliminates the possibility of quick and easy answers. In the final analysis, conclusions often are built through a synthesis of several different interpretations, but, even then, they may be partial and tentative.

The study of history in a pluralistic society allows each citizen the opportunity to reach independent conclusions about the past. Since most, if not all, historical issues affect the present and future, understanding the past becomes essential to social progress. Many of today's problems have a direct connection with the past. Additionally, other contemporary issues may lack obvious direct antecedents, but historical investigation can provide illuminating analogies. At first it may appear confusing to read and to think about opposing historical views, but the survival of our democratic society depends on such critical thinking by acute and discerning minds.

PART 1

Colonial Society

Colonial settlement took place in the context of conditions that were unique to that time and place. The ethnic identity of the colonists affected their relations with Native Americans and Africans, as well as with each other. Many of the attitudes, ideals, and institutions that emerged from the colonial experience served the early settlers well and are still emulated today. Others, such as slavery and racism, have left a less positive legacy.

- Was Colonial Culture Uniquely American?

- Were the English Colonists Guilty of Genocide?

- Was the Salem Witchcraft Hysteria Caused by a Fear of Women?

- Did American Slaves Develop a Distinct African American Culture in the Eighteenth Century?

- Was There a Great Awakening in Mid-Eighteenth-Century America?

ISSUE 1

Was Colonial Culture Uniquely American?

YES: Gary B. Nash, from *Race, Class, and Politics: Essays on American Colonial and Revolutionary Society* (University of Illinois Press, 1986)

NO: David Hackett Fischer, from *Albion's Seed: Four British Folkways in America* (Oxford University Press, 1989)

ISSUE SUMMARY

YES: Professor of history Gary B. Nash argues that colonial American culture emerged from a convergence of three broad cultural traditions—European, Native American, and African—which produced a unique triracial society in the New World.

NO: Professor of history David Hackett Fischer contends that the cultural traditions of colonial America and the United States were derived from English folkways transported by migrants from four different regions in the British Isles.

Michel-Guillaume Jean de Crevecoeur was a French immigrant who became a naturalized subject of the colony of New York in 1764. He married an American woman, and the couple settled on a comfortable estate in New York. In 1782, Crevecoeur published a volume entitled *Letters from an American Farmer* in which he attempted to analyze the culture and national character of his adopted land. In probing the unique quality of the American, Crevecoeur wrote: "What then is the American, this new man? He is either an European, or the descendent of an European, hence that strange mixture of blood, which you will find in no other country. . . . *He* is an American who, leaving behind him all his ancient prejudices and manners, receives new ones from the new mode of life he has embraced, the new government he obeys, and the new rank he holds. He becomes an American by being received in the broad lap of our great *Alma Mater.* Here individuals of all nations are melted into a new race of men, whose labors and posterity will one day cause great changes in the world." A half century later another Frenchman, the aristocratic Alexis de Tocqueville, explored the distinctiveness of America by emphasizing the twin components of democracy and equality. But it was an American historian, Frederick Jackson Turner, who captured the attention of generations of scholars and students by characterizing the unique qualities of life in America and distinguishing that life from Old World culture. For Turnerians, it was the American frontier experience that was most responsible for Crevecoeur's "new man."

Historians continue to express interest in the nature of American culture as they explore the Old World and New World roots of the American people and the society they created beginning in the seventeenth century. Just how new was that early American culture? How much did it depart from the cultural heritage of those tens of thousands of immigrants who arrived in England's North American colonies prior to the American Revolution? Modern-day students who are unfamiliar with the writings of Crevecoeur, Tocqueville, and Turner should find it worthwhile to explore the basic components of the American culture that emerged in the colonial period. By understanding the nature of that culture, Americans obtain a better grasp of who they are.

For Gary B. Nash, the main problem in developing a clear picture of colonial American culture has been the tendency of past generations of scholars to operate from a male-dominated and highly ethnocentric framework. In Nash's view, those who ignore important segments of the population that played significant roles in colonial social development fail to describe that development accurately. His essay makes clear that while white male Europeans were prominent in carving a cultural base for the American people, they were assisted by their female counterparts, as well as Native Americans and Africans of both sexes. That culture was unique, he suggests, primarily because it was a triracial composite, not one simply transferred intact from Europe.

Not all scholars, however, agree with this notion of American distinctiveness. In the nineteenth century, historian Herbert Baxter Adams and his followers insisted that American culture was best understood as an extension of England or Europe. Contemporary historian David Hackett Fischer presents an intriguing modification of this so-called germ theory. According to Fischer, American society was germinated by four waves of British immigrants, each of which brought with them the shared characteristics of the English as well as the distinctive folkways of their respective regions. These four different sets of folkways, he concludes, account for the distinctiveness of regional cultures in the New World colonies, but each remains a direct product of English culture. In his essay, Fischer focuses upon the different ways in which the concept of freedom is defined in American society. These differences, says Fischer, reflect the varying "freedom ways" of immigrants from eastern England, the southern and western counties, the North Midlands, and the borders of North Britain and northern Ireland, who settled in British North America between 1629 and 1775.

YES   Gary B. Nash

THE SOCIAL DEVELOPMENT OF
COLONIAL AMERICA

The history of social development in colonial America—portrayed in this paper primarily as the history of social relations between groups of people defined by race, gender, and class—is in glorious disarray. Disarray because all of the old paradigms have collapsed under the weight of the last generation of scholarship. Glorious because a spectacular burst of innovative scholarship, the product of those who have crossed disciplinary boundaries, transcended filiopietism, and been inspired in the best sense by the social currents of their own times, has left us with vastly more knowledge of the first century and a half of American history than we ever had before....

So much creative work has been done during the last generation that it may seem that the time has arrived to build new models of social development. Yet this still may be premature because in spite of their many virtues, the innovative studies of the past two decades are so male-centered and oblivious to the black and native American peoples of colonial society that any new synthesis would necessarily be constructed with materials that present a skewed and incomplete picture of the social process in the prerevolutionary period.

If social development is defined as changing social relations between different groups in society, then the foundation of any such study must be rigorous analysis of the structural arrangements that did not strictly govern most human interaction but set the boundaries for it in the preindustrial period, as between masters and slaves, men and women, parents and children, employers and employees. Those relationships, moreover, must be examined within the context of a triracial society. This marks a fundamental difference between social development in England and America or in France and America. Of course other differences existed as well, but perhaps none was so great as that produced by the convergence of three broad cultural groups on the North American coastal plain in the seventeenth and eighteenth centuries. Some of the best work in colonial social history has been unmindful of this, drawing conceptually on European historical studies as if the colonies were pure offshoots of English society.... We must regard the social development of colonial America as *sui generis* because of the triracial environment in which most colonists lived their lives. This racial intermingling had profound effects on the social formation of the colonies....

NATIVE AMERICANS

Ideally, a discussion of the role of native American societies in the social development of eastern North America should be regionally organized because there was no unified "Indian" experience and the various tribal histories that ethnohistorians have reconstructed are closely related to the histories of European colonizers in particular areas. But space limitations permit only some general remarks about the underdeveloped field of native American history and its connection to the history of the colonizers. It is important to differentiate between coastal and interior tribes: even though disease and warfare thoroughly ravaged the numerous seaboard tribes by the third generation of settlement in every colony, these small societies profoundly affected the shaping of settler communities.

The process of decimation, dispossession, and decline among the Indian societies of the coastal areas occurred in different ways during the first century of European colonization. Everywhere that Europeans settled, a massive depopulation occurred as the invaders' diseases swept through biologically defenseless native societies. Yet this rarely broke the resistance of the native peoples. In New England that occurred only after the stronger coastal tribes, such as the Wampanoags and Narragansetts, finally succumbed in a long war of attrition to an enemy who sought no genuine accommodation. In Virginia and Maryland the tidewater tribes genuinely strove for ac-

commodation following their unsuccessful resistance movements of 1622 and 1644. But, as in New England, their inability to function in any way that served European society finally led to conflict initiated by whites. Even as friendly colonized people they were obstacles in the path of an acquisitive and expanding plantation society. In South Carolina it was not dead Indians but Indians alive and in chains that benefited the white settlers. The build-up of the colonizer population was slow enough, and the desire among the Indians for trade goods intense enough, that the white Carolinians, most of them transplanted from Barbados, where they had learned to trade in human flesh, could lure the coastal tribes into obliterating each other in the wars for slaves.

The result was roughly the same in all the colonies along the seaboard. By the 1680s in the older colonies and by the 1720s in the new ones the coastal tribes were shattered. Devastated by disease and warfare, the survivors either incorporated themselves as subjects of stronger inland groups or entered the white man's world as detribalized servile dependents. Their desire for European trade goods, which kept them in close contact with European colonizers, and the persistence of ancient intertribal hostilities, which thwarted pan-tribal resistance, sealed their fate once the growth of the settler population made it apparent that their value as trading partners was incidental in comparison with the value of the land that their destruction would convert to European possession.

Although they were defeated, the coastal cultures served a crucial function for tribes farther inland. Their prolonged resistance gave interior societies time to adapt to the European presence and to devise strategies of survival as the white societies grew in size and strength. "People like the Iroquois," T.J.C. Brasser has pointed out, "owed a great deal to the resistance of the coastal Algonkians, and both peoples were well aware of this." The coastal tribes provided a buffer between the interior Indians and the Europeans, and when the coastal tribes lost their political autonomy, their remnants were often incorporated into the larger inland tribes. This was important in the much stronger opposition that the Iroquois, Cherokees, and Creeks offered to European encroachment—a resistance so effective that for the first century and a half of European settlement the white newcomers were restricted to the coastal plain, unable to penetrate the Appalachians, where the interior tribes, often allied with the French, held sway.

During the first half of the eighteenth century the interior Indian societies demonstrated their capacity for adapting to the presence of Europeans and for turning economic and political interaction with them to their own advantage. Drawing selectively from European culture, they adopted through the medium of the fur, skin, and slave trade European articles of clothing, weapons, metal implements, and a variety of ornamental objects. To some extent this incorporation of material objects robbed the Indians of their native skills. But agriculture, fishing, and hunting, the mainstays of Indian subsistence before the Europeans came, remained so thereafter. European implements such as the hoe only made Indian agriculture more efficient. The knife and fishhook enabled the natives to fish and trap with greater intensity in order to obtain the commodities needed in the barter system. However, pottery making declined, and the hunter became more dependent upon the gun.

Yet, interaction with European societies over many generations sowed seeds of destruction within tribal villages. It is not necessary to turn Indians into acquisitive capitalists to explain their desire for trade goods. They did not seek guns, cloth, kettles, and fishhooks out of a desire to become part of bourgeois culture, accumulating material wealth from the fur trade, but because they recognized the advantages, within the matrix of their own culture, of goods fashioned by societies with a more complex technology. The utility of the Europeans' trade goods, not the opportunities for profit provided by the fur trade, drew native Americans into it, and from the Indian point of view, trade was carried on within the context of political and social alliance.

Nonetheless, the fur trade required native Americans to reallocate their human resources and reorder their internal economies. Subsistence hunting turned into commercial hunting, and consequently males spent more time away from the villages trapping and hunting. Women were also drawn into the new economic organization of villages, for the beaver, marten, or fox had to be skinned and the skins scraped, dressed, trimmed, and sewn into robes. Among some tribes the trapping, preparation, and transporting of skins became so time-consuming that food resources had to be procured in trade from other tribes. Ironically, the reorientation of tribal economies toward the fur trade dispersed villages and weakened the localized basis of clans and lineages. Breaking up in order to be nearer the widely dispersed trapping grounds, Indian villages moved closer to the nomadic woodland existence that Europeans had charged them with at the beginning of contact.

Involvement in the fur trade also altered the relationship of native Americans to their ecosystem. The tremendous destruction of animal life triggered by the advent of European trade undermined the spiritual framework within which hunting had traditionally been carried out and repudiated the ancient emphasis on living in balance with the natural environment. Trade also broadened vastly the scale of intertribal conflict. With Europeans competing for client tribes who would supply furs to be marketed throughout Europe, Indian societies were sucked into the rivalry of their patrons. As furs became depleted in the hunting grounds of one tribe, they could maintain the European trade connection only by conquering more remote tribes whose hunting grounds had not yet been exhausted or by forcibly intercepting the furs of other tribes as they were transported to trading posts. Thus, the Iroquois decimated the Hurons of the Great Lakes region in the mid-seventeenth century as part of their drive for beaver hegemony.

While the interior tribes were greatly affected by contact with the colonizers, they nonetheless rejected much of what the newcomers presented to them as a superior way of life. Tribes such as the Iroquois, Creeks, and Cherokees were singularly unimpressed with most of the institutions of European life and saw no reason to replace what they valued in their own culture with what they disdained in the culture of others. This applied to the newcomers' political institutions and practices, system of law and justice, religion, education, family organization, and child-rearing practices. Many aspects of Indian life were marked by cultural persistency in the long period of interaction with Europeans. Indian societies incorporated what served them well and rejected what made no sense within the framework of their own values and modes of existence.

Despite their maintenance of their traditional culture in many areas of life, the native Americans' involvement in the European trade network hastened the spread of epidemic diseases, raised the level of warfare, depleted ecozones of animal life, and drew Indians into a market economy that over a long period of time constricted their economic freedom. The interior tribes reorganized productive relations within their own communities to serve a trading partner who, through the side effects of trade, became a trading master.

Social development within the British mainland colonies proceeded in some unexpected ways because of the Indian presence. Unable to coordinate themselves militarily and politically in the first 150 years of settlement, English colonizers were unable to conquer or dislodge from their tribal homelands—as did their Spanish counterparts to the south—the powerful interior native American societies. Hence, the settler's societies, restricted to the coastal plain, developed differently than if they had been free to indulge their appetite for land and their westward yearning. Higher mortality rates associated with the spread of epidemic diseases in more densely settled areas, the rise of tenancy in rural areas, underemployment in the cities at the end of the colonial period, the decline of indentured servitude because of the growing pool of landless free laborers, and the rise of class tensions in older seaboard communities are some of the social phenomena that may be attributed in part to the limitations placed upon westward movement by the controlling hand of the major eastern tribes in the trans-Allegheny and even the Piedmont region. The native American was also of primary importance in forging an "American" identity among English, Scotch-Irish, German, and other European immigrants in North America. In their relations with the native people of the land the colonizers in British North American served a long apprenticeship in military affairs. Far more populous than the settlers of New France and therefore much more covetous of Indian land, they engaged in hundreds of military confrontations ranging from localized skirmishes to large-scale regional wars. The allegiance of the diverse immigrants to the land, the annealing of an American as distinct from an English identity, had much to do with the myriad ways in which the colonists interacted with a people who were culturally defined as "the others" but were inextricably a part of the human landscape of North America.

AFRO-AMERICANS

Unless we wish to continue picturing some one million Africans brought to or born in America before the Revolution as mindless and cultureless drones, it will be necessary to push forward recent work on the social development of black society and then to incorporate this new corpus of scholarship into an overall analysis of colonial social development. It bears noting that a large majority of the persons who crossed the Atlantic to take up life in the New World in the three hundred years before the American Revolution were Africans. Their history is still largely untold because so much attention has been paid to the kind of slave systems Europeans fashioned in the New World—the black codes they legislated, their treatment of slaves, the economic development they directed— that the slaves themselves, as active participants in a social process, are often forgotten.

In attempting to remedy this gap, historians have borrowed heavily from the work of anthropologists. The encounter model of Sidney Mintz and Richard Price, developed with reference to the Caribbean world, is especially useful because it explores how Africans who found themselves in the possession of white masters five thousand miles from their homeland created institutions and ways of life that allowed them to live as satisfactorily as possible under the slave regimen imposed upon them by the master class. In their New World encounter with European colonizers the problem was not one of merging a West African culture with a European culture, because the human cargoes aboard slave ships were not a single collective African people but rather a culturally heterogenous people from many tribes and regions. Hence, arriving slaves did not form "communities" of people at the outset but could only become communities through forging a new life out of the fragments of many old cultures combined with elements of the dominant European culture that now bounded their existence. "What the slaves undeniably shared at the outset," according to Mintz and Price, "was their enslavement; all—or nearly all —else had to be created by them."

Major strides have been taken in tracing this process of social adaptation in the Chesapeake region and along the rice coast of South Carolina and Georgia, though much remains to be done. Already, it is apparent that in this process of adaptation there was a premium on cultural innovations and creativity, both because slaves had to adjust rapidly to the power of the master class and because of the initial cultural heterogeneity of the Africans. Unlike the European colonizers, Africans were immediately obliged "to shift their primary cultural and social commitment from the Old World to the New." This required rapid adaptation, learning new ways of doing things that would ensure survival. It is not surprising, therefore, that Africans developed local slave cultures rather than a unified Afro-American culture. In adapting to North American slavery, they adopted "a general openness to ideas and usages from other cultural traditions, a special tolerance (within the West African context) of cultural differences." Of all the people converging in seventeenth- and eighteenth-century North America, the Africans, by the very conditions of their arrival, developed the greatest capacity for cultural change.

The complexity of black culture in America cannot be understood without considering the evolution of distinct, regional black societies as they developed over the long course of slavery. One of the accomplishments of the new social historians of the colonial South is to have broken much new ground on the life cycle, family formation, and cultural characteristics of the black population, which was increasingly creole, or American-born, as the eighteenth century progressed. This work makes it possible already to go beyond earlier studies of slave life in the colonies, which were based largely on studies of nineteenth-century sources, when discussing the development of Afro-American society in the eighteenth-century colonies.

How much of African culture survived under eighteenth-century slavery is an oft-debated question. There can be little doubt that slave masters were intent on obliterating every Africanism that reduced the effectiveness of slaves as laborers and that they had some success in this. It is also true that slavery eliminated many of the cultural differences among slaves, who came from a wide variety of African cultural groups—Fulanis, Ibos, Yorubas, Malagasies, Ashantis, Mandingos, and others. At the same time, it must be remembered that throughout the eighteenth century, unlike the nineteenth, large numbers of new Africans arrived each year. Slave importations grew rapidly in the eighteenth century, so that probably never more than half the adult slaves were American-born. This continuous infusion of African culture kept alive many of the elements that would later be transmuted almost beyond recognition. Through fashioning their own distinct culture within the limits established by the rigors of the slave system, blacks were able to forge their own religious forms, their own music and dance, their own family life, and their own beliefs and values. All of these proved indispensable to survival in a system of forced labor. All were part of the social development of black society. And all affected the social development of white society as well.

WOMEN

One final aspect of social development, occasionally alluded to in this essay but indispensable to the work that lies ahead, concerns social relations defined by gender. In the last ten years, and especially in the last four or five, a wave of new work has appeared, some of it defined as women's history and some as demographic or family history. This work shows how rich the possibilities are for those who wish to study the lives of women and female-male relationships. It is crucial to the construction of new paradigms of social development that these studies of women's productive and reproductive lives, which need to be studied with class, racial, and regional differences in mind, be pushed forward at an accelerated pace and then integrated with the studies of the much better understood male half of the population. It is out of the convergence of the already completed demographic and community studies and the studies of women, blacks, and native Americans still remaining to be done that a new understanding of the social development of colonial America will emerge.

NO

David Hackett Fischer

ALBION'S SEED

In Boston's Museum of Fine Arts, not far from the place where English Puritans splashed ashore in 1630, there is a decidedly unpuritanical painting of bare-breasted Polynesian women by Paul Gauguin. The painting is set on a wooded riverbank. In the background is the ocean, and the shadowy outline of a distant land. The canvas is crowded with brooding figures in every condition of life—old and young, dark and fair. They are seen in a forest of symbols, as if part of a dream. In the corner, the artist has added an inscription: "D'ou venons nous? Qui sommes nous? Ou allons nous?"

That painting haunts the mind of this historian. He wonders how a Polynesian allegory found its way to a Puritan town which itself was set on a wooded riverbank, with the ocean in the background and the shadow of another land in the far distance. He observes the crowd of museumgoers who gather before the painting. They are Americans in every condition of life, young and old, dark and fair. Suddenly the great questions leap to life. Where do *we* come from? Who are we? Where are we going?

The answers to these questions grow more puzzling the more one thinks about them. We Americans are a bundle of paradoxes. We are mixed in our origins, and yet we are one people. Nearly all of us support our republican system, but we argue passionately (sometimes violently) among ourselves about its meaning. Most of us subscribe to what Gunnar Myrdal called the American Creed, but that idea is a paradox in political theory. As Myrdal observed in 1942, America is "conservative in fundamental principles... but the principles conserved are liberal and some, indeed, are radical."

We live in an open society which is organized on the principle of voluntary action, but the determinants of that system are exceptionally constraining. Our society is dynamic, changing profoundly in every period of American history; but it is also remarkably stable. The search for the origins of this system is the central problem in American history....

The organizing question here is about what might be called the determinants of a voluntary society. The problem is to explain the origins and stability of a social system which for two centuries has remained stubbornly democratic in its politics, capitalist in its economy, libertarian in its laws, individualist in its society and pluralistic in its culture.

Much has been written on this subject —more than anyone can possibly read. But a very large outpouring of books and articles contains a remarkably small number of seminal ideas. Most historians have tried to explain the determinants of a voluntary society in one of three ways: by reference to the European culture that was transmitted to America, or to the American environment itself, or to something in the process of transmission.

During the nineteenth century the first of these explanations was very much in fashion. Historians believed that the American system had evolved from what one scholar called "Teutonic germs" of free institutions, which were supposedly carried from the forests of Germany to Britain and then to America. This idea was taken up by a generation of historians who tended to be Anglo-Saxon in their origins, Atlantic in their attitudes and Whiggish in their politics. Most had been trained in the idealist and institutional traditions of the German historical school.

For a time this Teutonic thesis became very popular—in Boston and Baltimore. But in Kansas and Wisconsin it was unkindly called the "germ theory" of American history and laughed into oblivion. In the early twentieth century it yielded to the Turner thesis, which looked to the American environment and especially to the western frontier as a way of explaining the growth of free institutions in America. This idea appealed to scholars who were middle western in their origins, progressive in their politics, and materialist in their philosophy.

In the mid-twentieth century the Turner thesis also passed out of fashion. Yet another generation of American historians became deeply interested in processes of immigration and ethnic pluralism as determinants of a voluntary society. This third approach was specially attractive to scholars who were not themselves of Anglo-Saxon stock. Many were central European in their origin, urban in their residence, and Jewish in their religion. This pluralistic "migration model" is presently the conventional interpretation.

Other explanations have also been put forward from time to time, but three ideas have held the field: the germ theory, the frontier thesis, and the migration model.

This [essay] returns to the first of those explanations, within the framework of the second and third. It argues a modified "germ thesis" about the importance for the United States of having been British in its cultural origins. The argument is complex, and for the sake of clarity might be summarized in advance. It runs more or less as follows.

During the very long period from 1629 to 1775, the present area of the United States was settled by at least four large waves of English-speaking immigrants. The first was an exodus of Puritans from the east of England to Massachusetts during a period of eleven years from 1629 to 1640. The second was the migration of a small Royalist elite and large numbers of indentured servants from the south of England to Virginia (ca. 1642–75). The third was a movement from the North Midlands of England and Wales to the Delaware Valley (ca. 1675–1725). The fourth was a flow of English-speaking people from the borders of North Britain and northern Ireland to the

Appalachian backcountry mostly during the half-century from 1718 to 1775.

These four groups shared many qualities in common. All of them spoke the English language. Nearly all were British Protestants. Most lived under British laws and took pride in possessing British liberties. At the same time, they also differed from one another in many other ways: in their religious denominations, social ranks, historical generations, and also in the British regions from whence they came. They carried across the Atlantic four different sets of British folkways which became the basis of regional cultures in the New World.

By the year 1775 these four cultures were fully established in British America. They spoke distinctive dialects of English, built their houses in diverse ways, and had different methods of doing much of the ordinary business of life. Most important for the political history of the United States, they also had four different conceptions of order, power and freedom which became the cornerstones of a voluntary society in British America.

Today less than 20 percent of the American population have any British ancestors at all. But in a cultural sense most Americans are Albion's seed, no matter who their own forebears may have been [Albion was the first recorded name for the island of Britain]. Strong echoes of four British folkways may still be heard in the major dialects of American speech, in the regional patterns of American life, in the complex dynamics of American politics, and in the continuing conflict between four different ideas of freedom in the United States. The interplay of four "freedom ways" has created an expansive pluralism which is more libertarian than any unitary culture alone could be. That is the central

thesis of this [essay]: the legacy of four British folkways in early America remains the most powerful determinant of a voluntary society in the United States today....

MASSACHUSETTS FREEDOM WAYS: THE PURITAN IDEA OF ORDERED LIBERTY

The public life of New England was... shaped by an idea of liberty which was peculiar to the Puritan colonies. To understand its nature, one might begin with the word itself. From the generation of John Winthrop (1558–1649) to that of Samuel Adams (1722–1803), the noun "liberty" was used throughout New England in at least four ways which ring strangely in a modern ear.

First, "liberty" often described something which belonged not to an individual but to an entire community. For two centuries, the founders and leaders of Massachusetts wrote of the "liberty of New England," or the "liberty of Boston" or the "liberty of the Town." This usage continued from the great migration to the War of Independence and even beyond. Samuel Adams, for example, wrote more often about the "liberty of America" than about the liberty of individual Americans.

This idea of collective liberty, or "publick liberty" as it was sometimes called, was thought to be consistent with close restraints upon individuals. In Massachusetts these individual restrictions were numerous, and often very confining. During the first generation, nobody could live in the colony without approval of the General Court. Settlers even of the highest rank were sent prisoners to England for expressing "divers dangerous opinions," or merely because the Court judged them to be "persons unmeet to inhabit here." Others were not allowed to move within the colony except by special permission of the General Court. For a time, the inhabitants of Dedham, Sudbury and Concord were forbidden to move out of their towns, because the General Court believed that those frontier settlements were dangerously underpopulated....

New Englanders also used the word "liberty" in a second way which is foreign to our own time. When it referred to individuals, it often became a plural noun—"liberties" rather than "liberty." These plural liberties were understood as specific exemptions from a condition of prior restraint—an idea which had long existed in East Anglia and in many other parts of the western world. In the manor of Hengrave (Suffolk), for example, tenants were granted a specific "liberty" of fishing in the river Lark. Such a liberty was not universal or absolute; the river was closed to all other people. There were a great many of these liberties in East Anglian communities during the early seventeenth century. A person's status was defined by the number and nature of liberties to which he was admitted.

The idea of plural liberties as specific exemptions from a condition of prior constraint was carried to Massachusetts. The General Court, for example, enacted laws which extended "liberties and privileges of fishing and fowling" to certain inhabitants, and thereby denied them to everyone else. One person's "liberty" in this sense became another's restraint. In Massachusetts, as in England, a person's rank was defined by the liberties that he possessed, and vice versa.

The laws of the Bay Colony granted some liberties to all men, others to all free men, and a few only to gentlemen. For example, a "true gentleman" and "any man equal to a gentleman," was granted the liberty not to be punished by whipping "unless his crime be very shameful, and his course of life vicious and profligate." Other men had a lesser liberty, not to be whipped more than forty stripes. Other liberties were assigned not to individuals at all, but to churches and towns and other social groups....

New England Puritans also used the word "liberty" in a third meaning, which became urgently important to the founders of Massachusetts. This was the idea of "soul liberty," or "Christian liberty," an idea of high complexity. Soul liberty was freedom to serve God in the world. It was freedom to order one's own acts in a godly way—but not in any other. It made Christian freedom into a form of obligation.

The founding generation in Massachusetts often wrote of "soul liberty," "Christian liberty" or "liberty of conscience." Many moved to the New World primarily in hopes of attaining it. What they meant was not a world of religious freedom in the modern sense, or even of religious toleration, but rather of freedom for the true faith. In their minds, this idea of religious liberty was thought to be consistent with the persecution of Quakers, Catholics, Baptists, Presbyterians, Anglicans and indeed virtually everyone except those within a very narrow spectrum of Calvinist orthodoxy. Soul liberty also was thought to be consistent with compulsory church attendance and rigorous Sabbath laws. Even the Indians were compelled to keep the Puritan Sabbath in Massachusetts. To the founders of that colony, soul freedom meant that they were free to persecute others in their own way.... To others of different persuasions, the Puritans' paradoxical idea of "soul freedom" became a cruel and bloody contradiction. But to the Puritans themselves "soul liberty" was a genuinely libertarian principle which held that a Christian community should be free to serve God in the world. Here was an idea in which the people of Massachusetts deeply believed, and the reason why their colony was founded in the first place.

The words "liberty" and also "freedom" were used in yet a fourth way by the builders of the Bay Colony. Sometimes, the people of Massachusetts employed the word "freedom" to describe a collective obligation of the "body politicke," to protect individual members from the tyranny of circumstance. This was conceived not in terms of collective welfare or social equality but of individual liberty. It was precisely the same idea that a descendant of the Massachusetts Puritans, Franklin Roosevelt, conceived as the Four Freedoms. That way of thinking was not his invention. It appeared in Massachusetts within a few years of its founding. The Massachusetts poor laws, however limited they may have been, recognized every individual should be guaranteed a freedom from want in the most fundamental sense. The General Court also explicitly recognized even a "freedom of fear." Its language revealed a libertarian conception of social problems (and solutions) that was characteristic of English-speaking people as early as the seventeenth century.

These four libertarian ideas—collective liberty, individual liberties, soul liberty and freedom from the tyranny of circumstance—all had a common denominator. They were aspects of a larger conception which might be called ordered liberty. This principle was deeply embedded in Puritan ideas and also in East Anglian realities. It came to be firmly established in Massachusetts even before the end of the great migration. For many years it continued to distinguish the culture of New England from other parts of British America. Even today, in much modified forms, it is still a living tradition in parts of the United States. But this principle of "ordered liberty" is also opposed by other libertarian ideas, which were planted in different parts of British America....

VIRGINIA FREEDOM WAYS: THE ANGLICAN IDEA OF HEGEMONIC LIBERTY

"How is it," Dr. Samuel Johnson asked, "that we hear the loudest yelps for liberty among the drivers of negroes?" That famous question captured a striking paradox in the history of Virginia. Like most other colonists in British America, the first gentlemen of Virginia possessed an exceptionally strong consciousness of their English liberties, even as they took away the liberty of others. Governor William Berkeley himself, notwithstanding his reputation for tyranny, wrote repeatedly of "prized liberty" as the birthright of an Englishman. The first William Fitzhugh often wrote of Magna Carta and the "fundamental laws of England," with no sense of contradiction between his Royalist politics and libertarian principles. Fitzhugh argued that Virginians were both "natural subjects to the king" and inheritors of the "laws of England," and when they ceased to be these things, "then we are no longer freemen but slaves."

Similar language was used by many English-speaking people in the seventeenth and eighteenth century. The fine-spun treatises on liberty which flowed so abundantly from English pens in this era were rationales for political folkways deeply embedded in the cultural condition of Englishmen.

These English political folkways did not comprise a single libertarian tradition. They embraced many different and even contradictory conceptions of freedom. The libertarian ideas that took root in Virginia were very far removed from those that went to Massachusetts. In place of New England's distinctive idea of ordered liberty, the Virginians thought of liberty as a hegemonic condition of dominion over others and—equally important—dominion over oneself....

Virginia ideas of hegemonic liberty conceived of freedom mainly as the power to rule, and not to be overruled by others. Its opposite was "slavery," a degradation into which true-born Britons descended when they lost their power to rule....

It never occurred to most Virginia gentlemen that liberty belonged to everyone. It was thought to be the special birthright of free-born Englishmen—a property which set this "happy breed" apart from other mortals, and gave them a right to rule less fortunate people in the world. Even within their own society, hegemonic liberty was a hierarchical idea. One's status in Virginia was defined by the liberties that one possessed. Men of high estate were thought to have more liberties than others of lesser rank. Servants possessed few liberties, and slaves none at all. This libertarian idea had nothing to do with equality. Many years later, John Randolph of Roanoke summarized his ancestral creed in a sentence: "I am an aristocrat," he declared, "I love liberty; I hate equality."

In Virginia, this idea of hegemonic liberty was thought to be entirely consistent with the institution of race slavery. A planter demanded for himself the liberty to take away the liberties of others —a right of *laisser asservir*, freedom to enslave. The growth of race slavery in turn deepened the cultural significance of hegemonic liberty, for an Englishman's rights became his rank, and set him apart from others less fortunate than himself. The world thus became a hierarchy in which people were ranked according to many degrees of unfreedom, and they received their rank by the operation of fortune, which played so large a part in the thinking of Virginians. At the same time, hegemony over others allowed them to enlarge the sphere of their own personal liberty, and to create the conditions within which their special sort of libertarian consciousness flourished....

Hegemonic liberty was a dynamic tradition which developed through at least three historical stages. In the first it was linked to Royalist cause in the English Civil War. The Virginia gentleman Robert Beverley boasted that the colony "was famous, for holding out the longest for the Royal Family, of any of the English Dominions." Virginia was the last English territory to relinquish its allegiance to Charles I, and the first to proclaim Charles II king in 1660 even before the Restoration in England. Speeches against the Stuarts were ferociously punished by the county courts. The Assembly repeatedly expressed its loyalty to the Crown, giving abundant thanks for "his Majesty's most gracious favors towards us, and Royal Condescensions to anything requisite."

In the second stage, hegemonic liberty became associated with Whiggish politics, and with an ideology of individual independence which was widely shared throughout the English-speaking world.

In Virginia, many families who had been staunch Royalists in the seventeenth century became strong Whigs in eighteenth century; by the early nineteenth century they would be Jeffersonian Republicans. Their principles throughout tended to be both elitist and libertarian—a clear expression of a cultural ethic which was capable of continuing expansion....

In the nineteenth and twentieth centuries, the tradition of hegemonic liberty entered a third stage of development, in which it became less hierarchical and more egalitarian. Such are the conditions of modern life that this idea is no longer the exclusive property of a small elite, and the degradation of others is no longer necessary to their support. The progress of political democracy has admitted everyone to the ruling class. In America and Britain today, the idea of an independent elite, firmly in command of others, has disappeared. But the associated idea of an autonomous individual, securely in command of self, is alive and flourishing....

DELAWARE FREEDOM WAYS: THE QUAKER IDEA OF RECIPROCAL LIBERTY

Quakers believed in an idea of reciprocal liberty that embraced all humanity, and was written in the gold rule.

This Christian idea was reinforced in Quaker thinking by an exceptionally strong sense of English liberties. As early as 1687, William Penn ordered the full text of the Magna Carta to be reprinted in Philadelphia, together with a broad selection of other constitutional documents. His purpose was to remind the freeholders of Pennsylvania to remember their British birthright....

On the subject of liberty, the people of Pennsylvania needed no lessons from their Lord Proprietor. Few public questions were introduced among the colonists without being discussed in terms of rights and liberties. On its surface, this libertarian rhetoric seemed superficially similar to that of Massachusetts and Virginia. But the founders of Pennsylvania were a different group of Englishmen—a later generation, from another English region, with a special kind of Christian faith. Their idea of liberty was not the same as that which came to other parts of British America.

The most important of these differences had to do with religious freedom —"liberty of conscience." William Penn called it. This was not the conventional Protestant idea of liberty to do only that which is right. The Quakers believed that liberty of conscience extended even to ideas that they believed to be wrong. Their idea of "soul freedom" protected every Christian conscience.

The most articulate spokesman for this idea was William Penn himself. Of nearly sixty books and pamphlets that Penn wrote before coming to America, half were defenses of liberty of conscience. Some of these works were among the most powerful statements ever written on this subject. One ended with a revealing personal remark: " ... tis a matter of great satisfaction to the author that he has so plainly cleared his conscience in pleading for the liberty of other men's." ...

William Penn's personal experience of religious persecution gave him other reasons for believing in religious liberty. His own sufferings convinced him that the coercion of conscience was not merely evil but futile, and deeply dangerous to true faith. "They subvert all true religion," Penn wrote, " ... where men believe, not because 'tis false, but so commanded by their superiors."

These memories and experiences were not Penn's alone. In the period from 1661 to 1685, historians estimate that at least 15,000 Quakers were imprisoned in England, and 450 died for their beliefs. As late as the year 1685, more than 1,400 Quakers were still languishing in English jails. Most "books of sufferings" recorded punishments that continued well into the eighteenth century—mostly fines and seizures for nonpayment of tithes....

Many Quaker immigrants to Pennsylvania had experienced this religious persecution; they shared a determination to prevent its growth in their own province. The first fundamental law passed in Pennsylvania guaranteed liberty of conscience for all who believed in "one Almighty God," and established complete freedom of worship. It also provided penalties for those who "derided the religion of others." The Quaker founders of Pennsylvania were not content merely to restrain government from interfering with rights of conscience. They also made it an instrument of positive protection. Here was a reciprocal idea of religious liberty which they actively extended to others as well as themselves.

Liberty of conscience was one of a large family of personal freedoms which Quakers extended equally to others. William Penn recognized three secular "rights of an Englishman": first, a "right and title to your own lives, liberties and estates; second, representative government; third, trial by jury." In Pennsylvania, these liberties went far beyond those of Massachusetts, Virginia and old England itself....

The Quakers of the Delaware Valley also differed from other English-speaking people in regard to race slavery. The question was a difficult one for them. The first generation of Quakers had been deeply troubled by slavery, but many were not opposed outright. The problem was compounded in the Delaware Valley by the fact that slavery worked well as an economic institution in this region. Many Quakers bought slaves. Even William Penn did so. Of the leaders of the Philadelphia Yearly Meeting for whom evidence survives, 70 percent owned slaves in the period from 1681 to 1705.

But within the first decade of settlement a powerful antislavery movement began to develop in the Delaware Valley. As early as 1688, the Quakers of Germantown issued a testimony against slavery on the ground that it violated the golden rule. In 1696, two leading Quakers, Cadwalader Morgan and William Southeby, urged the Philadelphia Yearly Meeting to forbid slavery and slave trading. The meeting refused to go that far, but agreed to advise Quakers "not to encourage the bringing in of any more Negroes." As antislavery feeling expanded steadily among Friends, slaveowning declined among leaders of the Philadelphia Yearly Meeting—falling steadily from 70 percent before 1705, to only 10 percent after 1756.

The Pennsylvania legislature took action in 1712, passing a prohibitive duty on the importation of slaves. This measure was disallowed by the English Crown, which had a heavy stake in the slave trade. In 1730 the Philadelphia Yearly Meeting cautioned its members, but still a few Friends continued to buy slaves. Other Quaker antislavery petitions and papers followed in increasing number.... The argument came down to the reciprocal principle of the gold rule. Quakers argued that if they did not wish to be slaves themselves, they had no right to enslave others....

The Quakers radically redefined the "rights of Englishmen" in terms of their Christian beliefs. But they never imagined that they were creating something new. Penn and others in the colony wrote always of their rights as "ancient" and "fundamental" principles which were rooted in the immemorial customs of the English-speaking people and in the practices of the primitive church.

In the conservative cast of their libertarian thinking, the Quakers were much the same as Puritans and Anglicans. But in the substance of their libertarian thought they were very different. In respect to liberty of conscience, trial by jury, the rights of property, the rule of representation, and race slavery, Quakers genuinely believed that every liberty demanded for oneself should also be extended to others....

BACKCOUNTRY FREEDOM WAYS: THE BORDER IDEA OF NATURAL LIBERTY

The backsettlers, no less than other colonists in every part of British America, brought with them a special way of thinking about power and freedom, and a strong attachment to their liberties. As early as the middle decades of the eighteenth century their political documents contained many references to liberty as their British birthright. In 1768, the people of Mecklenberg County, North Carolina, declared, "We shall ever be more ready to support the government under which we find the most liberty."

No matter whether they came from... England or Scotland or Ireland, their libertarian ideas were very much alike —and profoundly different from no-

tions of liberty that had been carried to Massachusetts, Virginia and Pennsylvania. The traveler Johann Schoepf was much interested in ideas of law and liberty which he found in the backcountry. "They shun everything which appears to demand of them law and order, and anything that preaches constraint," Schoepf wrote of the backsettlers. "They hate the name of a justice, and yet they are not transgressors. Their object is merely wild. Altogether, natural freedom... is what pleases them."

This idea of "natural freedom" was widespread throughout the southern back settlements. But it was not a reflexive response to the "frontier" environment, nor was it "mere wild," as Schoepf believed. The backcountry idea of natural liberty was created by a complex interaction between the American environment and a European folk culture. It derived in large part from the British border country, where anarchic violence had long been a condition of life. The natural liberty of the borderers was an idea at once more radically libertarian, more strenuously hostile to ordering institutions than were the other cultures of British America....

A leading advocate of natural liberty in the eighteenth century was Patrick Henry, a descendant of British borderers, and also a product of the American backcountry. Throughout his political career, Patrick Henry consistently defended the principles of minimal government, light taxes, and the right of armed resistance to authority in all cases which infringed liberty....

Patrick Henry's principles of natural liberty were drawn from the political folkways of the border culture in which he grew up. He imbibed them from his mother, a lady who described the American Revolution as merely another set of "lowland troubles." The libertarian phrases and thoughts which echoed so strongly in the backcountry had earlier been heard in the borders of North Britain. When the backcountry people celebrated the supremacy of private interests they used the same thoughts and words as William Cotesworth, an English borderer who in 1717 declared: "... you know how natural it is to pursue private interest even against that Darling principle of a more general good.... It is the interest of the Public to be served by the man that can do it cheapest, though several private persons are injured by it."

This idea of natural liberty was not a reciprocal idea. It did not recognize the right of dissent or disagreement. Deviance from cultural norms was rarely tolerated; opposition was suppressed by force. One of Andrew Jackson's early biographers observed that "It appears to be more difficult for a North-of-Irelander than for other men to allow an honest difference of opinion in an opponent, so that he is apt to regard the terms opponent and enemy as synonymous."

When backcountrymen moved west in search of that condition of natural freedom which Daniel Boone called "elbow room," they were repeating the thought of George Harrison, a North Briton who declared in the borderlands during the seventeenth century that "every man at nature's table has a right to elbow room." The southern frontier provided space for the realization of this ideal, but it did not create it.

This libertarian idea of natural freedom as "elbow room" was very far from the ordered freedom of New England towns, the hegemonic freedom of Virginia's county oligarchs, and the reciprocal freedom of Pennsylvania Quakers. Here was yet another freedom way which came to be rooted in the culture of an American region, where it flourished for many years to come.

POSTSCRIPT

Was Colonial Culture Uniquely American?

Although Nash and Fischer approach the issue of American exceptionalism from different perspectives, both recognize a certain uniqueness in American society. Fischer's America is the product of an Old World English cultural heritage. However, by emphasizing the impact on America of the distinct folkways of peoples migrating from four different geographical regions in the British Isles, Fischer reinforces the notion of a unique quality to American culture, one grounded in British customs. Unfortunately, this Anglocentric argument leaves no room for cultural contributions from either Native Americans and Africans or Germans, Dutch, and Swedes. Nash, on the other hand, suggests that we examine the numerous non-English and non-European elements of American culture. His appreciation of cultural pluralism is developed in greater detail in *Red, White, and Black: The Peoples of Early America*, 2d ed. (Prentice Hall, 1974).

Another significant issue in the study of America's cultural origins is the question of their impact on the American character. Frederick Jackson Turner's "The Significance of the Frontier in American History," a paper read at the annual meeting of the American Historical Association in 1893, reflects the views of Crevecoeur and Tocqueville by asserting that a unique national character developed out of America's frontier experience. The Turner thesis remained a hot topic of historical debate for three quarters of a century as Turnerians and anti-Turnerians debated the fine details of the impact of the frontier on American national character. The staunchest disciple of Turner was Ray Allen Billington, whose *The Far Western Frontier, 1830–1860* (Harper & Row, 1956), *The Frontier Heritage* (Holt, Rinehart & Winston, 1966), and *Frederick Jackson Turner* (Oxford University Press, 1973) should be examined. An important extension of the Turner thesis is offered in David M. Potter, *People of Plenty: Economic Abundance and the American Character* (University of Chicago Press, 1954), which identifies another factor contributing to the distinctive American character. Michael Kammen's *People of Paradox: An Inquiry Concerning the Origins of American Civilization* (Alfred A. Knopf, 1972) argues that American distinctiveness is derived from the contradiction produced by a culture created from an interaction of Old and New World patterns. Students interested in pursuing these questions of culture and character should examine Michael McGiffert, ed., *The Character of Americans: A Book of Readings*, rev. ed. (Dorsey Press, 1970), and David Stannard, "American Historians and the Idea of a National Character," *American Quarterly* (May 1971).

ISSUE 2

Were the English Colonists Guilty of Genocide?

YES: David E. Stannard, from *American Holocaust: Columbus and the Conquest of the New World* (Oxford University Press, 1992)

NO: Steven T. Katz, from "The Pequot War Reconsidered," *The New England Quarterly* (June 1991)

ISSUE SUMMARY

YES: David E. Stannard, a professor of American studies, insists that the colonists carried out a conscious militaristic policy to exterminate the Native Americans. He maintains that this policy—combined with the devastating impact of epidemic diseases—resulted in the virtual elimination of the indigenous populations in the Atlantic coastal colonies within the first century of contact.

NO: Steven T. Katz, a professor of Near Eastern studies, contends that the historical record relative to the Pequot War offers little support for revisionist claims that this event was premeditated genocide carried out by New Englanders against their Native American opponents.

Relations between Native Americans and Europeans were marred by the difficulties arising from people of very different cultures encountering each other for the first time. These encounters led to inaccurate perceptions, misunderstandings, and failed expectations. While at first the American Indians deified the explorers, experience soon taught them to do otherwise. European opinion ran the gamut from admiration to contempt: some European poets and painters expressed admiration for the Noble Savage; other Europeans rationalized aggressive assaults against the New World's indigenous residents with the sentiment "The only good savage is a dead one."

Spanish, French, and English treatments of Native Americans differed and were based to a considerable extent on each nation's hopes about the New World and how it could be subordinated to the Old. The Spanish exploited the Indians most directly, taking their gold and silver, transforming their government, religion, and society, and even occasionally enslaving them. The French posed a lesser threat than did the others because there were fewer of them and because many French immigrants were itinerant trappers and priests rather than settlers. In the long run, emigration from England was the most threatening of all. Entire families came from England, and they were determined to establish a permanent home in the wilderness.

The juxtaposition of Native American and English from the Atlantic to the Appalachians resulted sometimes in coexistence, other times in enmity. Attempts at peaceful coexistence did not smooth over the tension between the English and the Indians. They did not see eye to eye, for example, about the uses of the environment. Indian agriculture, in the eyes of English settlers, was neither intense nor efficient. Native Americans observed that white settlers consumed large amounts of food per person and cultivated crops not only for themselves but also for towns and villages that bought the surplus. Subsistence farming collided with the market economy.

Large-scale violence erupted in Virginia in the 1620s, the 1640s, and the 1670s. In the latter decade, frontiersmen in the Virginia piedmont led by Nathaniel Bacon attacked tribes living in the Appalachian foothills. In New England, from the 1630s through the 1670s, Pequots, Wampanoags, Narragansetts, Mohegans, Podunks, and Nipmucks united to stop the encroachments into their woodlands and hunting grounds. King Philip's War erupted in June 1675 and lasted until September 1676, with isolated raids stretching on until 1678. Casualties rose into the hundreds, and Anglo-Indian relations deteriorated.

In the next century Spain, France, and England disputed each other's North American claims, and Native Americans joined sides, usually allying with France against England. These great wars of the eighteenth century ended in 1763 with England claiming the victory, but disputes over territorial expansion continued. Colonial officials objected to the Proclamation of 1763 by which King George III's imperial government forbade his subjects from settling west of the Appalachian watershed. The area from those mountains to the Mississippi River, acquired by the British from France under the terms of the peace negotiated in Paris in 1763, was designated as an Indian reservation. From 1763 to 1783, as Anglo-colonial relations moved from disagreement to combat to independence, the London government consistently sided with the Native Americans.

The following essays analyze the consequences of the New World encounters between English colonists and Native Americans. David E. Stannard examines conflicts between Native Americans and colonists in Virginia and New England over the course of the first century of colonization in British North America and concludes that the English settlers followed a conscious, concerted effort to exterminate the indigenous peoples who stood in their way. Steven T. Katz, however, asserts that an objective examination of the record of the Pequot War reveals a rather diverse reaction by the English settlers to this particular conflict and, thus, negates the allegations of revisionist scholars such as Stannard that this incident was the product of a premeditated policy of genocide.

YES

David E. Stannard

PESTILENCE AND GENOCIDE

When the first 104 English settlers arrived at Jamestown in April of 1607, the number of Indians under [Indian chief] Powhatan's control was probably upwards of 14,000—a fraction of what it had been just a few decades earlier, because of English, French, and Spanish depredations and disease (Estimates of the region's native population prior to European contact extend upwards of 100,000.) By the time the seventeenth century had passed, those 104 settlers had grown to more than 60,000 English men and women who were living in and harvesting Virginia's bounty, while Powhatan's people had been reduced to about 600, maybe less. More than 95 percent of Powhatan's people had been exterminated—beginning from a population base in 1607 that already had been drastically reduced, perhaps by 75 percent or more, as a result of prior European incursions in the region.

Powhatan's Empire was not the only Indian nation in Virginia, of course, but his people's fate was representative of that of the area's other indigenous societies. In 1697 Virginia's Lieutenant Governor Andros put the number of Indian warriors in the entire colony at just over 360, which suggests a total Indian population of less than 1500, while John Lawson, in his *New Voyage to Carolina*, claimed that more than 80 percent of the colony's native people had been killed off during the previous fifty years alone. In time, a combination plan of genocide and enslavement, as initially proposed by the colony's Governor William Berkeley, appeared to quiet what had become a lingering controversy over whether it was best to kill all the Indians or to capture them and put them to forced labor: Berkeley's plan was to slaughter all the adult Indian males in a particular locale, "but to spare the women and children and sell them," says Edmund Morgan. This way the war of extermination "would pay for itself," since it was likely that a sufficient number of female and child slaves would be captured "to defray the whole cost."

By the time this clever enterprise was under way in Virginia, the British had opened colonies in New England as well. As usual, earlier visits by Europeans already had spread among the Indians a host of deadly plagues. The Patuxet peoples, for example, were effectively exterminated by some of these diseases, while other tribes disappeared before they were even seen by any white men. Others were more fortunate, suffering death rates of 50 and 60 percent—a good deal greater than the proportion of Europeans killed by the Black Death pandemic of the fourteenth century, but still far short of total liquidation. These were rates, however, for any given *single* epidemic, and in New England's sixteenth and seventeenth centuries few epidemics traveled by themselves. The extant descriptions of what life and death were like at times like these are rare, but the accounts we do have of the viral and bacteriological assaults are sobering indeed, reminiscent of the earlier Spanish and Portuguese accounts from Mesoamerica and Brazil. Wrote Plymouth Colony's Governor William Bradford, for instance, of a smallpox epidemic from which huge numbers of Indians "died most miserably":

For want of bedding and linen and other helps they fall into a lamentable condition as they lie on their hard mats, the pox breaking and mattering and running one into another, their skin cleaving by reason thereof to the mats they lie on. When they turn them, a whole side will flay off at once as it were, and they will be all of a gore blood, most fearful to behold. And then being very sore, what with cold and other distempers, they die like rotten sheep. The condition of this people was so lamentable and they fell down so generally of this disease as they were in the end not able to help one another, no not to make a fire nor to fetch a little water to drink, nor any to bury the dead. But would strive as long as they could, and when they could procure no other means to make fire, they would burn the wooden trays and dishes they ate their meat in, and their very bows and arrows,

And some would crawl out on all fours to get a little water, and sometimes die by the way and not be able to get in again.

While "very few" of the Indians escaped this scourge, including "the chief sachem... and almost all his friends and kindred," Bradford reported, "by the marvelous goodness and providence of God, not one of the English was so much as sick or in the least measure tainted with this disease." Time and again Old World epidemics such as this coursed through the veins of the native peoples of the North Atlantic coast, even before the arrival of the first great waves of British settlers, leaving in their wake so many dead that they could not be buried, so many piles of skeletal remains that one early colonist referred to the land as "a new found Golgotha." But it was a Golgotha the Puritans delighted in discovering, not only because the diseases they brought with them from England left the Puritans themselves virtually unaffected, but because the destruction of the Indians by these plagues was considered an unambiguous sign of divine approval for the colonial endeavor. As the first governor of the Massachusetts Bay Colony wrote in 1634, the Puritan settlers, numbering at the time "in all about four thousand souls and upward," were in remarkably good health: "through the Lord's special providence... there hath not died above two or three grown persons and about so many children all the last year, it being very rare to hear of any sick of agues or other diseases." But, he noted in passing, as "for the natives, they are near all dead of the smallpox, so as the Lord hath cleared our title to what we possess."

God, however, was not enough. At some point the settlers would have to take things into their own hands. For, terribly destructive though the Old World diseases were, some Indians remained alive. The danger posed by these straggling few natives was greatly exaggerated by the English (as it remains exaggerated in most history textbooks today), not only because their numbers had been so drastically reduced, but because their attitudes toward the colonists and their very means of warfare were so comparatively benign. . . .

Not surprisingly, then, the highly disciplined and ideologically motivated British expressed contempt for what Captain John Mason called the Indians' "feeble manner . . . [that] did hardly deserve the name of fighting." Warfare among the native peoples had no "dissipline" about it, complained Captain Henry Spelman, so that when Indians fought there was no great "slawter of nether side"; instead, once "having shott away most of their arrows," both sides commonly "weare glad to retier." Indeed, so comparatively harmless was inter-tribal fighting, noted John Underhill, that "they might fight seven yeares and not kill seven men." Added Roger Williams: "Their Warres are farre lesse bloudy, and devouring than the cruell Warres of Europe; and seldome twenty slain in a pitched field. . . . When they fight in a plaine, they fight with leaping and dancing, that seldome an Arrow hits, and when a man is wounded, unlesse he that shot followes upon the wounded, they soone retire and save the wounded." In addition, the Indians' code of honor "ordinarily spared the women and children of their adversaries."

In contrast, needless to say, the British did very little in the way of "leaping and dancing" on the field of battle, and more often than not Indian women and children were consumed along with everyone and everything else in the conflagrations that routinely accompanied the colonists' assaults. Their purpose, after all, was rarely to avenge an insult to honor—although that might be the stipulated rationale for a battle—but rather, when the war was over, to be able to say what John Mason declared at the conclusion of one especially bloody combat: that "the Lord was pleased to smite our Enemies in the hinder Parts, and to *give us their Land for an Inheritance.*" Because of his readers' assumed knowledge of the Old Testament, it was unnecessary for Mason to remind them that this last phrase is derived from Deuteronomy, nor did he need to quote the words that immediately follow in that biblical passage: "Thou shalt save alive nothing that breatheth. . . . But thou shalt utterly destroy them."

The brutish and genocidal encounter to which Mason was referring was the Pequot War. Its first rumblings began to be heard in July of 1636—two years after a smallpox epidemic had devastated the New England natives "as far as any Indian plantation was known to the west," said John Winthrop—when the body of a man named John Oldham was found, apparently killed by Narragansett Indians on Block Island, off the Rhode Island coast. Although he held positions of some importance, Oldham was not held in high regard by many of the English settlers—he had been banished from Plymouth Colony and described by its Governor Bradford as "more like a furious beast than a man"—and those whites who found his body had proceeded to murder more than a dozen Indians who were found at the scene of the crime, whether or not they were individually responsible. Even in light of the colonists' grossly disproportionate sense of retribution when one of their own had been killed by Indians, this should have been sufficient revenge, but it was not. The colonists simply wanted to kill Indians. Despite the pledge of the Narragansetts' chief to mete out punishment to Oldham's murderers—a pledge he began to fulfill by sending 200 warriors to Block Island in search of the culprits—New England's Puritan leaders wanted more.

Led by Captain John Endicott, a heavily armed and armored party of about a hundred Massachusetts militiamen soon attacked the Block Island Indians. Their plan was to kill the island's adult males and make off with the women and children; as with Governor Berkeley's later scheme in Virginia, the venture would pay for itself since, as Francis Jennings puts it, "the captured women and children of Block Island would fetch a tidy sum in the West Indies slave markets." The Indians scattered, however, realizing they had no hope against the colonists' weapons and armor, so the frustrated soldiers, able to kill only an odd few Narragansetts here and there, had to content themselves with the destruction of deserted villages. "We burnt and spoiled both houses and corn in great abundance," recalled one participant.

From Block Island the troops headed back to the mainland where, following the directions of their colony's governor, they sought out a confrontation with some Pequot Indians. The Pequots, of course, had nothing to do with Oldham's death (the excuse for going after them was the allegation that, two years earlier, some among them may have killed two quarrelsome Englishmen, one of whom had himself tried to murder the Governor of Plymouth Colony), so when the soldiers first appeared along the Pequots' coastline the Indians ran out to greet them. As Underhill recalled: "The Indians spying of us came running in multitudes along the water side, crying, what cheere, Englishmen, what cheere, what doe you come for: They not thinking we intended warre, went on cheerefully untill they come to Pequeat river." It soon became evident to the Pequots what the soldiers had come for, even if the cause of their coming remained a mystery, so after some protracted efforts at negotiation, the Pequots melted back into the forest to avoid a battle. As they had on Block Island, the troops then went on a destructive rampage, looting and burning the Indians' villages and fields of corn.

Once the Massachusetts troops left the field and returned to Boston, the Pequots came out of the woods, made a few retaliatory raids in the countryside, and then attacked nearby Fort Saybrook. Casualties were minimal in all of this, as was normal in Indian warfare, and at one point—presumably feeling that their honor had been restored—the Pequots fell back and asked the fort's commander if he felt he had "fought enough." The commander, Lieutenant Lion Gardiner, made an evasive reply, but its meaning was clear: from that day forward there would be no peace. Next, the Pequots asked if the English planned to kill Indian women and children. Gardiner's reply was that "they should see that hereafter."

For a time small troubles continued in the field, while in Hartford the Connecticut General Court met and declared war against the Pequots. John Mason was appointed commander of the Connecticut troops. Rather than attack frontally, as the Massachusetts militia had, Mason led his forces and some accompanying Narragansetts (who long had been at odds with the Pequots) in a clandestine assault on the main Pequot village just before dawn. Upon realizing that Mason was planning nothing less than a wholesale massacre, the Narragansetts dissented and withdrew to the rear. Mason regarded them with contempt, saying that they could "stand at what distance they pleased, and see whether *English Men* would now fight or not." Dividing his forces in half, Mason at the head of one party, Underhill leading the other, under cover of darkness they attacked the unsuspecting Indians from two directions at once. The Pequots, Mason said, were taken entirely by surprise, their "being in a dead indeed their last Sleep."

The British swarmed into the Indian encampment, slashing and shooting at anything that moved. Caught off guard, and with apparently few warriors in the village at the time, some of the Pequots fled, "others crept under their Beds," while still others fought back "most courageously," but this only drove Mason and his men to greater heights of fury. "*We must burn them,*" Mason later recalled himself shouting, whereupon he "brought out a Fire Brand, and putting it into the Matts with which they were covered, set the Wigwams on Fire." At this, Mason says, "the Indians ran as Men most dreadfully Amazed":

And indeed such a dreadful Terror did the Almighty let fall upon their Spirits, that they would fly from us and run into the very Flames, where many of them perished.... [And] God was above them, who laughed his Enemies and the Enemies of his People to Scorn, making them as a fiery Oven: Thus were the Stout Hearted spoiled, having slept their last Sleep, and none of their Men could find their Hands: Thus did the Lord judge

among the Heathen, filling the Place with dead Bodies!

It was a ghastly sight—especially since we now know, as Francis Jennings reminds us, that most of those who were dying in the fires, and who were "crawling under beds and fleeing from Mason's dripping sword were women, children, and feeble old men." Underhill, who had set fire to the other side of the village "with a traine of Powder" intended to meet Mason's blaze in the center, recalled how "great and doleful was the bloudy sight to the view of young soldiers that never had been in war, to see so many souls lie gasping on the ground, so thick, in some places, that you could hardly pass along." Yet, distressing though it may have been for the youthful murderers to carry out their task, Underhill reassured his readers that "sometimes the Scripture declareth women and children must perish with their parents." Just because they were weak and helpless and unarmed, in short, did not make their deaths any less a delight to the Puritan's God. For as William Bradford described the British reaction to the scene:

It was a fearful sight to see them thus frying in the fire and the streams of blood quenching the same, and horrible was the stink and scent thereof; but the victory seemed a sweet sacrifice, and they gave the praise thereof to God, who had wrought so wonderfully for them, thus to enclose their enemies in their hands and give them so speedy a victory over so proud and insulting an enemy.

Added the Puritan divine Cotton Mather, as he celebrated the event many years later in his *Magnalia Christi Americana*: "In a little more than one hour, five or six hundred of these barbarians were dismissed from a world that was burdened with them." Mason himself counted the Pequot dead at six or seven hundred, with only seven taken captive and seven escaped. It was, he said joyfully, "the just Judgment of God."

The Narragansetts who had accompanied the Puritans on their march did not share the Englishmen's joy. This indiscriminate carnage was not the way warfare was to be carried out. "Mach it, mach it," Underhill reports their shouting; "that is," he translates, "It is naught, it is naught, because it is too furious, and slays too many men." Too many Indians, that was. Only two of the English died in the slaughter.

From then on the surviving Pequots were hunted into near-extermination. Other villages were found and burned. Small groups of warriors were intercepted and killed. Pockets of starving women and children were located, captured, and sold into slavery. If they were fortunate. Others were bound hand and foot and thrown into the ocean just beyond the harbor. And still more were buried where they were found, such as one group of three hundred or so who tried to escape through a swampland, but could make "little haste, by reason of their Children, and want of Provision," said Mason. When caught, as Richard Drinnon puts it, they "were literally run to ground," murdered, and then "tramped into the mud or buried in swamp mire."

The comparative handful of Pequots who were left, once this series of massacres finally ended, were parceled out to live in servitude. John Endicott and his pastor, for example, wrote to the governor asking for "a share" of the captives, specifically "a yong woman or girle and a boy if you thinke good."

The last of them, fifteen boys and two women, were shipped to the West Indies for sale as slaves, the ship captain who carried them there returning the next year with what he had received in exchange: some cotton, some salt, some tobacco, "and Negroes, etc." The word "Pequot" was then removed from New England's maps: the river of that name was changed to the Thames and the town of that name became New London. Having virtually eradicated an entire people, it now was necessary to expunge from historical memory any recollection of their past existence.

Some, however, remembered all too well. John Mason rode the honor of his butchery to the position of Major General of Connecticut's armed forces. And Underhill, as Drinnon notes, "put his experience to good use" in selling his military prowess to the Dutch. On one subsequent occasion "with his company of Dutch troops Underhill surrounded an Indian village outside Stamford, set fire to the wigwams, drove back in with saber thrusts and shots those who sought to escape, and in all burned and shot five hundred with relative ease, allowing only about eight to escape— statistics comparable to those from the Pequot fort."

Meanwhile, the Narragansetts, who had been the Pequots' rivals, but who were horrified at this inhuman carnage, quietly acknowledged the English domination of the Pequots' lands—their "widowed lands," to borrow a phrase from Jennings. That would not, however, prove sufficient. The English towns continued to multiply, the colonists continued to press out into the surrounding fields and valleys. The Narragansetts' land, and that of other tribes, was next.

To recount in detail the story of the destruction of the Narragansetts and such others as the Wampanoags, in what has come to be known as King Philip's War of 1675 and 1676, is unnecessary here. Thousands of native people were killed, their villages and crops burned to the ground. In a single early massacre 600 Indians were destroyed. It was, says the recent account of two historians, "a seventeenth-century My Lai" in which the English soldiers "ran amok, killing the wounded men, women, and children indiscriminately, firing the camp, burning the Indians alive or dead in their huts." A delighted Cotton Mather, revered pastor of the Second Church in Boston, later referred to the slaughter as a "barbeque." More butchery was to follow. Of these, one bloodbath alongside the Connecticut River was typical. It is described by an eyewitness:

Our souldiers got thither after an hard March just about break of day, took most of the Indians fast asleep, and put their guns even into their Wigwams, and poured in their shot among them, whereupon the Indians that durst and were able did get out of their Wigwams and did fight a little (in which fight one Englishman only was slain) others of the Indians did enter the River to swim over from the English, but many of them were shot dead in the waters, others wounded were therein drowned, many got into Canoes to paddle away, but the paddlers being shot, the Canoes over-set with all therein, and the stream of the River being very violent and swift in the place near the great Falls, most that fell over board were born by the strong current of that River, and carried upon the Falls of Water from those exceeding high and steep Rocks, and from thence tumbling down were broken in pieces; the English did

afterwards find of their bodies, some in the River and some cast a-shore, above two hundred.

The pattern was familiar, the only exception being that by the latter seventeenth century the Indians had learned that self-defense required an understanding of some English ideas about war, namely, in Francis Jennings's words: "that the Englishmen's most solemn pledge would be broken whenever obligation conflicted with advantage; that the English way of war had no limit of scruple or mercy; and that weapons of Indian making were almost useless against weapons of European manufacture. These lessons the Indians took to heart," so for once the casualties were high on both sides. There was no doubt who would win, however, and when raging epidemics swept the countryside during the peak months of confrontation it only hastened the end.

Once the leader of the Indian forces, "a doleful, great, naked, dirty beast," the English called him, was captured—and cut in pieces—the rest was just a mop-up operation. As one modern celebrant of the English puts it: "Hunting redskins became for the time being a popular sport in New England, especially since prisoners were worth good money, and the personal danger to the hunters was now very slight." Report after report came in of the killing of hundreds of Indians, "with the losse only of one man of ours," to quote a common refrain. Equally common were accounts such as that of the capture of "about 26 Indians, most Women and Children brought in by our Scouts, as they were ranging the Woods about Dedham, almost starved." All this, of course, was "God's Will," says the British reporter of these events, "which will at last give us cause to say, How Great is his Goodness! and how great is his Beauty!" As another writer of the time expressed the shared refrain, "thus doth the Lord Jesus make them to bow before him, and to lick the Dust."

Typical of those being made to bow and lick the dust by this time was "a very decrepit and harmless Indian," too old and too weak to walk, who was captured by the Puritan troops. For a time, says the eyewitness account of John Easton, the soldiers contented themselves with merely "tormenting" the old man. Finally, however, they decided to kill him: "some would have had him devoured by dogs," wrote Easton, "but the tenderness of some of them prevailed to cut off his head."

The only major question remaining as King Philip's war drew to its inevitable close was how to deal with the few natives who still were alive. So many Indians had been "consumed ... by the Sword & by Famine and by Sickness," wrote Cotton Mather's father Increase, "it being no unusual thing for those that traverse the woods to find dead Indians up and down ... there hath been none to bury them," that there now were "not above an hundred men left of them who last year were the greatest body of Indians in New England." As to what to do with that handful of survivors, only two choices—as always—enjoyed any support among the English colonists: annihilation or enslavement. Both approaches were tried. Allegedly dangerous Indians (that is, adult males) were systematically executed, while women and children were either shipped off to the slave markets of Spain or the West Indies, or were kept as servants of the colonists themselves. The terms of captured child slaves within Connecticut were to end

once they reached the age of twenty-six. But few saw their day of liberation. Either they died before reaching their twenty-sixth birthday, or they escaped. And those who escaped and were caught usually then were sold into foreign slavery, with the blessing of the Connecticut General Court that had passed specific postwar legislation with this end in mind.

One final bit of business that required clearing up concerned the fates of those scattered Indians who had been able to hide out on islands in Narragansett Bay that were under the colonial jurisdiction of Rhode Island. Rhode Island had remained neutral during the war, and both the Indians and the leaders of the other colonies knew there was less likelihood of homicidal or other barbarous treatment for native refugees found in Rhode Island's domain. This infuriated the colonists in Connecticut, Massachusetts, and Plymouth, not only because of their continuing blood lust, but because the Rhode Islanders were themselves reducing escaped Indians to servitude, even if they were not methodically executing them. The other colonies, "mindful of the cash value of prisoners," writes Douglas Edward Leach, felt that the Rhode Islanders were thus unfairly "now reaping the benefits which others had sowed in blood and treasure." Rhode Island's response was that the number of Indians within their territory was greatly exaggerated. And it appears that they were right, so successful had been the extermination campaign against the native people.

By the beginning of the eighteenth century the indigenous inhabitants of New England, and of most other northeastern Indian lands, had been reduced to a small fraction of their former number and were living in isolated, squalid enclaves.

Cotton Mather called these defeated and scattered people "tawny pagans" whose "inaccessible" homes were now nothing more than "kennels." And Mather's views, on this at least, were widely shared among the colonists. The once-proud native peoples, who had shown the English how to plant and live in the difficult environs of New England, were now regarded as animals, or at most, to quote one Englishwoman who traveled from Boston to New York in 1704, as "the most salvage of all the salvages of that kind that I have ever Seen."

It had started with the English plagues and ended with the sword and musket. The culmination, throughout the larger region, has been called the Great Dispersal. Before the arrival of the English —to choose an example further north from the area we have been discussing —the population of the western Abenaki people in New Hampshire and Vermont had stood at about 12,000. Less than half a century later approximately 250 of these people remained alive, a destruction rate of 98 percent. Other examples from this area tell the same dreary tale: by the middle of the seventeenth century, the Mahican people— 92 percent destroyed; the Mohawk people—73 percent destroyed; the eastern Abenaki people—78 percent destroyed; the Maliseet-Passamaquoddy people— 67 percent destroyed. And on, and on. Prior to European contact the Pocumtuck people had numbered more than

18,000; fifty years later they were down to 920—95 percent destroyed. The Quiripi-Unquachog people had numbered about 30,000; fifty years later they were down to 1500—95 percent destroyed. The Massachusett people had numbered at least 44,000; fifty years later they were down to barely 6000—81 percent destroyed.

This was by mid-century. King Philip's War had not yet begun. Neither had the smallpox epidemics of 1677 and 1678 occurred yet. The devastation had only started. Other wars and other scourges followed. By 1690, according to one count, the population of Norridgewock men was down to about 100; by 1726 it was down to 25. The same count showed the number of Androscoggin men in 1690 reduced to 160; by 1726 they were down to 10. And finally, the Pigwacket people: by 1690 only 100 men were left; by 1726 there were 7. These were the last ones, those who had fled to Canada to escape the English terrors. Once hostilities died down they were allowed to return to the fragments of their homelands that they still could say were theirs. But they hesitated "and expressed concern," reports a recent history of the region, "lest the English fall upon them while they were hunting near the Connecticut and Kennebec Rivers." The English— who earlier had decorated the seal of the Massachusetts Bay Colony with an image of a naked Indian plaintively urging the colonists to "Come over and help us"— had taught the natives well.

NO

Steven T. Katz

THE PEQUOT WAR RECONSIDERED

It is well known that in the 1970s and 1980s traditional scholarly analyses and judgments of the motives and events surrounding the Pequot War of 1637 came to be revised. In place of the view that the English were simply protecting themselves by preemptively attacking the Pequots, the revisionists argued that the Europeans used earlier, limited threats against them as cause to bring mass destruction on the Pequots. That assault is then taken to be a harbinger, a symbol of a larger, premeditated exterminatory intent that characterized the invasion of the New World. While there is surely room for a more penetrating critical reconstruction of the meaning of America's conquest and settlement than has yet appeared, one must be cautious in allowing legitimate moral outrage at the treatment of the Indians to substitute for a careful sorting of the evidence about the Pequot War. If we examine the facts closely and try to analyze them within their particular historical context, our judgments of the wrongs done the Native Americans will be more nuanced, balanced, and discriminating than radicalizing polemics allow and thus ultimately will better serve our efforts to understand the processes and consequences of colonization.

* * *

My first cautionary comment regarding the war is that it should not be viewed in strictly racial or ethnic terms of Red vs. White. I do not dispute that the colonists viewed the Indians through racial stereotypes, or that those stereotypes affected their behavior, but the particular circumstances of the Pequot War certainly seem to argue against the charge that it was a universal offensive against "Indianness" per se. The most telling of these circumstances is the presence of rival Indian groups on the side of the colonists. The crucial role of the Narragansetts, first in rejecting Pequot overtures to join a pan-Indian front against the English and then, in October 1636, in allying with the English against the Pequot, is but the earliest and most prominent case of European-Indian collaboration in the conflict. Following this alliance, the Mohegans, the Massachusetts and River Tribes, and later the Mohawks all sided with the British. Although the reasons for these alliances have been

From Steven T. Katz, "The Pequot War Reconsidered," *The New England Quarterly*, vol. 64 (June 1991). Copyright © 1991 by *The New England Quarterly*. Reprinted by permission. Notes omitted.

disputed for three centuries, seventeenth-century evidence—for example, the "Remonstrance of New Netherland," John Winthrop's *History of New England,* and John De Forest's *History of the Indians*—is clear that at least intermittent hostility between the Pequots and the Narragansetts and their tributaries preceded the war.

Once we are able to hold our charges of racism in reserve, we can attend to the specifics of the war. Our distance from the events obviously blurs our vision. Many facts about the war have been contested, including the particular causes for the outbreak of hostilities; however, there can be no doubt that both sides had cause to feel aggrieved. From the perspective of most Indians, exceptions notwithstanding, the very presence of the European was an act of aggression. Filling in the outlines of this generalized aggression was an already considerable and well-documented body of particular crimes committed by unscrupulous individuals like John Oldham, whose murder in 1636 set in motion the events that led to the war. Oldham was not, moreover, the only Englishman the Pequots or their tributaries had murdered. In 1634 they had killed two English captains, including the notorious and disreputable John Stone, who had kidnapped and held several Indians for ransom, and in the next two years they had killed at least six more colonists. Alternatively, the English leadership was disturbed that the Pequots had taken no action against the guilty among them and disheartened that the Pequots had abrogated the terms of the treaty they had signed. Fears increased when Jonathan Brewster, a Plymouth trader, passed word that Uncas,

sachem of the Mohegans, had reported that

> the Pequents have some mistrust, that the English will shortly come against them (which I take is by indiscreet speeches of some of your people here to the Natives) and therefore out of desperate madnesse doe threaten shortly to sett upon both Indians [Mohegans] and English, joyntly.

Uncas may well have fabricated the rumor, but the colonists were certainly in a frame of mind to take it seriously. Their numbers were small, and news of the Virginia uprising of 1622, with its 350 casualties, had still not faded from memory. What the Puritans sought was a stratagem that would put an end to unpredictable, deadly annoyances as well as forestall any larger, more significant Indian military action like that suggested by Uncas's report. However one estimates the "good faith" or lack thereof of the Massachusetts leadership, efforts were made to negotiate, but these efforts failed, or at least were perceived to have failed. The colonists then chose as their best course of action a retaliatory raid, intended both to punish and to warn, on the Indians of Block Island, who were specifically charged with Oldham's murder. The Pequots were involved, according to William Hubbard, because the murderers had "fled presently to the Pequods, by whom they were sheltered, and so became also guilty themselves of his blood."

Ninety Englishmen participated in the raid commanded by John Endecott. John Winthrop noted that Endecott was ordered

> to put to death the men of Block Island, but to spare the women and children, and to bring them away, and to take

possession of the Island; and from thence to go to the Pequods to demand the murderers of Capt. Stone and other English, and one thousand fathom of wampom for damages, etc., and some of their children as hostages.

None of the mainland Pequot at Pequot Harbor were to be harmed if they capitulated to his demands. In the event, the raid on Block Island turned into an extensive assault, and the Indian settlement there was looted and burned. However, although property was destroyed and several Indians were wounded, "the Naymen killed not a man, save that one Kichomiquim, an Indian Sachem of the Bay, killed a Pequot." The fact that only one Indian was killed seems to confirm John Winthrop's belief that the colonists "went not to make war upon [the Pequots] but to do justice." Not all colonists defined "justice" as Winthrop did, however, for the Endecott raid on the Harbor Indians was condemned by the colonial leaders of Plymouth, Connecticut, and Fort Saybrook.

In response to Endecott's assaults, the Pequots plagued the settlers with a series of raids, ambushes, and annoyances. On 23 April, Wethersfield, Connecticut, was attacked. Nine were killed, including a woman and child, and two additional young women were captured. A number of other raids claimed the lives of thirty Europeans, or five percent of all the settlers in Connecticut. In addition to these offensive actions, the Pequot set about developing alliances, particularly with the Narragansett, to galvanize support for a war to destroy European settlement in their territory, if not in New England entirely. Many colonists who learned of the plan for a broad effort against them, which was frustrated only at the last

minute through the intervention of Roger Williams, rightly felt, given their demographic vulnerability, that their very survival was threatened. Even Francis Jennings, the most severe critic of Puritan behavior, acknowledges that "Had these [Pequot] proposals [for alliance with the Narragansetts] been accepted by the Narragansetts, there would have without a doubt arisen a genuine Indian menace.... Whether the colonies could long have maintained themselves under such conditions is open to serious question."

The Pequot War was the organized reaction of the colonists of Connecticut and Massachusetts to these intimidating events. In choosing to make war, they were choosing to put an end to threats to their existence as individuals and as a community. They did not decide to fight out of some a priori lust for Indian blood based on some metaphysical doctrine of Indian inferiority, however much they may have held that view, or some desire for further, even complete, control over Indian territory, much as they coveted such land. They fought, initially, a defensive war. They may well have provoked events, as even Winthrop tacitly acknowledged, by their over-reactive raid on Block Island, but, in the early stages of the conflict, they did not intend to enter into a full-scale war with the Pequot until the Pequot raised the stakes with their response to the events at Block Island and Pequot Harbor. Of course the Indians cannot be blamed for so replying, for they too saw themselves as acting legitimately in self-defense, both narrowly and more generally in defense of traditional Indian rights to their own native lands. In effect, both sides acted to defend what they perceived as rightly theirs. In this context, if either side can be said to have harbored larger geo-political ambitions, it was the Pequot, though defeat would certainly bury those desires.

The major action of the war was an attack by 70 Connecticut and 90 Massachusetts colonists along with 60 Mohegans, plus some scattered Narragansett and Eastern Niantics, against the Pequot Fort at Mystic, which held an Indian population of between 400 and 700, including women and children. The colonists and their Indian allies surprised the Pequots and burned their fort to the ground. During the battle two English soldiers were killed and about 20 were wounded, while almost half the Indians allied with them were killed or wounded; almost all the Pequots were killed.

Richard Drinnon, in his *Facing West: The Metaphysics of Indian Hating and Empire Building* (1980), has argued that the unusual violence of the operation signals the colonists' "genocidal intentions." In evaluating the behavior of the English in this particular instance, however, it should be recognized that the tactics employed were neither so unconventional nor so novel that they can be taken to mark a turning point in Puritan-Indian relations, nor were they so distinctive as to indicate a transformation in Puritan awareness of the otherness of their adversaries. Given the relative strength of the enemy, the inexperience of the colonial forces, and the crucial fact that Sassacus, chief of the Pequot, and his warriors were camped only five miles from Mystic Fort and were sure to arrive soon, as in fact they did, one need not resort to dramatic theories of genocidal intentionality to explain the actions of the English. The simple, irrefutable fact is that had the battle been prolonged, Sassacus would have had time to reach Mystic and deflect the English attack.

* * *

Although he does not use the term *genocide* per se, it is clear from the rhetorical thrust of his argument and his use of phrases like "deliberate massacre" [in *The Invasion of America: Indians, Colonialism, and the Cant of Conquest* (W. W. Norton, 1976)] that Francis Jennings is an insistent advocate of the genocidal thesis. Given the force of his prose, the popularity of his work, and its long-standing influence, it is useful to deconstruct Jennings's argument to evaluate the legitimacy of the heinous charge leveled against the English colonists.

Jennings attributes to Capt. John Mason, the expedition's leader, an overt, *ab initio* [from the beginning] desire to massacre the Indians. "Mason proposed," he writes,

> to avoid attacking Pequot warriors, which would have overtaxed his unseasoned, unreliable troops. Battle, as such, was not his purpose. Battle is only one of the ways to destroy an enemy's will to fight. Massacre can accomplish the same end with less risk, and Mason had determined that massacre would be his objective.

Ignoring all other reports of Mason's intentions and actions, Jennings bases his conclusions on Mason's own terse account of the event. Jennings cites Mason's reasons for his strategy, with special reference to his concluding " 'and also some other [reasons],' " which he says " 'I shall forebear to trouble you with.' " Even Jennings labels this comment cryptic, but he still does not forebear using it as unambiguous evidence of a hidden, premeditated plan to massacre all the Indians at Fort Mystic.

Jennings also refers to Mason's discussion with his colleagues Lt. Lion Gardiner and Capt. John Underhill as well as with the expedition's Chaplain Stone. He takes Mason's request that the chaplain "'commend our Condition to the Lord, that night, to direct how in what manner we should demean our selves'" to be a covert reference to the existence of a plan to massacre the Indians the next day. But on the eve of such a battle, especially given Puritan sensibilities, such a request is neither surprising nor, given the text before us, indicative of any special intent; to read it as an implicit confession of genocidal desire, Jennings has to overinterpret the brief original source dramatically.

Jennings charges that "all the secondary accounts of the Pequot conquest squeamishly evade confessing the deliberateness of Mason's strategy, and some falsify to conceal it." What Jennings adduces as confirmation of both the premeditated plot to massacre and the later conscious suppression of that fact emerges in the course of a curious argument, which I quote in full.

> Mason's own narrative is the best authority on this point. The Massachusetts Puritans' William Hubbard brazened out his own misquotation by telling his readers to "take it as it was delivered in writing by that valiant, faithful, and prudent Commander Capt. Mason." With this emphatic claim to authority he quoted Mason as saying, "We had resolved a while not to have burned it [the village], but being we could not come at them, I resolved to set it on fire." Despite Hubbard's assurance, these were not Mason's words. His manuscript said bluntly, "we had formerly concluded to destroy them by the Sword and save the Plunder."

Jennings's conclusion does not follow logically from the texts he cites nor from his juxtaposition of them. They neither suggest premeditation to massacre nor falsification of the record; instead, Hubbard's paraphrase of Mason's words accords perfectly with his stated intent to plunder the settlement. Jennings himself recognizes that such economic motives were central to the Block Island raid, as well as other actions by the English. Burning Fort Mystic would, of course, severely limit its economic potential; the sword was a less efficient tool of human destruction but would preserve goods of value to the English. In fact, Mason's vow to "destroy" the Pequots "by the Sword" is a phrase not at all unusual to the language of military conflict and in that context such comments almost always signal not the annihilation of the enemy but the disruption of its capacity to fight. This understanding of Mason's comment is supported by the Puritans' further prosecution of the war.

Jennings continues to press home his point in his increasingly confused and confusing reconstruction of events. I quote:

> The rest of Mason's manuscript revealed what sort of inhabitants had been occupying the Mystic River village and proved conclusively that mere victory over them was not enough to satisfy Mason's purpose. After telling how the attack was launched at dawn of May 26, and how entrance to the village was forced, the account continued thus:
>
>> At length William Heydon espying the Breach in the Wigwam, supposing some English might be there, entred; but in his Entrance fell over a dead Indian; but speedily recovering himself, the Indians some fled, others crept under their Beds: the Captain [Mason] going out of the Wigwam saw many Indians in the Lane or Street; he making to-

wards them, they fled, were pursued to the End of the Lane, where they were met by Edward Pattison, Thomas Barber, with some others; where seven of them were Slain, as they said. The Captain facing about, Marched a slow Pace up the Lane he came down, perceiving himself very much out of Breath; and coming to the other End near the Place where he first entred, saw two Soldiers standing close to the Pallizado with their Swords pointed to the Ground: The Captain told them that We should never kill them after that manner: The Captain also said, WE MUST BURN THEM: and immediately stepping into the Wigwam where he had been before, brought out a Fire Brand, and putting it into the Matts with which they were covered, set the Wigwams on Fire.

From this sparse, unsophisticated description, Jennings concludes that "It is terribly clear... that the village, stockaded though it was, had few warriors at home when the attack took place." Mason himself, however, asserts that just the day before the English attack, 150 braves had reinforced the Indian garrison holding the fort, but Jennings cavalierly dismisses this claim in a marvelous display of selective reading. The reasons he musters for denying Mason's express testimony on such a vital matter are offered both in Jennings's text and in a dizzying footnote. The burden of the main argument is that insofar as Mason's account portrays Indians fleeing and creeping under their beds for protection, those so described could only have been "women, children, and feeble old men," who had no other recourse but to resort to such cowardly stratagems. Surely 150 warriors—and the Pequots had already well demonstrated "their willingness to fight to the death"—

would not have "suddenly and uncharacteristically turned craven." At the end of this convoluted denial of part—and only part, indeed the most straightforward and factual part—of Mason's account is Jennings's assumption that Mason marched on Fort Mystic because he had received advance intelligence from Narragansett allies that "there were no 'reinforcements.'" Destroying the "wretches" would be easily accomplished.

But the original narratives of the battle suggest a very different reading. Mason indicates that he found his first plan unworkable, that only after the attack had begun did he realize how costly it might prove for the English; only then, in self-protection, did he make the decision to burn rather than to plunder the settlement. This analysis of events is confirmed by [John] Underhill's record of the battle, which also has the virtue of emphasizing the bravery of the Indians involved. "Most courageously," he writes, "these Pequots behaved themselves." Only when the battle grew too intense did the British, out of necessity, torch the fort. Even then, Underhill states, "many courageous fellows were unwilling to come out and fought most desperately through the palisadoes... and so perished valiantly. Mercy did they deserve for their valor, could we have had opportunity to bestow it." Jennings does not cite Underhill's crucial and disarming testimony; instead, he engages in some more verbal sleight of hand, carefully choosing the texts he wishes to manipulate.

In a footnote he replays his charge against Mason. Leaving out only the citations, I quote in full:

... Underhill and [William] Hubbard omitted the reinforcements assertion.

Winthrop assigned as Pequot casualties "two chief sachems, and one hundred and fifty fighting men, and about one hundred and fifty old men, women, and children." ... Mason's and Winthrop's "reinforcements" thus became Winthrop's total of warrior casualties. Even if this is true, it means that Mason planned the attack before those warriors arrived, but the likelihood of its truth is remote. No matter how these wriggly texts are viewed, they testify to Mason's deliberate purpose of massacring noncombatants. He had advance information of the Pequot dispositions.

First, it should be recognized that because Underhill and Hubbard do not mention the 150 Indian reinforcements, Jennings uses their silence as confirmation of the dishonesty of Mason's account. But arguments from silence "say" very little, and extreme caution should be exercised in employing them, especially in the face of explicit testimony to the contrary. Jennings next uses Winthrop's narrative, which supports Mason's claim about reinforcements, to diminish that claim by impugning Winthrop's veracity. But such double-think will not do, for if Winthrop is unreliable, the truth of his account "remote," he cannot serve to discredit Mason; if he is reliable, his depiction of events cannot be taken lightly. Then, out of this morass of conflicting facts and conclusions, Jennings draws the non sequitur that Mason was intent on massacring noncombatant Pequots; in fact, all contemporary accounts simply state that noncombatants were massacred, not that there was any premeditated plan to do so. It appears that Jennings would have us believe that his highly ambiguous, contradictory reconstruction of the facts proposed 340 years after the event and premised on a dubi-

ous dialectical analysis of silence, a great deal of hermeneutical confusion, and a series of non sequiturs is to be given precedence over the description of circumstances provided by several contemporary and first-person accounts in our possession. Assuredly, the Connecticut militiamen acted reprehensibly and with unnecessary severity against noncombatants that spring day in 1637, but they did not do so for the reasons, nor in the manner, advanced in Jennings's moving, but untrue, retelling of the tale.

* * *

Following the destruction of Mystic Fort, the colonists and their Indian allies pursued the surviving Pequots. In the first major encounter of this subsequent stage in the conflict, approximately 200 Indians were captured, of whom 22 or 24 were adult males; these braves were executed. The remaining women and children, almost 80 percent of the total captured, were parceled up about evenly, as was common Indian practice, among the victorious Indian allies and the colonists of Massachusetts Bay. A second and larger engagement took place on 14 July near modern Southport, Connecticut, where Sassacus and the majority of the remaining Pequots, numbering several hundred, were surrounded. In the ensuing battle, women, children, and old men, again a majority of the Pequots present, were allowed to seek sanctuary while about 80 warriors fought to their death. In the final phase of the war, various Indian tribes in the area, vying for English friendship and seeking to settle old tribal debts, hunted down and murdered Pequot braves while dispersing their womenfolk and children. Sassacus was killed, and in early August the Mohawks sent his head to the British in Hartford.

Alden Vaughan describes the aftermath of these events:

> Toward the end of 1637 the few remaining sachems begged for an end to the war, promising vassalage in return for their lives. A peace convention was arranged for the following September. With the Treaty of Hartford, signed on September 21, 1638, the Pequots ceased to exist as an independent polity.

The treaty arrangement as well as the previous pattern of killing all adult males suggests that the anti-Pequot forces, both Indian and European, were determined to eliminate the Pequot threat once and for all. The 180 Pequots captured in the assault on Sassacus were parceled out among the victors: 80 to the Narragansett, 80 to the Mohegans, and 20 to the Eastern Niantics. The survivors were now no longer to be known as Pequots or to reside in their tribal lands, and the Pequot River was renamed the Thames and the Pequot village, New London. These treaty stipulations, which required the extinction of Pequot identity and the assignment of Pequot survivors to other tribes, and some to slavery, suggest an overt, unambiguous form of *cultural* genocide, here employed in the name of military security. However, the dispersement of the remaining communal members—the elderly, the women, and the children, almost certainly a majority of the tribe as a whole—directly contradicts the imputation of any intent to commit *physical* genocide, as some revisionists insist.

A more constrained reading of events would not deny that the Puritans, as their post-war writings reflect, were conscious that they had acted with great, perhaps even excessive, destructive force. Almost certainly composed as responses to English and Indian critics, these after-the-fact appraisals should not, however, be misconstrued as evidence of either genocidal intent prior to the event or even of genocidal behavior during and after the war. Rather, given the Puritan mentality, saturated as it was with concerns to detect God's providential design in temporal matters, these post-hoc accountings, even were we to call them rationalizations, were attempts to satisfy the Puritans' own internal axiological demand that their taking of lives on such a large scale, and in such a bloody way, was justified. Puritans had to know, and they wanted their critics to know, that what they had done was sanctioned by heaven. This concern for ethical legitimation should not be mistaken as evidence that the Puritans, however aware they were *after the event* of the contentious nature of the massacre they had wrought, looked upon this happening as signaling some fundamental re-orientation in their relationship either to their New World surroundings in general or with their New England Indian neighbors in particular. Neither Edward Johnson's approval of the Puritan preachers' exhortation to "execute vengeance upon the heathen," nor William Bradford's description of the burning of the inhabitants at Fort Mystic as a "sweet sacrifice" to the Lord, nor Underhill's appeal to scriptural precedent that in conquering a grossly evil people, such as the Pequot, "women and children must perish with their parents" are proof to the contrary. Indeed, they are exactly the sort of theological pronouncements one would expect within the Puritan conceptual environment, fed as it was by recycled scriptural paradigms.

In general, the English did not relish their victory in an unseemly way. John

Mason, for example, "refused to publish his accounts of his exploits, deeming them too immodest and likely to detract from the glory ascribed to God in those events." Captain Underhill, by contrast, did publish his version of the tale, but as Richard Slotkin has written, "Captain Underhill was a man clearly out of step with the Massachusetts way and one proscribed and exiled by the Puritan community." Underhill's "enthusiasms," in fact, were repeatedly met with censure rather than emulation. Mason, by contrast, the modest, self-effacing, God-extolling leader, was considered a worthy model in early American literature.

* * *

When the actions of the Puritans are placed in their appropriate context, when they are deconstructed as part and parcel of the historical reality of the seventeenth century, the accusations of genocide leveled against them are recognized to be exaggerations. However excessive the force wielded by the colonists, they had already seen—and would continue to see—their own die at the hands of the Indians. The Virginia Indian uprisings of 1622 have already been mentioned. In April 1644, a second uprising took the lives of approximately 500 whites, and in 1675, 300 more colonists were killed. The bloody events of King Philip's War (1675–76) would certainly have intensified the fears that had long plagued those living at the edge of the frontier. Much Indian violence was, of course, a response to English greed, but for those charged with protecting the members of expanding English communities, the violence had to be stopped at all costs. In the New World—an environment so uncertain, so hostile—the colonists' need to limit threats to their survival was intense.

Their responses could be excessive, but their fears were not unfounded.

From our point of view, it is easy to sympathize with the Pequots and to condemn the colonists' actions, but the scope of our condemnation must be measured against the facts. After the Treaty of Hartford was signed, Pequots were not physically harmed. Indeed, in 1640 the Connecticut leadership "declared their dislike of such as would have the Indians rooted out," that is, murdered. Before the Pequots capitulated, many of their tribe had died, but the number killed probably totaled less than half the entire tribe. Sherburne Cook's estimate is even lower: "If the initial population [of Pequots] was 3,000 and 750 were killed, the battle loss was twenty-five percent of the tribe."

While many Pequots were absorbed by other tribes—it is estimated that Uncas's Mohegan tribe, for example, received hundreds—evidence clearly indicates that soon after the conclusion of the war, the Pequot began to regroup as a tribe. By 1650 four special towns were created to accommodate them, each ruled by a Pequot governor, and in 1667 Connecticut established permanent reservations for the tribe, which by 1675 numbered approximately 1,500–2,000 members. That year, no more than two generations after the Pequot War had ended, the Pequots allied with the colonists to fight King Philip's War. As recently as the 1960s, Pequots were still listed as a separate group residing in Connecticut. Such factors suggest that while the British could certainly have been less thorough, less severe, less deadly in prosecuting their campaign against the Pequots, the campaign they actually did carry out, for all its vehemence, was not, either in intent or execution, genocidal.

This revision of the revisionists is not meant to deny the larger truth that the conquest of the New World entailed the greatest demographic tragedy in history. The wrongs done to the Native Americans, the suffering they experienced, the manifest evil involved in the colonial enterprise is in no way to be deflected or minimized. However, this sorry tale of despoliation and depopulation needs to be chronicled aright, with an appropriate sense of the actuality of seventeenth-century colonial existence. False, if morally impassioned, judgments cannot substitute for carefully nuanced and discriminating appraisals. Thus, while it is appropriate to censure the excesses, the unnecessary carnage, of the Pequot War, to interpret these events through the radicalizing polemic of accusations of genocide is to rewrite history to satisfy our own moral outrage.

POSTSCRIPT

Were the English Colonists Guilty of Genocide?

Some contemporary scholars have charged that Christopher Columbus and the subsequent waves of European immigrants to America committed a long list of crimes against humanity and the environment. Many observers, however, dismiss these allegations of wrongdoing as the products of political correctness. Nevertheless, the complexities associated with the relations between Native Americans and colonists from Europe—evident in the essays by Stannard and Katz—show how difficult it is to generalize about the clash of cultures that occurred on New World shores.

A case in point is the history of Indian-white relations in early Virginia. The colonists participating in the Jamestown expedition, for example, were attacked by a group of Indians almost as soon as they set foot on American soil. A few months later, however, Powhatan, the dominant chief in the region, provided essential food supplies to the Jamestown residents who were suffering from disease and hunger. By the latter part of 1608, however, the colonists, under the leadership of John Smith, had begun to take an antagonistic stance toward Powhatan and his people. Smith attempted to extort food supplies from the Indians by threatening to burn their villages and canoes. These hostilities continued long after Smith's departure from Virginia and did not end until the 1640s, when colonial leaders signed a formal treaty with the Powhatan Confederacy.

Extensive literature addresses the relationship between Native Americans and Europeans in the seventeenth and eighteenth centuries. Gary Nash, *Red, White, and Black: The Peoples of Early America*, 2d ed. (Prentice Hall, 1982), is an excellent survey for the colonial period. James Axtell, *After Columbus: Essays in the Ethnohistory of Colonial North America* (Oxford University Press, 1988) is indispensable. Karen Ordahl Kupperman, *Settling With the Indians: The Meeting of English and Indian Cultures in America, 1580–1640* (Rowman & Littlefield, 1980) and Bernard Sheehan, *Savagism and Civility: Indians and Englishmen in Colonial Virginia* (Cambridge University Press, 1980) offer conflicting explanations for the nature of Indian-white relations in the colonies. The themes of coexistence and coercion in relation to contacts between Native Americans and Englishmen in New England are assessed in Neal E. Salisbury, *Manitou and Providence: Indians, Europeans, and the Beginnings of New England* (Oxford University Press, 1982). Every student interested in the history of Native American societies should read Anthony F. C. Wallace's classic anthropological and historical work *The Death and Rebirth of the Seneca* (Alfred A. Knopf, 1970).

ISSUE 3

Was the Salem Witchcraft Hysteria Caused by a Fear of Women?

YES: Carol F. Karlsen, from *The Devil in the Shape of a Woman: Witchcraft in Colonial New England* (Random House, 1987)

NO: Kai T. Erikson, from *Wayward Puritans: A Study in the Sociology of Deviance* (John Wiley & Sons, 1966)

ISSUE SUMMARY

YES: Associate professor of history Carol F. Karlsen contends that the belief that women were evil existed implicitly at the core of Puritan culture and that it explains why alleged witches, as threats to the desired order of society, were generally seen as women.

NO: Professor of sociology Kai T. Erikson argues that the Salem witchcraft hysteria was a product of the Puritan colonists' efforts to restore a common sense of mission, which they believed had eroded over the first 60 years of settlement.

For most people, the images of witches are confined to television and movie screens or perhaps to the theatrical stage on which Shakespeare's *MacBeth* is being performed. The popular image of witches can be seen in the annual television presentation of *The Wizard of Oz* and in reruns of "Bewitched," as well as in the form of black-garbed, broomstick-toting children who appear on our doorsteps at Halloween. Although such apparitions rarely elicit fear, such was not always the case.

Prehistoric paintings on the walls of caves throughout Europe reveal that witchcraft was of immediate and serious concern to many of our ancestors. The most intense eruptions in the long history of witchcraft, however, appeared during the sixteenth and seventeenth centuries. In the British North American colonies, there were over 100 witchcraft trials in seventeenth-century New England alone, and 40 percent of those accused were executed. For most Americans the events that began in the kitchen of the Reverend Samuel Parris in Salem, Massachusetts, in 1692 are the most notorious.

A group of young girls, with the assistance of Parris's West Indian slave, Tituba, were attempting to see into the future by "reading" messages in the white of a raw egg they had suspended in a glass. The tragic results of this seemingly innocent diversion scandalized the Salem community and reverberated all the way to Boston. One of the participants insisted she saw the specter of a coffin in the egg white, and soon after, the girls began to display the hysterical symptoms of the possessed. Following intense interrogation by adults, Tituba, Sarah Good, and Sarah Osborne were accused of practicing magic and were arrested. Subsequently, Tituba confessed her guilt and acknowledged the existence of other witches but refused to name them. Accusations spread as paranoia enveloped the community. Between May and September 1692 hundreds of people were arrested. Nineteen were convicted and hanged (not burned at the stake, as is often assumed), and another, a man who refused to admit either guilt or innocence, was pressed to death under heavy weights. Finally, Sir William Phips, the new royal governor of the colony, halted court proceedings against the accused (which included his wife), and in May 1693 he ordered the release of those who were still in jail.

Throughout history, witchcraft accusations have tended to follow certain patterns, most of which were duplicated in Salem. Usually, they occurred during periods of political turmoil, economic dislocation, or social stress. In Salem a political impasse between English authorities and the Massachusetts Bay Colony, economic tensions between commercial and agricultural interests, and disagreements between Salem Town and Salem Village all formed the backdrop to the legal drama of 1692. In addition, the events in Salem fit the traditional pattern that those accused of witchcraft were almost always women. To what extent did sexism play the central role in the Salem witchcraft hysteria of 1692? Are there other, equally valid explanations that place little or no weight on the gender of the accused?

In the selections that follow, Carol F. Karlsen and Kai T. Erikson offer two varying interpretations of the events that occurred in Salem 300 years ago. For Karlsen, gender is the key factor. Negative views of women as the embodiment of evil were deeply imbedded in the Puritan (and European) world view. But through most of the seventeenth century, according to Karlsen, New Englanders avoided explicit connections between women and witchcraft. Nevertheless, the attitudes that depicted witches as women remained self-evident truths and sprang to the surface in 1692. Erikson, in opposition, focuses upon the societal tensions that had produced among many New Englanders the feeling that their sense of mission had eroded by the last decade of the seventeenth century. Confronted by this loss of purpose, they imagined a conspiracy of witches, which provided them at least temporary targets against which they could rally as a unified community once again.

YES

Carol F. Karlsen

HANDMAIDENS OF THE LORD

There is a curious paradox that students of New England witchcraft encounter. The characteristics of the New England witch—demographic, economic, religious, and sexual—emerge from *patterns* found in accusations and
in the life histories of the accused; they are not visible in the content of individual accusations or in the ministerial literature. No colonist ever explicitly
said why he or she saw witches as women, or particularly as older women.
No one explained why some older women were suspect while others were
not, why certain sins were signs of witchcraft when committed by women
but not when committed by men, or why specific behaviors associated with
women aroused witchcraft fears while specific behaviors associated with men
did not. Indeed, New Englanders did not openly discuss most of their widely
shared assumptions about women-as-witches.

This cultural silence becomes even more puzzling when we consider that
many of these assumptions had once been quite openly talked about in the
European witchcraft tradition. In the late fifteenth and early sixteenth centuries especially, defenders of the Christian faith spelled out in elaborate
detail why they believed women rather than men were likely to join Satan's
forces. The reasons they gave are not very different from those evident in the
patterns the New England sources reveal. This presses upon us a question of
some consequence: why had once-explicit beliefs about women's proclivity
to witchcraft become implicit in their New England setting?

We can probe this question by following the lead of the anthropologist
Mary Douglas and other scholars who have explored the social construction of knowledge. In Douglas's analysis, human societies relegate certain
information to the category of self-evident truths. Ideas that are treated as
self-evident, "as too true to warrant discussion," constitute a society's implicit knowledge. At one time explicit, implicit ideas have not simply been
forgotten, but have been "actively thrust out of the way" because they conflict
with ideas deemed more suitable to the social order. But the conflict is more
apparent than real. In the "elusive exchange" between implicit and explicit
knowledge, the implicit is "obliquely affirmed" and the society is shielded
from challenges to its world view. The implicit resides in a society's symbols,

rituals, and myths, which simultaneously describe, reflect, and mask that world view. To understand these processes, implicit and explicit knowledge must be examined together and in the context of their social environment.

In colonial New England, the many connections between "women" and "witchcraft" were implicitly understood. In Europe, several generations before, the connections had still been explicit. Over time, these established "truths" about women's sinfulness had increasingly come into conflict with other ideas about women—ideas latent in Christian thought but brought to the fore by the Reformation and the political, economic, and social transformations that accompanied it. For the Puritans who emigrated to New England in the early seventeenth century, once-explicit assumptions about why witches were women were already self-evident.

The swiftly changing conditions of early settlement left it uncertain at first whether, or how, witchcraft would serve the goals of New England society. Though men in positions of authority believed that certain women were working against the new colonies' interests, others did not see these women as witches. By the late 1640s, however, New Englanders embraced a witchcraft belief system as integral to their social order. Over the course of the seventeenth century, Puritan rituals, symbols, and myths perpetuated the belief that women posed ever-present dangers to human society, but the newer, post-Reformation ideas about women forced colonists to shrink from explicitly justifying this belief. They therefore continued to assume the complex of ideas about women-as-witches as self-evident truths....

* * *

The fundamental tenet of European witchcraft—that women were innately more evil than men—did not fit with other ideas Puritans brought with them to their new world. This tenet was still as necessary to Puritans as it had been for their Catholic predecessors, but it was incompatible with the emphasis Puritanism placed on the priesthood of all believers, on the importance of marriage and family relations, and on the status of women within those relations.

Puritanism took shape in late sixteenth- and early seventeenth-century England amidst a heated controversy over the nature of women, the value of marriage, and the propriety of women's social roles. The dominant attitude toward women in the popular press and on stage did not differ very much from the views of Catholic witch-hunters except that overall it was less virulent, delivered as often in the form of mockery as invective. According to this opinion, women were evil, whorish, deceitful, extravagant, angry, vengeful, and, of course, insubordinate and proud. Women "are altogether a lumpe of pride," one author maintained in 1609—"a masse of pride, even altogether made of pride, and nothing else but pride, pride." Considering the nature of women, marriage was at best man's folly; at worst, it was the cause of his destruction.

The problem, as some writers of this school had it, was women's increasing independence, impudence, "masculine" dress, and "masculine" ways. The presence of women in the streets and shops of the new commercial centers was merely symptomatic of their newly found "forwardness" and desire for "liberties." But more than likely it was not so much women's increasing independence in the wake of commercial development that troubled these commentators; rather it was the increasing visibility of women within their traditional but increasingly commercialized occupations. Solutions to the problem, when offered, echoed a 1547 London proclamation that enjoined husbands to "keep their wives in their houses."

Other writers argued that women were equal if not superior to men, called for recognition of the abuse women suffered under men's tyranny, and intimated that society would be better served if economic power resided in women's hands —but their voices were few and barely heard. More often, defenders of women simply took exception to the worst of the misogynists' charges and recounted the contributions women made to the welfare of their families and their society. The most serious challenge to prevailing opinion, however, came from a group of men who shared some of the concerns and goals of women's most avid detractors. Most of these men were Protestant ministers, and they entered the debate indirectly, through their sermons and publications on domestic relations. Though not primarily interested in bettering women's position in society, they found certain transformations in attitudes toward women essential to their own social vision. Among them, it was the Puritan divines—in both old and New England—who mounted the most cogent, most sustained, and most enduring attack on the contemporary wisdom concerning women's inherent evil.

From the publication of Robert Cleaver's *A Godly Form of Householde Government* in 1598 until at least the appearance of John Cotton's *A Meet Help* in 1699, a number of Puritan ministers did battle with "Misogynists, such as cry out against all women." If they were not unanimous on every point, most of them agreed with John Cotton that women were not "a necessary Evil," but "a necessary good." For justification of this belief, they turned to the Scriptures, to the story of the Creation. God in his infinite wisdom, John Robinson contended, had created woman from man and for man, when he "could find none fit and good enough for the man... amongst all the good creatures which he had made." He had made woman *from* man's rib, Samuel Willard noted, "Partly that all might derive Originally from One; Partly that she might be the more Dear and Precious to him, and Beloved by him as a piece of himself." He had made her *for* "man's conveniency and comfort," Cotton said, to be a helpmeet in all his spiritual and secular endeavors and "a most sweet and intimate companion." It followed from both the means and purposes of God's Creation that women and men were "joynt Heirs of salvation," that marriage was an honorable, even ideal state, and that women who fulfilled the purposes of their creation deserved to be praised, not vilified by godly men. In 1598, Cleaver called men foolish who detested women and marriage. For Cotton, a century later, such men were "a sort of Blasphemers."

What had happened? Why did Puritans (along with their reforming brethren) insist on a shift in attitude that would by the nineteenth century result in a full reversal of a number of sixteenth-century notions about the "innate" qualities of men and women? We can begin to answer this question by considering a few elements critical in bringing about the transformation.

The Puritan challenge to the authority of church and state covered many issues, but one point not in dispute was the necessity of authority itself. Puritans were as disturbed by the lack of order in their society as were their enemies and were as fully committed to the principle of hierarchy. Though Puritanism developed during the period of upheavel that followed the breakup of the feudal order, Puritans were nevertheless determined to smother the sources of upheaval. Like other propertied Englishmen, Puritan men worried especially about masterlessness—insubordination in women, children, servants, vagabonds, beggars, and even in themselves.

Where they differed with other men of property was in their belief that existing authority was both ineffective and misplaced. "Faced with the ineffectuality of authorities in everyday life," one historian has argued, "the Puritans dramatically and emphatically denied the chain of authority in the church and enthroned conscience in its place.... The radical solution to social deterioration was not the strengthening of external authority. It was, rather, the internalization of authority itself." Foremost among the lessons Puritans taught was God's insistence on complete submission to divine will as expressed in the Bible and interpreted by ministers and magistrates. Outward compliance was not enough. Individuals who were fully committed to following the laws of God were *self*-controlled, needing only the Scriptures and an educated ministry to guide them on the path of right behavior. Submission to God's will had to be not only complete but voluntary. External discipline was still necessary to control the ungodly, but even they could be taught a measure of self-discipline.

The internal commitment to God's laws was to be inculcated primarily within the family, under the guidance and watchful eye of the head of the household, who conducted family prayer and instilled moral values in his dependents. It was not easy for family heads to ensure willing submission in their dependents, Puritans readily admitted. Minister John Robinson was talking specifically about children when he said that the "stubbornness, and stoutness of mind arising from natural pride... must... be broken and beaten down,... [the] root of actual rebellion both against God and man... destroyed," but his remarks reflect the larger Puritan belief in the difficulty of curbing human willfulness. For subordinates to accept their places in the hierarchical order, they must first be disciplined to accept the *sin* in their very tendency to rebel. From there, it was possible to develop enlightened consciences.

The family was also crucial as a symbol of a hierarchical society. Functioning as both "a little Church" and "a little Commonwealth," it served as a model of relationships between God and his creatures and as a model for all social relations. As husband, father, and master to wife, children, and servants, the head of the household stood in the same relationship to them as the minister did to his congregants and as the magistrate did to his subjects. Also, his relationship to them mirrored God's to him. Indeed, the authority of God was vested in him as household head, and his relationship to God was immediate: he served God directly. There was therefore no need for a priesthood to mediate between God and family heads. Other household members had immortal souls and could pray to God directly, but they served God indirectly by serving their superiors within the domestic frame. This model enhanced the position of all male heads of household and made any challenge to their authority a challenge to God's authority. It thereby more firmly tied other family members into positions of subordination.

The relationship of household heads to other family members fit within a larger Puritan world view. God had created the world, Puritans maintained, in the form of a great "Chain of Being" in which man was both above other creatures and subordinate to the Deity. God had ordained that human relationships were to be similarly patterned, with husbands superior to wives, parents to children, masters to servants, ministers to congregants, and magistrates to subjects. All, however, were subordinate to God. In each of these relations, inferiors served God by serving their superiors. While Puritans viewed the parent-child relation as a natural one, all other unequal relationships were described as voluntary, based on a covenant between the individuals concerned. God also required that family heads enter into another contractual relationship, called a "family covenant." Under this agreement, men promised to ensure obedience in all their dependents, in return for God's promise of prosperity.

Finally, the family also guided children in the right selection of their "particular callings." For the English divine William Perkins, particular callings were of two types. The first was God's call to individuals to enter into one or more of the several kinds of unequal social relations (husband/wife/parent/child, master/servant, and so on), relations that were "the essence and foundation of any society, without which the society cannot be." The second was God's call to specific kinds of employment by which individuals earned their livelihoods. In each case, God did the calling, but children had to endeavor to know what God had in mind for them, and parents were responsible to see that their charges made appropriate choices. Once chosen, callings were to be attended to conscientiously, not for honor or material reward but in the service of God. What Perkins did not say was that for Puritans the second sort of calling did not apply to females. Woman was called for only one employment, the work of a wife....

* * *

As the old idea of woman as a necessary evil was gradually transformed into the idea of woman as a necessary good, the fear and hostility that men felt toward women remained. The old view of woman was suppressed, but it made its presence known in the many faults and tensions that riddled Puritan formulations on woman. Though largely unspoken, the old assumptions modified the seemingly more enlightened knowledge Puritans imparted. The new discourse, "first uttered out of the pulpit," was in fact dedicated to affirming the beliefs of the old, but in ways that would better serve male interests in a society that was itself being transformed.

The belief that woman was evil continued to reside in the myth at the core of Puritan culture—the biblical tale of human origins. Really two myths in one, it is the story of Creation in the Garden of Eden and the story of Adam and Eve's fall from grace. Our concern is mostly with the latter, but the two tales are nonetheless interdependent—the joys of Paradise making comprehensible the agonies of Paradise lost.

In their version of human origins, the Puritan clergy were more ambiguous than usual about when they were discussing "man, male and female," and when they were discussing men only. Despite its many contradictions, this creation myth allowed the Puritans to establish their two most cherished truths: hierarchy and order. Even before the Fall, they maintained, God had designated woman as both inferior to and destined to serve man—though her original inferiority was based "in innocency" and without "grief." Woman's initial identity was not —like man's—as a separate individual, but as a wife in relation to a husband. The very purpose of her creation allowed Puritans to extend the idea of her subordination *as wife* to her subordination *as woman*, in much the same manner as Anglican minister Matthew Griffiths did when he observed: "No sooner was she a Woman, but presently a Wife; so that Woman and Wife are of the same standing." So interchangeable were these terms in the minds of the clergy that they could barely conceive of woman's relationship to God except through a husband.

Woman's position in the Puritan version of Eden was analogous to that of the angels and the animals. Angels were formed before Creation as morally perfect spiritual beings. Though angels were clearly above man in the hierarchy of Creation, and though man was not to have dominion over them, God would require the angels to "minister for man." Animals were even closer to the position of woman since they too were created specifically to serve man.

The Puritan account of the Fall follows the standard Christian version in its general outlines. Discontented with their position in the hierarchical order, Adam and Eve succumbed to the Devil's temptation to eat the forbidden fruit, thus challenging God's supremacy over them and rebelling against the order of Creation. Guilty of pride, both were punished, but Eve doubly because she gave in to the temptation first, thereby causing man's downfall.

Puritan elaborations on this tale are revealing. According to Samuel Willard, Adam and Eve were both principal causes of man's fall, but there were also three instrumental causes: the serpent, the Devil, and the woman. Exonerating the serpent as a creature lacking the ability to reason, he went on to discuss the two "blamable Causes," the Devil and Eve. The events of the Fall originated with the Devil, he said, explaining that the word "Devil" was a collective term for a group of apostate angels. Filled with pride in their positions as the most noble of God's creations, discontented that they were assigned to serve "such a peasant as man," envious of what they saw as a "greater honour conferred upon him," and consumed with malice against God and man, the apostate angels sought revenge by plotting man's downfall. What motivated them was not their displeasure at their place in the hierarchical order, Willard claimed, for only God was above them. Rather it was their "supreme contempt for their employment." United by their evil intentions, they are called "Satan" in the Scriptures as a sign that they had traded their natural subjection to God for a diabolical subjection to the "Prince of Evil." In the process of accomplishing their ends, they were the first to speak falsehoods in Eden, becoming in the process blasphemers against God and murderers of the bodies and souls of men. "They seduced them... and thus in procuring of man's fall, they compleated their own; in making of him miserable, they made themselves Devils."

Eve's story—and her motivations—were more complex. Entering the body of the serpent, the Devil addressed himself to Eve, Willard said, suggesting to her that if she ate the fruit he offered, she would become godlike. Her senses suddenly deluded, she gave in to her lusts: "the lusts of the flesh, in giving way to carnal appetite, good for food; the lust of the eye, in entertaining the desirable aspect of the forbidden fruit, pleasant to the eyes; [and] the lusts of pride, in aspiring after more wisdom than God saw meet to endow a creature withal, to make one wise." Easily seduced, she in turn seduced Adam, thereby implicating him in her guilt. She commended the fruit, "makes offers to him, insinuates herself into him, backs all that the Serpent had said, and attracts him to joint consent with her in the great Transgression." Eve was moved not only by her sensuality but, like Satan, by pride. Her action bespoke the pride of a desire for knowledge, and by extension for God's position, rather than the resentment of her obligation to serve man.

Adam and Eve were both punished for the sin of pride, for rebelling against the order of Creation, but Eve rebelled both as part of man and as man's "other." For this reason, Willard called her both a principal and an instrumental cause of man's fall. According to Willard, when God commanded man not to eat the fruit of the tree of knowledge, "though their prohibition be expresst as given to Adam in the singular [necessarily so, as Eve had yet to be created in the chapter Willard was citing]... yet Eve understood it as comprehending them both." Thus she shared with Adam responsibility as a principal in the matter. "Yet, looking upon her as made for the man, and by the Creators law owing a subordination to him, so she may also be looked upon as instrumental." Elaborating on this point, Willard argued that having been created as his helpmeet, she ought to have encouraged and fortified him in that obedience which God had required of them both. Instead she became a mischief, "an occasion, yea a blamable cause of his ruin." For this, the Lord placed his "special curse" upon the female sex: "Unto the woman he said, I will greatly multiply thy sorrow and thy conception: in sorrow shalt thou bring forth children: and thy desire shall be to thy husband, and he shall rule over thee."

Part of woman's sin, then, was the seduction of man; another part was her failure to serve man. Though Willard never explicitly charged woman with having the same sinister motives as Satan, he did strengthen the association between these two instruments of man's fall by defining her as the Devil's willing agent: she acted "upon deliberation," he said, "and was voluntary in what she did."

In contrast, Adam (as distinguished from "man") lacked any motive for his sin. His role in the Fall was essentially passive. When God confronted the pair about their sin Adam defended himself by pointing the accusatory finger at his mate: "the woman which thou gavest to be with me, she gave me of the tree, and I did eat." Willard exonerated Adam by supporting his disclaimer and by describing him as an unwitting victim of his temptress wife: "Adam was not deceived, but the woman being deceived, was in the transgression." The burden of Adam's guilt was thereby lifted, and the blame placed on Eve. If "man's" sin in the Garden of Eden was pride, it was woman subsumed in man who committed it. Her male counterpart deserved a share of the punishment, but merely for allowing himself to be made "a servant of servants." Willard reinforced this point in his description of the sins that made human beings like devils. It is by now a familiar list: pride, discontent, envy, malice, lying, blasphemy, seduction, and murder. Some were explicitly Eve's, others implicitly hers; none were attributed to Adam.

* * *

Eve was the main symbol of woman-as-evil in Puritan culture. She was, in many ways, the archetypal witch. Whatever the new beliefs affirmed about women's potential goodness, the persistence of Eve as a figure in the Puritan cosmology signals the endurance of older if more covert beliefs. Women could be taught to internalize the authority of men, Puritans thought—but they knew that the sweeping denial of self they demanded of women was "too bitter a pill to be well digested," that it had to "be sweetened" before it could "be swallowed." The story of the Fall taught the lesson that female submission would not come easily —not, certainly, through a theological reformulation alone. Their continuing references to the Fall bespeak Puritan belief that the subjection of the daughters of Eve, whether religious, economic, or sexual, would have to be coerced. That was the message of Eve's punishment.

Ever fearful that women's conversion to virtuous womanhood was incomplete, ministers sometimes resorted to more vivid images of physical and psychological coercion. They warned the Puritan husband that he should not "bee satisfied that hee hath robed his wife of her

virginitie, but in that hee hath possession and use of her will." Women tempted to abandon their chastity, and therefore their God, were told to resolve that if ever these Other Lords do after this Obtain any thing from you, it shall be by the Violence of a Rape." For women who had yet to learn the necessity of subjection came the ever-present threat of additional punishment: "Christ will sorely revenge the rebellion of evill wives." Though the clergy protested again and again that the position of wives was different from that of servants, when they tried to picture what husbands' position would be like if the power relations within marriage were reversed, they envisioned men kept as vassals or enchained as slaves.

Ministers described this reversal of the sexual order as a complete perversion of the laws of God and the laws of nature. The most frequently employed symbols of female usurpers were perversions of those other beings destined to serve man: angels and animals. For woman to be "a man-kinde woman or a masterly wife" conjured up images of fallen angels, demons, and monsters, distortions of nature in every respect.

The tensions within the new ideology suggest that Puritans could no more resolve the ambivalence in their feelings than they could the contradictions in their thought. There was a deep and fundamental split in the Puritan psyche where women were concerned: their two conflicting sets of beliefs about women coexisted, albeit precariously, one on a conscious level, the other layers beneath. If woman was good—if she was chaste, submissive, deferential—then who was this creature whose image so frequently, if so fleetingly, passed through the mind and who so regularly controlled the night? Who was this female figure who was so clearly what woman was not? The ministers were not the only ones who lived with this tension, of course. The dual view of women affected everyone, male and female alike. Still, as the primary arbiters of culture in an age when God still reigned supreme, the clergy played the crucial role not only in creating the virtuous wife but in perpetuating belief in her malevolent predecessor.

* * *

In colonial New England, the intensity of this psychic tension is best seen in the writings of Cotton Mather—perhaps simply because he wrote so much, perhaps because his own ambivalence was so extreme.

In 1692, Mather published his lengthiest treatise on womanhood, *Ornaments for the Daughters of Zion*. His purpose, as he stated in his preface, was "to advocate virtue among those who can not forget their Ornaments and to promote a fear of God in the female sex." He was concerned both with women's behavior and with their relationship to God. He devoted much of his attention to the celebration of individual women, mostly biblical figures, whose lives were distinguished by quiet piety and godly ways. He presented them as models for New England women to emulate.

That same year, Mather completed *Wonders of the Invisible World*, his major justification for the Salem witchcraft trials and executions. Mather's focus here was on the behavior of witches and their relationships with the Devil—particularly women's complicity in Satan's attempts to overthrow the churches of New England. The book featured the witchcraft testimony presented against five of the accused at Salem, four of whom were women.

The nearly simultaneous publication of these two mirror-image works was not, it would seem, merely coincidental. Though Mather's witchcraft book does not explicitly address the reason why most of his subjects are women, his witches are nonetheless embodiments of peculiarly female forms of evil. Proud, discontented, envious, and malicious, they stood in direct contrast to the embodiments of female good in *Ornaments*, all of whom fully accepted the place God had chosen for them and regarded a willing and joyous submission to his will as the ultimate expression of their faith. Unable to ignore the profound uneasiness these two diametrically opposed views generated, Mather, like other New Englanders, relegated the still-powerful belief in women's evil to witches, on whom his fear and hatred could be unleashed. He was thereby freed to lavish praise on virtuous women—women who repressed the "witch" in themselves. Though his resolution allowed him to preserve man's superior position in the universe, Mather's heavy reliance in *Ornaments* on figures of Eve reveals how very delicate the balance was.

* * *

Mather's resolution was also his culture's. In the late sixteenth and seventeenth centuries, Puritans and other like-minded Protestants were engaged in the task of transforming an ideology, formulating beliefs that would better serve them in a world in which many of the old hierarchies and truths were no longer useful or plausible. They devised a new conception of man which, though drawn from the old, increasingly conceived him as an individual in relation to his God and his neighbors. It was a formulation that better fit the new economic order. The new man required a new woman: not an individual like himself, but a being who made possible his mobility, his accumulation of property, his sense of self-importance, and his subjection to new masters. By defining women as capable and worthy of the helpmeet role, the Puritan authorities offered a powerful inducement for women to embrace it. But they also recognized that the task they had set for themselves was a difficult one. If women were to repress their own needs, their own goals, their own interests—and identify with the needs, goals, and interests of the men in their families—then the impulse to speak and act on their own behalf had to be stifled.

As the witchcraft trials and executions show, only force could ensure such a sweeping denial of self. New England witches were women who resisted the new truths, either symbolically or in fact. In doing so, they were visible—and profoundly disturbing—reminders of the potential resistance in all women.

Puritans' witchcraft beliefs are finally inseparable from their ideas about women and from their larger religious world view. The witch was both the negative model by which the virtuous woman was defined and the focus for Puritan explanations of the problem of evil. In both respects, Puritan culture resembles other cultures with witchcraft beliefs: the witch image sets off in stark relief the most cherished values of these societies. A central element in these cosmologies, witches explain the presence of not only illness, death, and personal misfortune, but of attitudes and behavior antithetical to the culture's moral universe.

For Puritans, hierarchy and order were the most cherished values. People who did not accept their place in the social order were the very embodiments of evil. Disorderly women posed a greater threat than disorderly men because the male/female relation provided the very model of and for all hierarchical relations, and because Puritans hoped that the subordination of women to men would ensure men's stake in maintaining those relations. Many years ago the anthropologist Monica Hunter Wilson said that witchcraft beliefs were "the standardized nightmare of a group, and... the comparative analysis of such nightmares... one of the keys to the understanding of society." New England's nightmare was what the historian Natalie Zemon Davis has called "women on top": women as the willing agents of the Prince of Evil in his effort to topple the whole hierarchical system.

NO

Kai T. Erikson

THE SHAPES OF THE DEVIL

THE WITCHES OF SALEM VILLAGE

Between the end of the Quaker persecutions in 1665 and the beginning of the Salem witchcraft outbreak in 1692, the [Massachusetts Bay] colony had experienced some very trying days. To begin with, the political outlines of the commonwealth had been subject to sudden, often violent, shifts, and the people of the colony were quite uncertain about their own future. The King's decrees during the Quaker troubles had provoked only minor changes in the actual structure of the Puritan state, but they had introduced a note of apprehension and alarm which did not disappear for thirty years; and no sooner had Charles warned the Massachusetts authorities of his new interest in their affairs then he dispatched four commissioners to the Bay to look after his remote dominions and make sure that his occasional orders were being enforced. From that moment, New England feared the worst. The sermons of the period were full of dreadful prophecies about the future of the Bay, and as New England moved through the 1670's and 1680's, the catalogue of political calamities grew steadily longer and more serious. In 1670, for example, a series of harsh arguments occurred between groups of magistrates and clergymen, threatening the alliance which had been the very cornerstone of the New England Way. In 1675 a brutal and costly war broke out with a confederacy of Indian tribes led by a wily chief called King Philip. In 1676 Charles II began to review the claims of other persons to lands within the jurisdiction of Massachusetts, and it became increasingly clear that the old charter might be revoked altogether. In 1679 Charles specifically ordered Massachusetts to permit the establishment of an Anglican church in Boston, and in 1684 the people of the Bay had become so pessimistic about the fate of the colony that several towns simply neglected to send Deputies to the General Court. The sense of impending doom reached its peak in 1686. To begin with, the charter which had given the colony its only legal protection for over half a century was vacated by a stroke of the royal pen, and in addition the King sent a Royal Governor to represent his interests in the Bay who was both an Anglican and a man actively hostile to the larger goals of New

England. For the moment, it looked as if the holy experiment was over; not only had the settlers lost title to the very land they were standing on, but they ran the very real risk of witnessing the final collapse of the congregational churches they had built at so great a cost.

The settlers were eventually rescued from the catastrophes of 1686, but their margin of escape had been extremely narrow and highly tentative. In 1689 news began to filter into the Bay that William of Orange had landed in England to challenge the House of Stuart, and hopes ran high throughout the colony; but before the people of the Bay knew the outcome of this contest in England, a Boston mob suddenly rose in protest and placed the Royal Governor in chains. Luckily for Massachusetts, William's forces were successful in England and the Boston insurrection was seen as little more than a premature celebration in honor of the new King. Yet for all the furor, little had changed. At the time of the witchcraft hysteria, agents of Massachusetts were at work in London trying to convince William to restore the old charter, or at least to issue a new one giving Massachusetts all the advantages it had enjoyed in the past, but everyone knew the colony would never again operate under the same autonomy. As the people of the Bay waited to hear about the future of their settlement, then, their anxiety was understandably high.

Throughout this period of political crisis, an even darker cloud was threatening the colony, and this had to do with the fact that a good deal of angry dissension was spreading among the saints themselves. In a colony that depended on a high degree of harmony and group feeling, the courts were picking their way through a maze of land disputes and personal feuds, a complicated tangle of litigations and suits. Moreover, the earnest attempts at unanimity that had characterized the politics of Winthrop's era [from 1629 to 1648, during which John Winthrop served as governor of Massachusetts Bay Colony on 12 separate terms] were now replaced by something closely resembling open party bickering. When John Josselyn visited Boston in 1668, for instance, he observed that the people were "savagely factious" in their relations with one another and acted more out of jealousy and greed than any sense of religious purpose. And the sermons of the day chose even stronger language to describe the decline in morality which seemed to darken the prospects of New England. The spirit of brotherhood which the original settlers had counted on so heavily had lately diffused into an atmosphere of commercial competition, political contention, and personal bad feeling.

Thus the political architecture which had been fashioned so carefully by the first generation and the spiritual consensus which had been defended so energetically by the second were both disappearing. At the time of the Salem witchcraft mania, most of the familiar landmarks of the New England Way had become blurred by changes in the historical climate, like signposts obscured in a storm, and the people of the Bay no longer knew how to assess what the past had amounted to or what the future promised. Massachusetts had become, in Alan Heimert's words, "a society no longer able to judge itself with any certainty."

In 1670, the House of Deputies took note of the confusion and fear which was beginning to spread over the country and prepared a brief inventory of the troubles facing the Bay:

> Declension from the primitive foundation work, innovation in doctrine and worship, opinion and practice, an invasion of the rights, liberties and privileges of churches, an usurpation of a lordly and prelatical power over God's heritage, a subversion of the gospel order, and all this with a dangerous tendency to the utter devastation of these churches, turning the pleasant gardens of Christ into a wilderness, and the inevitable and total extirpation of the principles and pillars of the congregational way; these are the leaven, the corrupting gangrene, the infecting spreading plague, the provoking image of jealousy set up before the Lord, the accursed thing which hath provoked divine wrath, and doth further threaten destruction.

The tone of this resolution gives us an excellent index to the mood of the time. For the next twenty years, New England turned more and more to the notion that the settlers must expect God to turn upon them in wrath because the colony had lost its original fervor and sense of mission. The motif introduced in this resolution runs like a recurrent theme through the thinking of the period: the settlers who had carved a commonwealth out of the wilderness and had planted "the pleasant gardens of Christ" in its place were about to return to the wilderness. But there is an important shift of imagery here, for the wilderness they had once mastered was one of thick underbrush and wild animals, dangerous seasons and marauding Indians, while the wilderness which awaited them contained an entirely different sort of peril. "The Wilderness thro' which we are passing to the Promised Land," Cotton Mather wrote in a volume describing the state of New England at the time of the witchcraft difficulties, "is all over fill'd with Fiery flying serpents.... All our way to Heaven, lies by the Dens of Lions, and the Mounts of Leopards; there are incredible Droves of Devils in our way." ... Massachusetts had lost much of its concern for institutions and policies and had begun to seek some vision of its future by looking into a ghostly, invisible world.

It was while the people of the colony were preoccupied with these matters that the witches decided to strike. ...

* * *

Historically, there is nothing unique in the fact that Massachusetts Bay should have put people on trial for witchcraft. As the historian [George L.] Kittredge has pointed out, the whole story should be seen "not as an abnormal outbreak of fanaticism, not as an isolated tragedy, but as a mere incident, a brief and transitory episode in the biography of a terrible, but perfectly natural, superstition."

The idea of witchcraft, of course, is as old as history; but the concept of a malevolent witch who makes a compact with Satan and rejects God did not appear in Europe until the middle of the fourteenth century and does not seem to have made a serious impression on England until well into the sixteenth. The most comprehensive study of English witchcraft, for example, opens with the year 1558, the first year of Elizabeth's reign, and gives only passing attention to events occurring before that date.

In many ways, witchcraft was brought into England on the same current of change that introduced the Protestant Reformation, and it continued to draw nourishment from the intermittent religious quarrels which broke out during the next century and a half. Perhaps no other form of crime in history has been a better index to social disruption and change, for outbreaks of witchcraft mania have generally taken place in societies which are experiencing a shift of religious focus—societies, we would say, confronting a relocation of boundaries. Throughout the Elizabethan and early Stuart periods, at any rate, while England was trying to establish a national church and to anchor it in the middle of the violent tides which were sweeping over the rest of Europe, increasing attention was devoted to the subject. Elizabeth herself introduced legislation to clarify the laws dealing with witchcraft, and James I, before becoming King of England, wrote a textbook on demonology which became a standard reference for years to come.

But it was during the Civil Wars in England that the witchcraft hysteria struck with full force. Many hundreds, probably thousands of witches were burned or hung between the time the Civil Wars began and Oliver Cromwell emerged as the strong man of the Commonwealth, and no sooner had the mania subsided in England than it broke out all over again in Scotland during the first days of the Restoration. Every important crisis during those years seemed to be punctuated by a rash of witchcraft cases. England did not record its last execution for witchcraft until 1712, but the urgent witch hunts of the Civil War period were never repeated.

With this background in mind, we should not be surprised that New England, too, should experience a moment of panic; but it is rather curious that this moment should have arrived so late in the century.

During the troubled years in England when countless witches were burned at the stake or hung from the gallows, Massachusetts Bay showed but mild concern over the whole matter. In 1647 a witch was executed in Connecticut, and one year later another woman met the same fate in Massachusetts. In 1651 the General Court took note of the witchcraft crisis in England and published an almost laconic order that "a day of humiliation" be observed throughout the Bay, but beyond this, the waves of excitement which were sweeping over the mother country seemed not to reach across the Atlantic at all. There was no shortage of accusations, to be sure, no shortage of the kind of gossip which in other days would send good men and women to their lonely grave, but the magistrates of the colony did not act as if a state of emergency was at hand and thus did not declare a crime wave to be in motion. In 1672, for example, a curious man named John Broadstreet was presented to the Essex County Court for "having familiarity with the devil," yet when he admitted the charge the court was so little impressed that he was fined for telling a lie. And in 1674, when Christopher Brown came before the same court to testify that he had been dealing with Satan, the magistrates flatly dismissed him on the grounds that his confession seemed "inconsistent with truth."

So New England remained relatively calm during the worst of the troubles in England, yet suddenly erupted into a terrible violence long after England lay exhausted from its earlier exertions.

* * *

In many important respects, 1692 marked the end of the Puritan experiment in Massachusetts, not only because the original charter had been revoked or because a Royal Governor had been chosen by the King or even because the old political order had collapsed in a tired heap. The Puritan experiment ended in 1692, rather, because the sense of mission which had sustained it from the beginning no longer existed in any recognizable form, and thus the people of the Bay were left with few stable points of reference to help them remember who they were. When they looked back on their own history, the settlers had to conclude that the trajectory of the past pointed in quite a different direction than the one they now found themselves taking: they were no longer participants in a great adventure, no longer residents of a "city upon a hill," no longer members of that special revolutionary elite who were destined to bend the course of history according to God's own word. They were only themselves, living alone in a remote corner of the world, and this seemed a modest end for a crusade which had begun with such high expectations.

In the first place, as we have seen, the people of the colony had always pictured themselves as actors in an international movement, yet by the end of the century they had lost many of their most meaningful contacts with the rest of the world. The Puritan movement in England had scattered into a number of separate sects, each of which had been gradually absorbed into the freer climate of a new regime, and elsewhere in Europe the Protestant Reformation had lost much of its momentum without achieving half the goals set for it. And as a result, the colonists had lost touch with the background against which they had learned to assess their own stature and to survey their own place in the world.

In the second place, the original settlers had measured their achievements on a yardstick which no longer seemed to have the same sharp relevance. New England had been built by people who believed that God personally supervised every flicker of life on earth according to a plan beyond human comprehension, and in undertaking the expedition to America they were placing themselves entirely in God's hands. These were men whose doctrine prepared them to accept defeat gracefully, whose sense of piety depended upon an occasional moment of failure, hardship, even tragedy. Yet by the end of the century, the Puritan planters could look around them and count an impressive number of accomplishments. Here was no record of erratic providence; here was a record of solid human enterprise, and with this realization, as Daniel Boorstin suggests, the settlers moved from a "sense of mystery" to a "consciousness of mastery," from a helpless reliance on fate to a firm confidence in their own abilities. This shift helped clear the way for the appearance of the shrewd, practical, self-reliant Yankee as a figure in American history, but in the meantime it left the third generation of settlers with no clear definition of the status they held as the chosen children of God.

In the third place, Massachusetts had been founded as a lonely pocket of civilization in the midst of a howling wilderness, and as we have seen, this idea remained one of the most important themes of Puritan imagery long after the underbrush had been cut away and the wild animals killed. The settlers had lost sight of their local frontiers, not only in the sense that colonization had spread beyond the Berkshires into what is now upper state New York, but also in the sense that the wilderness which had held the community together by pressing in on it from all sides was disappearing. The original settlers had landed in a wilderness full of "wild beasts and wilder men"; yet sixty years later, sitting many miles from the nearest frontier in the prosperous seaboard town of Boston, Cotton Mather and other survivors of the old order still imagined that they were living in a wilderness—a territory they had explored as thoroughly as any frontiersmen. But the character of this wilderness was unlike anything the first settlers had ever seen, for its dense forests had become a jungle of mythical beasts and its skies were thick with flying spirits. In a sense, the Puritan community had helped mark its location in space by keeping close watch on the wilderness surrounding it on all sides; and now that the visible traces of that wilderness had receded out of sight, the settlers invented a new one by finding the shapes of the forest in the middle of the community itself.

And as the wilderness took on this new character, it seemed that even the Devil had given up his more familiar disguises. He no longer lurked in the underbrush, for most of it had been cut away; he no longer assumed the shape of hostile Indians, for most of them had retreated inland for the moment; he no longer sent waves of heretics to trouble the Bay, for most of them lived quietly under the protection of toleration; he no longer appeared in the armies of the Counter-Reformation, for the old battlefields were still and too far away to excite the imagination. But his presence was felt everywhere, and when the colonists began to look for his new hiding places they found him crouched in the very heart of the Puritan colony. Quite literally, the people of the Bay began to see ghosts, and soon the boundaries of the New England Way closed in on a space full of demons and incubi, spectres and evil spirits, as the settlers tried to find a new sense of their own identity among the landmarks of a strange, invisible world. Cotton Mather, who knew every disguise in the Devil's wardrobe, offered a frightening catalogue of the Devil's attempts to destroy New England.

I believe, there never was a poor Plantation, more pursued by the wrath of the Devil, than our poor New-England.... It was a rousing alarm to the Devil, when a great Company of English Protestants and Puritans, came to erect Evangelical Churches, in a corner of the world, where he had reign'd without control for many ages; and it is a vexing Eye-sore to the Devil, that our Lord Christ should be known, and own'd and preached in this howling wilderness. Wherefore he has left no Stone unturned, that so he might undermine his Plantation, and force us out of our Country.

First, the Indian Powawes, used all their Sorceries to molest the first Planters here; but God said unto them, Touch them not! Then, Seducing spirits came to root in this Vineyard, but God so rated them off, that they have not prevail'd much farther than the edges of our Land. After this, we have had a continual blast upon some of our principal Grain, annually diminishing a vast part of our ordinary Food. Herewithal, wasting Sicknesses, especially Burning and Mortal Agues, have Shot the Arrows of Death in at our Windows. Next, we have had many Adversaries of our own Language, who have been perpetually assaying to deprive us of those English Liberties, in the encouragement whereof these Territories have been settled. As if this had not been enough; the Tawnies among whom we came have watered our Soil with the Blood of many Hundreds of Inhabitants.... Besides all which, now at last the Devils are (if I may so speak) in

Person come down upon us with such a Wrath, as is justly much, and will quickly be more, the Astonishment of the World.

And this last adventure of the Devil has a quality all its own.

Wherefore the Devil is now making one Attempt more upon us; an Attempt more Difficult, more Surprising, more snarl'd with unintelligible Circumstances than any that we have hitherto Encountered.... An Army of Devils is horribly broke in upon the place which is the center, and after a sort, the First-born of our English Settlements: and the Houses of the Good People there are fill'd with the doleful shrieks of their Children and Servants, Tormented by Invisible Hands, with Tortures altogether preternatural.

The witchcraft hysteria occupied but a brief moment in the history of the Bay. The first actors to take part in it were a group of excited girls and a few of the less savory figures who drifted around the edges of the community, but the speed with which the other people of the Bay gathered to witness the encounter and accept an active role in it, not to mention the quality of the other persons who were eventually drawn into this vortex of activity, serves as an index to the gravity of the issues involved. For a few years, at least, the settlers of Massachusetts were alone in the world, bewildered by the loss of their old destiny but not yet aware of their new one, and during this fateful interval they tried to discover some image of themselves by listening to a chorus of voices which whispered to them from the depths of an invisible wilderness.

POSTSCRIPT

Was the Salem Witchcraft Hysteria Caused by a Fear of Women?

The Salem witch trials represent one of the most thoroughly studied episodes in American history. Several scholars have concluded that the enthusiasm for learning more about the Salem witches and their accusers far outweighs the importance of the event, yet, essays and books continue to roll off the presses. As suggested in the introduction to this issue, the selections by Karlsen and Erikson summarize only two of the many interpretations of the incident at Salem. Those interested in pursuing this topic further should examine Marion Starkey's *The Devil in Massachusetts: A Modern Enquiry into the Salem Witch Trials* (Alfred A. Knopf, 1949), which blames the episode on lies told by the accusers. An intriguing alternative is Chadwick Hansen's *Witchcraft at Salem* (George Braziller, 1969), in which the author insists that several Salem residents did practice black magic, thereby heightening the fears of their neighbors. Paul Boyer and Stephen Nissenbaum, in *Salem Possessed: The Social Origins of Witchcraft* (Harvard University Press, 1974), emphasize the conflicts between the residents of Salem Town and Salem Village. Recent studies include Enders A. Robinson, *The Devil Discovered: Salem Witchcraft, 1692* (Hippocrene Books, 1991) and Larry Gragg, *The Salem Witch Crisis* (Praeger, 1992).

Karlsen's work reflects a growing interest in the status of colonial American women. Students in American history classes have for generations read of the founding of the colonies in British North America, their political and economic development, and the colonists' struggle for independence without ever being confronted by a female protagonist. Only in the last two decades have discussions of the role of women in the development of American society made their appearance in standard textbooks. Consequently, it is useful to explore the status of women in colonial America. Surveys of American women's history that address the colonial period include June Sochen, *Herstory: A Woman's View of American History* (Alfred, 1974) and Nancy Woloch, *Women and the American Experience* (Alfred A. Knopf, 1984). The idea that colonial American women enjoyed a higher status than their European counterparts is supported in Richard B. Morris, *Studies in the History of American Law*, 2d ed. (Octagon Books, 1964); Roger Thompson, *Women in Stuart England and America: A Comparative Study* (Routledge & Kegan, 1974); and Page Smith, *Daughters of the Promised Land: Women in American History* (Little, Brown, 1977). For a contrary view of women in the age of the American Revolution, see Linda K. Kerber, *Women of the Republic: Intellect and Ideology in Revolutionary America* (University of North Carolina Press, 1980).

ISSUE 4

Did American Slaves Develop a Distinct African American Culture in the Eighteenth Century?

YES: Allan Kulikoff, from *Tobacco and Slaves: The Development of Southern Cultures in the Chesapeake, 1680–1800* (University of North Carolina Press, 1986)

NO: Jean Butenhoff Lee, from "The Problem of Slave Community in the Eighteenth-Century Chesapeake," *William and Mary Quarterly* (July 1986)

ISSUE SUMMARY

YES: Professor of history Allan Kulikoff claims that Chesapeake slaves developed their own social institutions and a distinct indigenous culture in the years between 1740 and 1790.

NO: Associate professor of history Jean Butenhoff Lee emphasizes the difficult and often unsuccessful efforts of slaves to create a stable family and community life in eighteenth-century Maryland.

The arrival at Jamestown, Virginia, in 1619 of a Dutch frigate carrying 20 Africans marked a momentous event for the future development of England's North American colonies. The introduction of a new racial component generated political, economic, and social repercussions that are still felt in modern America. With the development of black slavery, American colonists set the stage for a long-term moral dilemma that ultimately produced the bloodshed and destruction of civil war.

In the last 30 years, historians have given considerable attention to colonial American slavery. Their research, however, has left unresolved a question regarding those first Africans in Jamestown: Were the first blacks in England's North American colonies immediately bound out as slaves? While the evidence is inconclusive, there is strong reason to believe that the first Africans brought to Jamestown became indentured servants and were freed after fulfilling their contracts to their masters. These individuals formed the basis for the nation's free black population, which by 1860 would number approximately 500,000.

If slavery did not originate with those first Africans, when did the institution appear? The process was remarkably gradual in the Chesapeake where the first slave codes were not enacted by the Virginia and Maryland legislatures until the 1660s. Some extant records, however, suggest that the status of "slave" was being given to black servants at least 20 years prior to the appearance of a *de jure* system. In 1640, John Punch, a black servant, was arrested with two white fellow servants for running away. All were found guilty, and the two white men were whipped and given additional time to serve on their indentures. Punch, however, was only whipped. The court record revealed that since he was already serving his master for life, no time could be added on. In other words, John Punch was a slave.

By 1750, the institution of slavery had emerged in all the British colonies in North America. The preponderance of male bondsmen, however, prevented American slave populations from expanding naturally. Masters, therefore, depended upon shipments from Africa for new slaves until the sex ratio achieved greater parity. In addition, heavy concentrations of slaves did not appear until the rise of large plantations. In New England, such plantations were limited to Rhode Island's Narragansett Valley; in the Middle colonies, New Yorkers and Pennsylvanians acquired some extensive lands worked by slaves; and in the South, large plantations cultivating tobacco and rice appeared in the eighteenth century.

This, however, tells us little about the slaves themselves. How did they live? What was the scope of their lives? Was there a slave community in the colonial period?

In the following essays, Allan Kulikoff contends that only with a more equal sex ratio, large plantations, and concentrated numbers of bondsmen could slaves develop a community life apart from that of their masters. These characteristics emerged in the Chesapeake area between 1740 and 1790 and permitted slaves to establish a recognizable, autonomous African American culture. Jean Butenhoff Lee agrees that the development of African American slave community life was a gradual process, but she challenges Kulikoff's conclusions regarding the emergence of an autonomous slave community. By focusing on a single county, Lee determines that African American family and communal life was quite fragile and subject to constant disruption. The contacts among slaves on a single plantation or on adjacent plantations, she asserts, were so limited as to preclude the kind of community life Kulikoff describes.

YES
Allan Kulikoff

ORIGINS OF BLACK SOCIETY

Although the eighteenth-century Chesapeake planter looked upon newly enslaved Africans as strange and barbaric folk, he knew that American-born slaves could be taught English customs. Hugh Jones, a Virginia cleric, commented in 1724 that "the languages of the new Negroes are various harsh jargons" but added that slaves born in Virginia "talk good English, and affect our language, habits, and customs." How readily did slaves in Maryland and Virginia accept English ways? Did the preponderance of whites in the region's population and their power force slaves to accept Anglo-American beliefs, values, and skills? Or did slaves succeed in creating their own institutions despite white repression? . . .

How readily slaves could form their own culture depended upon both the pattern of forced African immigration to the Americas and the economic and demographic environment that awaited new slaves. Black forced immigrants came from hundreds of different communities and did not have a common culture. Their religious beliefs, kinship systems, and forms of social organization differed substantially. Nevertheless, West Africans did share some values and experiences. For example, each West African group developed different kinship practices, but throughout the region each person located his place in society by his position in his kin group and lineage. When Africans arrived in the New World, their cultural differences were initially of greater significance than the values they shared. They shared only their experience as slaves and labored to make a new society out of their common beliefs and values. The features of the society they formed depended upon the demands of the white masters, the characteristics of the economy, the demography of slave and white populations, and the extent of ethnic division among blacks. As they interacted daily, slaves learned to cope with ordinary problems of working, eating, marrying, and child rearing under the adverse conditions of slavery. The social institutions they developed were neither imposed by Europeans nor directly taken from African communities, but were a unique combination of elements borrowed from the European enslavers and from the common values of various African societies. As soon as slaves formed

From Allan Kulikoff, *Tobacco and Slaves: The Development of Southern Cultures in the Chesapeake, 1680–1800* (University of North Carolina Press, 1986). Copyright © 1986 by University of North Carolina Press. Reprinted by permission.

social institutions, internal conflict diminished, and blacks could place a new Afro-American culture into a settled social context.

The size of working units that masters organized, the number of Africans they bought from slavetraders, and the crops they grew, as well as the rules they required their slaves to follow, influenced the kind of communities their slaves could form. Economic decisions by thousands of masters determined both the density of the black population and the proportion of whites in the population, and these demographic patterns in turn set limits on the intensity of slave community life. The choice of crops was crucial. Some crops required large plantations; others could be grown on small farms. Since large plantations needed more slaves than small farms, large planters purchased greater numbers of African slaves, and consequently, regions dominated by large plantations had greater concentrations of slaves and a larger proportion of Africans in their slave population than regions dominated by farms. Slaves who lived on a large plantation in a region where a substantial majority of the people were enslaved and the density of the slave population was high probably had more opportunities to worship their gods, begin stable families, and develop their own communities than did slaves who lived on small quarters in a preponderantly white country. A slave who lived with many Africans in a place where continual heavy importation of blacks kept the proportion of Africans high was more likely to adopt African customs than the slave who lived where importation was sporadic, the proportion of immigrants among black adults low, and the number of whites great.

This model explains the development of black society in the Chesapeake colonies quite well. African and Afro-American slaves developed a settled life there very slowly. Three stages of community development can be discerned. From roughly 1650 to 1690, blacks assimilated the norms of white society, but the growth of the number of blacks also triggered white repression. The period from 1690 to 1740 was an era of heavy slave imports, small plantation sizes, and social conflicts among blacks. The infusion of Africans often disrupted newly formed slave communities. Finally, from 1740 to 1790, imports declined and then stopped, plantation sizes increased, the proportion of blacks in the population grew, and divisions among slaves disappeared. Consequently, native blacks formed relatively settled communities....

TOWARD AFRO-AMERICAN SLAVE COMMUNITIES

The demographic conditions that prevented blacks from developing a cohesive social life before 1740 changed during the quarter of a century before the Revolution, as immigration of Africans to the Chesapeake declined sharply. Only 17 percent of Virginia's adult blacks in 1750 and 15 percent in 1755 had arrived within the previous ten years, and these newcomers went in relatively greater numbers to newer piedmont counties than had their predecessors....

As the number of enslaved Africans in tidewater declined, the internal division among blacks diminished. These recent arrivals were under greater pressure than their predecessors to acquire the language, values, and beliefs of the dominant native majority. Like new Negroes before them, they sometimes ran away, but with less success. On arrival, they found themselves isolated and alone. Olaudah Equiano, for example, was brought to Virginia in 1757 at age twelve. "I was now exceedingly miserable," he later wrote, "and thought myself worse off than any... of my companions; for they could talk to each other, but I had no person to speak to that I could understand. In this state I was constantly grieving and pining, and wishing for death." But once slaves like Equiano learned English, they became part of the Afro-American community. Bob, twenty-nine, and Turkey Tom, thirty-eight, were new Negroes who lived on the home plantation of Charles Carroll of Carrollton in 1773. Since Bob and Tom were apparently the only two recent immigrant slaves on any of Carroll's many plantations, they both could participate fully in plantation life. Bob was a smith, a position usually reserved for natives; he married the daughter of a carpenter and lived with her and their two children. Tom, a laborer, also found a place in the plantation's kinship networks: his wife was at least a third-generation Marylander. Very few Africans probably ever became artisans, but so few Africans were imported that most Africans in tidewater could find wives among the native majority....

The size of quarters increased after 1740 throughout tidewater, providing greater opportunities for slaves to develop a social life of their own. The proportion who lived on units of more than twenty slaves doubled in St. Mary's County, increased by half in York and Anne Arundel counties, and grew, though more slowly, in Prince George's. In the 1780s, one-third to two-thirds of the slaves in eleven tidewater counties lived on farms of more than twenty slaves,

and only a sixth to a tenth lived on units of fewer than six. If these counties were typical, 44 percent of tidewater's blacks lived on farms of more than twenty slaves, and another 26 percent lived on medium-sized units of eleven to twenty. The number of very large quarters also grew. Before 1740 few quarters housed more than thirty slaves, but by the 1770s and 1780s the wealthiest gentlemen ran home plantations with more than one hundred slaves and quarters with thirty to fifty....

Because plantation sizes increased, more lived on quarters away from the master's house and his direct supervision. On small plantations the quarter could be located in an outbuilding or in a single dwelling. On large plantations, the quarters resembled small villages. Slave houses and the yards that surrounded them were centers of domestic activity. The houses were furnished with straw bedding, barrels for seats, pots, pans, and usually a grindstone or handmill for beating corn into meal. Agricultural tools and livestock were scattered outside the houses, and the quarter was surrounded by plots of corn and tobacco cultivated by the slaves.

Afro-Americans made the quarters into little communities, usually organized around families. Because the African slave trade largely ceased, the adult sex ratio decreased. Almost all men and women could marry, and by the 1770s many slaves had native grandparents and great-grandparents. The quarter was the center of family activity every evening and on Sundays and holidays, for except during the harvest, slaves had these times to themselves. Nonresident fathers visited their wives and children; runaways stayed with friends or kinfolk. In the evenings native men sometimes traveled to other quarters, where they passed the night talking, singing, smoking, and drinking. On occasional Sundays they held celebrations at which they danced to the banjo and sang bitter songs about their treatment by the master....

After 1740, the density of the black population and the proportion of slaves in the population of tidewater both increased, and, as a result, the area's slave society gradually spread out to embrace many neighboring plantations in a single network. Ironically, masters provided slaves with several tools they could use to extend these cross-quarter networks. Slave sales tore black families asunder, but as masters sold and transferred their slaves, more and more kinfolk lived on neighboring quarters, and naturally they retained ties of affection after they were separated. Whites built numerous roads and paths to connect their farms and villages, and their slaves used these byways to visit friends or run away and evade recapture. By the 1770s and 1780s, Afro-Americans numerically dominated many neighborhoods and created many cross-plantation networks....

Quarters were connected by extensive networks of roads and paths, which grew remarkably complex during the eighteenth century. For example, Prince George's County had about 50 miles of public roads in 1700, but 478 in 1762, or one mile of public road for every square mile of taxed land in the county. This elaboration of roads made it easier for slaves to visit nearby plantations. Whites could not patrol all these roads, let alone private paths not maintained by the county, without a general mobilization of the white population....

The Afro-Americans made good use of these opportunities to create their own society. In the years before the Revo-lution, they developed a sense of community with other slaves both on their own plantations and in the neighborhood. This social solidarity can be shown in several ways. In the first place, Afro-Americans often concealed slaves from within the neighborhood on their quarters. Since masters searched the neighborhood for runaways and placed notices on public buildings before advertising in a newspaper, many runaways, especially truants who were recaptured or returned voluntarily after a few days' absence, were not so advertised. The increasing appearance of such advertisements in the *Maryland Gazette* during the thirty years before the Revolution suggests that slaves were becoming more successful in evading easy recapture. The numbers of runaways in southern Maryland rose in each five-year period between 1745 and 1779, except the years 1765–1769, and the increase was especially great during the Revolution, when some escaped slaves were able to reach British troops....

The slave community, of course, had its share of conflicts, and on occasion a slave assaulted or stole from another slave. Nonetheless, accounts of several of these incidents suggest that the rest of the slave community united against the transgressors. Slaves sometimes refused to testify against their fellows, especially when blacks stole goods from whites, but when a member of the black community was hurt, slaves testified against the guilty person to protect themselves or their property. In May 1763 Jack poisoned Clear with a mixture of rum and henbane; she became ill and died the following February. Six slaves who belonged to Clear's master informed him of the act and testified against Jack in Prince George's court. They were joined by three slaves who lived on nearby plantations. The jury found Jack guilty, and he was sentenced to hang. Similarly, when Tom (owned by Richard Snowden, a prominent ironmaker) broke into Weems's quarter (near the Snowden ironworks) in Anne Arundel County and took goods belonging to Weems's slaves, six men and women owned by James and David Weems testified against him. He was found guilty and hanged.

There were limits to slave solidarity. Though native-born slaves often remained loyal to immediate kinfolk and friends on their own quarters, to more distant kinfolk, and to slaves on nearby or distant plantations, these loyalties sometimes clashed with each other or with the demands of the master. Then slaves had to choose sides in intricate master-slave conflicts. The development of these alliances can be seen in the response of Landon Carter and of his slaves when Simon, Carter's ox-carter, ran away in March 1766. Carter had Simon outlawed, and joined the militia to hunt for him. Simon was aided directly by at least six residents of his quarter, including an uncle, a brother, and a sister-in-law. Nonetheless, several other kinfolk, who lived on other quarters, were forced by Carter to inform against him. Finally, after two weeks, Talbot (another of Carter's slaves who lived some distance from Simon) shot Simon in the leg and, with the aid of several other slaves, recaptured him.

THE ORIGINS OF AFRO-AMERICAN CULTURE

Slaves in the Chesapeake, unlike those in the West Indies, took several generations to form a semiautonomous Afro-American culture. West Africans needed settled communities to develop the bundle of common values and beliefs they brought over with them into a syncretic culture, but the demographic environment of the early eighteenth-century Chesapeake was extremely hostile to the formation of settled communities. Heavily white populations, high black sex ratios, continually declining proportions of Africans among slaves, conflicts between African and creole slaves, and small unit sizes all made the development of both slave communities and slave culture difficult. African forced migrants did not forget these values, however, but used behavioral symbols of them whenever they could. These Africans practiced their beliefs in disconnected and often private episodes, not in daily social interaction with many other slaves. African slaves in the Chesapeake made tribal drums, strummed on their banjos, poisoned their enemies as did African witches and cunning men, passed on a few African words to their descendants, and sometimes engaged in private devotions to Allah or their tribal gods.

Afro-American slaves had developed strong community institutions on their quarters by the 1760s and 1770s, but the values and beliefs they held are difficult to ascertain. Since blacks in the Chesapeake region did not achieve a settled social life until after a heavy African slave trade stopped and since whites continued to live in even the most densely black areas, one would expect slave culture in the region to reflect white values and beliefs. Even native-born slaves had little choice either about their work or about the people who lived with them in their quarters. Nevertheless, they had a small measure of self-determination in their family life, in their religion, and in the ways they celebrated and mourned. When they could choose, Afro-American slaves simultaneously borrowed from whites and drew on the values and beliefs their ancestors brought from West Africa to form a culture not only significantly different from that of Anglo-Americans but also different from the culture of any West African group or any other group of North American slaves.

The ways Afro-American slaves organized their family life indicates most clearly how they used both African and Euro-American forms to create a new institution compatible with their life under slavery. By the time of the Revolution, most slaves lived in families, and slave households were similar to those of their white masters. About as many creole slaves as whites lived in two-parent and extended households. Whites lived in monogamous families, and only scattered examples of the African custom of polygyny can be found among creole blacks. Slavery forced the kinfolk of extended families to live very close to one another on large plantations, where they played and worked together. By contrast, whites only occasionally visited their extended kinfolk and worked in the fields only with their children, not with adult brothers and sisters. This closeness fostered a sense of kin solidarity among Afro-Americans. They named their children after both sides of the family (but interestingly enough, daughters were not often named after their mothers). And they sometimes refused to marry within the plantation even when sex ratios were equal: many of the available potential partners were first cousins, and black slaves apparently refused to marry first cousins. This may have represented a transformation of African marriage taboos that differed from tribe to tribe but tended to be stricter than those of Chesapeake whites, who frequently married first cousins.

West African religions varied remarkably among themselves, yet enslaved Africans shared a similar way of viewing the world, which they passed on to their native black children. All activities, Africans believed, were infused with sacredness, each in its own particular way. Religion was not universal but was practiced only within a communal context. God, spirits, animals, and plants were all seen in relation to people in the community, and certain men—rainmakers, medicine men, priests, sorcerers—had special powers over spirits or material life not available to most people.

In contrast, the Anglican faith practiced by most slaveholders in the Chesapeake before the Revolution radically separated the sacred from the secular: Anglicans attended church services in isolated buildings on Sundays but often ignored religious ceremonies the rest of the week. Although native slaves occasionally accepted the outward signs of Christian belief, few became convinced Protestants. Their children were baptized, and sometimes they received religious instruction. All three Anglican clergymen of Prince George's County reported in 1724 that they baptized slave children and adults (especially native-born adults) and preached to those who would listen. In 1731 one Prince George's minister baptized blacks "where perfect in their Catechism" and "visit[ed] them in their sickness and married them when called upon." Similar work continued in Virginia and Maryland in the generation before the Revolution. Nonetheless, Thomas Bacon, a Maryland cleric and publisher of a compendium of the colony's laws, believed that these baptized slaves were often "living in as profound Ignorance of what Christianity really is, (except as to a few outward Ordinances) as if they had remained in the midst of those barbarous Heathen Countries from whence their parents had been first imported."

Native-born slaves continued to observe African forms of mourning and celebrating, but they did not place these forms within the structure of Anglican religion, nor did masters give them time enough to expand these occasional ceremonies into an indigenous Afro-American religion. Whites sometimes observed these strange practices. Thomas Bacon, for instance, preached to blacks on Maryland's Eastern Shore in the 1740s at services they directed "at their *funerals* (several of which I have attended)—and to such small congregations as their *marriages* have brought together." Two early nineteenth-century observers connected similar services they saw to the slaves' remote African past. Henry Knight, who traveled to Virginia in 1816, explained that masters permitted slaves a holiday to mourn the death of a fellow slave. The day of the funeral, "perhaps a month after the corpse is interred, is a jovial day with them; they sing and dance and drink the dead to his new home, which some believe to be in old Guinea," the home of their grandparents and great-grandparents. A Charlotte County, Virginia, cleric saw more solemn but equally emotional services. He contended that there were "many remains... of the savage customs of Africa. They cry and bawl and howl around the grave and roll in the dirt, and make many expressions of the most frantic grief... sometimes the noise they make may be heard as far as one or two miles."

The slaves' music and dance, though often unconnected to their religion, displayed a distinctly African character. Afro-American slaves continued to make and to play two instruments (the banjo and balafo) of African origin. In 1774 Nicholas Cresswell, a British visitor, described slave celebrations in Charles County, Maryland. On Sundays, he wrote, the blacks "generally meet together and amuse themselves with Dancing to the Banjo. This musical instrument... is made of a Gourd something in the imitation of a Guitar, with only four strings." "Their poetry," Cresswell reported, "is like the music—Rude and uncultivated. Their Dancing is most violent exercise, but so irregular and grotesque. I am not able to describe it." Cresswell's reaction to the dancing suggests that it contained African rhythms unknown in European dance. If the form was African, it was placed in an American context: the slave songs Cresswell heard "generally relate the usage they have received from their Masters or Mistresses in a very satirical stile and manner."

Native slaves retained folk beliefs that may have been integral parts of West African religions. Slaves sometimes turned to magic, sorcery, and witchcraft to resolve conflicts within their own community or to strike back at harsh or unreasonable masters. Some African medicine men, magicians, sorcerers, and witches migrated and passed on their skills to other slaves. These men were spiritual leaders (or powerful, if evil men) in many African communities, including those of the Ibos, and they continued to practice among creole slaves who believed in their powers. Several examples suggest the prevalence of these beliefs. William Grimes was born in King George County, Virginia, in 1784;

his narrative of his life as a runaway suggests that he was terrified by a woman he thought was a witch, that he feared sleeping in the bed of a dead man, and that he consulted fortune-tellers. Dissatisfied slaves might consult conjurers to discover how to poison their masters. In 1773, for instance, Sharper was accused by his master, Peter Hansbrough of Stafford County, Virginia, of "Endeavouring to Procuring Poison from a Negroe Doctor or Conjurer as they are Call'd" for an unknown but dangerous purpose after Hansbrough had "discovered Some behaviour in... Sharper which occasioned [him] to be more Strict in inquiring into... where he Spent his time in his absent hours." Similarily, two slave blacksmiths in Spotsylvania County were convicted of attempting to poison their master in 1797, but seventy-six local residents petitioned the state for clemency because the slaves had been influenced by "a Negro Wench, or conjurer of Mr. James Crawford."

Afro-American slaves did not transform these disparate fragments of African cultures into a new slave religion until the development of white evangelical religion during the decades before and after the Revolution. Revivalist preachers permitted and even encouraged slaves to adapt African forms to the Christian faith. The most intensive black religious activity was in southside and central piedmont Virginia, areas with the Chesapeake's highest concentrations of new Negroes. The first evangelical mission to slaves began in 1755, when two white Baptists organized a black congregation on William Byrd's plantation in Mecklenburg County; that group of Christians lasted until the Revolution. Samuel Davies, a Presbyterian clergyman who practiced in Hanover County, and

several of his colleagues converted as many as a thousand slaves to evangelical Protestantism in the 1750s. Davies thought that these blacks were true Christians, not only acquainted with "the important doctrines of the Christian Religion, but also a deep sense of things upon their spirits, and a life of the strictest Morality and Piety." They placed African music into Protestant liturgy: "The Negroes," Davies commented, "above all of the human species that ever I knew, have an ear for Music, and a kind of delight in Psalmody." Some of his converts even "lodged all night in my kitchen; and sometimes, when I have awakened about two or three a-clock in the morning, a torrent of sacred harmony poured into my chamber, and carried my mind to heaven."

The numbers of Afro-Americans attracted to evangelical Protestantism rose slowly in the 1770s and then increased rapidly during the awakenings of the 1780s and 1790s. By 1790, about 7 percent of Virginia's black adults were members of Baptist or Methodist churches, and far more were affected by the revivals in both piedmont and tidewater counties. Slave work patterns and the authority of masters might be affected by this new and all-encompassing religiosity. For instance, some members of the Episcopal church in King George County complained in the mid-1780s that "Preachers or Exhorters" daily gathered "together Multitudes of People in the Woods most of them Slaves, alienating their minds from their Daily Labour and their Masters Interest."

Blacks accepted the exhortations of Baptist and Methodist preachers in the 1780s and 1790s far more enthusiastically than did whites. They answered the preacher's call with crying, shouting, shaking, and trembling. Their reaction was perhaps in part dictated by their African past: the ceremonies of revivals were similar to those of some African religions, and African forms meshed well with the emerging theology of evangelical Protestantism. Revivals, unlike the liturgy of rational religion, allowed slaves to reduce the distinctions between sacred and secular and return to a holistic, African kind of religiosity.

Afro-American slaves developed their own social institutions and indigenous culture during the second half of the eighteenth century. A period of great disruptions among blacks early in the century was followed by a time of settled communities. Newly enslaved Africans came to the Chesapeake colonies in large enough numbers to cause conflicts between native slaves and new Negroes, but the migration was too small to allow Africans to develop syncretic communities and cultures. It was only when native adults began to predominate that earlier conflicts among blacks were contained and families and quarter communities began to emerge. The culture these creole slaves forged put African forms of behavior into Euro-American familial and religious structures. Creole slaves by that time were two or three generations removed from Africa and (except in southside Virginia) infrequently saw Africans. They may not have been aware of the complicated origins of their behavior.

For the slaves, the origins of their culture were less important than its autonomy. White observers agreed that the music, dance, and religiosity of black slaves differed remarkably from those of whites. The emergence of black culture, and especially the beginnings of Afro-Christianity, played an important role in the development of slave solidarity. Slaves possessed little power over their lives: they suffered the expropriation of the fruits of their labor by their masters; they could be forced to move away from family and friends at a moment's notice; they were subject to the whip for any perceived transgressions. The practice of a distinctive culture within their own quarters gave them some small power over their own lives and destinies they otherwise would not have possessed.

The development of an indigenous black community life and culture had a great impact upon the social structure of the entire region. Afro-Americans became both an enslaved working class and a racial caste, separate from their white masters. They had their own system of social relations among themselves, within the context of slavery. Even though whites continued to possess remarkable power over blacks, they had to relate to slaves as a group with a structure and culture they could not entirely control. Afro-American communal life and culture, then, set minimal bounds on white behavior and encouraged black solidarity.

NO

Jean Butenhoff Lee

THE PROBLEM OF SLAVE COMMUNITY IN THE EIGHTEENTH-CENTURY CHESAPEAKE

In the spring of 1774, a young Englishman named Nicholas Cresswell crossed the Atlantic, entered Chesapeake Bay, and came to safe anchorage on the Rappahannock River. From there, three black oarsmen rowed him north on the bay as far as the broad mouth of the Potomac River, then upriver along the shores of St. Mary's and Charles counties, Maryland. On the afternoon of May 21, Cresswell reached his destination, the tiny village of Nanjemoy in southwestern Charles County.

A week later, as he was becoming acquainted with the sights and sounds of the Tobacco Coast, Cresswell attended what he called a "Negro Ball" near Nanjemoy. "Sundays being the only days these poor creatures have to themselves," he wrote, "they generally meet together and amuse themselves with Dancing to the Banjo," a four-stringed gourd "something in the imitation of a Guitar." Some of the slaves also sang "very droll music indeed," songs in which "they generally relate the usage they have received from their Masters or Mistresses in a very satirical stile and manner." The newcomer pronounced the music and verse "Rude and uncultivated," the dancing "most violent excercise... irregular and grotesque." With a hint of disbelief he concluded that the slaves "all appear to be exeedingly happy at these merry-makings and seem as if they had forgot or were not sensible of their miserable condition."

Cresswell's account is the kind of infrequent literary evidence that historians of the black experience in early America cherish for its clues to social intercourse among the enslaved, to their distinctive and expressive folk art, their use of leisure hours, and their resistance to the slave labor system, if only in lyrical satire. That Sunday in 1774 the Englishman observed a manifestation of what several scholars have argued was a recent development in the Chesapeake tidewater: stable Afro-American communities, a distinctive amalgam forged in the demographic experience of blacks during the preceding century. By the era of the American Revolution, it is argued, slave population growth had proceeded far enough that many blacks could exercise

From Jean Butenhoff Lee, "The Problem of Slave Community in the Eighteenth-Century Chesapeake," *William and Mary Quarterly*, 3rd ser., vol. 43 (July 1986). Copyright © 1986 by Jean Butenhoff Lee. Reprinted by permission.

substantial control over their labor and leisure. They maintained reasonably stable family lives, extensive kin networks, and social intercourse that transcended plantation boundaries. The present article describes this interpretation more fully, offers a general critique of it, and employs quantifiable and narrative sources to examine slave life in the heavily black tidewater county that Cresswell observed. The evidence from Charles County does not deny that slaves sought to create communal life but emphasizes what a difficult—and often unsuccessful—effort it must have been.

* * *

Relying on probate inventories compiled between 1658 and 1730 in Charles and three adjacent counties on Maryland's lower Western Shore, Russell R. Menard has suggested that the few slaves who lived there in the seventeenth century must have endured an isolated and dehumanizing existence. Most were adult males. Housed mainly on small plantations, they lived out their brief lives in a dreary round of clearing land, tending livestock, and growing tobacco and corn. They were cut off from their African culture, no longer part of kin groups through which African societies were organized, and often unable to find wives and form families. Importation of large numbers of Africans during the late seventeenth and early eighteenth centuries exacerbated the sexual imbalance among blacks, for adult males predominated in slave cargoes.

Allan Kulikoff hypothesizes that skewed sex ratios, small plantations, and the presence of many Africans persisted until about 1740. These conditions, he holds, impeded the development of a distinctive Afro-American culture because the experiences of Chesapeake and African slaves were different. Blacks who were born in the Chesapeake or who lived there for some time presumably were more or less assimilated to life in the white-dominated society of the Tobacco Coast. Periodically their lives were disrupted by the arrival of newcomers fresh from Africa, people of many ethnic groups who spoke a babel of languages, worshiped an array of deities, were bereft of family ties, and had to learn new ways of life and labor. Successive infusions of Africans, Kulikoff argues, therefore delayed formation of a society that was distinctively Afro-American.

Menard and Kulikoff agree that important demographic changes in the eighteenth century heralded the emergence of more settled social conditions and greater cultural homogeneity among slaves. First, the black population began to grow by natural increase, and importations from Africa declined. As a result, the proportion of children increased, and the ratio of men to women improved. In other words, as the slave population changed from largely immigrant to native-born, it gradually acquired more normal demographic characteristics. Second, slave population density increased, as did the number of large plantations. These factors allegedly led to widened opportunities within bondage. Some slaves escaped wearisome toil in the fields to become artisans or domestics. Others gained a measure of autonomy over their lives by being assigned to quarters where whites were not regularly present. For many more, a growing, sexually balanced, and largely native-born population clustered on large plantations was conducive, in Menard's words, to "social contact, intimate personal relationships, and a stable family life." By 1790, Kulikoff contends, "native blacks formed relatively settled communities," both within and among plantations. The linchpin of this argument is demographic change: as a native-born, sexually balanced black population experienced natural growth, and as population density and plantation size also increased, these conditions provided the basis for family and community life, occupational diversity, and autonomy.

Kulikoff has located this important transition in the years 1740 to 1790. He has also attempted to establish the distribution of the Chesapeake slave population and to explore some of the social and cultural consequences. He cautions that research on the region is incomplete, that his conclusions are based at least partly on unprovable assumptions, and that relationships between demographic and economic conditions, on the one hand, and slave society and culture, on the other, are "difficult to determine." He nevertheless believes that between 1740 and the American Revolution, in the area from "just north of the Patuxent" River in Anne Arundel and Prince George's counties, Maryland, "to just south of the James" River in Virginia, "plantations were large, black population density was high, few whites were present," and "well developed" road networks linked plantations. Slaves in this broad region "could create a rudimentary cross-plantation society," a process whites facilitated by selling slaves within their neighborhoods. Whereas blacks rarely lived in groups of more than thirty before 1740, "by the 1770s and 1780s the wealthiest gentlemen ran home plantations with more than one hundred slaves and quarters with thirty to fifty." By the 1780s, Kulikoff argues, perhaps 44 percent of the enslaved resided on large quarters (those with more than twenty blacks);

another 4 percent were men on smaller units located near "many large quarters." Yet another 26 percent lived on middling plantations, in groups of eleven to twenty, "and could participate in the family and community activities of their quarters." Composing the last one-fourth of the slaves, he contends, were "women and children who lived on small plantations ... [and] usually did not travel from quarter to quarter but had to wait for husbands and fathers to visit them."

Kulikoff holds that, before the Revolution, slaves "developed strong community institutions on their quarters" and formed complex, cross-plantation kin networks. Balanced sex ratios enabled most men and women to marry, and by the 1770s the majority of Afro-Americans lived in families and had households "similar to those of their white masters. About as many creole slaves as whites lived in two-parent and extended households." Grandparents and even great-grandparents were common. A family or two usually inhabited the small plantations, while "extended families in which most residents were kinfolk" occupied the large units. Because slave dwellings on large plantations usually were located, Kulikoff claims, at some distance from the master's house, their occupants spent many hours of their lives free of direct white supervision. By the 1780s, one-half to three-fourths of the slaves living in the Chesapeake tidewater "enjoyed some sort of social life not controlled by their masters." Slaves socialized with one another, tended gardens located in the yards surrounding their quarters, sang and danced at gatherings like the one Nicholas Cresswell witnessed in 1774, traveled from one plantation to another to visit friends and relatives, gave food and other help to runaways, and protected themselves from harm at the hands of fellow bondsmen and bondswomen.

* * *

This conception of black life now dominates discussion of slavery in the eighteenth-century Chesapeake. Yet it remains unproven. The obscurity in which most slaves lived obstructs historians' efforts to reconstruct their lives, nor have scholars made full use of the sources that are available. Information on the number of Africans carried to Maryland and Virginia—blacks who allegedly intruded upon existing slave communities—is incomplete. Data on their dispersal are fragmentary. Historians have little notion who purchased the Africans, whether they were bought singly or in groups, and whether they joined preexisting black households. The rate at which Africans reproduced, when natural increase began, and when a largely native-born black population emerged in the Chesapeake have not been determined with any precision.

Attempts to identify Afro-American family connections, moreover, often prove futile. Marriage and birth registers are rare for slaves. Masters' wills and inventories of estates only occasionally reveal kinship ties among a decedent's human chattels; when they do, these sources often link only a mother and her youngest child. The disruptions to which slaves were subjected—assignment to outlying quarters, hiring out, sale, and dispersal through gift or bequest—preclude any confident expectation that blacks who lived near one another were necessarily related. Nor does procreation by itself signify marriage or other enduring family commitments. The best evidence for slave families comes from the papers of a few great planters, but it is ques-

tionable whether kin connections that can be identified on some of the largest units were duplicated elsewhere, especially on smaller plantations.

The ruling interpretation leaves many questions to be answered with greater specificity. One would expect that growing population densities enhanced blacks' abilities to interact, find spouses, raise families, and create an Afro-American culture. But how dense was the slave population in the eighteenth-century Chesapeake? How many tidewater planters managed home plantations with more than one hundred blacks and quarters with thirty to fifty? How distant, typically, were slave dwellings from the master's house? If one-half to three-fourths of the blacks had "some sort of social life not controlled by their masters," is it believable that masters entirely controlled the lives of the rest of the enslaved?

Another problem concerns slaves' ability to interact across plantation boundaries. Road networks, high black population densities, and the practice of selling or otherwise disposing of slaves—especially relatives and friends—within neighborhoods obviously increased opportunities for contact. How often contacts were actually made is, of course, another matter. As yet we know little about how slaves were dispersed geographically, about the extent of road and path networks across the Chesapeake, or about how easily slaves could travel—either furtively or with their masters' permission—from one plantation to another. We shall never know how many mothers walked through the night in order to lie with their children for a few hours, as Frederick Douglass remembered his mother doing in the nineteenth century. Nor shall we ever know how often a slave hurried to a neighboring plantation to warn a relative of imminent danger, as Charles Ball's grandfather did in the late eighteenth century when he learned that his son was about to be sold to a slave dealer. But we can be reasonably certain that most of the black laborers of the Chesapeake spent no more than a small part of their time en route to or visiting friends and relatives who were not housed on their own quarters. For most of their lives, slaves' chances for social interaction were limited to the fields and meadows, the quarters and woods, of their home plantations.

It is to the groups in which slaves passed most of their daily lives, then, that we need to look for whatever *regular* occasions existed for family life and social interaction. The first Federal census of 1790, which is extant for Maryland but not Virginia, offers an opportunity to glimpse the spatial distribution of blacks. The returns show that, for the end of the eighteenth century, generalizations about large plantations, high slave density, and the presence of few whites are overdrawn. Whites were not few; they outnumbered slaves by 43,091 to 42,681 in the five lower Western Shore counties of the Maryland sector of the Patuxent-to-James region. The average number of whites in slaveholding families was 5.2 to 5.5 by county; these families possessed an average of 7.8 to 11.4 blacks. Nor were large plantations the norm: the proportion of slaveholding families with 20 or more slaves was less than one in ten in three of the four counties for which such data are extant. In the other, Prince George's, 15.5 percent of the plantations can be classified as large. When families that did not have slaves are included, the percentages fall below 10 percent in all four counties. These figures hardly convey the impression that few whites

and large plantations characterized the Maryland portion of the region. Before drawing conclusions, then, about opportunities for family formation and the development of Afro-American society and culture in the eighteenth-century Chesapeake, the spatial distribution of slaves deserves closer attention. Here is a subject for which many data exist, in the form of tax lists, censuses, and estate inventories. In fact, for the majority of blacks who toiled in the Chesapeake before 1800, the most common, often the only, documentary record we have of their existence, is their aggregate numbers. We need to get these numbers straight.

Charles County, in the heart of the region, is an advantageous place to examine the distribution of slaves. Its planters were heavily committed to tobacco production and slave labor. Furthermore, during the eighteenth century the number of large plantations, the proportion of slaves whose masters owned more than twenty blacks, and the ratio of blacks to whites in the whole population and in slaveholding households all increased. By 1790, black slaves were approaching a majority, and the county ranked third in Maryland in the number of black inhabitants, second in percentage of blacks, and first in the proportion of slaveowning families....

For Charles County, the extant list enumerated two-thirds of both the white and slave populations. The distribution of slaves in 1782 exhibited some marked similarities to that of the 1750s. So far as can be documented, the proportion of households with adult slave laborers was about the same at the end of the War for Independence as it had been thirty years earlier. The highest concentration of blacks was still found in the lower hundred of William and Mary Parish, the lowest in Durham Parish in the western part of the country. In Pomonkey Hundred, slaveholding still hovered around 50 percent. Yet if the proportion of slaveholders and the concentration of blacks in the civil subdivisions of the county look much alike in the 1750s and early 1780s, the distribution of blacks among households does not. The taxable labor force became more heavily black during the intervening years. Moreover, the proportion of slaves whose masters owned more than ten taxable blacks increased, while the proportion whose masters held five or fewer declined. We also find that 81.4 percent of plantations had five taxable slaves or fewer in 1758, but that figure fell to 57.4 percent a generation later. And while less than 1 percent... of the plantations accounted for in the earlier set of tax records had adult slave labor forces in excess of twenty men and women, in 1782 the percentage stood at 5.8....

During the era of the Revolution, then, Charles County slaves were experiencing the kind of demographic change that Menard predicted and Kulikoff has affirmed for the Chesapeake—a movement toward larger plantations where the possibilities for communal ties, family formation, and the sharing of tribulation and joy, of dreams and despair, presumably were significantly greater than in the period before 1730 when plantations were small and the average slave population density was much lower. How does the 1782 distribution of slaves in the ten hundreds of the county compare with what Kulikoff believes likely for the Chesapeake tidewater generally by the 1780s? First, notwithstanding the growth of the slave population, whites remained numerically dominant, 6,457 to 5,411. Second, Kulikoff's conjectures on plantation size, if applied to Charles County, consistently exaggerate the extent to which basic spatial distribution enhanced opportunities for slave family and communal life. His figures appreciably underestimate the proportion of slaves living in small groups of ten or fewer (44.9 percent in the county, 26 percent according to Kulikoff), are closer to the mark for the percentage living in groups of eleven to twenty (30.2 versus 26 percent), and significantly overestimate the proportion living on large plantations (25 percent versus 44 percent). Finally, no slaveowner held one hundred or more persons in bondage. Rather, the largest holding was sixty.

The 1782 assessment itself probably *overstates* the size of some slave groups because of the way it was taken. If a master had slaves in more than a single hundred of the county, they were counted for the hundred where they lived. But the tax lists do not reveal whether or how masters divided their slaves *within* hundreds. Owners of large tracts of land or separate tracts may well have stationed blacks on several quarters. In addition, slaves who were hired out were nevertheless credited to the master. Thus slaves were probably more scattered and less able to maintain regular contact with one another than the records disclose.

The wealth of data in the 1782 assessment enables one to move beyond generalizations about the number of slaves per master and to scrutinize at closer range 776 groups containing a total of 5,411 persons. Every slave, whether living in daily isolation from other blacks or in the largest group, can be placed in one of five age categories, and those in the most productive years of life can be distinguished by gender. From this evidence of the distribution of the youngest children and those who survived early childhood, of the comparative numbers of women and men of reproductive age, and of the proportion of slaves whose age and condition reduced their economic value, the most elementary boundaries of slave life emerge....

Only on plantations with slaves in all five age/gender categories could the full range of daily contacts occur, between young and old, male and female, parent and child and perhaps grandparents. More than one-half of the slaves... tallied in the tax lists did *not* have that opportunity. Among the rest..., the opportunity was realized only if none of the groups was fragmented among quarters or through hiring out—a highly improbable circumstance. When one examines the age and gender groups plantation by plantation, moreover, it becomes obvious that many blacks endured a truncated existence of one kind or another, even if masters kept them all together. Examination of the holdings of masters who owned slaves in up to three of the age/gender categories reveals some distinctly constricted living arrangements in Charles County. On some quarters, children were without regular parental supervision and guidance. On others, men and women returning from the fields did not hear the voices of black children. Older slaves had no audience of young listeners to whom they could pass along memories of Africa, religious instruction, or advice about making the most of bondage. Women and children or, less commonly, men and children were the only occupants of some quarters; there young Afro-Americans lacked continuous contact not only with one parent but with any black adult of the absent gender who could serve as a model....

The tax records demonstrate constraints that plantation agriculture placed upon blacks' ability to live in groups that, although not of their own choosing, at least included friends and relatives, males and females, young and old. The drawback of these records is that they yield a static picture. They reveal nothing about the experiences of slaves at other times in their lives, and they cannot even hint at the dislocations slaves endured at the whim of masters who hired or loaned them out, used them to satisfy debts, gave them away, or sold them for financial reasons or because they were recalcitrant. As probate records disclose, dislocation also occurred when masters died—a point deserving attention. In Charles County during the eighteenth century, slaves and land were the most valuable forms of wealth. Of these, the former were movable and easily more divisible. When a master died intestate, Maryland law prescribed that the slaves in the estate be divided among the widow, the surviving children, and the lineal descendants of children who had predeceased the parent. When masters wrote wills, they, too, customarily adopted partible inheritance of slave property. Significantly, among all parent-testators whose wills were filed for probate in the county between 1740 and 1784, daughters received a higher proportion of slave bequests than did sons. And it was daughters who, at marriage, usually moved to their husbands' land and took their slaves with them. Thus, for numerous reasons, no slave family or community escaped the threat of being torn apart....

Many owners probably broke up slave groups with no more disquietude than merchant Thomas Howe Ridgate expressed when he wrote, "so adieu to [the] Negro's." When the tobacco crop was in the shed, when funds had to be raised to satisfy a debt or pay for a child's education, when children came of age, daughters married, or a widow died, when a slave mother weaned her infant, or when "any of the negroes shou'd misbehave, or... my Executors shou'd think it more to the advantage of my children that some of the negroes should be sold," then blacks who had endured bondage together were torn apart. In 1768 Roger Smith bequeathed to his wife a lifetime estate in two slave families, a couple with seven children and a woman with two. When Mrs. Smith remarried, her blacks came under the mastery of her new husband, though he could not sell or mortgage them. At her death these families descended intact to her brother-in-law, Basil Smith; but when he died in 1774, just six years after the initial bequest, the two slave families were parceled out in four lots. Another testator, Ann Dent, in 1764 gave mulatto Tom to one married daughter, Tom's wife Cate to a second married daughter, and the couple's son to a granddaughter. Whether or how often this slave family thereafter was allowed to reunite, even briefly, thus depended upon the location and decision of three different masters. Such parceling out, repeated again and again through several generations, certainly established dispersed kin networks, but how successful Afro-Americans were in using those networks, or how often they simply lost contact with parents, siblings, and spouses, is unknown.

The 1782 tax assessment lists and testamentary evidence show that it was not uncommon for children to be separated from their mothers, even at an early age. Sometimes masters planned to dispose of children still in the womb; at other times they deliberated what to do with a woman's "future increase." Ann Cornish decided that "as she had not a negroe apiece for each of her Grand Children she wou[ld] give them as they came into the World." Cebberamous, a bondswoman of Elizabeth Askin, was destined to lose "the first Child that... [she] shall bring to good." Theodocia Speake's slave Sue was similarly to be stripped of "the first Child that... [she] Brings that liveth a year & if in Case it Dieth in a year then the next Child the aforesaid negro Sue bringeth." Mothers—and fathers, too, if they were present—whose children remained with them only a year abruptly lost them just as they were beginning to explore the world on foot. Richard Maston's pregnant slave Venus kept her infant until it could babble and toddle but then had to relinquish it to a white couple who were to "take the Child... under their own immediate Care so soon as it... shall arrive at the Age of two years." Almost as if he were dealing out cards, Maximillion Matthews of Durham Parish in 1770 gave the first child of his slave woman Henny to his daughter, the second to his wife, and the third to his son, "and so Alternatively and respectively for all the increase that the said negro Henny may have."

Members of slave communities who were allocated among masters' wives, sons, daughters, and grandchildren could hope to see one another at least occasionally. And blacks who were temporarily hired out could look forward to returning to their home plantations at the termination of their contracts. Slave sales, especially public auctions, were a different matter. Masters who had a surplus of blacks or needed to raise funds, and executors who needed to clear an estate of debt, could not afford to be much concerned about ties among blacks.

Nor would they have gone to the trouble and expense of advertising in the *Maryland Gazette* and Virginia newspapers had they expected to dispose of slaves entirely in the immediate neighborhood.

Dispersal of Benjamin Fendall's blacks illustrates what could happen among even the largest slaveholders. Fendall owned a well-developed plantation on the Potomac River, rented some of his lands to tenants, and operated several mills and a bakery that sold ship bread to passing vessels. In addition to field hands, his slaves included a blacksmith, an "ingenious fellow" who "is a Carpenter, Cooper, Shoemaker, and Tanner," a waiter, and "a fine Cook Wench, who is a good Seamstress, and can do any Kind of House-work." During his lifetime Fendall gave some of his slaves to his adult children. At his death in 1764, twenty-nine remained. These he willed to be sold, with the rest of his estate, to pay his debts and provide legacies for two children who were minors. Sale of the slaves was not swift: it was accomplished in two public auctions held six months apart. At the first, in the midst of the growing season in July 1764, seven males aged fourteen and above, one woman, and three children were sold. Then in January 1765 the executors disposed of all but one of the remaining slaves: eight males aged fourteen and above, six women, and four children. The twenty-nine slaves went to seventeen different masters....

* * *

Until recently, historians have portrayed North American slavery with too little sensitivity to time or place, so that it appeared a static rather than dynamic institution. They have also studied slavery mainly at what Ira Berlin has called its point of maturity: the antebellum years, which composed less than one-quarter of the time the institution existed in North America. Recent scholarship has helped to redress that imbalance by focusing on the preceding, formative centuries, and in that regard a paradigm based on Chesapeake demographic conditions is valuable. For most blacks in the Chesapeake before 1800, the only documentary evidence of their existence is their aggregate numbers set down in census and tax records and—for those listed in estate inventories—their names, gender, and age. The eighteenth-century data from Charles County suggest that it is time to refine and clarify the paradigm —to examine Chesapeake slave distribution more fully at the plantation level, to be sensitive to regional variations, and to establish more precisely the timing of demographic change.

In Charles County, the development of stable slave communities proceeded much more slowly than Menard or Kulikoff hypothesized in their pioneering work. Demographic encouragement of stability, moreover, never seems to have been as favorable as the current paradigm would suggest. True, the number of large plantations, the proportion of slaves living on those plantations, and the proportion of slaves in the county's population increased during the eighteenth century. Nonetheless, it would distort reality to apply to the county the prevailing interpretation of slave distribution in the Chesapeake tidewater. As late as 1782, large plantations, few whites, and high black population densities did not characterize Charles County. Rather, 45 percent of the enslaved were held by masters who owned ten or fewer slaves, and another 30 percent by masters who had eleven to twenty. Whites continued to outnumber blacks, as they had throughout the eighteenth century. These demographic factors need to be considered in relation to masters' treatment of slaves as property, to be acquired and disposed of at pleasure. The result was an Afro-American family and communal life that was markedly fragile and subject to disruption.

POSTSCRIPT

Did American Slaves Develop a Distinct African American Culture in the Eighteenth Century?

The essays by Kulikoff and Lee both suggest that the emergence of a cohesive African American community life was a gradual process that occurred over the course of two centuries. They differ not on the question of whether or not slaves attempted to create a communal life for themselves in the Chesapeake but rather on the degree of success achieved by bond servants in gaining control over their community institutions. Kulikoff's conclusions are supported by Russell Menard, whose demographic studies provide a wealth of information on the colonial Chesapeake region. See "From Servants to Slaves: The Transformation of the Chesapeake Labor System," *Southern Studies* (Winter 1977). You can examine further support for the Kulikoff thesis in William D. Piersen, *Black Yankees: The Development of an Afro-American Subculture in Eighteenth-Century New England* (University of Massachusetts Press, 1988).

How much African American culture was inspired by African survivers? How much cultural baggage did Africans bring with them to the New World? Anthropologist Melville Herskovits argued in *The Myth of the Negro Past* (1941) that numerous elements of West African culture survived the "middle passage" and were adapted by slaves to their New World environment.

Despite the fact that historians of slavery have generally focused upon the antebellum period, there is a significant body of literature pertaining to the colonial period. The details of the Atlantic slave trade are treated best in Basil Davidson, *Black Mother: The African Slave Trade: Precolonial History, 1450–1850* (Little, Brown, 1961); Daniel P. Mannix, *Black Cargoes: A History of the Atlantic Slave Trade, 1518–1865* (Viking Press, 1962); and Philip D. Curtin, *The Atlantic Slave Trade: A Census* (University of Wisconsin, 1969). The origins of slavery in the British mainland colonies are debated in Oscar and Mary Handlin, "The Origins of the Southern Labor System," *William and Mary Quarterly* (April 1950); Carl N. Degler, "Slavery and the Genesis of American Race Prejudice," *Comparative Studies in History and Society* (October 1959); and Winthrop Jordan, "Modern Tensions and the Origins of American Slavery," *Journal of Southern History* (February 1962). The development of black slavery in various British mainland colonies is treated in Mechal Sobel, *The World They Made Together: Black and White Values in Eighteenth-Century Virginia* (Princeton University Press, 1987), and Peter H. Wood, *Black Majority: Negroes in Colonial South Carolina from 1670 Through the Stono Rebellion* (Alfred A. Knopf, 1974).

ISSUE 5

Was There a Great Awakening in Mid-Eighteenth-Century America?

YES: Patricia U. Bonomi, from *Under the Cope of Heaven: Religion, Society, and Politics in Colonial America* (Oxford University Press, 1986)

NO: Jon Butler, from "Enthusiasm Described and Decried: The Great Awakening as Interpretative Fiction," *Journal of American History* (September 1982)

ISSUE SUMMARY

YES: Professor of history Patricia U. Bonomi defines the Great Awakening as a period of intense revivalistic fervor that laid the foundation for socio-religious and political reform by spawning an age of contentiousness in the British mainland colonies.

NO: Professor of American history Jon Butler argues that to describe the colonial revivalistic activities of the eighteenth century as the "Great Awakening" is to seriously exaggerate their extent, nature, and impact on pre-Revolutionary American society and politics.

Although generations of American schoolchildren have been taught that the British colonies in North America were founded by persons fleeing religious persecution in England, the truth is that many of those early settlers were motivated by other factors, some of which had little to do with theological preferences. To be sure, the Pilgrims and Puritans of New England sought to escape the proscriptions established by the Church of England. Many New Englanders, however, did not adhere to the precepts of Calvinism and were therefore viewed as outsiders. The Quakers who populated Pennsylvania were mostly fugitives from New England, where they had been victims of religious persecution. But to apply religious motivations to the earliest settlers of Virginia, South Carolina, or Georgia is to engage in a serious misreading of the historical record. Even in New England the religious mission of (the first governor of Massachusetts Bay Colony) John Winthrop's "city upon a hill" began to erode as the colonial settlements matured and stabilized.

Although religion was a central element in the lives of the seventeenth- and eighteenth-century Europeans who migrated to the New World, proliferation of religious sects and denominations, emphasis upon material gain in all parts of the colonies, and the predominance of reason over emotion that is associated with the Deists of the Enlightenment period all contributed to a gradual but obvious movement of the colonists away from the church and clerical authority. William Bradford (the second governor of Plymouth Colony), for example, expressed grave concern that many Plymouth residents were following a path of perfidy, and William Penn (the founder of Pennsylvania) was certain that the "holy experiment" of the Quakers had failed. Colonial clergy, fearful that a fall from grace was in progress, issued calls for a revival of religious fervor. Therefore, the spirit of revivalism that spread through the colonies in the 1730s and 1740s was an answer to these clerical prayers.

The episode known as the First Great Awakening coincided with the Pietistic movement in Europe and England and was carried forward by dynamic preachers such as Gilbert Tennant, Theodore Frelinghuysen, and George Whitefield. They promoted a religion of the heart, not of the head, in order to produce a spiritual rebirth. These revivals, most historians agree, reinvigorated American Protestantism. Many new congregations were organized as a result of irremediable schisms between "Old Lights" and "New Lights." Skepticism about the desirability of an educated clergy sparked a strong strain of anti-intellectualism. Also, the emphasis on conversion was a message to which virtually everyone could respond, regardless of age, sex, or social status. For some historians, the implications of the Great Awakening extended beyond the religious sphere into the realm of politics and were incorporated into the American Revolution.

In the following selections, Patricia U. Bonomi writes from the traditional assumption that a powerful revivalistic force known as the Great Awakening occurred in the American colonies in the mid-eighteenth century. Following a survey of the converging forces that served as precursors to this revivalistic movement, she explains that the Great Awakening grew out of clerical disputes among Presbyterians and quickly spread to other denominations throughout the colonies, abetted by dynamic itinerant preachers such as George Whitefield. Before the enthusiasm subsided, she concludes, the Awakening had instilled a tradition of divisiveness that would affect a number of American social, political, and religious structures.

Jon Butler claims that closer scrutiny of the Great Awakening reveals that the revivals were regional episodes that did not affect all of the colonies equally and, hence, had only a modest impact on American colonial religion. Butler suggests that because the mid-eighteenth-century revivals did not produce the kinds of dramatic changes, religious or political, frequently ascribed to them, historians should abandon the concept of the Great Awakening altogether.

YES

Patricia U. Bonomi

"THE HOSANNAS OF THE MULTITUDE": THE GREAT AWAKENING IN AMERICA

The Great Awakening—that intense period of revivalist tumult from about 1739 to 1745—is one of the most arresting subjects of American history. The eighteenth century, and the latter part of the seventeenth, were of course punctuated with religious episodes that seemed to erupt without warning and draw entire communities into a vortex of religious conversions and agitations of soul. Yet those episodes tended not to spread beyond the individual churches or towns in which they originated. By the third decade of the eighteenth century, however, a number of currents were converging to prepare the way for an unprecedented burst of religious fervor and controversy.

The two major streams of thought shaping western religious belief in the eighteenth century—Enlightenment rationalism and Continental pietism—were by the 1720s reaching increasing numbers of Americans through the world of print, transatlantic learned societies, and such recently arrived spokesmen as the Anglican moderate George Berkeley, on the one side, and the Dutch Reformed pietist Theodore Frelinghuysen, on the other. By the 1730s, American clergymen influenced by the spiritual intensity and emotional warmth of Reformed pietism were vigorously asserting that religion was being corrupted by secular forces; in their view a conversion experience that touched the heart was the only road to salvation. The rationalists demurred, preferring a faith tempered by "an enlightened Mind ... not raised Affections." This contest between reason and innate grace was in one sense as old as Christianity itself. In New England, where it was often cast as a competition between Arminians and Antinomians, only the Calvinists' ability to hold the two elements in exquisite balance had averted a schism. Rationalist attitudes ... were sufficiently prevalent in the eighteenth-century South to obstruct the development of heart religion there until the later colonial years. In the Middle Colonies, every point of view was heard, though by the 1730s tension was rising between the entrenched ministers of more orthodox opinion and incoming clergymen who insisted on conversion as the *sine qua non* of vital religion.

Adding to currents of religious unease in the early eighteenth century were a number of other developments: an accelerating pace of commercial growth; land shortages as well as land opportunities; the unprecedented diversity of eighteenth-century immigration; and a rapid climb in total population. Population growth now created dense settlements in some rural as well as urban areas, facilitating mass public gatherings. Moreover, the proliferation of churches and sects, intensifying denominational rivalries, and smallpox and earthquake alarms that filled meetinghouses to overflowing all contributed to a sense of quickening in church life.

Into this volatile and expectant environment came some of the most charismatic and combative personalities of the age. And as the electricity of a Tennent crackled, and the thunder of a Whitefield rolled, a storm broke that, in the opinion of many, would forever alter American society. The Great Awakening created conditions uniquely favorable to social and political, as well as religious, reform by piercing the facade of civility and deference that governed provincial life to usher in a new age of contentiousness. By promoting church separations and urging their followers to make choices that had political as well as religious implications, the Awakeners wrought permanent changes in public practices and attitudes. Before it subsided, the revival had unsettled the lives of more Americans and disrupted more institutions than any other single event in colonial experience to that time. To see how a religious movement could overspill its boundaries to reshape cultural understanding and political expectations, we must take a closer look at some of the churches and people caught up in the revival.

PRESBYTERIAN BEGINNINGS

The Great Awakening began not as a popular uprising but as a contest between clerical factions. Thus only those churches with a "professional" clergy and organized governing structure—the Presbyterian, Congregational, Dutch Reformed, and eventually the Anglican—were split apart by the revival. The newer German churches and the sects, having little structure to overturn, remained largely outside the conflict. These events have usually been viewed from the perspective of New England Congregationalism, though the first denomination to be involved in the Awakening was the Presbyterian Church in the Middle Colonies. All of the strains and adjustments experienced by other colonial denominations over a longer time span were compressed, in the Presbyterian case, into the fifty years from the beginning of Ulster immigration around 1725 to the Revolution. Thus the Presbyterian example serves as a kind of paradigm of the experience of all churches from their initial formation through the Great Awakening and its aftermath. It reveals too how a dispute between ministers rapidly widened into a controversy that tested the limits of order and introduced new forms of popular leadership that challenged deferential traditions.

Presbyterians looked to the future with reasonably high hopes by the third decade of the eighteenth century. To all appearances they possessed a more stable and orderly church structure than any of their middle-colony competitors. Unlike the Anglicans, they required no bishop to perform the essential rites of ordination and confirmation; nor did they suffer quite the same shortage of ministers as the German churches. The supply of Presbyterian clergy, if never adequate, had at least been sufficient to support the formation of a rudimentary governing structure. Three presbyteries and the Synod of Philadelphia were in place before the first wave of immigration from Ulster reached the Delaware basin, enabling the twenty-five to thirty ministers active in the Middle Colonies to direct growth and protect professional standards in the period of expansion after 1725. Congregations were under the care of laymen ordained to the office of "elder" and, when available, ministers. Supervising presbyteries in each region maintained oversight of local congregations and ordained and disciplined the clergy. At the top was the synod, which provided a forum where clerical disputes over church doctrine and governing authority could be resolved *in camera* [secretly].

Yet the controls imposed by the Presbyterian hierarchy were hardly all that they appeared to be. Beneath orderly processes were tensions which had been expanding steadily before finally bursting forth in fratricidal strife and schism after 1739. Any reading of eighteenth-century Presbyterian records discloses at least three kinds of strains beneath the surface: between parishioners, between people and minister, and within the professional clergy itself.

The Presbyterian Church was the focal point and mediator of Scotch-Irish community life from the late 1720s on, when thousands of Ulster Scots began entering the colonies annually. As the westward-migrating settlers moved beyond the reach of government and law, the Presbyterian Church was the only institution that kept pace with settlement. By stretching resources to the limit, the synod, and especially the presbyter-

ies, kept in touch with their scattered brethren through itinerant preachers and presbyterial visitations. Ministers, invariably the best educated persons on the early frontier, were looked to for leadership in both religious and community affairs, and they often took up multiple roles as doctors, teachers, and even lawyers. So closely did the Scotch-Irish identify with the Kirk [Church] that it was often said they "could not live without it."

But if the church was a vital center it was also an agency of control. Presbyterian ministers—whom some regarded as a "stiff-necked... [and] pedantick crew"—expected to guide their parishioners' spiritual growth and moral safety in America as they had done in the Old Country, and at first, by and large, they succeeded. Congregations gathered spontaneously in Scotch-Irish settlements, much as they did in immigrant German communities. A major difference between the two societies was that from an early stage lay Presbyterians submitted themselves to clerical authority. As soon as a Presbyterian congregation was formed, it requested recognition and the supply of a minister from the local presbytery. Often the presbytery could provide only a probationer or itinerant preacher for the Sabbath, and many settlements were fortunate to hear a sermon one or two Sundays a month. The congregations nonetheless proceeded to elect elders, deacons to care for the poor and sick, and trustees to oversee the collection of tithes for the minister's salary. The governing "session," comprised of elders and minister, functioned as a kind of court, hearing charges and ruling on a variety of matters, including disputes between parishioners over land or debt, domestic difficulties, and church doctrine.

The main responsibility of the session was to enforce moral discipline. Its rulings could be appealed to the supervising presbytery. The presbytery minutes consequently have much to tell us about the quality of clerical authority. But they also disclose the growing undercurrent of resistance that such authority aroused among the freer spirits in the Scotch-Irish settlements....

NEW SIDES VS. OLD SIDES

The Great Awakening split the Presbyterian Church apart, and through the cracks long-suppressed steam hissed forth in clouds of acrimony and vituperation that would change the face of authority in Pennsylvania and elsewhere. As the passions of the Awakening reached their height in the early 1740s, evangelical "New Side" Presbyterians turned on the more orthodox "Old Sides" with the ferocity peculiar to zealots, charging them with extravagant doctrinal and moral enormities. The internecine spectacle that ensued, the loss of proportion and professional decorum, contributed to the demystification of the clergy, forced parishioners to choose between competing factions, and overset traditional attitudes about deference and leadership in colonial America.

The division that surfaced in 1740–1741 had been developing for more than a decade. Presbyterian ministers had no sooner organized their central association, the Synod of Philadelphia, in 1715 than the first lines of stress appeared, though it was not until a cohesive evangelical faction emerged in the 1730s that an open split was threatened. Most members of the synod hoped to model American Presbyterianism along orderly lines, and in 1729 an act requiring all ministers and ministerial candidates to subscribe publicly to the Westminster Confession had been approved. In 1738 the synod had further ruled that no minister would be licensed unless he could display a degree from a British or European university, or from one of the New England colleges (Harvard or Yale). New candidates were to submit to an examination by a commission of the synod on the soundness of their theological training and spiritual condition. The emergent evangelical faction rightly saw these restrictions as an effort to control their own activities. They had reluctantly accepted subscription to the Westminster Confession, but synodical screening of new candidates struck them as an intolerable invasion of the local presbyteries' right of ordination.

The insurgents were led by the Scotsman William Tennent, Sr., and his sons, William, Jr., Charles, John, and Gilbert. William, Sr. had been educated at the University of Edinburgh, receiving a bachelor's degree in 1693 and an M.A. in 1695. He may have been exposed to European pietism at Edinburgh, where new ideas of every sort were brewing in the last quarter of the seventeenth century. Though ordained a minister of the Anglican church in 1706, Tennent did not gain a parish of his own, and in 1718 he departed the Old World for the New. When he applied for a license from the Synod of Philadelphia in 1718, Tennent was asked his reasons for leaving the Church of England. He responded that he had come to view government by bishops as anti-scriptural, that he opposed ecclesiastical courts and plural benefices, that the church was leaning toward Arminianism, and that he disapproved of "their ceremonial way of worship." All this seemed sound enough to the Presbyterians, and Tennent was licensed forthwith. Having a strong interest in scholarship and pedagogy, Tennent built a one-room schoolhouse in about 1730 in Neshaminy, Bucks County —the Log College, as it was later derisively called—where he set about training young men for the ministry. Exactly when Tennent began to pull away from the regular synod leadership is unclear, but by 1736 his church at Neshaminy was split down the middle and the anti-evangelical members were attempting to expel him as minister.

In 1739 the synod was confronted with a question on professional standards that brought the two factions closer to a complete break. When the previous year's synod had erected commissions to examine the education of all ministerial candidates not holding degrees from approved universities, Gilbert Tennent had charged that the qualification was designed "to prevent his father's school from training gracious men for the Ministry." Overriding the synod's rule in 1739, the radical New Brunswick Presbytery licensed one John Rowland without reference to any committee, though Rowland had received "a private education"—the synod's euphemism for the Log College. Sharply criticizing the presbytery for its disorderly and divisive action, the synod refused to approve Rowland until he agreed to submit himself for examination, which he in turn refused to do.

* * *

Since education was central to the dispute, it is unfortunate that no Log College records have survived to describe the training given the remarkable group of men that came under William Tennent, Sr.'s tutelage. We do know that they emerged to become leaders of the revivalist movement, and would in turn prepare other religious and educational leaders of the middle and southern colonies. The little existing evidence casts doubt on the synod's charge that Tennent and his followers were "destroyers of good learning" who persisted in foisting unlettered Log College students upon an undiscriminating public. As Gilbert Tennent insisted, the insurgents "desired and designed a well-qualified Ministry as much as our Brethren." To be sure, their theological emphasis was at variance with that of the Old Side clergy, and there may have been parts of the traditional curriculum they did not value as highly, as had been true with the innovative dissenting academies in Britain. But as competition between the two factions intensified, restrained criticism gave way to enmity. Thus when the synod charged that Gilbert Tennent had called "Physicks, Ethicks, Metophysicks and Pnuematicks [the rubric under which Aristotelian philosophy was taught in medieval universities] meer Criticks, and consequently useless," its members could not resist adding that he did so "because his Father cannot or doth not teach them."

Yet there is much that attests to both William Tennent, Sr.'s learning and his pedagogical talents. That he was a polished scholar of the classics, spoke Latin and English with equal fluency, and was a master of Greek was confirmed by many who knew him. He also "had some acquaintance with the ... Sciences." A hint of the training Tennent offered comes from the licensing examination given his youngest son Charles in 1736 by the Philadelphia Presbytery, among whose members were several who would later emerge as chief critics of the Tennents. Young Charles was tested on his "ability in prayer [and] in the

Languages," in the delivery of a sermon and exegesis, and on his answers to "various suitable questions on the arts and sciences, especially Theology and out of Scripture." He was also examined on the state of his soul. Charles Tennent was apparently approved without question.

The strongest evidence of the quality of a Log College education comes, however, from the subsequent careers and accomplishments of its eighteen to twenty-one "alumni." Their deep commitment to formal education is demonstrated by the number of academies they themselves founded, including Samuel Blair's "classical school" at Faggs Manor in Pennsylvania, Samuel Finley's academy at Nottingham, and several others. Two early presidents of the College of New Jersey (Princeton) were Samuel Finley and Samuel Davies (the latter having been educated by Blair at Faggs Manor). Moreover, the published sermons and essays of Samuel Finley, Samuel Blair, and Gilbert Tennent not only pulse with evangelical passion but also display wide learning. In the opinion of a leading Presbyterian historian the intellectual accomplishments of the Log College revivalists far outshone those of the Old Side opposers, among whom only the scholarly Francis Alison produced significant writings. As George Whitefield observed when he visited Neshaminy in 1739 and saw the rough structure of logs that housed the school: "All that we can say of most universities is, that they are glorious without."

* * *

But the distinction that the Log College men would achieve was still unknown in 1739, when the New Brunswick Presbytery defied the synod by licensing John Rowland. It was at this juncture, more-over, that the twenty-six-year-old English evangelist, George Whitefield, made his sensational appearance. Whitefield's visits to New Jersey and Pennsylvania in the winter of 1739–1740 provided tremendous support for the Presbyterian insurgents, as thousands of provincials flocked to hear him and realized, perhaps for the first time, something of what the American evangelists had been up to. The public support that now flowed to Tennent and the New Side exhilarated its members, inciting them to ever bolder assaults on the synod.

The revivalists had to this point preached only in their own churches or in temporarily vacant pulpits, but that winter they began to invade the territory of the regular clergy. This action raised the issue of itinerant preaching, perhaps the thorniest of the entire conflict, for it brought the parties face to face on the question of who was better qualified to interpret the word of God. It was in this setting that Gilbert Tennent was moved on March 8, 1740 to deliver his celebrated sermon, *The Danger of an Unconverted Ministry,* to a Nottingham congregation engaged in choosing a new preacher. It was an audacious, not to say reckless, attack on the Old Side clergy, and Tennent would later qualify some of his strongest language. But the sermon starkly reveals the gulf that separated the two factions by 1740. It also demonstrates the revivalists' supreme disregard for the traditional limits on public discussion of what amounted to professional questions....

In this influential and widely disseminated sermon Tennent set forth the three principal issues over which Presbyterians would divide: the conversion experience, education of the clergy, and itinerant preaching. While his tone may have owed something to Whitefield's recent influence—humility was never a strong point with the evangelists—it also reflected the growing self-confidence of the insurgents, as a wave of public support lifted them to popular heights. During the synod of 1740 the anti-revivalist clergy, in a demonstration of their reasonableness, agreed to certain compromises on the issues of itinerancy and licensing, but when the revivalists continued to denounce them publicly as carnal and unconverted, their patience came to an end.

The break between Old Side and New Side Presbyterians came during the synod of 1741 when a protest signed by twelve ministers and eight elders demanded that the revivalists be expelled from the synod. In a preemptive move, the New Side clergy voluntarily withdrew from the Philadelphia Synod to their presbyteries, where their work continued with great zeal and met with success that would outshine that of their rivals. In 1745 the evangelical party, joined by other friends of the revival from the Middle Colonies, formed the Synod of New York, which would sustain a lively existence until 1758 when the Presbyterian schism was finally repaired.

* * *

Disagreements over theological emphasis, professional standards, and centralized authority were the most immediate causes of the Presbyterian schism, but other differences between Old and New Sides had the effect of making the conflict sharper. Disparities in education, age (and therefore career expectations), and cultural bias are of special interest.

The twelve Old Sides who moved to expel the revivalist radicals in 1741 have sometimes been labeled the "Scotch-Irish" party for good reason. Nine were born in Northern Ireland, and two in Scotland (the birthplace of the twelfth is unknown). All were educated abroad, mainly in Scotland, and especially at the University of Glasgow. Most came to the colonies between the ages of twenty-eight and thirty-two, after having completed their education. The typical Old Side clergyman was about forty-two at the time of the schism. The New Side ministers who formed the Synod of New York in 1745 numbered twenty-two. Of the twenty-one whose places of birth can be ascertained, ten were born in New England or on eastern Long Island, one in Newark, New Jersey, eight in Northern Ireland (including Gilbert, William, Jr., and Charles Tennent), one in Scotland, and one in England. Most of those born abroad emigrated to the colonies during their middle teens; Charles Tennent was but seven, and the oldest was William Robinson, the son of an English Quaker doctor, who emigrated at about twenty-eight after an ill-spent youth. The educational profile of the New Side preachers is in striking contrast to that of the Old. Of the twenty-two, nine received degrees from Yale College, two were Harvard men, and ten were educated at the Log College. One had probably gone to a Scottish university. The typical New Side minister was about thirty-two at the time of the schism, or a decade younger than his Old Side counterpart.

Several tendencies suggest themselves. The Old Sides, more mature than their adversaries, were also more settled in their professional careers; further, their Scottish education and early professional experiences in Ulster may have instilled a respect for discipline and ecclesiastical order that could not easily be cast aside. They knew it was difficult to keep up standards in provincial societies, especially the heterodox Middle Colonies where competition in religion, as in everything else, was a constant challenge to good order. Still, it was irritating to be treated as intruders by the resident notables, or by such as the Anglicans, who pretended to look down on the Presbyterians as "men of small talents and mean education." There was security in knowing that the first generation of Presbyterian leaders had been educated and licensed in accordance with the most exacting Old World criteria. But the tradition must be continued, for succeeding generations would gain respect only if the ministry were settled on a firm professional base. Though Harvard and Yale were not Edinburgh and Glasgow, they did pattern their curricula after the British universities and to that extent could serve until the Presbyterian Church was able to establish a college of its own. And only if Presbyterian leaders could control the education and admission of candidates to the ministry might they hold their heads high among rival religious groups. A professional ministry was thus crucial to the "Scotch-Irish" party's pride and sense of place.

The New Side party, on the other hand, cared less about professional niceties than about converting sinners. Its members were at the beginning of their careers, and most, being native-born or coming to the colonies in their youth, were not so likely to be imbued with an Old World sense of prerogative and order. They never doubted that an educated clergy was essential, but education had to be of the right sort. By the 1730s Harvard and Yale were being guided, in their view, by men of rationalist leanings who simply did not provide the type of training wanted by the revivalists. Thus

the New Sides chafed against the controls favored by their more conservative elders, controls that restricted their freedom of action, slowed their careers, and were in their opinion out of touch with New World ways.

The anti-institutionalism of the revivalists caused some critics to portray them as social levellers, though there were no significant distinctions in social outlook or family background between Old and New Sides. But as with any insurgent group that relies in part on public support for its momentum, the New Sides tended to clothe their appeals in popular dress. At every opportunity they pictured the opposers as "the Noble & Mighty" elders of the church, and identified themselves with the poor and "common People"— images reinforced by the Old Sides' references to the evangelists' followers as an ignorant and "wild Rabble."

The revivalists may not have been deliberate social levellers, but their words and actions had the effect of emphasizing individual values over hierarchical ones. Everything they did, from disrupting orderly processes and encouraging greater lay participation in church government, to promoting mass assemblies and the physical closeness that went with them, raised popular emotions. Most important, they insisted that there were choices, and that the individual himself was free to make them.

The people, it might be suspected, had been waiting for this. The long years of imposed consensus and oversight by the Kirk had taken their toll, and undercurrents of restlessness had strengthened as communities stabilized and Old World values receded. Still, the habit of deferring to the clergy was deeply rooted in Presbyterian culture, making inertia an accomplice of church authority. By 1740, however, with the clergy themselves, or a part of them, openly promoting rebellion, many Presbyterians "in imitation of their example," as it was said, joined the fray. The result was turbulence, shattered and divided congregations, and a rash of slanderous reports against Old Side clergymen. Most such charges were either proved false or are deeply suspect, owing to their connection with the factional conflict. But aspersions against the ministerial character had now become a subject of public debate, suggesting that the schisms of the Awakening were effectively challenging the old structures of authority....

* * *

So volatile had the revival become that it could no longer be contained within a single region. Thus when George Whitefield carried the crusade northward, the tumults and divisions that had seized the Presbyterian Church spread to the Congregational meetinghouses of New England.

THE "DIVINE FIRE" KINDLED IN NEW ENGLAND

Whitefield's initial visit to Boston in September 1740 was greeted with tremendous interest, for the "Grand Itinerant" was the first figure of international renown to tour the colonies. During an eleven-day period he preached at least nineteen times at a number of different churches and outdoor sites, including New South Church where the huge crowd was thrown into such a panic that five were killed and many more injured. Fifteen thousand persons supposedly heard Whitefield preach on Boston Common. Even allowing for an inflated count, these were surely the largest crowds ever assembled in Boston or any other colonial city. As Samuel Johnson once said, Whitefield would have been adored if he wore a nightcap and preached from a tree. Whitefield's tours outside of Boston, and then into western Massachusetts and Connecticut, were attended by similar public outpourings. No one, it seems, wanted to miss the show. In December Gilbert Tennent arrived in Boston, having been urged by Whitefield to add more fuel to the divine fires he had kindled there. Tennent's preaching, which lacked Whitefield's sweetness but none of his power, aroused a popular fervor that matched or exceeded that inspired by the Englishman.

Most Congregational ministers, including those at Boston, had welcomed Whitefield's tour as an opportunity to stimulate religious piety. Tennent's torrid preaching may have discomfited some, but it was not until 1742 that three events led to a polarization of the clergy into "New Light" supporters and "Old Light" opposers of the Great Awakening. First came the publication in Boston of Tennent's sermon, *The Danger of an Unconverted Ministry*, which one Old Light would later blame for having "sown the Seeds of all that Discord, Intrusion, Confusion, Separation, Hatred, Variance, Emulations, Wrath, Strife, Seditions, Heresies, &c. that have been springing up in so many of the Towns and Churches thro' the Province...." Another was the publication of Whitefield's 1740 *Journal*, in which he criticized "most" New England preachers for insufficient piety and observed of Harvard and Yale that "their Light is become Darkness." The final provocation was the arrival in Boston on June 25, 1742 of the Reverend James Davenport, a newly fledged evangelist who already had Connecticut in an uproar and would soon have all Boston by the ears.

Davenport had been expelled from Connecticut on June 3 after being adjudged "disturbed in the rational Faculties of his Mind." Now the twenty-six-year-old evangelist was determined to share his special insights with the people of Boston. Forewarned about Davenport's odd behavior, the ministers of Boston and Charlestown (the majority of whom favored the Awakening) requested that the intruder restrain his "assuming Behavior... especially in judging the spiritual State of Pastors and People," and decided not to offer him their pulpits. Davenport was undeterred. He preached on the Common and in the rain on Copp's Hill; he proclaimed first three and then nine more of Boston's ministers "by name" to be unconverted; and he announced that he was "ready to drop down dead for the salvation of but one soul." Davenport was followed, according to one critic, by a "giddy Audience... chiefly made up of idle or ignorant Persons" of low rank. To some of Boston's soberer citizens the crowd appeared "menacing," and one newspaper essayist found Davenport's followers "so red hot, that I verily believe they would make nothing to kill Opposers." Such was the anarchy threatened by religious enthusiasm....

In the months that followed, New Englanders, like middle-colony Presbyterians before them, would witness and then be drawn into a fierce struggle between the two factions, as their once-decorous ministers impugned the intelligence and integrity of their rivals in public sermons and essays. The Old Light writers were especially bellicose, losing no opportunity to rebuke the "enthusias-tic, factious, censorious Spirit" of the revivalists. Schisms were threatened everywhere, and as early as 1742 some congregations had "divided into Parties, and openly and scandalously separated from one another." As the Connecticut Old Light, Isaac Stiles, warned, the subversion of all order was threatened when "Contempt is cast upon Authority both Civil and Ecclesiastical." Most distressing to those who believed that "Good Order is the Strength and Beauty of the World," was the Awakening's tendency to splinter New England society. "Formerly the People could bear with each other in Charity when they differ'd in Opinion," recalled one writer, "but they now break Fellowship and Communion with one another on that Account."

Indeed, awakened parishioners were repeatedly urged to withdraw from a "corrupt ministry." "O that the precious Seed might be preserved and *separated* from all gross Mixtures!" prayed the Connecticut New Light Jonathan Parsons. And spurred on by Parsons and other New Lights, withdraw they did. In Plymouth and Ipswich, from Maine to the Connecticut River Valley, the New England separatist movement gained momentum from 1743 onward....

* * *

The Great Awakening, as Richard Hofstadter put it, was "the first major intercolonial crisis of the mind and spirit" in eighteenth-century America. No previous occurrence in colonial history compared with it in scale or consequences. True, the floodtide of evangelical fervor soon subsided, but nothing could quite restore the old cultural landscape. The unitary ideal of the seventeenth century continued to be eroded in the post-Awakening years by further church separations. Moreover, as the Reverend William Shurtleff noted in 1745, the "dividing Spirit is not confin'd to those that are Friends" of the revival. Nor was it confined to the religious sphere. That "dividing Spirit" would be manifested everywhere after mid-century in the proliferation of religious and political factions.

NO

Jon Butler

ENTHUSIASM DESCRIBED AND DECRIED: THE GREAT AWAKENING AS INTERPRETATIVE FICTION

In the last half century, the Great Awakening has assumed a major role in explaining the political and social evolution of prerevolutionary American society. Historians have argued, variously, that the Awakening severed intellectual and philosophical connections between America and Europe (Perry Miller), that it was a major vehicle of early lower-class protest (John C. Miller, Rhys Isaac, and Gary B. Nash), that it was a means by which New England Puritans became Yankees (Richard L. Bushman), that it was the first "intercolonial movement" to stir "the people of several colonies on a matter of common emotional concern" (Richard Hofstadter following William Warren Sweet), or that it involved "a rebirth of the localistic impulse" (Kenneth Lockridge).

American historians also have increasingly linked the Awakening directly to the Revolution. Alan Heimert has tagged it as the source of a Calvinist political ideology that irretrievably shaped eighteenth-century American society and the Revolution it produced. Harry S. Stout has argued that the Awakening stimulated a new system of mass communications that increased the colonists' political awareness and reduced their deference to elite groups prior to the Revolution. Isaac and Nash have described the Awakening as the source of a simpler, non-Calvinist protest rhetoric that reinforced revolutionary ideology in disparate places, among them Virginia and the northern port cities. William G. McLoughlin has even claimed that the Great Awakening was nothing less than "the Key to the American Revolution."

These claims for the significance of the Great Awakening come from more than specialists in the colonial period. They are a ubiquitous feature of American history survey texts, where the increased emphasis on social history has made these claims especially useful in interpreting early American society to twentieth-century students. Virtually all texts treat the Great Awakening as a major watershed in the maturation of prerevolutionary American society. *The Great Republic* terms the Awakening "the greatest event in the history of

From Jon Butler, "Enthusiasm Described and Decried: The Great Awakening as Interpretative Fiction," *Journal of American History,* vol. 69 (September 1982). Copyright © 1982 by *Journal of American History.* Reprinted by permission. Notes omitted.

religion in eighteenth-century America." *The National Experience* argues that the Awakening brought "religious experiences to thousands of people in every rank of society" and in every region. *The Essentials of American History* stresses how the Awakening "aroused a spirit of humanitarianism," "encouraged the notion of equal rights," and "stimulated feelings of democracy" even if its gains in church membership proved episodic. These texts and others describe the weakened position of the clergy produced by the Awakening as symptomatic of growing disrespect for all forms of authority in the colonies and as an important catalyst, even cause, of the American Revolution. The effect of these claims is astonishing. Buttressed by the standard lecture on the Awakening tucked into most survey courses, American undergraduates have been well trained to remember the Great Awakening because their instructors and texts have invested it with such significance.

Does the Great Awakening warrant such enthusiasm? Its puzzling historiography suggests one caution. The Awakening has received surprisingly little systematic study and lacks even one comprehensive general history. The two studies, by Heimert and Cedric B. Cowing, that might qualify as general histories actually are deeply centered in New England. They venture into the middle and southern colonies only occasionally and concentrate on intellectual themes to the exclusion of social history. The remaining studies are thoroughly regional, as in the case of books by Bushman, Edwin Scott Gaustad, Charles Hartshorn Maxson, Dietmar Rothermund, and Wesley M. Gewehr, or are local, as with the spate of articles on New England towns and Jonathan Edwards or Isaac's articles and

book on Virginia. The result is that the general character of the Great Awakening lacks sustained, comprehensive study even while it benefits from thorough local examinations. The relationship between the Revolution and the Awakening is described in an equally peculiar manner. Heimert's seminal 1966 study, despite fair and unfair criticism, has become that kind of influential work whose awesome reputation apparently discourages further pursuit of its subject. Instead, historians frequently allude to the positive relationship between the Awakening and the Revolution without probing the matter in a fresh, systematic way.

The gap between the enthusiasm of historians for the social and political significance of the Great Awakening and its slim, peculiar historiography raises two important issues. First, contemporaries never homogenized the eighteenth-century colonial religious revivals by labeling them "the Great Awakening." Although such words appear in Edwards's *Faithful Narrative of the Surprising Work of God*, Edwards used them alternately with other phrases, such as "general awakening," "great alteration," and "flourishing of religion," only to describe the Northampton revivals of 1734–1735. He never capitalized them or gave them other special emphasis and never used the phrase "the Great Awakening" to evaluate all the prerevolutionary revivals. Rather, the first person to do so was the nineteenth-century historian and antiquarian Joseph Tracy, who used Edwards's otherwise unexceptional words as the title of his famous 1842 book, *The Great Awakening*. Tellingly, however, Tracy's creation did not find immediate favor among American historians. Charles Hodge discussed the Presbyterian revivals in his *Constitutional History of the Presbyterian Church* without describing them as part of a "Great Awakening," while the influential Robert Baird refused even to treat the eighteenth-century revivals as discrete and important events, much less label them "the Great Awakening." Baird all but ignored these revivals in the chronological segments of his *Religion in America* and mentioned them elsewhere only by way of explaining the intellectual origins of the Unitarian movement, whose early leaders opposed revivals. Thus, not until the last half of the nineteenth century did "the Great Awakening" become a familiar feature of the American historical landscape.

Second, this particular label ought to be viewed with suspicion, not because a historian created it—historians legitimately make sense of the minutiae of the past by utilizing such devices—but because the label itself does serious injustice to the minutiae it orders. The label "the Great Awakening" distorts the extent, nature, and cohesion of the revivals that did exist in the eighteenth-century colonies, encourages unwarranted claims for their effects on colonial society, and exaggerates their influence on the coming and character of the American Revolution. If "the Great Awakening" is not quite an American Donation of Constantine, its appeal to historians seeking to explain the shaping and character of prerevolutionary American society gives it a political and intellectual power whose very subtlety requires a close inspection of its claims to truth.

How do historians describe "the Great Awakening"? Three points seem especially common. First, all but a few describe it as a Calvinist religious revival in which converts acknowledged their sinfulness without expecting salvation. These colonial converts thereby distinguished themselves from Englishmen caught up in contemporary Methodist revivals and from Americans involved in the so-called Second Great Awakening of the early national period, both of which imbibed Arminian principles that allowed humans to believe they might effect their own salvation in ways that John Calvin discounted. Second, historians emphasize the breadth and suddenness of the Awakening and frequently employ hurricane metaphors to reinforce the point. Thus, many of them describe how in the 1740s the Awakening "swept" across the mainland colonies, leaving only England's Caribbean colonies untouched. Third, most historians argue that this spiritual hurricane affected all facets of prerevolutionary society. Here they adopt Edwards's description of the 1736 Northampton revival as one that touched "all sorts, sober and vicious, high and low, rich and poor, wise and unwise," but apply it to all the colonies. Indeed, some historians go farther and view the Great Awakening as a veritable social and political revolution itself. Writing in the late 1960s, Bushman could only wonder at its power: "We inevitably will underestimate the effect of the Awakening on eighteenth-century society if we compare it to revivals today. The Awakening was more like the civil rights demonstrations, the campus disturbances, and the urban riots of the 1960s combined. All together these may approach, though certainly not surpass, the Awakening in their impact on national life."

No one would seriously question the existence of "the Great Awakening" if historians only described it as a short-lived Calvinist revival in New England during the early 1740s. Whether stimulated by Edwards, James Davenport, or the British itinerant George Whitefield, the New England revivals between 1740 and 1745 obviously were Calvinist ones. Their sponsors vigorously criticized the soft-core Arminianism that had reputedly overtaken New England Congregationalism, and they stimulated the ritual renewal of a century-old society by reintroducing colonists to the theology of distinguished seventeenth-century Puritan clergymen, especially Thomas Shepard and Solomon Stoddard.

Yet, Calvinism never dominated the eighteenth-century religious revivals homogenized under the label "the Great Awakening." The revivals in the middle colonies flowed from especially disparate and international sources. John B. Frantz's recent traversal of the German revivals there demonstrates that they took root in Lutheranism, German Reformed Calvinism (different from the New England variety), and Pietism (however one wants to define it). Maxson stressed the mysticism, Pietism, Rosicrucianism, and Freemasonry rampant in these colonies among both German and English settlers. In an often overlooked observation, Maxson noted that the Tennents' backing for revivals was deeply linked to a mystical experience surrounding the near death of John Tennent and that both John Tennent and William Tennent, Jr., were mystics as well as Calvinists. The revivals among English colonists in Virginia also reveal eclectic roots. Presbyterians brought Calvinism into the colony for the first time since the 1650s, but Arminianism underwrote the powerful Methodist awakening in the colony and soon crept into the ranks of the colony's Baptists as well.

"The Great Awakening" also is difficult to date. Seldom has an "event" of such magnitude had such amorphous beginnings and endings. In New England, historians agree, the revivals flourished principally between 1740 and 1743 and largely ended by 1745, although a few scattered outbreaks of revivalism occurred there in the next decades. Establishing the beginning of the revivals has proved more difficult, however. Most historians settle for the year 1740 because it marks Whitefield's first appearance in New England. But everyone acknowledges that earlier revivals underwrote Whitefield's enthusiastic reception there and involved remarkable numbers of colonists. Edwards counted thirty-two towns caught up in revivals in 1734–1735 and noted that his own grandfather, Stoddard, had conducted no less than five "harvests" in Northampton before that, the earliest in the 1690s. Yet revivals in Virginia, the site of the most sustained such events in the southern colonies, did not emerge in significant numbers until the 1750s and did not peak until the 1760s. At the same time, they also continued into the revolutionary and early national periods in ways that make them difficult to separate from their predecessors.

Yet even if one were to argue that "the Great Awakening" persisted through most of the eighteenth century, it is obvious that revivals "swept" only some of the mainland colonies. They occurred in Massachusetts, Connecticut, Rhode Island, Pennsylvania, New Jersey, and Virginia with some frequency at least at some points between 1740 and 1770. But New Hampshire, Maryland, and Georgia witnessed few revivals in the same years, and revivals were only occasionally important in New York, Delaware, North Carolina, and South Carolina. The revivals also touched only certain segments of the population in the colonies where they occurred. The best example of the phenomenon is Pennsylvania. The revivals there had a sustained effect among English settlers only in Presbyterian churches where many of the laity and clergy also opposed them. The Baptists, who were so important to the New England revivals, paid little attention to them until the 1760s, and the colony's taciturn Quakers watched them in perplexed silence. Not even Germans imbibed them universally. At the same time that Benjamin Franklin was emptying his pockets in response to the preaching of Whitefield in Philadelphia—or at least claiming to do so—the residents of Germantown were steadily leaving their churches, and Stephanie Grauman Wolf reports that they remained steadfast in their indifference to Christianity at least until the 1780s.

Whitefield's revivals also exchanged notoriety for substance. Colonists responded to him as a charismatic performer, and he actually fell victim to the Billy Graham syndrome of modern times: his visits, however exciting, produced few permanent changes in local religious patterns. For example, his appearances in Charleston led to his well-known confrontation with Anglican Commissary Alexander Garden and to the suicide two years later of a distraught follower named Anne LeBrasseur. Yet they produced no new congregations in Charleston and had no documented effect on the general patterns of religious adherence elsewhere in the colony. The same was true in Philadelphia and New York City despite the fact that Whitefield preached to enormous crowds in both places. Only Bostonians responded differently. Supporters organized in the late 1740s a new "awakened" congregation that reputedly met with considerable initial success, and opponents adopted a defensive posture exemplified in the writings of Charles Chauncy that profoundly

affected New England intellectual life for two decades.

Historians also exaggerate the cohesion of leadership in the revivals. They have accomplished this, in part, by overstressing the importance of Whitefield and Edwards. Whitefield's early charismatic influence later faded so that his appearances in the 1750s and 1760s had less impact even among evangelicals than they had in the 1740s. In addition, Whitefield's "leadership" was ethereal, at best, even before 1750. His principal early importance was to serve as a personal model of evangelical enterprise for ministers wishing to promote their own revivals of religion. Because he did little to organize and coordinate integrated colonial revivals, he also failed to exercise significant authority over the ministers he inspired.

The case against Edwards's leadership of the revivals is even clearer. Edwards defended the New England revivals from attack. But, like Whitefield, he never organized and coordinated revivals throughout the colonies or even throughout New England. Since most of his major works were not printed in his lifetime, even his intellectual leadership in American theology occurred in the century after his death. Whitefield's lack of knowledge about Edwards on his first tour of America in 1739–1740 is especially telling on this point. Edwards's name does not appear in Whitefield's journal prior to the latter's visit to Northampton in 1740, and Whitefield did not make the visit until Edwards had invited him to do so. Whitefield certainly knew of Edwards and the 1734–1735 Northampton revival but associated the town mainly with the pastorate of Edwards's grandfather Stoddard. As Whitefield described the visit in his journal: "After a little refreshment, we crossed the ferry to Northampton, where no less than three hundred souls were saved about five years ago. Their pastor's name is Edwards, successor and grandson to the great Stoddard, whose memory will be always precious to my soul, and whose books entitled 'A Guide to Christ,' and 'Safety of Appearing in Christ's Righteousness,' I would recommend to all."

What were the effects of the prerevolutionary revivals of religion? The claims for their religious and secular impact need pruning too. One area of concern involves the relationship between the revivals and the rise of the Dissenting denominations in the colonies. Denomination building was intimately linked to the revivals in New England. There, as C. C. Goen has demonstrated, the revivals of the 1740s stimulated formation of over two hundred new congregations and several new denominations. This was accomplished mainly through a negative process called "Separatism," which split existing Congregationalist and Baptist churches along prorevival and antirevival lines. But Separatism was of no special consequence in increasing the number of Dissenters farther south. Presbyterians, Baptists, and, later, Methodists gained strength from former Anglicans who left their state-supported churches, but they won far more recruits among colonists who claimed no previous congressional membership.

Still, two points are important in assessing the importance of revivals to the expansion of the Dissenting denominations in the colonies. First, revivalism never was the key to the expansion of the colonial churches. Presbyterianism expanded as rapidly in the middle colonies between 1710 and 1740 as between 1740 and 1770. Revivalism scarcely produced the remarkable growth that the Church

of England experienced in the eighteenth century unless, of course, it won the favor of colonists who opposed revivals as fiercely as did its leaders. Gaustad estimates that between 1700 and 1780 Anglican congregations expanded from about one hundred to four hundred, and Bruce E. Steiner has outlined extraordinary Anglican growth in the Dissenting colony of Connecticut although most historians describe the colony as being thoroughly absorbed by the revivals and "Separatism."

Second, the expansion of the leading evangelical denominations, Presbyterians and Baptists, can be traced to many causes, not just revivalism or "the Great Awakening." The growth of the colonial population from fewer than three hundred thousand in 1700 to over two million in 1770 made the expansion of even the most modestly active denominations highly likely. This was especially true because so many new colonists did not settle in established communities but in new communities that lacked religious institutions. As Timothy L. Smith has written of seventeenth-century settlements, the new eighteenth-century settlements welcomed congregations as much for the social functions they performed as for their religious functions. Some of the denominations reaped the legacy of Old World religious ties among new colonists, and others benefited from local anti-Anglican sentiment, especially in the Virginia and Carolina backcountry. As a result, evangelical organizers formed many congregations in the middle and southern colonies without resorting to revivals at all. The first Presbyterian congregation in Hanover County, Virginia, organized by Samuel Blair and William Tennent, Jr., in 1746, rested on an indigenous lay critique of Anglican theology that had turned residents to the works of Martin

Luther, and after the campaign by Blair and Tennent, the congregation allied itself with the Presbyterian denomination rather than with simple revivalism.

The revivals democratized relations between ministers and the laity only in minimal ways. A significant number of New England ministers changed their preaching styles as a result of the 1740 revivals. Heimert quotes Isaac Backus on the willingness of evangelicals to use sermons to "insinuate themselves into the affections' of the people" and notes how opponents of the revivals like Chauncy nonetheless struggled to incorporate emotion and "sentiment" into their sermons after 1740. Yet revivalists and evangelicals continued to draw sharp distinctions between the rights of ministers and the duties of the laity. Edwards did so in a careful, sophisticated way in *Some Thoughts concerning the Present Revival of Religion in New England*. Although he noted that "disputing, jangling, and contention" surrounded "lay exhorting," he agreed that "some exhorting is a Christian duty." But he quickly moved to a strong defense of ministerial prerogatives, which he introduced with the proposition that "the Common people in exhorting one another ought not to clothe themselves with the like authority, with that which is proper for ministers." Gilbert Tennent was less cautious. In his 1740 sermon *The Danger of an Unconverted Ministry*, he bitterly attacked "Pharisee-shepherds" and "Pharisee-teachers" whose preaching was frequently as "unedifying" as their personal lives. But Gilbert Tennent never attacked the ministry itself. Rather, he argued for the necessity of a *converted* ministry precisely because he believed that only preaching brought men and women to Christ and that only ordained

ministers could preach. Thus, in both 1742 and 1757, he thundered against lay preachers. They were "of dreadful consequence to the Church's peace and soundness in principle. . . . [F]or Ignorant Young Converts to take upon them authoritatively to Instruct and Exhort publickly tends to introduce the greatest Errors and the greatest anarchy and confusion."

The 1740 revival among Presbyterians in New Londonderry, Pennsylvania, demonstrates well how ministers shepherded the laity into a revival and how the laity followed rather than led. It was Blair, the congregation's minister, who first criticized "dead Formality in Religion" and brought the congregation's members under "deep convictions" of their "natural unregenerate state." Blair stimulated "soul exercises" in the laity that included crying and shaking, but he also set limits for these exercises. He exhorted them to "moderate and bound their passions" so that the revival would not be destroyed by its own methods. Above this din, Blair remained a commanding, judgmental figure who stimulated the laity's hopes for salvation but remained "very cautious of expressing to People my Judgment of the Goodness of their States, excepting where I had pretty clear Evidences from them, of their being savingly changed." . . .

Nor did the revivals change the structure of authority within the denominations. New England Congregationalists retained the right of individual congregations to fire ministers, as when Northampton dismissed Edwards in 1750. But in both the seventeenth and eighteenth centuries, these congregations seldom acted alone. Instead, they nearly always consulted extensively with committees of ordained ministers when firing as well as when hiring ministers. In the middle colonies, however, neither the prorevival Synod of New York nor the antirevival Synod of Philadelphia tolerated such independence in congregations whether in theory or in practice. In both synods, unhappy congregations had to convince special committees appointed by the synods and composed exclusively of ministers that the performance of a fellow cleric was sufficiently dismal to warrant his dismissal. Congregations that acted independently in such matters quickly found themselves censured, and they usually lost the aid of both synods in finding and installing new ministers.

Did the revivals stir lower-class discontent, increase participation in politics, and promote democracy in society generally if not in the congregations? Even in New England the answer is, at best, equivocal. Historians have laid to rest John C. Miller's powerfully stated argument of the 1930s that the revivals were, in good part, lower-class protests against dominant town elites. The revivals indeed complicated local politics because they introduced new sources of potential and real conflict into the towns. New England towns accustomed to containing tensions inside a single congregation before 1730 sometimes had to deal with tensions within and between as many as three or four congregations after 1730. Of course, not all of these religious groups were produced by the revivals, and, as Michael Zuckerman has pointed out, some towns never tolerated the new dissidents and used the "warning out" system to eject them. Still, even where it existed, tumult should not be confused with democracy. Social class, education, and wealth remained as important after 1730 in choosing town and church officers as they had been before 1730, and Edward M. Cook, Jr., notes that after 1730 most new re-

vival congregations blended into the old order: "dissenters [took] their place in town affairs once they stopped threatening the community and symbolically became loyal members of it." ...

What, then, ought we to say about the revivals of religion in prerevolutionary America? The most important suggestion is the most drastic. Historians should abandon the term "the Great Awakening" because it distorts the character of eighteenth-century American religious life and misinterprets its relationship to prerevolutionary American society and politics. In religion it is a deus ex machina that falsely homogenizes the heterogeneous; in politics it falsely unites the colonies in slick preparation for the Revolution. Instead, a four-part model of the eighteenth-century colonial revivals will highlight their common features, underscore important differences, and help us assess their real significance.

First, with one exception, the prerevolutionary revivals should be understood primarily as regional events that occurred in only half the colonies. Revivals occurred intermittently in New England between 1690 and 1745 but became especially common between 1735 and 1745. They were uniformly Calvinist and produced more significant local political ramifications—even if they did not democratize New England—than other colonial revivals except those in Virginia. Revivals in the middle colonies occurred primarily between 1740 and 1760. They had remarkably eclectic theological origins, bypassed large numbers of settlers, were especially weak in New York, and produced few demonstrable political and social changes. Revivals in the southern colonies did not occur in significant numbers until the 1750s, when they were limited largely to Virginia, missed Maryland almost entirely, and did not occur with any regularity in the Carolinas until well after 1760. Virginia's Baptist revivalists stimulated major political and social changes in the colony, but the secular importance of the other revivals has been exaggerated. A fourth set of revivals, and the exception to the regional pattern outlined here, accompanied the preaching tours of the Anglican itinerant Whitefield. These tours frequently intersected with the regional revivals in progress at different times in New England, the middle colonies, and some parts of the southern colonies, but even then the fit was imperfect. Whitefield's tours produced some changes in ministerial speaking styles but few permanent alterations in institutional patterns of religion, although his personal charisma supported no less than seven tours of the colonies between 1740 and his death in Newburyport, Massachusetts, in 1770.

Second, the prerevolutionary revivals occurred in the colonial backwaters of Western society where they were part of a long-term pattern of erratic movements for spiritual renewal and revival that had long characterized Western Christianity and Protestantism since its birth two centuries earlier. Thus, their theological origins were international and diverse rather than narrowly Calvinist and uniquely American. Calvinism was important in some revivals, but Arminianism and Pietism supported others. This theological heterogeneity also makes it impossible to isolate a single overwhelmingly important cause of the revivals. Instead, they appear to have arisen when three circumstances were present—internal demands for renewal in different international Christian communities, charismatic preachers, and special, often unique, local circumstances

that made communities receptive to elevated religious rhetoric.

Third, the revivals had modest effects on colonial religion. This is not to say that they were "conservative" because they did not always uphold the traditional religious order. But they were never radical, whatever their critics claimed. For example, the revivals reinforced ministerial rather than lay authority even as they altered some clergymen's perceptions of their tasks and methods. They also stimulated the demand for organization, order, and authority in the evangelical denominations. Presbyterian "New Lights" repudiated the conservative Synod of Philadelphia because its discipline was too weak, not too strong, and demanded tougher standards for ordination and subsequent service. After 1760, when Presbyterians and Baptists utilized revivalism as part of their campaigns for denominational expansion, they only increased their stress on central denominational organization and authority.

Indeed, the best test of the benign character of the revivals is to take up the challenge of contemporaries who linked them to "outbreaks of enthusiasm" in Europe. In making these charges, the two leading antirevivalists in the colonies, Garden of Charleston and Chauncy of Boston, specifically compared the colonial revivals with those of the infamous "French Prophets" of London, exiled Huguenots who were active in the city between 1706 and about 1730. The French Prophets predicted the downfall of English politicians, raised followers from the dead, and used women extensively as leaders to prophesy and preach. By comparison, the American revivalists were indeed "conservative." They prophesied only about the millennium, not about local politicians, and described only the necessity, not the certainty, of salvation. What is most important is that they eschewed radical change in the position of women in the churches. True, women experienced dramatic conversions, some of the earliest being described vividly by Edwards. But, they preached only irregularly, rarely prophesied, and certainly never led congregations, denominations, or sects in a way that could remotely approach their status among the French Prophets.

Fourth, the link between the revivals and the American Revolution is virtually nonexistent. The relationship between prerevolutionary political change and the revivals is weak everywhere except in Virginia, where the Baptist revivals indeed shattered the exclusive, century-old Anglican hold on organized religious activity and politics in the colony. But, their importance to the Revolution is weakened by the fact that so many members of Virginia's Anglican aristocracy also led the Revolution. In other colonies the revivals furnished little revolutionary rhetoric, including even millennialist thought, that was not available from other sources and provided no unique organizational mechanisms for anti-British protest activity. They may have been of some importance in helping colonists make moral judgments about eighteenth-century English politics, though colonists unconnected to the revivals made these judgments as well.

In the main, then, the revivals of religion in eighteenth-century America emerge as nearly perfect mirrors of a regionalized, provincial society. They arose erratically in different times and places across a century from the 1690s down to the time of the Revolution. Calvinism underlay some of them, Pietism and Arminianism others. Their leadership was local and, at best, regional, and they helped reinforce—but were not the key to—the proliferation and expansion of still-regional Protestant denominations in the colonies. As such, they created no intercolonial religious institutions and fostered no significant experiential unity in the colonies. Their social and political effects were minimal and usually local, although they could traumatize communities in which they upset, if only temporarily, familiar patterns of worship and social behavior. But the congregations they occasionally produced usually blended into the traditional social system, and the revivals abated without shattering its structure. Thus, the revivals of religion in prerevolutionary America seldom became proto-revolutionary, and they failed to change the timing, causes, or effects of the Revolution in any significant way.

Of course, it is awkward to write about the eighteenth-century revivals of religion in America as erratic, heterogeneous, and politically benign. All of us have walked too long in the company of Tracy's "Great Awakening" to make our journey into the colonial past without it anything but frightening. But as Chauncy wrote of the Whitefield revivals, perhaps now it is time for historians "to see that Things have been carried too far, and that the Hazard is great... lest we should be over-run with *Enthusiasm*."

POSTSCRIPT

Was There a Great Awakening in Mid-Eighteenth-Century America?

Butler's critique of efforts to link the Great Awakening with the American Revolution is part of a longstanding historical debate. Butler suggests that there is not enough evidence to support, for example, William McLoughlin's thesis that the revivals were a "key" that opened the door to the War for Independence. If Butler is correct, however, there is still room to argue that the Revolution was not without its religious elements.

In his book *Religion in America: Past and Present* (Prentice Hall, 1961), Clifton E. Olmstead argues for a broader application of religious causes to the origins of the American Revolution. First—and consistent with McLoughlin, Bonomi, and others—Olmstead contends that the Great Awakening did foster a sense of community among American colonists, thus providing the unity required for an organized assault on English control. Moreover, the Great Awakening further weakened existing ties between the colonies and England by drawing adherents of the Church of England into the evangelical denominations that expanded as a result of revivalistic Protestantism. Second, tensions were generated by the demand that an Anglican bishop be established in the colonies. Many evangelicals found in this plan evidence that the British government wanted further control over the colonies. Third, the Quebec Act, enacted by Parliament in 1774, not only angered American colonists by nullifying their claims to western lands, but it also heightened religious prejudice in the colonies by granting tolerance to Roman Catholics. Fourth, ministers played a significant role in encouraging their parishioners to support the independence movement. Olmstead claims that this revolutionary movement in the colonies was defended overwhelmingly by Congregationalist, Presbyterian, Dutch Reformed, and Baptist ministers. Finally, many of the Revolutionaries, imbued with the American sense of mission, believed that God was ordaining their activities.

Further support for these views can be found in Rhys Isaac, *The Transformation of Virginia, 1740–1790* (University of North Carolina Press, 1982); Ruth H. Bloch, *Visionary Republic* (Cambridge University Press, 1985); and Harry S. Stout, *The New England Soul: Preaching and Religious Culture in Colonial New England* (Oxford University Press, 1986). Students interested in further analyses of the Great Awakening should consult Edwin Scott Gaustad, *The Great Awakening in New England* (Peter Smith, 1957); David S. Lovejoy, *Religious Enthusiasm and the Great Awakening* (Prentice Hall, 1969); and Marilyn J. Westerkamp, *Triumph of the Laity: Scots-Irish Piety and the Great Awakening, 1625–1760* (Oxford University Press, 1987).

PART 2

Revolution and the New Nation

The American Revolution led to independence from England and to the establishment of a new nation. As the United States matured, its people and leaders struggled to implement fully the ideals that had sparked the Revolution. What had been abstractions before the formation of the new government had to be applied and refined in day-to-day practice. The nature of post-Revolutionary America, government stability, the transition of power against the backdrop of political factionalism, and the extension of democracy had to be worked out.

- Was the American Revolution a Conservative Movement?

- Were the Founding Fathers Democratic Reformers?

- Was President Jefferson a Political Compromiser?

- Did the Bank War Cause the Panic of 1837?

ISSUE 6

Was the American Revolution a Conservative Movement?

YES: Carl N. Degler, from *Out of Our Past: The Forces That Shaped Modern America*, 3rd ed. (Harper & Row, 1970)

NO: Gordon S. Wood, from *The Radicalism of the American Revolution* (Alfred A. Knopf, 1991)

ISSUE SUMMARY

YES: Pulitzer Prize–winning author Carl N. Degler argues that upper-middle-class colonists led a conservative American Revolution that left untouched the prewar economic and social class structure of an upwardly mobile people.

NO: Prize-winning historian Gordon S. Wood argues that the American Revolution was a far-reaching, radical event that produced a unique democratic society in which ordinary people could make money, pursue happiness, and be self-governing.

Was the American Revolution a true revolution? The answer may depend on how the term *revolution* is defined. *Strict constructionists*, for example, perceive revolution as producing significant and deep societal change, while *loose constructionists* define the term as "any resort to violence within a political order to change its constitution, rulers, or policies." Historians agree that American Revolutionaries fulfilled the second definition because they successfully fought a war that resulted in the overthrow of their British rulers and established a government run by themselves. However, historians disagree over the amount of social and economic changes that took place in America.

Early historians did not concern themselves with the social and economic aspects of the American Revolution. They instead argued over the causes of the Revolution and refought the political arguments advanced by the rebelling colonists and the British government. George Bancroft was the first historian to advance the *Whig*, or *pro-American*, interpretation of the war. America won, he said, because God was on our side. Much of Bancroft's 10-volume *History of the United States* (1834–1874) was written during the period of Jacksonian democracy, when belief that it was the Manifest Destiny of the United States to spread the ideas of freedom, progress, and democracy across the North American continent was highest.

Bancroft's view remained unchallenged until the beginning of the twentieth century, when a group of *imperialist* historians analyzed the Revolution from the perspective of the British empire. These historians tended to be sympathetic to the economic and political difficulties that Great Britain faced in running an empire in the late eighteenth century.

Both the Whig and the imperialist historians assumed that the Revolution was an *external* event whose primary cause was the political differences between the colonists and their British rulers. In 1909, however, historian Carl Becker paved the way for a different interpretation of the Revolution when he concluded in his study of colonial New York that an *internal* revolution had taken place. The American Revolution, said Becker, created a struggle not only for home rule but also one for who should rule at home. This *progressive*, or *conflict*, interpretation dominated most of the writings on the American Revolution from 1910 through 1945. During this time progressive historians searched for the social and economic conflicts among groups struggling for political power.

Since World War II, most professional historians have rejected what they considered to be an oversimplified conflict interpretation of the Revolution by the previous generation of progressive historians. Robert E. Brown, in his studies on colonial Massachusetts and Virginia, argued that America had become a middle-class democracy before the American Revolution. Consequently, Brown maintained, there was no need for a social revolution. Most influential have been the works of Harvard professor Bernard Bailyn, who used a *neo-Whig* approach in analyzing the Revolution. In *Ideological Origins of the American Revolution* (Harvard University Press, 1968), Bailyn took ideas seriously once again and saw the colonists implementing the views of radical British thinkers in their struggle for independence.

In the first selection, Carl N. Degler argues the neo-Whig view of the American Revolution, maintaining that the upper-middle-class colonists led a conservative Revolution that left untouched the prewar economic and social class structure of an upwardly mobile people. This essay is an excellent example of the loose constructionist definition of revolution.

Gordon S. Wood has given a new dimension to studies of the Revolutionary era. In his book *The Radicalism of the American Revolution,* he argues the strict constructionist view that the Revolution produced major social changes. In the second selection, taken from this book, Wood maintains that the American Revolution was a radical event because America was the first nation to hold democratic values allowing ordinary people to make money, pursue happiness, and rule themselves.

YES

Carl N. Degler

A NEW KIND OF REVOLUTION

CONSERVATIVES CAN BE INNOVATORS

Like fabled genii grown too big to be imprisoned in their bottles, wars and revolutions frequently take on a life of their own irrespective of their first purposes. The overarching considerations of survival or victory distort or enlarge the narrow and limited aims for which the conflict was begun. The American War for Independence was such an event. Begun for only limited political and constitutional purposes, the war released social forces which few of the leaders ever anticipated, but which have helped to mold the American tradition.

One such unforeseen result was the rapid and final disestablishment of the Anglican Church, heretofore the state-supported religion in all of the colonies south of Mason and Dixon's Line and in parts of New York and New Jersey as well.[1] In knocking out the props of the State from beneath the Anglican Church, the states provided the occasion for wider and more fundamental innovations. Virginia in 1786, in disestablishing the Anglican Church, put no other church in its place and instead passed a law guaranteeing religious freedom. This law, with which Madison and Jefferson had so much to do, prepared the ground for the ultimate triumph of the American doctrine of separation of Church and State.

The ratification of the federal Constitution in 1788 constituted the first step in the acceptance of the principle that a man's religion was irrelevant to government, for the Constitution forbade all religious tests for officeholding.[2] Then in 1791, when the first ten amendments were added, Congress was enjoined from legislating in any manner "respecting an establishment of religion or prohibiting the free exercise thereof." These legalistic and now commonplace phrases had centuries of man's religious history packed within them; upon their implementation western Christendom reached a milestone in its long quest for a viable accommodation between man's religious conscience and *raison d'état*.

For millennia a man's religion had been either a passport or a barrier to his freedom and the opportunity to serve his State; it had always mattered

Excerpted from Carl N. Degler, *Out of Our Past: The Forces That Shaped Modern America*, 3rd ed. (Harper & Row, 1970). Copyright © 1959, 1970 by Carl N. Degler. Reprinted by permission of HarperCollins Publishers, Inc. Some notes omitted.

how a man worshiped God. Since Emperor Theodosius in the fourth century of the Christian era, religious orthodoxy had been considered necessary for good citizenship and for service to the state. All this weighty precedence was boldly overthrown by Americans in 1789–91 when they erected a government wherein "a man's religious tenets will not forfeit the protection of the Laws nor deprive him of the right of attaining and holding the highest offices that are known in the United States," as George Washington said.

In the course of the early nineteenth century, the federal example of a strict divorce of State and Church was emulated by the individual states. At the time of the Revolution many states had demanded Christian and often Protestant affiliations for officeholding, and some had even retained a state-supported Church. Gradually, however, and voluntarily—Massachusetts was last in 1833—all the states abandoned whatever connections they might have had with the churches. The doctrine of separation has been more deeply implanted in our tradition in the twentieth century by the Supreme Court, which has declared that separation is a freedom guaranteed by the Fourteenth Amendment to the Constitution and therefore obligatory upon the states as well as the federal government. Thus the two extremes of the American political spectrum—the popular state governments and the august Supreme Court—have joined in sanctioning this doctrine born out of the Revolution by the liberalism of the Enlightenment.

It was a remarkably novel and even unique approach to the question of the relation between the State and religion. Although the doctrine repudiates any connection between the State and the Church, the American version has little in common with the practice in countries like revolutionary France and Mexico and atheistic Soviet Russia, where separation has been so hostile to religion as to interfere, at times, with freedom of worship. The American conception is not antireligious at all. Our Presidents invoke the Deity and offer Thanksgiving prayers, our armies and legislatures maintain chaplains, and the state and federal governments encourage religion through the remission of taxes. In America the State was declared to be secular, but it continued to reflect the people's concern with religion. The popular interest in religion was still evident in 1962 and 1963 when the Supreme Court invoked the principle of separation of church and state to ban prayers and Bible-reading from the public schools. In both Congress and the public press there was a loud protest against such a close and allegedly antireligious interpretation of the principle. But efforts to amend the Constitution in order to circumvent the Supreme Court's interpretation have yet to get beyond advocacy by a few conservative congressmen.

In the eighteenth century the American principle of separation of Church and State was indeed an audacious experiment. Never before had a national state been prepared to dispense with an official religion as a prop to its authority and never before had a church been set adrift without the support of the state. Throughout most of American history the doctrine has provided freedom for religious development while keeping politics free of religion. And that, apparently, had been the intention of the Founding Fathers.

As the principle of the separation of Church and State was a kind of social side effect of the Revolution, so also was the assertion in the Declaration of Independence that "all men are created equal." These five words have been sneered at as idealistic, refuted as manifestly inaccurate, and denied as preposterous, but they have, nonetheless, always been capable of calling forth deep emotional response from Americans. Even in the Revolutionary era, their power was evident. In 1781 the Supreme Judicial Court of Massachusetts declared slavery at an end in that state because it "is inconsistent with our own conduct and Constitution" which "set out with declaring that all men are born free and equal...." The Reverend Samuel Hopkins told the Continental Congress that it was illogical to "be holding so many hundreds of blacks in slavery... while we are maintaining this struggle for our own and our Children's liberty." In 1782 William Binford of Nenrico County, Virginia, set free twelve slaves because he was "fully persuaded that freedom is the natural right of all mankind." Another Virginian, a few years later, freed all his slaves which had been "born after the Declaration of Independence." Such efforts to reconcile the theory of the Declaration with the practices of life represent only the beginnings of the disquieting echoes of the celebrated phrase.

The idea of equality also worked its influence on the position of women, if only because women were active participants in the Revolutionary struggle. During the days of the Association, or boycott of British goods, women were conspicuous in carrying out the policy. Mary Beth Norton in her recent study of women during the Revolution tells of women who pointedly refused to serve tea, or gave up tea even when ill, though Revolutionary Committees made exceptions for those who were sick. Many women became directly involved in the cause, as in the case of a woman who wrote: "Tho a female I was born a patriot and cant help it If I would." More pointed still was Mary Willing Byrd, who applied the patriotic philosophy to her own situation: "I have paid my taxes and have not been Personally, nor Virtually represented. My property is taken from me and I have no redress." Norton noted that during the discussions of the 1760's, women commentators on the political scene often apologized for their forwardness; but in the 1780's they were making no apologies. The Revolutionary experience had changed all that. Some women even broke up their marriages over politics, Norton observes. Indeed, thanks to the demands of the war, many wives now had to take on responsibilities once denied them. A husband might begin by asking male relatives or friends to handle his affairs while he was away, but as time passed the tendency was to turn things over to his wife, the result of which was to enhance her capabilities in his eyes. "This war which has so often and long separated us," wrote Timothy Pickering to his wife in 1783, "has taught me how to value you."

Prominent among the women who took the emerging new order at its face value was Abigail Adams, the wife of John. Early in the struggle she asked him, in a well-known letter, to "remember the ladies" when he was helping to devise a new society. "Do not put such unlimited power into the hands of Husbands," she urged. "Remember all Men would be tyrants if they could." What she was asking was that the rights of women within the family be expanded in the name of the Revolution. Although John Adams ridiculed his wife's suggestion, women's position in the family did alter after the Revolution. Divorce became a little easier for women. In Connecticut, for example, where divorce was commoner than in other states, more women either deserted or divorced their husbands than before. More women, too, had the courage to sue for separations on the ground of their husbands' adultery. And by the 1790's, women were asking for property settlements, something that had been extremely rare as recently as the 1770's. Even after the Revolution, however, divorce was still not very common; of all the new states, only Pennsylvania included the right to divorce in its new constitution. But those limited changes were quite in line with the most striking improvement in women's position after the Revolution, namely the great expansion of education for girls.

Although John Adams boasted in the late colonial period of the widespread literacy in the English colonies, he could not have been thinking of women. For at the time of the Revolution about 80 per cent of males could read and write, but only about 40 per cent of women could. Soon after the Revolution, however, women themselves began to call for schooling, though previously, Mary Beth Norton reports, almost no complaints about the lack of education for women were heard. During the 1780's and 1790's a number of schools for girls were founded, and as publicly supported schools were established, girls were included in them along with boys. The result was that the literacy level of women began to rise, until in the middle years of the nineteenth century it reached that of men. The role of the Revolutionary experience in bringing about this significant shift is reflected in the frequent public discussions during the 1790's and after about the responsibilities of mothers to rear patriot sons and daughters for the new Republic. If these mothers were to do their job right, obviously they would have to be educated. "For the first time," in the 1790's, writes Mary Beth Norton, "American daughters as well as sons were being told that they could 'improve.' "

Incalculably important for the future of women in America as the opening of schools to girls after the Revolution undoubtedly was, it nevertheless did not do more than lay the foundation for later changes. No new jobs, aside from teaching, were opened to women in the post-Revolutionary era, even though women were now more likely to be educated. And although a few female societies had been founded during the Revolutionary years, a true feminist or women's movement was still in the future. Yet that later movement would draw heavily upon the ideology of the Revolution for its arguments and rhetoric, just as the women of the Revolutionary era had drawn upon it to support their aspirations for greater freedom. It is surely not without significance that both blacks and women in the middle years of the nineteenth century would draw upon the words as well as the ideas of the Declaration of Independence to justify their claims to freedom and equality.

It would be wrong, however, to assume that the mere inclusion of the phrase "all men are created equal" in the Declaration worked the mighty influence implied in the foregoing changes; social values are not created so deliberately or so easily. Like so much else in the Declaration, this sentence was actually the distillation of a cherished popular sentiment into a ringing phrase, allegiance to which stemmed more from its prior acceptance than from its eloquence. The passionate belief in social equality which commentators and travelers in Jacksonian America would later find so powerful was already emergent in this earlier period. Indeed, we have already seen its lineaments during the colonial period. It was also expressed in the "country party" ideas that became the ideology of the Revolutionary fathers and the heart of republicanism. After 1776, the conviction was reinforced by the success of the Revolution and by the words of the great Declaration itself.

It was also supported by the facts of American social life. Despite the lowly position accorded the Negro, wrote the French traveler [Jacques-Pierre] Brissot in 1788, it still must be admitted "that the Americans more than any other people are convinced that all men are born free and equal." Moreover, he added, "we must acknowledge, that they direct themselves generally by this principle of equality." German traveler Johan Schoepf noticed that in Philadelphia "rank of birth is not recognized, is resisted with a total force.... People think, act, and speak here precisely as it prompts them...." And in the privacy of the Federal Convention of 1787, Charles Pinckney of South Carolina urged his fellow delegates to recognize the uniqueness of their country. "There is more equality of rank and fortune in America than in any other country under the sun," he told them.

There were other signs of what an earlier generation would have stigmatized as "leveling tendencies" in the new post-Revolutionary society. The attacks made in a number of states in the 1780's upon the privileged Order of the Cincinnati, because it was secret and confined to Revolutionary officers and their descendants, were obviously inspired by a growing egalitarian sentiment. French traveler Moreau de Saint-Méry recalled with disgust how Americans proudly told him that the hotel custom of putting strange travelers together in the same bed was "a proof of liberty." By the end of the century old social distinctions like rank-seating in churches and the differentiating title of esquire were fast passing out of vogue. On an economic level, this abiding American faith was translated as equality of opportunity, and here dour Federalist Fisher Ames could lock arms with his Republican opponents when he averred that "all cannot be rich, but all have a right to make the attempt."

In politics, too, even though the suffrage was not broadened very much, the years of the Revolution and after saw less deference at the voting place and a recognition of a broader definition of the people. Ordinary citizens now elected ordinary citizens to represent them, historian Jackson Turner Main has pointed out; no longer were "natural leaders" the only acceptable candidates. A significant measure of the new place of the people in the rural hinterlands was the shift of state capitals westward. Georgia, the two Carolinas, Virginia, Pennsylvania, New York, and New Hampshire all moved their capitals away from the established cities of the coast. The new governments also recognized the popular bases of their legitimacy by opening legislative sessions to the public for the first time and publishing the contents of the bills they were considering. The recording of votes in the legislature became a common practice only in the course of the Revolution. Thus began in the Revolution a movement toward a greater recognition of the role of the people in government, a movement that would receive a further and more striking impetus during the Age of Jackson.

Though economic grievances seem to have played a negligible role in bringing on the Revolution, this is not to say that there were no economic consequences. The economic stimulus afforded by the war demands and the freedom from English mercantilistic restrictions which victory made permanent provided adventuresome American merchants and entrepreneurs with wide opportunities for gaining new markets and new sources of profit. The expansion of the American economy, which was to be characteristic all through the nineteenth century, was thus begun.

But even when one has added together the new constitutions, the enlightened religious innovations, and the stimulus to equality, it is quickly apparent that the social consequences of the Revolution were meager indeed. In both purpose and implementation they were not to be equated with the massive social changes which shook France and Russia in later years. For the most part, the society of post-Revolutionary America was but the working out of social forces which were already evident in the colonial period.

It is significant, for example, that no new social class came to power through the door of the American Revolution. The men who engineered the revolt were largely members of the colonial ruling class. Peyton Randolph and Patrick Henry were well-to-do members of the Virginia Assembly; Washington, reputed to be the richest man in America, was an officer in the Virginia militia. The New York leaders John Morin Scott and Robert Livingston were judges on the Supreme Court of the colony, while William Drayton, a fire-eating radical of South Carolina, was a nephew of the lieutenant governor of the province, and himself a member of the Governor's Council until his anti-British activities forced his removal. Certainly Benjamin Franklin, citizen of the Empire, celebrated scientist, and long retired, well-to-do printer, was no submerged member of Philadelphia's society—or London's for that matter. Moreover, Franklin's natural son, William, was a Royal Governor at the outbreak of the Revolution. Hancock of Boston and Christopher Gadsden of Charleston were only two of the many respected and wealthy merchants who lent their support to the patriot cause. In fact, speaking of wealth, the Revolution in Virginia was made and led by the great landed class, and its members remained to reap the benefits. Farther down the social scale, in the backwoods of Massachusetts, it has been shown that the chief revolutionists in the western counties were the old leaders, so that no major shift in leadership took place there either, as a result of the Revolution.

This emphasis on position and wealth among the Revolutionary leaders should not be taken as a denial that many men of wealth and brains left the colonies in the exodus of the Loyalists. Certainly few patriots were the peers of Jared Ingersoll in the law, Jonathan Boucher in the Church, and Thomas Hutchinson and Joseph Galloway in government. But the Loyalist departure did not decapitate the colonial social structure, as some have suggested—it only removed those most attached to the mother country. A large part of the governing class remained to guide the Revolution and reap its favors. It is true that in the states of Georgia and Pennsylvania, where the radical democrats held sway in the early years of the Revolution, new men seemed to occupy positions of power. But these men were still unknowns on the periphery of government and business, and generally remained there; they cannot be compared with the Robespierres and the Dantons, the Lenins and the Trotskys, of the great continental eruptions.

A convenient gauge of the essential continuity of the governing class in America before and after the Revolution is to be found in an examination of the careers of the signers of the Declaration of Independence. Surely these fifty-five men are important patriot leaders and presumably among the chief beneficiaries of the Revolution they advocated. Yet they were by no means a disadvantaged lot. Fully 40 per cent of them attended college or one of the Inns of Court in England at a time when such a privilege was a rarity. An additional 21 per cent of them came from important families of their respective colonies, or, like Robert Morris and Joseph Hewes, were men of acquired wealth. Over 69 per cent of them held office under the colonial regimes, 29 per cent alone holding some office within the executive branch; truly these were not men held at arm's length from the plums of office.

Most striking about the careers of these men is the fact that so many of them held office before and after the dividing line of the Revolution. Of those who held an office under the state governments after the Revolution, 75 per cent had occupied offices before 1774, proving, if need be, that service in the colonial governments before the Revolution was no obstacle to political preferment for a patriot afterward. If those who held no office before 1774 are not counted —and several might be considered too young to be expected to have held office —then the continuity shows up even more clearly. Eighty-nine per cent of

those who filled an office before the Revolution also occupied an office under one of the new state governments. And if federal office after 1789 is included, then the proportion rises to 95 per cent. Add to this the fact that other leaders, not included in the group of signers, had similarly good social backgrounds— men like Washington, Robert Livingston, Gouverneur Morris, Philip Schuyler, and a dozen more—and the conclusion that the Revolution was a thoroughly upper-middle-class affair in leadership and aim is inescapable.

A further and perhaps more important conclusion should be drawn from this analysis of the political careers of the signers after the Revolution. These conservative, upper-class leaders who proclaimed the Revolution suffered no repudiation in the course of the struggle; no mass from the bottom rose and seized control of the Revolutionary situation to direct the struggle into new channels. Rather these men merely shifted, as it were, from their favored status under the colonial regimes to comparable, if not improved, positions after the Revolution.

As a colonial revolt against an alien power, such a development is not surprising. But certainly—for better or for worse—the continuity brought a degree of social and political stability to the new nation rarely associated with the word "revolution" and serves, once again, to illustrate the truly conservative nature of the American revolt.

Similarly, in the redistribution of land, which played such a crucial role in France and Russia, the American Revolution set no example of social motivation or consequence. The Crown's lands, it is true were confiscated, and—of greater import —so were the lands of the proprietors and those of the literally thousands of Tories.

But the disposition of these lands hardly constitutes a social revolution of major proportions. One can collect, of course, examples of the breakup of great estates, like the De Lancey manor in New York, which was sold to 275 individuals, or the 40,000-acre estate in North Carolina which was carved into scores of plots averaging 200 acres apiece, or the vast 21,000,000-acre proprietary lands of the Penns. But the more significant question to be answered is who got the land. And, from the studies which have been made, it would appear that most often the land went to speculators or men already possessing substantial acreage, not to the landless or even to the small holder. To be sure, much Tory land which first fell under the auctioneer's hammer to a speculator ultimately found its way into the hands of a yeoman, but such a procedure is a rather slow and orderly process of social revolution.

Furthermore, it is obvious from the Confiscation Acts in the several states and the commissioners who operated pursuant to them that the motive behind the acquisition of Tory lands was enhancement of the state revenues—as, indeed, the original resolution from Congress had suggested. Under such circumstances, pecuniary motives, not democratic theories of society, determined the configuration distribution would take. And it is here that we begin to touch upon the fundamental reason why the confiscation of the royal, proprietary, and Loyalist lands never assumed crucial social importance. Land was just too plentiful in America for these acres to matter. Speculators were loaded down with it; most men who wanted it already possessed it, or were on the way toward possession. One recent investigator of the confiscations in New York, for example, has pointed out that land there could be bought cheaper from speculators than from a former Tory estate.

Even the abolition of primogeniture in all the southern states by 1791 cannot be taken as a significant example of the Revolution's economic influence. The fact of the matter is that primogeniture had never appreciably affected land distribution, since it came into play only when the owner died intestate. Considering the notorious litigiousness of eighteenth-century Americans, it is hardly to be doubted that partible inheritance was the practice, if not the theory, long before primogeniture was wiped from the statute books. Furthermore, in almost half of the country—New Jersey, Pennsylvania, and all of the New England states—primogeniture never prevailed anyway.

As for the abolition of entail, it was frequently welcomed by owners of entailed estates, as was the case in Jefferson's Virginia, since it would permit the sale of otherwise frozen assets. These laws had not created a landed aristocracy in America and their repeal made no significant alteration in the social landscape.

Instead of being an abrupt break, the Revolution was a natural and even expected event in the history of a colonial people who had come of age. It is true that social and political changes accompanied the Revolution, some of which were destined to work great influence upon American institutions in the future, but many of them had been implicit in the pre-Revolutionary society, or had become aspirations of Americans in the course of developing their republican ideology in justification of their revolution. The fundamental outlines of society and thought were left untouched by the Revolution: the class structure, the capitalistic orientation of thought, the distribution of property, the conception of good government. Even Gary Nash in his recent study of the urban classes in the coming of the Revolution concedes that "no social revolution occurred in America in the 1770s," though he adds that there were social and economic conflicts among Americans over the distribution of wealth and power.

The absence of widespread, profound social and economic change is not surprising. For all their talk, these Americans had been largely a contented and prosperous people under the British Crown and they were, therefore, largely contented revolutionaries who wanted no more than to remain undisturbed in their accustomed ways. They were in no wise to be compared with the disgruntled lawyers, the frustrated bourgeois, the tyrannized workers, and the land-hungry peasants of the old regimes of France and Russia.

But once these Americans were disturbed, they began to fashion a conception of the future and of themselves that would proclaim a new order in the world, even a new model for mankind. This proclaiming of a new Age of Revolution was evident not only in the motto on the Great Seal of the United States: "A New Order in the World," but also, ... in a new approach to foreign policy based upon that self-conception. For no matter how conservative the origins of the Revolution may have been, it could never be forgotten that the United States was born in Revolution; never before had a people thrown over their colonial rulers. That basic event has become embedded in American folk culture and sophisticated thought alike. The pride that Americans took in these origins was apparent in the self-conscious, often naïve enthusiasm displayed by the American people and their statesmen in support of the colonial rebellions in South America and in Greece in the first two decades of the nineteenth century. Revolutionaries of the middle of the century, like Louis Kossuth [Hungary] and [Giuseppe] Garibaldi [Italy], garnered moral and material benefits from this continuing American friendship for rebellion. European exiles and revolutionaries of 1848 were entertained at the London residence of United States Minister James Buchanan. And it was still apparent in the middle of the twentieth century. The declarations of independence of Ho Chi Minh's Democratic Republic of (North) Vietnam in 1945 and Ian Smith's Rhodesia in 1965 both begin with quotations from the United States Declaration of Independence! And [President Gamal Abdel] Nasser of Egypt, at the time of the United States intervention in Lebanon in July, 1958, taunted Americans with their revolutionary tradition. "How can the United States, which pushed off British colonialism many years ago, forget its history?" he shouted to a crowd in Damascus.

An anticolonial tradition of such weight could not fail to leave its stamp on American policies.... The influence is also evident in the granting of statehood to the former colonies of Hawaii and Alaska, and in the granting of independence to the Philippines. Indeed, long before, during the era of Revolution itself, American leaders, profiting from the lessons of Britain's imperial difficulties, agreed in the Ordinance of 1787 and the Constitution that newly acquired territories could attain, in the natural course of events, equal constitutional status with the original thirteen states. Thus, in a single stroke, Americans sidestepped the tensions and divisions attendant upon a colonial empire and laid the enduring foundations for an expanding and united country.

Constitutional devices, however, no matter how clever or farsighted, cannot of themselves create a new people. The forces of economics and geography can wreak havoc with the best laid plans of Founding Fathers. Whether Americans would retain their independence and become a truly united people was to be determined only by time and the people themselves.

NOTES

1. This is not to say, however, that disestablishment of all churches was brought about by the Revolution. All of the New England states, with the exception of Rhode Island—still loyal to Roger Williams in this respect—continued to support the Congregational Church.

2. Just because the so-called conservatives dominated the Constitutional Convention, such religious indifference was possible. Generally the radials during the Revolutionary era were in favor of state support or recognition of some religion. Thus in the states where the radicals dominated, religious tests were part of the Constitution: Georgia (all members of the legislature had to be Protestants); North Carolina (no one could hold office who denied "God or the truth of the Protestant religion"); and Pennsylvania (the test oath demanded a belief in one God and his rewarding and punishing, and the acknowledgment that the Old and New Testaments were "given by Divine Inspiration"). The contrast with the Constitutional Convention of 1787 is striking. The Continental Congress, which had been dominated by the radicals, always opened its deliberations with chaplain-led prayers; the Convention of 1787, however, failed to have either a chaplain or prayers, though Franklin made an eloquent plea for both. He wrote later that "the Convention except three or four persons thought Prayers unnecessary." Whereas the Declaration of Independence refers to "God" and "Divine Providence," such words are completely absent from the "conservative" Constitution—much to the mystification of modern conservatives.

NO

Gordon S. Wood

THE RADICALISM OF THE AMERICAN REVOLUTION

This ... is part of a continuing inquiry into the democratization of early America that I have been engaged in during the past several decades. Few subjects are more important to Americans, and perhaps to the rest of the world as well. Americans were not born free and democratic in any modern sense; they became so—and largely as a consequence of the American Revolution. After eighteenth-century Americans threw off their monarchical allegiance in 1776, they struggled to find new attachments befitting a republican people. Living in a society that was already diverse and pluralistic, Americans realized that these attachments could not be the traditional ethnic, religious, and tribal loyalties of the Old World. Instead, they sought new enlightened connections to hold their new popular societies together. But when these proved too idealistic and visionary, they eventually found new democratic adhesives in the actual behavior of plain ordinary people—in the everyday desire for the freedom to make money and pursue happiness in the here and now. To base a society on the commonplace behavior of ordinary people may be obvious and understandable to us today, but it was momentously radical in the long sweep of world history up to that time. This book attempts to explain this momentous radicalism of the American Revolution. . . .

We Americans like to think of our revolution as not being radical; indeed, most of the time we consider it downright conservative. It certainly does not appear to resemble the revolutions of other nations in which people were killed, property was destroyed, and everything was turned upside down. The American revolutionary leaders do not fit our conventional image of revolutionaries—angry, passionate, reckless, maybe even bloodthirsty for the sake of a cause. We can think of Robespierre, Lenin, and Mao Zedong as revolutionaries, but not George Washington, Thomas Jefferson, and John Adams. They seem too stuffy, too solemn, too cautious, too much the gentlemen. We cannot quite conceive of revolutionaries in powdered hair and knee breeches. The American revolutionaries seem to belong in drawing rooms or legislative halls, not in cellars or in the streets. They made speeches, not bombs; they wrote learned pamphlets, not manifestos. They were not abstract theorists and they were not social levelers. They did not kill one another; they did not devour themselves. There was no reign of terror in the American Revolution and no resultant dictator—no Cromwell, no Bonaparte. The American Revolution does not seem to have the same kinds of causes—the social wrongs, the class conflict, the impoverishment, the grossly inequitable distributions of wealth—that presumably lie behind other revolutions. There were no peasant uprisings, no jacqueries, no burning of châteaux, no storming of prisons.

Of course, there have been many historians—Progressive or neo-Progressive historians, as they have been called—who have sought, as Hannah Arendt put it, "to interpret the American Revolution in the light of the French Revolution," and to look for the same kinds of internal violence, class conflict, and social deprivation that presumably lay behind the French Revolution and other modern revolutions. Since the beginning of the twentieth century these Progressive historians have formulated various social interpretations of the American Revolution essentially designed to show that the Revolution, in Carl Becker's famous words, was not only about "home rule" but also about "who was to rule at home." They have tried to describe the Revolution essentially as a social struggle by deprived and underprivileged groups against entrenched elites. But, it has been correctly pointed out, despite an extraordinary amount of research and writing during a good part of this century, the purposes of these Progressive and neo-Progressive historians—"to portray the origins and goals of the Revolution as in some significant measure expressions of a peculiar economic malaise or of the social protests and aspirations of an impoverished or

threatened mass population—have not been fulfilled." They have not been fulfilled because the social conditions that generically are supposed to lie behind all revolutions—poverty and economic deprivation—were not present in colonial America. There should no longer be any doubt about it: the white American colonists were not an oppressed people; they had no crushing imperial chains to throw off. In fact, the colonists knew they were freer, more equal, more prosperous, and less burdened with cumbersome feudal and monarchical restraints than any other part of mankind in the eighteenth century. Such a situation, however, does not mean that colonial society was not susceptible to revolution.

Precisely because the impulses to revolution in eighteenth-century America bear little or no resemblance to the impulses that presumably account for modern social protests and revolutions, we have tended to think of the American Revolution as having no social character, as having virtually nothing to do with the society, as having no social causes and no social consequences. It has therefore often been considered to be essentially an intellectual event, a constitutional defense of American rights against British encroachments ("no taxation without representation"), undertaken not to change the existing structure of society but to preserve it. For some historians the Revolution seems to be little more than a colonial rebellion or a war for independence. Even when we have recognized the radicalism of the Revolution, we admit only a political, not a social radicalism. The revolutionary leaders, it is said, were peculiar "eighteenth-century radicals concerned, like the eighteenth-century British radicals, not with the need to recast the social order nor with the problems of the economic inequality and the injustices of stratified societies but with the need to purify a corrupt constitution and fight off the apparent growth of prerogative power." Consequently, we have generally described the Revolution as an unusually conservative affair, concerned almost exclusively with politics and constitutional rights, and, in comparison with the social radicalism of the other great revolutions of history, hardly a revolution at all.

If we measure the radicalism of revolutions by the degree of social misery or economic deprivation suffered, or by the number of people killed or manor houses burned, then this conventional emphasis on the conservatism of the American Revolution becomes true enough. But if we measure the radicalism by the amount of social change that actually took place— by transformations in the relationships that bound people to each other—then the American Revolution was not conservative at all; on the contrary: it was as radical and as revolutionary as any in history. Of course, the American Revolution was very different from other revolutions. But it was no less radical and no less social for being different. In fact, it was one of the greatest revolutions the world has known, a momentous upheaval that not only fundamentally altered the character of American society but decisively affected the course of subsequent history.

It was as radical and social as any revolution in history, but it was radical and social in a very special eighteenth-century sense. No doubt many of the concerns and much of the language of that premodern, pre-Marxian eighteenth century were almost entirely political. That was because most people in that very different distant world could not as yet conceive of society apart from government. The social distinctions and

economic deprivations that we today think of as the consequence of class divisions, business exploitation, or various isms—capitalism, racism, etc.—were in the eighteenth century usually thought to be caused by the abuses of government. Social honors, social distinctions, perquisites of office, business contracts, privileges and monopolies, even excessive property and wealth of various sorts—all social evils and social deprivations—in fact seemed to flow from connections to government, in the end from connections to monarchical authority. So that when Anglo-American radicals talked in what seems to be only political terms—purifying a corrupt constitution, eliminating courtiers, fighting off crown power, and, most important, becoming republicans—they nevertheless had a decidedly social message. In our eyes the American revolutionaries appear to be absorbed in changing only their governments, not their society. But in destroying monarchy and establishing republics they were changing their society as well as their governments, and they knew it. Only they did not know —they could scarcely have imagined— how much of their society they would change. J. Franklin Jameson, who more than two generations ago described the Revolution as a social movement only to be roundly criticized by a succeeding generation of historians, was at least right about one thing: "the stream of revolution, once started, could not be confined within narrow banks, but spread abroad upon the land."

By the time the Revolution had run its course in the early nineteenth century, American society had been radically and thoroughly transformed. One class did not overthrow another; the poor did not supplant the rich. But social relationships

—the way people were connected one to another—were changed, and decisively so. By the early years of the nineteenth century the Revolution had created a society fundamentally different from the colonial society of the eighteenth century. It was in fact a new society unlike any that had ever existed anywhere in the world.

Of course, there were complexities and variations in early American society and culture—local, regional, sectional, ethnic, and class differences that historians are uncovering every day—that make difficult any generalizations about Americans as a whole. This study is written in spite of these complexities and variations, not in ignorance of them. There is a time for understanding the particular, and there is a time for understanding the whole. Not only is it important that we periodically attempt to bring the many monographic studies of eighteenth-century America together to see the patterns they compose, but it is essential that we do so—if we are to extend our still meager understanding of an event as significant as the American Revolution.

That revolution did more than legally create the United States; it transformed American society. Because the story of America has turned out the way it has, because the United States in the twentieth century has become the great power that it is, it is difficult, if not impossible, to appreciate and recover fully the insignificant and puny origins of the country. In 1760 America was only a collection of disparate colonies huddled along a narrow strip of the Atlantic coast—economically underdeveloped outposts existing on the very edges of the civilized world. The less than two million monarchical subjects who lived in these colonies still took for granted that society was and ought to be a hierarchy of ranks and degrees of depen-

dency and that most people were bound together by personal ties of one sort or another. Yet scarcely fifty years later these insignificant borderland provinces had become a giant, almost continent-wide republic of nearly ten million egalitarian-minded bustling citizens who not only had thrust themselves into the vanguard of history but had fundamentally altered their society and their social relationships. Far from remaining monarchical, hierarchy-ridden subjects on the margin of civilization, Americans had become almost overnight, the most liberal, the most democratic, the most commercially minded, and the most modern people in the world.

And this astonishing transformation took place without industrialization, without urbanization, without railroads, without the aid of any of the great forces we usually invoke to explain "modernization." It was the Revolution that was crucial to this transformation. It was the Revolution, more than any other single event, that made America into the most liberal, democratic, and modern nation in the world.

Of course, some nations of Western Europe likewise experienced great social transformations and "democratic revolutions" in these same years. The American Revolution was not unique; it was only different. Because of this shared Western-wide experience in democratization, it has been argued by more than one historian that the broader social transformation that carried Americans from one century and one kind of society to another was "inevitable" and "would have been completed with or without the American Revolution." Therefore this broader social revolution should not be confused with the American Revolution. America, it is said, would have emerged into the modern world as a liberal, democratic, and capitalistic society even without the Revolution. One could, of course, say the same thing about the relationship between the French Revolution and the emergence of France in the nineteenth century as a liberal, democratic, and capitalistic society; and indeed, much of the current revisionist historical writing on the French Revolution is based on just such a distinction. But in America, no more than in France, that was not the way it happened: the American Revolution and the social transformation of America between 1760 and the early years of the nineteenth century were inextricably bound together. Perhaps the social transformation would have happened "in any case," but we will never know. It was in fact linked to the Revolution; they occurred together. The American Revolution was integral to the changes occurring in American society, politics, and culture at the end of the eighteenth century.

These changes were radical, and they were extensive. To focus, as we are today apt to do, on what the Revolution did not accomplish—highlighting and lamenting its failure to abolish slavery and change fundamentally the lot of women—is to miss the great significance of what it did accomplish; indeed, the Revolution made possible the anti-slavery and women's rights movements of the nineteenth century and in fact all our current egalitarian thinking. The Revolution not only

radically changed the personal and social relationships of people, including the position of women, but also destroyed aristocracy as it had been understood in the Western world for at least two millennia. The Revolution brought respectability and even dominance to ordinary people long held in contempt and gave dignity to their menial labor in a manner unprecedented in history and to a degree not equaled elsewhere in the world. The Revolution did not just eliminate monarchy and create republics; it actually reconstituted what Americans meant by public or state power and brought about an entirely new kind of popular politics and a new kind of democratic officeholder. The Revolution not only changed the culture of Americans—making over their art, architecture, and iconography—but even altered their understanding of history, knowledge, and truth. Most important, it made the interests and prosperity of ordinary people—their pursuits of happiness—the goal of society and government. The Revolution did not merely create a political and legal environment conducive to economic expansion; it also released powerful popular entrepreneurial and commercial energies that few realized existed and transformed the economic landscape of the country. In short, the Revolution was the most radical and most far-reaching event in American history.

POSTSCRIPT

Was the American Revolution a Conservative Movement?

In arguing that the American Revolution was a conservative affair, Degler compares the American colonial leadership classes of lawyers, merchants, and planters with those who led similar revolutions later in France, Russia, and China. The American leadership was different, claims Degler, as most held positions in government both before and after the Revolution. The goals of the American leaders also appear tame compared to revolutionaries in other countries. The Americans got rid of mercantilism but preserved capitalism. Also, loyalists were dispatched to Canada and England, but an upper middle class of pre-Revolutionary leaders remained in power.

Degler challenges the views of the earlier progressive historian J. Franklin Jameson, who argues in *The American Revolution as a Social Movement* (1926; reprint, Princeton University Press, 1967) that a radical transformation had taken place in the postwar distribution of land. Jameson also argues that the abolition of the slave trade and the separation of church and state were radical results of the American Revolution.

Degler plays down the importance of the ideology of the American Revolution as an example to other nations and the fact that the American colonists fought the first successful anticolonial war of national liberation. For books that extend this argument, see Richard B. Morris, *The Emerging Nations and the American Revolution* (Harper & Row, 1970) and Robert R. Palmer, *The Age of the Democratic Revolution*, 2 vols. (Princeton University Press, 1959, 1964). Also see Alfred F. Young, ed., *The American Revolution: Explorations in the History of American Radicalism* (Northern Illinois University Press, 1976).

Wood concedes that the American Revolution brought no societal changes, such as those experienced in the later French Revolution. Nonetheless, he argues that the Revolution brought about major political and social changes among the masses of people. No longer would the commoners defer to the upper classes for political leadership; they wanted to rule themselves. In addition, the commoners took advantage of the rise of capitalism brought about by the market revolution in the early nineteenth century.

Students who wish to explore the historiographical controversies should consult some of the many readers in the field. Two of the best-edited collections are Richard Fulton, *The Revolution That Wasn't: A Contemporary Assessment of 1776* (Associated Faculty Press, 1981) and George Athan Billias, *The American Revolution: How Revolutionary Was It?* (Holt, Rinehart & Winston, 1965).

ISSUE 7

Were the Founding Fathers Democratic Reformers?

YES: John P. Roche, from "The Founding Fathers: A Reform Caucus in Action," *American Political Science Review* (December 1961)

NO: Michael Parenti, from *Democracy for the Few,* 5th ed. (St. Martin's Press, 1988)

ISSUE SUMMARY

YES: Political scientist John P. Roche believes that the Founding Fathers were not only revolutionaries but also superb democratic politicians who created a Constitution that supported the needs of the nation and at the same time was acceptable to the people.

NO: Political scientist Michael Parenti argues that the Constitution was framed by financially successful planters, merchants, and creditors in order to protect the rights of property rather than the rights and liberties of individuals.

The United States possesses the oldest written constitution of any major power. The 55 men who attended the Philadelphia Convention of 1787 could scarcely have dreamed that 200 years later the nation would venerate them as the most "enlightened statesmen" of their time. James Madison, the principal architect of the document, may have argued that the Founding Fathers had created a system that might "decide forever the fate of Republican Government which we wish to last for ages," but Madison also told Thomas Jefferson in October 1787 that he did not think the document would be adopted, and if it was, it would not work.

The enlightened statesmen view of the Founding Fathers, presented by nineteenth-century historians like John Fiske, became the accepted interpretation among the general public until the Progressive Era. In 1913 Columbia University professor Charles A. Beard's *An Economic Interpretation of the Constitution of the United States* (Free Press, 1913, 1986) caused a storm of controversy because it questioned the motivations of the Founding Fathers. The Founding Fathers supported the creation of a stronger central government, argued Beard, not for patriotic reasons but because they wanted to protect their own economic interests.

Beard's research method was fairly simple. Drawing upon a collection of old, previously unexamined treasury records in the National Archives, he discovered that a number of delegates to the Philadelphia Convention and, later, the state ratifying conventions, held substantial amounts of continental securities that would sharply increase in value if a strong national government were established. In addition to attributing economic motives to the Founding Fathers, Beard included a Marxist class conflict interpretation in his book. Those who supported the Constitution, he said, represented "personalty interests which had been adversely affected under the Articles of Confederation: money, public securities, manufactures, and trade and ship ping." Those who opposed ratification of the Constitution were the small farmers and debtors.

Beard's socioeconomic conflict interpretation of the supporters and opponents of the Constitution raised another issue: How was the Constitution ratified if the majority of Americans opposed it? Beard's answer was that most Americans could not vote because they did not own property. Therefore, the entire process, from the calling of the Philadelphia Convention to the state ratifying conventions, was nonrepresentative and nondemocratic.

An Economic Interpretation was a product of its times. Economists, sociologists, and political scientists had been analyzing the conflicts that resulted from the Industrial Revolution, which America had been experiencing at the turn of the twentieth century. Beard joined a group of progressive historians who were interested in reforming the society in which they lived and who also shared his discontent with the old-fashioned institutional approach. The role of the new historians was to rewrite history and discover the real reason why things happened. For the progressive historians, reality consisted of uncovering the hidden social and economic conflicts within society.

In the years between the world wars, the general public held steadfastly to the enlightened statesmen view of the Founding Fathers, but Beard's thesis on the Constitution became the new orthodoxy in most college texts on American history and government. The post–World War II period witnessed the emergence of the neoconservative historians, who viewed the Beardian approach to the Constitution as overly simplistic.

In the first selection, which is a good example of consensus history, John P. Roche presents a sophisticated version of the enlightened statesmen view of the Founding Fathers. The Founding Fathers may have been revolutionaries, says Roche, but they were also superb democratic politicians who framed a Constitution that supported the needs of the nation and at the same time was acceptable to the people. A good example of Beard's influence lasting into the 1980s can be found in the second selection, in which Michael Parenti argues that the Constitution is an elitist document that was framed by financially successful planters, merchants, and creditors in order to protect the rights of property over the rights and liberties of individuals.

YES

John P. Roche

THE FOUNDING FATHERS: A REFORM CAUCUS IN ACTION

The work of the Constitutional Convention and the motives of the Founding Fathers have been analyzed under a number of different ideological auspices. To one generation of historians, the hand of God was moving in the assembly; under a later dispensation, the dialectic (at various levels of philosophical sophistication) replaced the Deity: "relationships of production" moved into the niche previously reserved for Love of Country.... The Framers have undergone miraculous metamorphoses: at one time acclaimed as liberals and bold social engineers, today they appear in the guise of sound Burkean conservatives, men who in our time would subscribe to *Fortune*....

The "Fathers" have thus been admitted to our best circles; the revolutionary ferocity which confiscated all Tory property in reach ... has been converted ... into a benign dedication to "consensus" and "prescriptive rights." ... It is not my purpose here to argue that the "Fathers" were, in fact, radical revolutionaries; that proposition has been brilliantly demonstrated.... My concern is with the further position that not only were they revolutionaries, but also they were democrats. Indeed, in my view, there is one fundamental truth about the Founding Fathers ...: They were first and foremost superb democratic politicians.... As recent research into the nature of American politics in the 1780s confirms, they were committed (perhaps willy-nilly) to working within the democratic framework, within a universe of public approval.... The Philadelphia Convention was not a College of Cardinals or a council of Platonic guardians working within a manipulative, pre-democratic framework; it was a nationalist reform caucus which had to operate with great delicacy and skill in a political cosmos full of enemies to achieve the one definitive goal—popular approbation....

What they did was to hammer out a pragmatic compromise which would both bolster the "national interest" and be acceptable to the people. What inspiration they got came from their collective experience as professional politicians in a democratic society. As John Dickinson put it to his fellow delegates on August 13, "Experience must be our guide. Reason may mislead us."

From John P. Roche, "The Founding Fathers: A Reform Caucus in Action," *American Political Science Review*, vol. 55 (December 1961). Copyright © 1961 by The American Political Science Association. Reprinted by permission.

In this context, let us examine the problems they confronted and the solutions they evolved. The Convention has been described picturesquely as a counter-revolutionary junta and the Constitution as a coup d'état, but this has been accomplished by withdrawing the whole history of the movement for constitutional reform from its true context. No doubt the goals of the constitutional elite were "subversive" to the existing political order, but it is overlooked that their subversion could only have succeeded if the people of the United States endorsed it by regularized procedures....

I

When the Constitutionalists went forth to subvert the Confederation, they utilized the mechanisms of political legitimacy. And the roadblocks which confronted them were formidable. At the same time, they were endowed with certain potent political assets. The history of the United States from 1786 to 1790 was largely one of a masterful employment of political expertise by the Constitutionalists as against bumbling, erratic behavior by the opponents of reform. Effectively, the Constitutionalists had to induce the states, by democratic techniques of coercion, to emasculate themselves.... And at the risk of becoming boring, it must be reiterated that the only weapon in the Constitutionalist arsenal was an effective mobilization of public opinion.

The group which undertook this struggle was an interesting amalgam of a few dedicated nationalists with the self-interested spokesmen of various parochial bailiwicks. The Georgians, for example, wanted a strong central authority to provide military protection for their huge, underpopulated state against the Creek Confederacy; Jerseymen and Connecticuters wanted to escape from economic bondage to New York; the Virginians hoped to establish a system which would give that great state its rightful place in the councils of the republic. The dominant figures in the politics of these states therefore cooperated in the call for the Convention. In other states, the thrust towards national reform was taken up by opposition groups who added the "national interest" to their weapons system; in Pennsylvania, for instance, the group fighting to revise the Constitution of 1776 came out four-square behind the Constitutionalists, and in New York, [Alexander] Hamilton and the Schuyler [family] ambiance took the same tack against George Clinton. There was, of course, a large element of personality in the affair: there is reason to suspect that Patrick Henry's opposition to the Convention and the Constitution was founded on his conviction that Jefferson was behind both, and a close study of local politics elsewhere would surely reveal that others supported the Constitution for the simple (and politically quite sufficient) reason that the "wrong" people were against it....

What distinguished the leaders of the Constitutionalist caucus from their enemies was a "Continental" approach to political, economic and military issues. To the extent that they shared an institutional base of operations, it was the Continental Congress (thirty-nine of the delegates to the Federal Convention has served in Congress), and this was hardly a locale which inspired respect for the state governments.... Membership in the Congress under the Articles of Confederation worked to establish a continental frame of reference, that a Congressman from Pennsylvania and one from

North Carolina would share.... This was particularly true with respect to external affairs: the average state legislator was probably about as concerned with foreign policy than as he is today, but Congressmen were constantly forced to take the broad view of American prestige, were compelled to listen to the reports of Secretary John Jay and to the dispatches and pleas from their frustrated envoys in Britain, France and Spain. From considerations such as these, a "Continental" ideology developed which seems to have demanded a revision of our domestic institutions primarily on the ground that only by invigorating our general government could we assume our rightful place in the international arena....

Note that I am not endorsing the "Critical Period" thesis; on the contrary, Merrill Jensen seems to me quite sound in his view that for most Americans, engaged as they were in self-sustaining agriculture, the "Critical Period" was not particularly critical. In fact, the great achievement of the Constitutionalists was their ultimate success in convincing the elected representatives of a majority of the white male population that change was imperative. A small group of political leaders with a Continental vision and essentially a consciousness of the United States' international impotence, provided the matrix of the movement. To their standard other leaders rallied with their own parallel ambitions. Their great assets were (1) the presence in their caucus of the one authentic American "father figure," George Washington, whose prestige was enormous; (2) the energy and talent of their leadership (in which one must include the towering intellectuals of the time, John Adams and Thomas Jefferson, despite their absence abroad), and their communications "network," which

was far superior to anything on the opposition side; (3) the preemptive skill which made "their" issue The Issue and kept the locally oriented opposition permanently on the defensive; and (4) the subjective consideration that these men were spokesmen of a new and compelling credo: American nationalism, that ill-defined but nonetheless potent sense of collective purpose that emerged from the American Revolution....

The Constitutionalists got the jump on the "opposition" (a collective noun: oppositions would be more correct) at the outset with the demand for a Convention. Their opponents were caught in an old political trap: they were not being asked to approve any specific program of reform, but only to endorse a meeting to discuss and recommend needed reforms. If they took a hard line at the first stage, they were put in the position of glorifying the status quo and of denying the need for any changes. Moreover, the Constitutionalists could go to the people with a persuasive argument for "fair play"—"How can you condemn reform before you know precisely what is involved?" Since the state legislatures obviously would have the final say on any proposals that might emerge from the Convention, the Constitutionalists were merely reasonable men asking for a chance. Besides, since they did not make any concrete proposals at that stage, they were in a position to capitalize on every sort of generalized discontent with the Confederation.

Perhaps because of their poor intelligence system, perhaps because of overconfidence generated by the failure of all previous efforts to alter the Articles, the opposition awoke too late to the dangers that confronted them in 1787. Not only did the Constitutionalists manage to get every state but Rhode Island... to appoint delegates to Philadelphia, but when the results were in, it appeared that they dominated the delegations. Given the apathy of the opposition, this was a natural phenomenon: in an ideologically nonpolarized political atmosphere those who get appointed to a special committee are likely to be the men who supported the movement for its creation.... Much has been made of the fact that the delegates to Philadelphia were not elected by the people; some have adduced this fact as evidence of the "undemocratic" character of the gathering. But put in the context of the time, this argument is wholly specious: the central government under the Articles was considered a creature of the component states and in all the states but Rhode Island, Connecticut and New Hampshire, members of the national Congress were chosen by the state legislatures. This was not a consequence of elitism or fear of the mob; it was a logical extension of states'-rights doctrine to guarantee that the national institution did not end-run the state legislatures and make direct contact with the people.

II

With delegations safely named, the focus shifted to Philadelphia. While waiting for a quorum to assemble, James Madison got busy and drafted the so-called Randolph or Virginia Plan with the aid of the Virginia delegation. This was a political master-stroke. Its consequence was that once business got under way, the framework of discussion was established on Madison's terms. There was no interminable argument over agenda; instead the delegates took the Virginia Resolutions—"just for purposes of discussion"—as their point of departure. And

along with Madison's proposals, many of which were buried in the course of the summer, went his major premise: a new start on a Constitution rather than piecemeal amendment....

Standard treatments of the Convention divide the delegates into "nationalists" and "states'-righters" with various improvised shadings ("moderate nationalists," etc.), but these are a posteriori categories which obfuscate more than they clarify. What is striking to one who analyzes the Convention as a case-study in democratic politics is the lack of clearcut ideological divisions in the Convention. Indeed, I submit that the evidence—Madison's Notes, the correspondence of the delegates, and debates on ratification—indicates that this was a remarkably homogeneous body on the ideological level. [Robert] Yates and [John] Lansing [of New York], who favored the New Jersey Plan]... left in disgust on July 10.... Luther Martin, Maryland's bibulous narcissist, left on September 4 in a huff when he discovered that others did not share his self-esteem; others went home for personal reasons. But the hard core of delegates accepted a grinding regimen throughout the attrition of a Philadelphia summer precisely because they shared the Constitutionalist goal.

Basic differences of opinion emerged, of course, but these were not ideological; they were structural. If the so-called "states'-rights" group had not accepted the fundamental purposes of the Convention, they could simply have pulled out and by doing so have aborted the whole enterprise. Instead of bolting, they returned day after day to argue and to compromise. An interesting symbol of this basic homogeneity was the initial agreement on secrecy: these professional politicians did not want to become prisoners of publicity; they wanted to retain that freedom of maneuver which is only possible when men are not forced to take public stands in the preliminary stages of negotiation. There was no legal means of binding the tongues of the delegates: at any stage in the game a delegate with basic principled objections to the emerging project could have taken the stump (as Luther Martin did after his exit) and denounced the convention to the skies. Yet... the delegates generally observed the injunction. Secrecy is certainly uncharacteristic of any assembly marked by strong ideological polarization....

Commentators on the Constitution who have read *The Federalist* in lieu of reading the actual debates have credited the Fathers with the invention of a sublime concept called "Federalism."... Federalism, as the theory is generally defined, was an improvisation which was later promoted into a political theory. Experts on "federalism" should take to heart the advice of David Hume, who warned... "there is no subject in which we must proceed with more caution than in [history], lest we assign causes which never existed and reduce what is merely contingent to stable and universal principles." In any event, the final balance in the Constitution between the states and the nation must have come as a great disappointment to Madison....

It is indeed astonishing how those who have glibly designated James Madison the "father" of Federalism have overlooked the solid body of fact which indicates that he shared Hamilton's quest for a unitary central government. To be specific, they have avoided examining the clear import of the Madison-Virginia Plan, and have disregarded Madison's dogged inch-by-inch retreat from the bastions of centralization. The Virginia Plan envisioned a unitary national government effectively freed from and dominant over the states. The lower house of the national legislature was to be elected directly by the people of the states with membership proportional to population. The upper house was to be selected by the lower and the two chambers would elect the executive and choose the judges. The national legislature was to be empowered to disallow the acts of state legislatures, and the central government was vested, in addition to the powers of the nation under which the Articles of Confederation, with plenary authority wherever "... the separate States are incompetent or in which the harmony of the United States may be interrupted by the exercise of individual legislation." Finally, just to lock the door against state intrusion, the national Congress was to be given the power to use military force on recalcitrant states. This was Madison's "model" of an ideal national government, though it later received little publicity in *The Federalist*.

The interesting thing was the reaction of the Convention to this militant program for a strong autonomous central government. Some delegates were startled, some obviously leery of so comprehensive a project of reform, but nobody set off any fireworks and nobody walked out. Moreover, in the two weeks that followed, the Virginia Plan received substantial endorsement *en principe*; the initial temper of the gathering can be deduced from the approval "without debate or dissent," on May 31, of the Sixth Resolution which granted Congress the authority to disallow state legislation "... contravening in its opinion the Articles of Union." Indeed, an amendment was included to bar states from contravening national treaties.

The Virginia Plan may therefore be considered, in ideological terms, as the delegates' Utopia, but as the discussions continued and became more specific, many of those present began to have second thoughts.... They were practical politicians in a democratic society, and no matter what their private dreams might be, they had to take home an acceptable package and defend it—and their own political futures—against predictable attack. On June 14 the breaking point between dream and reality took place. Apparently realizing that under the Virginia Plan, Massachusetts, Virginia and Pennsylvania could virtually dominate the national government—and probably appreciating that to sell this program to "the folks back home" would be impossible—the delegates from the small states dug in their heels and demanded time for a consideration of alternatives....

Now the process of accommodation was put into action smoothly—and wisely, given the character and strength of the doubters. Madison had the votes, but this was one of those situations where the enforcement of mechanical majoritarianism could easily have destroyed the objectives of the majority: the Constitutionalists were in quest of a qualitative as well as a quantitative consensus;... it was a political imperative if they were to attain ratification.

III

According to the standard script, at this point the "states'-rights" group intervened in force behind the New Jersey Plan, which has been characteristically portrayed as a revision to the status quo under the Articles of Confederation with but minor modifications. A careful examination of the evidence indicates that only in a marginal sense is this an accurate description. It is true that the New Jersey Plan put the states back into the institutional picture, but one could argue that to do so was a recognition of political reality rather than an affirmation of states'-rights. A serious case can be made that the advocates of the New Jersey Plan, far from being ideological addicts of states'-rights, intended to substitute for the Virginia Plan a system which would both retain strong national power and have a chance of adoption in the states. The leading spokesman for the project asserted quite clearly that his views were based more on counsels of expediency than on principle.... In his preliminary speech on June 9, Paterson had stated "... to the public mind we must accommodate ourselves," and in his notes for this and his later effort as well, the emphasis is the same. The structure of government under the Articles should be retained:

> 2. Because it accords with the Sentiments of the People
>
>> [Proof:] 1. Coms. [Commissions from state legislatures defining the jurisdiction of the delegates]
>>
>> 2. News-papers—Political Barometer. Jersey never would have sent Delegates under the first [Virginia] Plan—
>
> Not here to sport Opinions of my own. Wt. [What] can be done. A little practicable Virtue preferrable to Theory.

This was a defense of political acumen, not of states'-rights....

In other words, the advocates of the New Jersey Plan concentrated their fire on what they held to be the political liabilities of the Virginia Plan—which were matters of institutional structure—rather than on the proposed scope of national authority. Indeed, the Supremacy Clause of the Constitution first saw the light of day in Paterson's Sixth Resolution; the New Jersey Plan contemplated the use of military force to secure compliance with national law; and finally Paterson made clear his view that under either the Virginia or the New Jersey systems, the general government would "... act on individuals and not on states." From the states'-rights viewpoint, this was heresy: the fundament of that doctrine was the proposition that any central government had as its constituents the states, not the people, and could only reach the people through the agency of the state government.

Paterson then reopened the agenda of the Convention, but he did so within a distinctly naturalist framework. Paterson's position was one of favoring a strong central government in principle, but opposing one which in fact put the big states in the saddle.

How attached would the Virginians have been to their reform principles if Virginia were to disappear as a component geographical unit (the largest) for representational purposes? Up to this point, the Virginians had been in the happy position of supporting high ideals with that inner confidence born of knowledge that the "public interest" they endorsed would nourish their private interest. Worse, they had shown little willingness to compromise. Now the delegates from the small states announced that they were unprepared to be offered up as sacrificial victims to a "national interest" which reflected Virginia's parochial ambition. Caustic Charles Pinckney was not far off when he remarked sardonically that "... the whole [conflict] comes to this: Give N. Jersey an equal vote, and she will dismiss her scruples, and concur in the Natil. system." What he rather unfairly did not add was that the Jersey delegates were not free agents who could adhere to their private convictions; they had to take back, sponsor and risk their reputations on the reforms approved by the Convention—and in New Jersey, not in Virginia....

IV

On Tuesday morning, June 19, ... James Madison led off with a long, carefully reasoned speech analyzing the New Jersey Plan which, while intellectually vigorous in its criticisms, was quite conciliatory in mood. "The great difficulty," he observed, "lies in the affair of Representation; and if this could be adjusted, all others would be surmountable." (As events were to demonstrate, this diagnosis was correct.) When he finished, a vote was taken on whether to continue with the Virginia Plan as the nucleus for a new constitution: seven states voted "Yes"; New York, New Jersey, and Delaware voted "No"; and Maryland, whose position often depended on which delegates happened to be on the floor, divided. Paterson, it seems, lost decisively; yet in a fundamental sense he and his allies had achieved their purpose: from that day onward, it could never be forgotten that the state governments loomed ominously in the background.... Moreover, nobody bolted the convention: Paterson and his colleagues took their defeat in stride and set to work to modify the Virginia Plan, particularly with respect to its provisions on representation in the national legislature. Indeed, they won an immediate rhetorical bonus; when Oliver Ellsworth of Connecticut rose to move that the word "national" be expunged from the Third Virginia Resolution ("Resolved that a national Government ought to be established consisting of a supreme Legislative, Executive and Judiciary"), Randolph agreed and the motion passed unanimously. The process of compromise had begun.

For the next two weeks, the delegates circled around the problem of legislative representation. The Connecticut delegation appears to have evolved a possible compromise quite early in the debates, but the Virginians and particularly Madison (unaware that he would later be acclaimed as the prophet of "federalism") fought obdurately against providing for equal representation of states in the second chamber.... On July 2, the ice began to break when through a number of fortuitous events—and one that seems deliberate—the majority against equality of representation was converted into a dead tie. The Convention had reached the stage where it was "ripe" for a solution (presumably all the therapeutic speeches had been made), and the South Carolinians proposed a committee. Madison and James Wilson wanted none of it, but with only Pennsylvania dissenting, the body voted to establish a working party on the problem of representation.

The members of this committee, one from each state, were elected by the delegates—and a very interesting committee it was. Despite the fact that the Virginia Plan had held majority support up to that date, neither Madison nor Randolph was selected (Mason was the Virginian) and Baldwin of Georgia, whose shift in position had resulted in the tie, was chosen. From the composition, it was clear that this was not to be a "fighting" committee: the emphasis in membership was on what might be described as "second-level political entrepreneurs." On the ba-

sis of the discussions up to that time, only Luther Martin of Maryland could be described as a "bitter-ender." Admittedly, some divination enters into this sort of analysis, but one does get a sense of the mood of the delegates from these choices—including the interesting selection of Benjamin Franklin, despite his age and intellectual wobbliness, over the brilliant and incisive Wilson or the sharp, polemical Gouverneur Morris, to represent Pennsylvania. His passion for conciliation was more valuable at this juncture than Wilson's logical genius, or Morris' acerbic wit....

It would be tedious to continue a blow-by-blow analysis of the work of the delegates; the critical fight was over representation of the states and once the Connecticut Compromise was adopted on July 17, the Convention was over the hump. Madison, James Wilson, and Gouverneur Morris of New York (who was there representing Pennsylvania!) fought the compromise all the way in a last-ditch effort to get a unitary state with parliamentary supremacy. But their allies deserted them.... Moreover, once the compromise had carried (by five states to four, with one state divided), its advocates threw themselves vigorously into the job of strengthening the general government's substantive powers—as might have been predicted, indeed, from Paterson's early statements. It nourishes an increased respect for Madison's devotion to the art of politics, to realize that this dogged fighter could sit down six months later and prepare essays for *The Federalist* in contradiction to his basic convictions about the true course the Convention should have taken.

V

Two tricky issues will serve to illustrate the later process of accommodation. The first was the institutional position of the Executive. Madison argued for an executive chosen by the National Legislature and on May 29 this had been adopted with a provision that after his seven-year term was concluded, the chief magistrate should not be eligible for reelection. In late July this was reopened and for a week the matter was argued from several different points of view.... One group felt that the states should have a hand in the process; another small but influential circle urged direct election by the people. There were a number of proposals: election by the people, election by state governors, by electors chosen by state legislatures, by the National legislature,... and there was some resemblance to three-dimensional chess in the dispute because of the presence of two other variables, length of tenure and reeligibility. Finally, after opening, reopening, and re-reopening the debate, the thorny problem was consigned to a committee for resolution.

The Brearley Committee on Postponed Matters was a superb aggregation of talent and its compromise on the Executive was a masterpiece of political improvisation. (The Electoral College, its creation, however, had little in its favor as an institution—as the delegates well appreciated.) The point of departure for all discussion about the presidency in the Convention was that in immediate terms, the problem was non-existent; in other words, everybody present knew that under any system devised, George Washington would be President. Thus they were dealing in the future tense and to a body of working politicians the merits of the Brearley proposal were obvious: everybody got a piece of cake. (Or to put it more academically, each viewpoint could leave the Convention and argue to its constituents that it had really won the day.) First, the state legislatures had the right to determine the mode of selection of the electors; second, the small states received a bonus in the Electoral College in the form of a guaranteed minimum of three votes while the big states got acceptance of the principle of proportional power; third, if the state legislatures agreed (as six did in the first presidential election), the people could be involved directly in the choice of electors; and finally, if no candidate received a majority in the College, the right of decision passed to the National Legislature with each state exercising equal strength. (In the Brearley recommendation, the election went to the Senate, but a motion from the floor substituted the House; this was accepted on the ground that the Senate already had enough authority over the executive in its treaty and appointment powers.)

This compromise was almost too good to be true, and the Framers snapped it up with little debate or controversy. No one seemed to think well of the College as an institution; indeed, what evidence there is suggests that there was an assumption that once Washington had finished his tenure as President, the electors would cease to produce majorities and the chief executive would usually be chosen in the House. George Mason observed casually that the selection would be made in the House nineteen times in twenty and no one seriously disputed this point. The vital aspect of the Electoral College was that it got the Convention over the hurdle and protected everybody's interests....

In short, the Framers did not in their wisdom endow the United States with a College of Cardinals—the Electoral College was neither an exercise in applied Platonism nor an experiment in indirect government based on elitist distrust of the masses. It was merely a jerry-rigged improvisation which has subsequently been endowed with a high theoretical content....

The second issue on which some substantial practical bargaining took place was slavery. The morality of slavery was, by design, not at issue; but in its other concrete aspects, slavery colored the arguments over taxation, commerce, and representation. The "Three-Fifths Compromise," that three-fifths of the slaves would be counted both for representation and for purposes of direct taxation (which was drawn from the past—it was a formula of Madison's utilized by Congress in 1783 to establish the basis of state contributions to the Confederation treasury) had allayed some Northern fears about Southern over-representation.... The Southerners, on the other hand, were afraid that Congressional control over commerce would lead to the exclusion of slaves or to their excessive taxation as imports. Moreover, the Southerners were disturbed over "navigation acts," i.e., tariffs or special legislation providing, for example, that exports be carried only in American ships; as a section depending upon exports, they wanted protection from the potential voracity of their commercial brethren of the Eastern states. To achieve this end, Mason and others urged that the Constitution include a proviso that navigation and commercial laws should require a two-thirds vote in Congress.

These problems came to a head in late August and, as usual were handed to a committee in the hope that, in Gouverneur Morris' words, "... these things may form a bargain among the Northern and Southern states." The Committee reported its measures of reconciliation on August 25, and on August 29 the package was wrapped up and delivered. What occurred can best be described in George Mason's dour version (he anticipated Calhoun in his conviction that permitting navigation acts to pass by majority vote would put the South in economic bondage to the North—it was mainly on this ground that he refused to sign the Constitution):

> The Constitution as agreed to till a fortnight before the Convention rose was such a one as he would have set his hand and heart to.... [Until that time] The 3 New England States were constantly with us in all questions... so that it was these three States with the 5 Southern ones against Pennsylvania, Jersey and Delaware. With respect to the importation of slaves, [decision-making] was left to Congress. This disturbed the two Southernmost States who knew that Congress would immediately suppress the importation of slaves. Those two States therefore struck up a bargain with the three New England States. If they would join to admit slaves for some years, the two Southern-most States would join in changing the clause which required the $2/3$ of the Legislature in any vote [on navigation acts]. It was done.

On the floor of the Convention there was a virtual love-feast on this happy occasion. Charles Pinckney of South Carolina attempted to overturn the committee's decision, when the compromise was reported to the Convention, by insisting that the South needed protection from the imperialism of the Northern states. But his Southern colleagues were not prepared to rock the boat and General C. C.

Pinckney arose to spread oil on the suddenly ruffled waters; he admitted that:

> It was in the true interest of the S[outhern] States to have no regulation of commerce; but considering the loss brought on the commerce of the Eastern States by the Revolution, their liberal conduct towards the views of South Carolina [on the regulation of the slave trade] and the interests the weak Southn. States had in being united with the strong Eastern states, he thought it proper that no fetters should be imposed on the power of making commercial regulations; and that his constituents, though prejudiced against the Eastern States, would be reconciled to this liberality. He had himself prejudices against the Eastern States before he came here, but would acknowledge that he had found them as liberal and candid as any men whatever.

Pierce Butler took the same tack, essentially arguing that he was not too happy about the possible consequences, but that a deal was a deal....

VI

Drawing on their vast collective political experience, utilizing every weapon in the politician's arsenal, looking constantly over their shoulders at their constituents, the delegates put together a Constitution. It was a makeshift affair; some sticky issues (for example, the qualification of voters) they ducked entirely; others they mastered with that ancient instrument of political sagacity, studied ambiguity (for example, citizenship), and some they just overlooked. In this last category, I suspect, fell the matter of the power of the federal courts to determine the constitutionality of acts of Congress. When the judicial article was formulated (Article III of the Constitution), deliberations were still in the stage where the legislature was endowed with broad power under the Randolph formulation, authority which by its own terms was scarcely amenable to judicial review. In essence, courts could hardly determine when "... the separate States are incompetent or... the harmony of the United States may be interrupted"; the National Legislature, as critics pointed out, was free to define its own jurisdiction. Later the definition of legislative authority was changed into the form we know, a series of stipulated powers, but the delegates never seriously reexamined the jurisdiction of the judiciary under this new limited formulation. All arguments on the intention of the Framers in this matter are thus deductive and a posteriori, though some obviously make more sense than others.

The Framers were busy and distinguished men, anxious to get back to their families, their positions, and their constituents.... They were trying to do an important job, and do it in such a fashion that their handiwork would be acceptable to very diverse constituencies. No one was rhapsodic about the final document, but it was a beginning, a move in the right direction, and one they had reason to believe the people would endorse. In addition, since they had modified the impossible amendment provisions of the Articles... to one demanding approval by only three-quarters of the states, they seemed confident that gaps in the fabric which experience would reveal could be rewoven without undue difficulty.

So with a neat phrase introduced by Benjamin Franklin (but devised by Gouverneur Morris) which made their decision sound unanimous, and an inspired benediction by the Old Doctor urging doubters to doubt their own infallibility, the Constitution was accepted and signed. Curiously, Edmund Randolph, who had played so vital a role throughout, refused to sign, as did his fellow Virginian George Mason and Elbridge Gerry of Massachusetts. Randolph's behavior was eccentric; ... the best explanation seems to be that he was afraid that the Constitution would prove to be a liability in Virginia politics, where Patrick Henry was burning up the countryside with impassioned denunciations. Presumably, Randolph wanted to check the temper of the populace before he risked his reputation, and perhaps his job, in a fight with both Henry and Richard Henry Lee. Events lend some justification to this speculation: after much temporizing... Randolph endorsed ratification in Virginia and ended up getting the best of both worlds....

The Constitution, then, was an apotheosis of "constitutionalism," a triumph of architectonic genius; it was a patchwork sewn together under the pressure of both time and events by a group of extremely talented democratic politicians. They refused to attempt the establishment of a strong, centralized sovereignty on the principle of legislative supremacy for the excellent reason that the people would not accept it. They risked their political fortunes by opposing the established doctrines of state sovereignty because they were convinced that the existing system was leading to national impotence and probably foreign domination. For two years, they worked to get a convention established. For over three months, in what must have seemed to the faithful participants an endless process of give-and-take, they reasoned, cajoled, threatened, and bargained amongst themselves. The result was a Constitution which the people, in fact, by democratic processes, did accept, and a new and far better national government was established....

To conclude, the Constitution was neither a victory for abstract theory nor a great practical success. Well over half a million men had to die on the battlefields of the Civil War before certain constitutional principles could be defined—a baleful consideration which is somehow overlooked in our customary tributes to the farsighted genius of the Framers and to the supposed American talent for "constitutionalism." The Constitution was, however, a vivid demonstration of effective democratic political action, and of the forging of a national elite which literally persuaded its countrymen to hoist themselves by their own boot straps.

NO

Michael Parenti

A CONSTITUTION FOR THE FEW

To help us understand the American political system, let us investigate its origins and its formal structure, the rules under which it operates, and the interests it represents, beginning with the Constitution and the men who wrote it. Why was a central government and a Constitution created? By whom? And for what purposes?

It is commonly taught that in the eighteenth and nineteenth centuries men of property preferred a laissez-faire government, one that kept its activities to a minimum. In actuality, while they wanted government to leave them free in all matters of trade and commerce, not for a moment did they desire a weak, inactive government. Rather, they strove to erect a civil authority that worked *for* rather than against the interests of wealth, and they frequently advocated an extension rather than a diminution of state power. They readily agreed with Adam Smith, who said that government was "instituted for the defense of the rich against the poor" and "grows up with the acquisition of valuable property."

CLASS POWER AND CONFLICT IN EARLY AMERICA

During the period between the Revolution and the Constitutional Convention, the "rich and the wellborn" played a dominant role in public affairs.

> Their power was born of place, position, and fortune. They were located at or near the seats of government and they were in direct contact with legislatures and government officers. They influenced and often dominated the local newspapers which voiced the ideas and interests of commerce and identified them with the good of the whole people, the state, and the nation. The published writings of the leaders of the period are almost without exception those of merchants, of their lawyers, or of politicians sympathetic with them.

The United States of 1787 has been described as an "egalitarian" society free from the extremes of want and wealth that characterized the Old World, but there were landed estates and colonial mansions that bespoke an impressive munificence. From the earliest English settlements, men of influence had received vast land grants from the crown. By 1700, three-fourths of the acreage in New York belonged to fewer than a dozen persons. In the interior of Virginia, seven persons owned a total of 1,732,000 acres. By 1760, fewer than 500 men in five colonial cities controlled most of the commerce, banking, mining, and manufacturing on the eastern seaboard and owned much of the land.

As of 1787, property qualifications left perhaps more than a third of the White male population disfranchised. Property qualifications for holding office were so steep as to prevent most voters from qualifying as candidates. Thus, a member of the New Jersey legislature had to be worth at least 1,000 pounds, while state senators in South Carolina were required to possess estates worth at least 7,000 pounds, clear of debt. In addition, the practice of oral voting, rather than use of a secret ballot, and an "absence of a real choice among candidates and programs" led to "widespread apathy." As a result, men of substance monopolized the important offices. Not long before the Constitutional Convention, the French *chargé d'affaires* wrote to his Foreign Minister:

> Although there are no nobles in America, there is a class of men denominated "gentlemen."... Almost all of them dread the efforts of the people to despoil them of their possessions, and, moreover, they are creditors, and therefore interested in strengthening the government, and watching over the execution of the law.... The majority of them being merchants, it is for their interest to establish the credit of the United States in Europe on a solid foundation by the exact payment of debts, and to grant to Congress powers extensive enough to compel the people to contribute for this purpose.

The Constitution was framed by financially successful planters, merchants, and creditors, many linked by kinship and marriage and by years of service in Congress, the military, or diplomatic service. They congregated in Philadelphia in 1787 for the professed purpose of revising the Articles of Confederation and strengthening the powers of the central government. They were aware of the weaknesses of the United States in its commercial and diplomatic dealings with other nations. There were also problems among the thirteen states involving trade, customs duties, and currency differences, but these have been exaggerated and in fact, some reforms were being instituted under the Articles.

Most troublesome to the framers of the Constitution was the increasingly insurgent spirit evidenced among the people. Fearing the popular takeover of state governments, the wealthy class looked to a national government as a means of protecting their interests. Even in states where they were inclined to avoid strong federation, the rich, once faced with the threat of popular rule "and realizing that a political alliance with conservatives from other states would be a safeguard if the radicals should capture the state government... gave up 'state rights' for 'nationalism' without hesitation."

The nationalist conviction that arose so swiftly among men of wealth during the 1780s was not the product of inspiration; it was not a "dream of nation-building" that suddenly possessed them. (If so, they kept it a secret in their public and private communications.) Rather, their newly acquired nationalism was a practical response to material conditions affecting them in a most immediate way. Their like-minded commitment to federalism was born of a common class interest that transcended state boundaries.

The populace of that day has been portrayed as irresponsible and parochial spendthrifts who never paid their debts and who believed in nothing more than timid state governments and inflated paper money. Most scholars say little about the actual plight of the common people, the great bulk of whom lived at a subsistence level. Most of the agrarian population consisted of poor freeholders, tenants, and indentured hands (the latter lived in conditions of servitude). Small farmers were burdened by heavy rents, ruinous taxes, and low incomes. To survive, they frequently had to borrow money at high interest rates. To meet their debts, they mortgaged their future crops and went still deeper into debt. Large numbers were caught in that cycle of rural indebtedness which is today still the common fate of agrarian peoples in many countries.

Throughout this period, newspapers complained of the "increasing numbers of young beggars in the streets." Economic prisoners crowded the jails. In 1786, one county jail in Massachusetts held eighty-eight persons of whom eighty-four were incarcerated for debts or nonpayment of taxes. Among the people there grew the feeling that the revolution against the English crown had been fought for naught. Angry armed crowds in several states began blocking foreclosures and forcibly freeing debtors from jail. Disorders of a violent but organized kind occurred in a number of states. In the winter of 1787, debtor farmers in western Massachusetts led by Daniel Shays took up arms. But their rebellion was forcibly put down by the state militia after several skirmishes that left eleven men dead and scores wounded.

CONTAINING THE SPREAD OF DEMOCRACY

The specter of Shays' Rebellion hovered over the delegates who gathered in Philadelphia three months later, confirming their worst fears. They were determined that persons of birth and fortune should control the affairs of the nation and check the "leveling impulses" of the propertyless multitude that composed "the majority faction." "To secure the public good and private rights against the danger of such a faction," wrote James Madison in *Federalist* No. 10, "and at the same time preserve the spirit and form of popular government is then the great object to which our inquiries are directed." Here Madison touched the heart of the matter: how to keep the *spirit* and *form* of popular government with only a minimum of the *substance*; how to construct a government that would win some popular support but would not tamper with the existing class structure, a government strong enough to service the growing needs of an entrepreneurial class while withstanding the democratic egalitarian demands of the popular class.

The framers of the Constitution could agree with Madison when he wrote in the same *Federalist* No. 10 that "the most common and durable source of faction has been the various and unequal distribution of property. Those who hold and those who are without property have ever formed distinct interests in society" and "the first object of government" is "the protection of different and unequal faculties of acquiring property." The framers were of the opinion that democracy was "the worst of all political evils," as Elbridge Gerry put it. Both he and Madison warned of "the danger of the leveling spirit." "The people," said

Roger Sherman, "should have as little to do as may be about the Government." And according to Alexander Hamilton, "All communities divide themselves into the few and the many. The first are the rich and the well-born, the other the mass of the people.... The people are turbulent and changing; they seldom judge or determine right."

The delegates spent many weeks debating their interests, but these were the differences of merchants, slave owners, and manufacturers, a debate of haves versus haves in which each group sought safeguards within the new Constitution for its particular concerns. Added to this were disagreements about how best to achieve agreed-upon ends. Questions of structure and authority occupied a good deal of the delegates' time: How much representation should the large and small states have? How might the legislature be organized? How should the executive be selected? What length of tenure should exist for the different officeholders? Yet questions of enormous significance, relating to the new government's ability to protect the interests of property, were agreed upon with surprisingly little debate. On these issues, there were no dirt farmers or poor artisans attending the convention to proffer an opposing viewpoint. The debate between haves and have-nots never occurred. Thus Article I, Section 8 of the Constitution, which gives the federal government the power to support commerce and protect the interests of property, was adopted within a few days with little debate. It empowered Congress to:

1. Regulate commerce among the states and with foreign nations and Indian tribes

2. Lay and collect taxes and impose duties and tariffs on imports but not on commercial exports
3. Establish a national currency and regulate its value
4. "Borrow Money on the credit of the United States"—a measure of special interest to creditors
5. Fix the standard of weights and measures necessary for trade
6. Protect the value of securities and currency against counterfeiting
7. Establish "uniform Laws on the subject of Bankruptcies throughout the United States"
8. "Pay the Debts and provide for the common Defence and general Welfare of the United States"

Congress was limited to powers specifically delegated to it by the Constitution or implied as "necessary and proper" for the performance of the delegated powers. Over the years, under this "implied power" clause, federal intervention in the private economy grew to an extraordinary magnitude.

Some of the delegates were land speculators who expressed a concern about western holdings. Accordingly, Congress was given the "Power to dispose of and make all needful Rules and Regulations respecting the Territory or other Property belonging to the United States." Some delegates speculated in highly inflated and nearly worthless Confederation securities. Under Article VI, all debts incurred by the Confederation were valid against the new government, a provision that allowed speculators to make enormous profits when their securities, bought for a trifling, were honored at face value.

By assuming this debt, the federal government—under the policies of the first Secretary of the Treasury, Alexander Hamilton—"monetarized" the economy, using the public treasury to create a vast amount of credit for a propertied class that could then invest further in commerce and industry. The eventual payment of this assumed debt would come out of the pockets of the general public. In effect, the government helped greatly to finance the early process of capital accumulation. In assuming the debt, Hamilton was using the federal power to bolster not only the special interests of speculators and creditors but also the overall interest of an emerging capitalist class.

In the interest of merchants and creditors, the states were prohibited from issuing paper money or imposing duties on imports and exports or interfering with the payment of debts by passing any "Law impairing the Obligation of Contracts." The Constitution guaranteed "Full Faith and Credit" in each state "to the Acts, Records, and judicial Proceedings" of other states, thus allowing creditors to pursue their debtors across state lines.

Slavery—another form of property—was afforded special accommodation in the Constitution. Three-fifths of the slave population in each state were to be counted when calculating representation in the lower house. The importation of slaves was given constitutional protection for another twenty years. And slaves who escaped from one state to another had to be delivered up to the original owner upon claim, a provision that was unanimously adopted at the Convention.

The framers believed the states acted with insufficient force against popular uprisings, so Congress was given the task of "organizing, arming, and disciplining the Militia" and calling it forth,

among other reasons, to "suppress Insurrections." The federal government was empowered to protect the states "against domestic Violence." Provision was made for "the Erection of Forts, Magazines, Arsenals, dock-Yards and other needful Buildings" and for the maintenance of an army and navy for both national defense and to establish an armed federal presence within the potentially insurrectionary states—a provision that was to prove a godsend to the industrial barons a century later when the army was used repeatedly to break strikes by miners and railroad and factory workers.

In keeping with their desire to contain the majority, the founders inserted "auxiliary precautions" *designed to fragment power without democratizing it.* By separating the executive, legislative, and judicial functions and then providing a system of checks and balances among the various branches, including staggered elections, executive veto, Senate confirmation of appointments and ratification of treaties, and a bicameral legislature, they hoped to dilute the impact of popular sentiments. They contrived an elaborate and difficult process for amending the Constitution, requiring proposal by two-thirds of both the Senate and the House, and ratification by three-fourths of the state legislatures. (Such strictures operate with anti-majoritarian effect to this day. Thus, although national polls show a substantial majority of Americans supports the Equal Rights Amendment, the proposal failed to make its way through the constitutional labyrinth.) To the extent that it existed at all, the majoritarian principle was tightly locked into a system of minority vetoes, making swift and sweeping popular action less likely.

The propertyless majority, as Madison pointed out in *Federalist* No. 10, must not be allowed to concert in common cause against the established social order. First, it was necessary to prevent a unity of public sentiment by enlarging the polity and then compartmentalizing it into geographically insulated political communities. The larger the nation, the greater the "variety of parties and interests" and the more difficult it would be for a majority to find itself and act in unison. As Madison argued, "A rage for paper money, for an abolition of debts, for an equal division of property, or for any other wicked project will be less apt to pervade the whole body of the Union than a particular member of it." An uprising of impoverished farmers may threaten Massachusetts at one time and Rhode Island at another, but a national government will be large and varied enough to contain each of these and insulate the rest of the nation from the contamination of rebellion.

Second, not only must the majority be prevented from finding horizontal cohesion, but its vertical force—that is, its upward thrust upon government— should be blunted by interjecting indirect forms of representation. Thus, senators from each state were to be elected by their respective state legislatures. The chief executive was to be selected by an electoral college voted by the people but, as anticipated by the framers, composed of political leaders and men of substance who would gather in their various states and choose a president of their own liking. It was believed that they would usually be unable to muster a majority for any one candidate, and that the final selection would be left to the House, with each state delegation therein having only one vote. The Supreme Court was to be elected by no one, its justices being appointed to life tenure by the president and confirmed by the Senate. In time, of course, the electoral college proved to be something of a rubber stamp, and the Seventeenth Amendment, adopted in 1913, provided for popular election of the Senate—demonstrating that the Constitution is modifiable in democratic directions, but only with great difficulty.

The only portion of government directly elected by the people was the House of Representatives. Many of the delegates would have preferred excluding the public entirely from direct representation: John Mercer observed that he found nothing in the proposed Constitution more objectionable than "the mode of election by the people. The people cannot know and judge of the characters of Candidates. The worst possible choice will be made." Others were concerned that demagogues would ride into office on a populist tide only to pillage the treasury and wreak havoc on all. "The time is not distant," warned Gouverneur Morris, "when this Country will abound with mechanics [artisans] and manufacturers [industrial workers] who will receive their bread from their employers. Will such men be the secure and faithful Guardians of liberty?... Children do not vote. Why? Because they want prudence, because they have no will of their own. The ignorant and dependent can be as little trusted with the public interest."

When the delegates finally agreed to having "the people" elect the lower house, they were referring to a select portion of the population. Property qualifications disfranchised the poorest White males in various states. Half the adult population was denied suffrage because they were women. American Indians had no access to the ballot. About one-fourth, both men and women, had no vote because they were held in bondage, and even of the Blacks who had gained their legal freedom, in both the North and the South, none was allowed to vote until the passage of the Fourteenth Amendment, after the Civil War.

PLOTTERS OR PATRIOTS?

The question of whether the framers of the Constitution were motivated by financial or national interest has been debated ever since Charles Beard published *An Economic Interpretation of the Constitution* in 1913. Beard believed that the "founding fathers" were guided by their class interests. Arguing against Beard are those who say that the framers were concerned with higher things than just lining their purses. True, they were moneyed men who profited directly from policies initiated under the new Constitution, but they were motivated by a concern for nation building that went beyond their particular class interests, the argument goes. To paraphrase Justice Holmes, these men invested their belief to make a nation; they did not make a nation because they had invested. "High-mindedness is not impossible to man," Holmes reminds us.

That is exactly the point: high-mindedness is a common attribute among people even when, or especially when, they are pursuing their personal and class interests. The fallacy is to presume that there is a dichotomy between the desire to build a strong nation and the desire to protect wealth and that the framers could not have been motivated by both. In fact, like most other people, they believed that what was good for themselves was ultimately good for the entire society. Their universal values and their class interests went hand in hand, and to discover the existence of the "higher" sentiment does not eliminate the self-interested one.

Most persons believe in their own virtue. The founders never doubted the nobility of their effort and its importance for the generations to come. Just as many of them could feel dedicated to the principle of "liberty for all" and at the same time own slaves, so could they serve both their nation and their estates. The point is not that they were devoid of the grander sentiments of nation building but that *there was nothing in their concept of nation that worked against their class interest and a great deal that worked for it.*

People tend to perceive issues in accordance with the position they occupy in the social structure; that position is largely—although not exclusively—determined by their class status. Even if we deny that the framers were motivated by the desire for personal gain that moves others, we cannot dismiss the existence of their class interest. They may not have been solely concerned with getting their own hands in the till, although enough of them did, but they were admittedly preoccupied with defending the wealthy few from the laboring many—for the ultimate benefit of all, as they understood it. "The Constitution," as Staughton Lynd noted, "was the settlement of a revolution. What was at stake for Hamilton, Livingston, and their opponents, was more than speculative windfalls in securities; it was the question, what kind of society would emerge from the revolution when the dust had settled, and on which class the political center of gravity would come to rest."

The small farmers and debtors, who opposed a central government that was even farther beyond their reach than the local and state governments, have been described as motivated by self-serving, parochial interests—unlike the supposedly higher-minded statesmen who journeyed to Philadelphia and others of their class who supported ratification. How and why the wealthy became visionary nation-builders is never explained. Not too long before, many of them had been proponents of laissez-faire and had opposed a strong central mercantile government. In truth, it was not their minds that were so much broader but their economic interests. Their motives were neither higher nor lower than those of any other social group struggling for place and power in the United States of 1787. They pursued their material interests as might any small freeholder. But possessing more time, money, information, and organization, they enjoyed superior results.

How could they have acted otherwise? For them to have ignored the conditions of governance necessary for the maintenance of the social order that meant everything to them would have amounted to committing class suicide—and they were not about to do that. They were a rising bourgeoisie rallying around a central power in order to develop the kind of national powers that would (a) better provide for the growing needs of a national commercial economy, (b) protect their overseas trading and diplomatic interests, and (c) defend their class interests from the competing claims of other classes within their own society. Some of us are quite willing to accept the existence of such a material-based nationalism in the history of other countries, but not in our own.

Finally, those who argue that the founders were motivated primarily by high-minded objectives consistently overlook the fact that the delegates repeatedly stated their intention to erect a government strong enough to protect the haves from the have-nots. They gave voice to the crassest class prejudices and never found it necessary to disguise the fact—as have latter-day apologists—that their concern was to diminish popular control and resist all tendencies toward class equalization (or "leveling," as it was called). Their opposition to democracy and their dedication to moneyed interests were unabashedly and openly avowed. Their preoccupation with their class interests was so pronounced that one delegate, James Wilson of Pennsylvania, did finally complain of hearing too much about how the sole or primary object of government was property. The cultivation and improvement of the human mind, he maintained, was the most noble object—a fine sentiment that evoked no opposition from his colleagues as they continued about their business.

If the founders sought to "check power with power," they seemed chiefly concerned with restraining mass power, while assuring the perpetuation of their own class power. They supposedly had a "realistic" opinion of the rapacious nature of human beings—readily evidenced when they talked about the common people—yet they held a remarkably sanguine view of the self-interested impulses of their own class, which they saw as inhabited largely by virtuous men of "principle and property." According to Madison, wealthy men (the "minority faction") would be unable to sacrifice "the rights of other citizens" or mask their "violence under the forms of the Constitution." They would never jeopardize the institution of property and wealth and the untrammeled uses thereof, which in the eyes of the framers constituted the essence of "liberty."

AN ELITIST DOCUMENT

More important than to conjecture about the framers' motives is to look at the Constitution they fashioned, for it tells us a good deal about their objectives. The Constitution was consciously designed as a conservative document, elaborately equipped with a system of minority checks and vetoes, making it easier for entrenched interests to endure. It provided ample power to build the services and protections of state needed by a growing capitalist class but made difficult the transition of rule to a different class. The Constitution was a historically successful ruling-class undertaking whose effects are still very much with us....

The Constitution championed the rights of property over the rights and liberties of persons. For the founders, liberty meant something different from and antithetical to democracy. It meant liberty to invest, speculate, trade, and accumulate wealth and to secure its possession without encroachment by sovereign or populace. The civil liberties designed to give all individuals the right to engage in public affairs won little support from the delegates. When Colonel Mason recommended that a committee be formed to draft "a Bill of Rights," a task he said could be accomplished "in a few hours," the other convention members offered little discussion on the motion and voted unanimously against it.

If the Constitution was so blatantly elitist, how did it manage to win ratification? Actually, it did not have a wide backing, initially being opposed in most of the states. But the same superiority of wealth, organization, and control of political office and the press that allowed the rich to monopolize the Philadelphia Convention enabled them to orchestrate a successful ratification campaign. The Federalists also used bribes, intimidation, and other discouragements against opponents of the Constitution. What's more, *the Constitution never was submitted to a popular vote.* Ratification was by state convention composed of delegates drawn mostly from the same affluent strata as the framers. Those who voted for these delegates were themselves usually subjected to property qualifications.

DEMOCRATIC CONCESSIONS

For all its undemocratic aspects, the Constitution was not without its historically progressive features. Consider the following:

1. The very existence of a written constitution with specifically limited powers represented an advance over more autocratic forms of government.

2. No property qualifications were required for any federal officeholder, unlike in England and most of the states. And salaries were provided for all officials, thus rejecting the common practice of treating public office as a voluntary service, which only the rich could afford.

3. The president and all other officeholders were elected for limited terms. No one could claim a life tenure on any office.

4. Article VI reads: "no religious Test shall ever be required as a Qualification to any Office or public Trust under the United States," a feature that represented a distinct advance over a number of state constitutions that banned Catholics, Jews, and nonbelievers from holding office.

5. Bills of attainder, the practice of declaring by legislative fiat a specific person or group of people guilty of an offense, without benefit of a trial, were made unconstitutional. Also outlawed were ex post facto laws, the practice of declaring an act a crime and punishing those who had committed it *before* it had been unlawful.

6. As noted earlier, the framers showed no interest in a Bill of Rights, but supporters of the new Constitution soon recognized their tactical error and pledged the swift adoption of such a bill as a condition for ratification. So, in the first session of Congress, the first ten amendments were swiftly passed and then adopted by the states; these rights included freedom of speech and religion; freedom to assemble peaceably and to petition for redress of grievances; the right to keep arms; freedom from unreasonable searches and seizures, self-incrimination, double jeopardy, cruel and unusual punishment, and excessive bail and fines; the right to a fair and impartial trial; and other forms of due process.

7. The Constitution guarantees a republican form of government and explicitly repudiates monarchy and aristocracy; hence, Article I, Section 9 states: "No title of Nobility shall be granted by the United States...." According to James McHenry, a delegate from Maryland, *at least twenty-one of the fifty-five delegates favored some form of monarchy.* Yet few dared venture in that direction out of fear of popular opposition. Furthermore, delegates like Madison believed that stability for their class order was best assured by a republican form of government. The time had come for the bourgeoisie to rule directly without the baneful intrusions of kings and nobles.

Time and again during the Philadelphia Convention, this assemblage of men who feared and loathed democracy found it necessary to show some regard for popular sentiment (as with the direct election of the lower house). If the Constitution was going to be accepted by the states and if the new government was to have any stability, it had to gain some measure of popular acceptance; hence, the founders felt compelled to leave something for the people. While the delegates and their class dominated the events of 1787–1789, they were far from omnipotent. The class system they sought to preserve was itself the cause of marked restiveness among the people.

Land seizures by the poor, food riots, and other violent disturbances occurred throughout the eighteenth century in just about every state and erstwhile colony. This popular ferment spurred the framers in their effort to erect a strong central government *but it also set a limit on what they could do.* The delegates "gave" nothing to popular interests, rather—as with the Bill of Rights—they reluctantly made concessions under the threat of democratic rebellion. They kept what they could and grudgingly relinquished what they felt they had to, driven not by a love of democracy but by a fear of it, not by a love of the people but by a prudent desire to avoid popular uprisings. The Constitution, then, was a product not only of class privilege but of class struggle—a struggle that continued and intensified as the corporate economy and the government grew.

POSTSCRIPT

Were the Founding Fathers Democratic Reformers?

Parenti is a radical political scientist. In *Democracy for the Few*, he extends the underlying assumption of Charles A. Beard's *An Economic Interpretation* throughout his own examination of the operations of the present-day American government. Like Beard, Parenti assumes that the Constitution was written to protect the economic interests of the upper classes. The checks and balances system, he argues, was designed to protect the property of the elite while pretending to give some political power to the masses.

Roche, on the other hand, stresses the political reasons for writing a new Constitution. In a spirited essay that reflects great admiration for the Founding Fathers as enlightened politicians, Roche describes the Constitution as "a triumph of architectonic genius; it was a patch-work sewn together under the pressure of both time and events by a group of extremely talented democratic politicians."

Roche narrates the events of the convention of 1787 with a clarity rarely seen in the writings on this period. He makes the telling point that once the dissenters left Philadelphia, the delegates were able to hammer out a new Constitution. All the Founding Fathers agreed to create a stronger national government, but differences centered around the shape the new government would take. The delegates' major concern was to create as strong a national government as possible that would be acceptable to all states. Had the ratifying conventions rejected the new Constitution, the United States might have disintegrated into 13 separate countries.

Roche's interpretation draws heavily upon the consensus interpretation of Richard Hofstadter's "The Founding Fathers: An Age of Realism," from Hofstadter's classic *The American Political Tradition and the Men Who Made It*, 2d ed. (Alfred A. Knopf, 1973). Roche also borrows some ideas from the nationalist synthesis of Stanley Elkins and Eric McKitrick's "The Fathers: Young Men of the Revolution," a widely reprinted article that first appeared in the June 1961 issue of the *Political Science Quarterly*.

One may quibble with several of Roche's interpretations. For example, does he overstate the democratic tendencies of the Founding Fathers? The new national government was actually a republic (indirect representation), not a democracy (direct ruling by the people). Only members of the House of Representatives were directly elected by the people; the president, U.S. senators, and Supreme Court justices were chosen by indirect means. It is also possible that Roche goes too far when he describes the Founding Fathers as twentieth-century, horse-trading politicians.

Historian Gordon S. Wood tries to recapture the eighteenth-century world in *The Creation of the American Republic, 1776–1787* (University of North Carolina Press, 1969), a seminal work that has replaced Beard as the starting point for scholarship on this topic. Wood has also summarized his major ideas in several essays. See "Democracy and the Constitution," in Robert A. Goldwin and William A. Schambra, eds., *How Democratic Is the Constitution?* (American Enterprise Institute for Public Policy Research, 1980).

Wood takes a position that differs from those of both Parenti and Roche. Although he agrees with the class conflict theories of Beard and Parenti regarding the supporters and opponents of the Constitution, he stresses social and ideological, not economic, motivations. Wood argues that the Federalists were upper-class aristocrats who believed that the national government, which they controlled, provided a more cosmopolitan and enlightened outlook than the local and provincial interests of the "humbler sort" who ran the state assemblies. "The Founding Fathers," he says, "argued for the new government in 'Democratic' language to avoid charges of setting up an 'aristocratic' government."

Wood's ideological interpretation of the Founding Fathers has not gone unchallenged. Michael MacGiffert has edited "A Symposium of Views and Reviews" on Woods's *The Creation of the American Republic, 1776–1787* for the *William and Mary Quarterly* (July 1987). A devastating critique of the methodological fallacies of Wood and other intellectual writers on this period can be found in Ralph Lerner's "The Constitution of the Thinking Revolutionary," in Richard Beeman et al., eds., *Beyond Confederation: Origins of the Constitution and American National Identity* (University of North Carolina Press, 1987).

The bicentennial celebration of the Constitution in the 1980s witnessed the publication of numerous works on this period. Three in particular stand out: Richard B. Morris, *The Forging of the Union, 1781–1789* (Harper & Row, 1987) summarizes a lifetime of scholarship by one of the most knowledgeable historians of this period; Michael Kammen, *A Machine That Would Go of Itself: The Constitution in American Culture* (Alfred A. Knopf, 1986) elaborates on the place the Constitution has occupied "in the public consciousness and symbolic life of the American people"; and Forrest McDonald places the Founding Fathers within the intellectual climate of the late eighteenth century in *Novus Ordo Seclorum: The Intellectual Origins of the Constitution* (University of Kansas Press, 1985).

Students should also consult the following works: Leonard W. Levy and Dennis J. Mahoney, eds., *The Framing and Ratification of the Constitution* (MacMillan, 1987), a series of short, scholarly essays on the subject; Peter S. Onaf's "Reflections on the Founding: Constitutional Historiography in Bicentennial Perspective," *William and Mary Quarterly* (April 1989), essential reading for advanced students because of its sophisticated analysis and voluminous references; and all essays written by Edmund S. Morgan on this period, particularly his review of 19 studies of the Constitutional period in the June 29, 1987, issue of *The New Republic*.

ISSUE 8

Was President Jefferson a Political Compromiser?

YES: Morton Borden, from "Thomas Jefferson," in Morton Borden, ed., *America's Eleven Greatest Presidents*, 2d ed. (Rand McNally, 1971)

NO: Lance Banning, from *The Jeffersonian Persuasion: Evolution of a Party Ideology* (Cornell University Press, 1978)

ISSUE SUMMARY

YES: Professor of history Morton Borden argues that President Thomas Jefferson was a moderate and pragmatic politician who placed the nation's best interests above those of the states.

NO: Professor of history Lance Banning argues that Jefferson and his supporters were ideologically committed to westward expansion, the elimination of the national debt, and the eradication of the pro-British trade policies incurred by his Federalist opponents.

"Jefferson still lives," stated John Adams as he died on July 4, 1826, the 50th anniversary of Independence Day. Unknown to Adams, Thomas Jefferson had passed away a few hours earlier on that same day. But Jefferson never really died. He was one of the few heroes of history to become a living legend.

There are two images of Jefferson. One is that of the true Renaissance man who knew a little about everything. "Not a sprig of grass shoots uninteresting to me," he once wrote to his daughter. As a philosopher who spoke to posterity, he waxed eloquent in his letters about civil liberties, the rights of man, the rights of the states, strict construction of the Constitution, and the virtues of the agrarian way of life. A practical man, he was an architect of the nation's capital, the University of Virginia, and his own home. A respected member of the Virginia aristocracy who owned about 10,000 acres and from 100 to 200 slaves, Jefferson ran his farm in a self-sufficient manner and carefully studied the efficiency of employing slave labor. When he traveled, he recorded everything he observed in detailed journals. The newest inventions —including steam engines, thermometers, and elevators—fascinated him.

The other image of Jefferson is that of the statesman who has been ranked among the top half-dozen U.S. presidents in every major poll taken by historians in the last 35 years. Whether or not Jefferson deserves such an honor depends on how the functions of the presidency are perceived. One role that Jefferson disdained was the function of chief of state. So important to the modern presidency, the ceremonial role could have been played by the tall, dignified Virginia aristocrat as well as it was by George Washington, had he so desired. But Jefferson hated formalities. He walked to his inauguration and refused to wear a hat. Because he was a widower, he abandoned the practice of holding large, formal parties (which he felt smacked too much of monarchy). He preferred instead intimate dinners with his intellectual friends and political cronies. A shy, soft-spoken individual, the author of the Declaration of Independence did not campaign for office, and he refused to deliver an annual address to Congress, preferring to send them a written message. If one uses modern terminology, Jefferson was not "mediagenic." In 1992 Jefferson might not have even been nominated by his party, much less elected to the presidency.

In the 1800 presidential election Jefferson barely defeated his Federalist opponent John Adams. A tie vote in the electoral college between Jefferson and his vice president, Aaron Burr, was erased in the 36th round in the House of Representatives when several Federalists broke the deadlock and voted for Jefferson.

In the first of the following selections, Professor Morton Borden substantiates the views of moderate Federalists who believed that Jefferson was a practical politician and, above all, a nationalist who incorporated Federalist policies with traditional Republican views in running his presidency. In the second selection, Professor Lance Banning sees major ideological differences between Jefferson and his Federalist opponents. According to Banning, Jefferson felt that his two predecessors to the presidency, George Washington and John Adams, and especially Federalist party leader Alexander Hamilton had corrupted governmental institutions with their "anglo-monarchical" views —a situation that Jefferson, once in power, worked to reverse.

YES   Morton Borden

THOMAS JEFFERSON

For twelve years the Constitution worked, after a fashion. From its inception the new document had been subjected to severe trials and divisive strains. A rebellion in Pennsylvania, a naval war with France, a demand for states' rights from Virginia and Kentucky, and various Western schemes of disunion —all had been surmounted. Had it not been for the great prestige of George Washington and the practical moderation of John Adams, America's second attempt at a federal union might have failed like the first. Partisan passions had run high in the 1790's, and any single factor on which men disagreed —Hamilton's financial plans or the French Revolution or the Sedition Act— might easily have caused a stoppage of the nation's political machinery.

The two-party system emerged during this decade, and on each important issue public opinion seemed to oscillate between Federalist and Democratic-Republican. Perhaps this was to be expected of a young nation politically adolescent. Year by year Americans were becoming more politically alert and active; if there was little room for middle ground between these two factions, yet opinions were hardly fixed and irrevocable. The culmination of partisan controversy and the test of respective strengths took place in the monumental election of 1800.

Jefferson was feared, honestly feared, by almost all Federalists. Were he to win the election, so they predicted, all the hard constructive gains of those twelve years would be dissipated. Power would be returned to the individual states; commerce would suffer; judicial power would be lessened; and the wonderful financial system of Hamilton would be dismantled and destroyed. Jefferson was an atheist, and he would attack the churches. Jefferson was a hypocrite, an aristocrat posing as democrat, appealing to the baser motives of human beings in order to obtain votes. Jefferson was a revolutionary, a Francophile and, after ruining the army and navy under the guise of economy measures, might very well involve the nation in a war with England. In short, it was doubtful if the Constitution could continue its successful course under such a president.

In like manner the Republicans feared another Federalist victory. To be sure, John Adams had split with Hamilton and had earned the enmity

From Morton Borden, "Thomas Jefferson," in Morton Borden, ed., *America's Eleven Greatest Presidents*, 2d ed. (Rand McNally, 1971). Copyright © 1971 by Morton Borden. Reprinted by permission.

of the Essex Junto. But would he not continue Hamilton's "moneyed system"? Did not Adams share the guilt of every Federalist for the despicable Alien and Sedition Acts? Was it not true that "His Rotundity" so admired the British system that he was really a monarchist at heart? Republicans were not engaging in idle chatter, nor were they speaking solely for effect, when they predicted many dire consequences if Adams were elected. A typical rumor had Adams uniting "his house to that of his majesty of Britain" and "the bridegroom was to be king of America."

Throughout the country popular interest in the election was intense, an intensity sustained over months of balloting. When the Republicans carried New York City, Alexander Hamilton seriously suggested that the results be voided. And when the breach between Adams and Hamilton became public knowledge, Republicans nodded knowingly and quoted the maxim: "When thieves fall out, honest men come by their own."

The Federalists were narrowly defeated. But the decision was complicated by a result which many had predicted: a tied electoral vote between the two Republican candidates, Aaron Burr and Thomas Jefferson. (Indeed, the Twelfth Amendment was adopted in 1804 to avoid any such recurrence.) A choice between the two would be made by the House of Representatives. At this moment, February, 1801, the Constitution seemed on the verge of collapse. Federalist members of the lower house united in support of Burr; Republicans were just as adamant for Jefferson. After thirty-five ballots, neither side had yet obtained the necessary majority. The issue seemed hopelessly deadlocked. What would happen on March 4, inauguration day?

One representative from Maryland, sick with a high fever, was literally carried into Congress on a stretcher to maintain the tied vote of his state. The Republican governor of Pennsylvania, Thomas McKean, threatened to march on Washington with troops if the Federalists persisted in thwarting the will of the people. Hamilton was powerless; his advice that Jefferson was the lesser evil went unheeded. So great was their hatred of the Virginian that most Federalists in Congress would have opposed him regardless of the consequences. After all, they reasoned, Jefferson would dismantle the federal government anyway. In the end, however, patriotism and common sense prevailed. For the choice was no longer Jefferson or Burr, but Jefferson or no president at all. A few Federalists, led by James A. Bayard of Delaware, could not accept the logic of their party, and threw the election to Jefferson.

What a shock it was, then, to read Jefferson's carefully chosen words in his inaugural address:

> But every difference of opinion is not a difference of principle. We have called by different names brethren of the same principle. We are all republicans—we are all federalists. If there be any among us who would wish to dissolve this Union or to change its republican form, let them stand undisturbed as monuments of the safety with which error of opinion may be tolerated where reason is left free to combat it. I know, indeed, that some honest men fear that a republican government cannot be strong; that this government is not strong enough. But would the honest patriot, in the full tide of successful experiment, abandon a government which has so far kept us free and firm, on the theoretic and visionary fear that this government, the world's best hope, may by possibility

want energy to preserve itself? I trust not. I believe this, on the contrary, the strongest government on earth. I believe it is the only one where every man, at the call of the laws, would fly to the standard of the law, and would meet invasions of the public order as his own personal concern. Sometimes it is said that man cannot be trusted with the government of himself. Can he, then, be trusted with the government of others? Or have we found angels in the form of kings to govern him? Let history answer this question.

The words were greeted with applause —and confusion. It was obvious that Jefferson wanted to salve the wounds of bitter factionalism. While many Federalists remained distrustful and some even regarded it as hypocritical, most men approved the tone of their new president's message.

But what did Jefferson mean? Were there no economic principles at stake in his conflicts with Hamilton? Were there no political and constitutional principles implicit in the polar views of the respective parties? And, in the last analysis, did not these differences reflect a fundamental philosophical quarrel over the nature of human beings? Was not the election of 1800 indeed a revolution? If not, then what is the meaning of Jeffersonianism?

For two terms Jefferson tried, as best he could, to apply the standards of his inaugural address. Naturally, the Alien and Sedition Acts were allowed to lapse. The new secretary of the treasury, Albert Gallatin, was instructed to devise an easily understood program to erase the public debt gradually. Internal taxes were either abolished or reduced. Frugality and economy were emphasized to an extreme. Elegant and costly social functions were replaced by simple and informal recep-

tions. The expense of maintaining ambassadors at the courts of Portugal, Holland, and Prussia was erased by withdrawing these missions. The army and navy were pared down to skeleton size. To be sure, Jefferson had to reverse himself on the matter of patronage for subordinate government posts. Originally he planned to keep these replacements to a minimum, certainly not to permit an individual's partisan opinions to be a basis for dismissal unless the man manifestly used his office for partisan purposes. This position was politically untenable, according to Jefferson's lieutenants, and they pressed him to accept a moderate number of removals. Indeed, Jefferson's handling of patronage is symbolic of what Hamilton once called his "ineradicable duplicity."

The Federalist leaders cried out in anguish at every one of these policy changes. The lowering of the nation's military strength would increase the danger of invasion. It was a rather risky gamble to assume that peace could be maintained while European war was an almost constant factor, and the United States was the major neutral carrier. The abolition of the excises, especially on distilled spirits, would force the government to rely on tariffs, on unpredictable source of revenue depending on the wind and waves. It was charged that several foreign ambassadors were offended by Jefferson's rather affected and ultrademocratic social simplicity. Most important, the ultimate payment of the public debt would reduce national power.

This time, however, the people did not respond to the Federalist lament of impending anarchy. After all, commerce prospered throughout most of Jefferson's administration. Somehow the churches remained standing. No bloodbaths took place. The Bank of the United States still operated. Peace was maintained. Certainly, some Federalist judges were under attack, but the judicial power passed through this ordeal to emerge unscathed and even enhanced. Every economic indicator—urban growth, westward expansion, agricultural production, the construction of canals, turnpikes and bridges —continued to rise, undisturbed by the political bickering in Washington.

At first the Federalists were confident that they would regain power. Alexander Hamilton's elaborate scheme for an organization to espouse Christianity and the Constitution, as the "principal engine" to restore Federalist power, was rejected out of hand. He was told that "our adversaries will soon demonstrate to the world the soundness of our doctrines and the imbecility and folly of their own." But hope changed to despair as the people no longer responded; no "vibration of opinion" took place as in the 1790's. Federalism was the party of the past, an antiquated and dying philosophy. "I will fatten my pigs, and prune my trees; nor will I any longer... trouble to govern this country," wrote Fisher Ames: "You federalists are only lookers-on." Jefferson swept the election of 1804, capturing every state except Connecticut and Delaware from the Federalist candidate, Charles C. Pinckney. "Federalism is dead," wrote Jefferson a few years later, "without even the hope of a day of resurrection. The quondam leaders indeed retain their rancour and principles; but their followers are amalgamated with us in sentiment, if not in name."

* * *

It is the fashion of some historians to explain the Federalist demise and Republican ascendancy in terms of a great change in Jefferson. A radical natural law

philosopher when he fought as minority leader, he became a first-rate utilitarian politician as president. The Virginian became an American. Revolutionary theory was cast aside when Jefferson faced the prosaic problem of having to run the country. He began to adopt some of the techniques and policies of the Federalists. Indeed, it is often observed that Jefferson "outfederalized the Federalists."

There is much to be said for this view. After all, less than three months after he assumed the presidency, Jefferson dispatched a naval squadron to the Mediterranean on a warlike mission, without asking the permission of Congress. Two members of his Cabinet, Levi Lincoln and Albert Gallatin, thought the action unconstitutional, and so advised the President. Almost from the moment of its birth the young nation had paid tribute, as did every European power, rather than risk a war with the Barbary pirates. But Jefferson could not abide such bribery. No constitutional scruples could delay for a moment his determination to force the issue. Later, Congress declared war, and in four years Barbary power was shattered. The United States under Jefferson accomplished an object that England, France, Spain, Portugal, and Holland had desired for more than a century—unfettered commerce in the Mediterranean. Here, then, in this episode, is a totally different Jefferson—not an exponent of states' rights and strict interpretation of the Constitution, but an American nationalist of the first order.

Perhaps the most frequently cited example of Jefferson's chameleon quality, however, was on the question of whether the United States should or should not purchase the Louisiana Territory from France. On this question the fundamental issue was squarely before Jefferson, and a choice could not be avoided. The purchase would more than double the size of the United States. Yet the Constitution did not specifically provide for such acquisition of foreign territory. Further, the treaty provided that this area would eventually be formed into states, full partners in the Union. Again, the Constitution did not specifically cover such incorporation. A broad interpretation of Article IV, Section III, however, might permit United States' ratification of the treaty. Should theory be sacrificed and an empire gained? Or were the means as important as the ends?

Broad or loose construction of the Constitution was the key to the growth of federal power. Federalists had argued in this vein to justify most of their legislation in the 1790's. To Jefferson, individual liberty and governmental power were on opposite ends of a seesaw, which the Federalists had thrown off balance. He believed that government, especially the central government, must be restricted within rather narrow and essential limits. Only by continually and rigidly applying strict construction to the Constitution could this tendency to overweening power be controlled and individual liberty be safeguarded. As early as 1777, Jefferson, then governor of Virginia, had warned that constitutions must be explicit, "so as to exclude all possible doubt;... [lest] at some future day ... power[s] should be assumed."

On the other hand, the purchase of Louisiana would fulfill a dream and solve a host of problems. Jefferson envisioned an American empire covering "the whole northern, if not the southern continent, with a people speaking the same language, governed in similar forms, and by similar laws." The purchase would be a giant step in the direction of democracy's inevitable growth. "Is it not better," asked Jefferson, "that the opposite bank of the Mississippi should be settled by our own brethren and children, than by strangers of another family?"

Of more immediate interest, westerners would be able to ship their goods down the Mississippi without fear that New Orleans might be closed. Indian attacks undoubtedly would taper off without the Spanish to instigate them. Uppermost in Jefferson's mind, however, was the freedom from England that the purchase would assure. He did not fear Spanish ownership. A feeble, second-rate nation like Spain on the frontier offered little threat to America's future security. The continued possession of Louisiana by an imperialistic France led by the formidable Napoleon, however, might force the United States into an alliance with England. At first Jefferson thought a constitutional amendment specifically permitting the purchase might solve the dilemma. But Napoleon showed signs of wavering. The treaty had to be confirmed immediately, with no indication of constitutional doubt. Jefferson asked the Republican leaders in the Senate to ratify it "with as little debate as possible, and particularly so far as respects the constitutional difficulty."

In still other ways Jefferson's presidency was marked by Federalist policies which encouraged the growth of central power. Internal improvements loomed large in Jefferson's mind. While many turnpikes and canals were financed by private and state capital, he realized that federal support would be necessary, especially in the western part of the nation. With the use of federal money obtained from the sale of public lands, and (later) aided by direct congressional appropriations, the groundwork for the famous Cumberland road was established during Jefferson's administration. He enthusiastically supported Gallatin's plan to spend twenty million dollars of federal funds on a network of national roads and canals. Other more pressing problems intervened, however, and it was left to later administrations to finance these local and interstate programs. If Hamilton had pressed for internal improvements in the 1790's (he suggested them in the *Report on Manufactures*), Jefferson probably would have raised constitutional objections.

Finally, is not Jefferson's change of tack further reflected in the political history of that era? Over the span of a few years it seemed as if each party had somehow reversed directions. In 1798–99 Jefferson and Madison penned the Virginia and Kentucky Resolutions as an answer to the Federalists' infamous Alien and Sedition Acts. In 1808–9 more radical but comparable rumblings of dissatisfaction emanated from some New England Federalists over Jefferson's Embargo Act. For the embargo, says one of Jefferson's biographers, was "the most arbitrary, inquisitorial, and confiscatory measure formulated in American legislation up to the period of the Civil War." Further, both parties splintered during Jefferson's administration. Many moderate Federalists, like John Quincy Adams, found themselves in closer harmony with administration policy than with Essex Junto beliefs. And Jefferson's actions alienated old comrades, like John Randolph, Jr., whose supporters were called the Tertium Quids. It is interesting to note that there is no historical consensus of why, when, how, or what precipitated the break between Randolph and Jefferson. Randolph is always referred to as brilliant but erratic; and whatever immediate reason is alleged, the cause somehow has to do with Randolph's personality and Jefferson's betrayal of the true doctrines.

* * *

It is part of Jefferson's greatness that he could inspire a myth and project an image. But one must not confuse myth and reality, shadow and substance. Thomas Jefferson as he was, and Thomas Jefferson as people perceived him, are quite different. While both concepts of course, are of equal value in understanding our past, it is always the historian's task to make the distinction. Too often, in Jefferson's case, this has not been done. Too often the biographers have described the myth—have taken at face value the popular view of Jefferson and his enemies, contained in the vitriolic newspaper articles and pamphlets, the passionate debates and fiery speeches of that period—and missed or misconstrued the reality.

This is understandable. Even the principals inevitably became involved and helped to propagate the exaggerated images of the 1790's and thus misunderstood one another's aims and motives. Jefferson, according to his grandson, never considered Federalist fulminations "as abusing him; they had never known him. They had created an imaginary being clothed with odious attributes, to whom they gave his name; and it was against that creature of their imaginations they had levelled their anathemas." John Adams, reminiscing in a letter to Jefferson, wrote: "Both parties have excited artificial terrors and if I were summoned as a witness to say upon oath, which party had excited … the most terror, and which had really felt the most, I could not give a more sincere answer, than in the vulgar style 'Put them in a bag and shake them, and then see which comes out first.' "

On March 4, 1801, following a decade of verbal violence, many Americans were surprised to hear that "We are all republicans—we are all federalists." Some historians act as if they, too, are surprised. These historians then describe Jefferson's administration as if some great change took place in his thinking, and conclude that he "outfederalized the Federalists." This is a specious view, predicated on an ultraradical Jefferson of the 1790's in constant debate with an ultraconservative Hamilton. Certainly Jefferson as president had to change. Certainly at times he had to modify, compromise, and amend his previous views. To conclude, however, that he outfederalized the Federalists is to miss the enormous consistency of Jefferson's beliefs and practices.

Jefferson was ever a national patriot second to none, not even to Hamilton. He always conceived of the United States as a unique experiment, destined for greatness so long as a sharp line isolated American civilization from European infection. Thus he strongly advised our youth to receive their education at home rather than in European schools, lest they absorb ideas and traits he considered "alarming to me as an American." From "Notes on Virginia" to his advice at the time of Monroe's doctrine, Jefferson thought of America first. It matters not that Hamilton was the better prophet; Jefferson was the better American. The French minister Adet once reported: "Although Jefferson is the friend of liberty... although he is an admirer of the efforts we have made to cast off our shackles... Jefferson, I say, is an American, and as such, he cannot sincerely be our friend. An American is the born enemy of all the peoples of Europe."

Jefferson's nature was always more practical than theoretical, more common-sensical than philosophical. Certainly the essence of his Declaration of Independence is a Lockean justification of revolution; but, said Jefferson, "It was... an expression of the American mind," meant "to place before mankind the common sense of the subject." Jefferson always preferred precision to "metaphysical subtleties." The Kentucky and Virginia Resolutions can be understood only as a specific rebuttal of the Sedition Act. "I can never fear that things will go far wrong," wrote Jefferson, "where common sense has fair play."

One must also remember that Hamilton's power lessened considerably in the last four years of Federalist rule. He had a strong coterie of admirers, but the vast body of Federalists sided with John Adams. Despite all Hamilton did to insure Adams' defeat, and despite the split in Federalist ranks, the fact that Jefferson's victory in 1801 was won by a narrow margin indicated Federalist approval of Adams' actions. Certainly the people at that time—Jefferson and Adams included—regarded 1801 as the year of revolution. But if historians must have a revolution, perhaps Adams' split with the Hamiltonians is a better date. "The mid-position which Adams desired to achieve," writes Manning Dauer, "was adopted, in the main, by Jefferson and his successors."

To be sure, the two men disagreed on many matters of basic importance. Jefferson placed his faith in the free election of a virtuous and talented natural aristocracy; Adams did not. Within the constitutional balance, Jefferson emphasized the power of the lower house; Adams would give greater weight to the executive and judiciary. Jefferson, as a general rule, favored a strict interpretation of the Constitution; Adams did not fear broad construction. Both believed that human beings enjoyed inalienable rights, but only Jefferson had faith in man's perfectability. Jefferson could say, "I like a little rebellion now and then. It is like a storm in the atmosphere"; Adams had grown more conservative since 1776. Jefferson always defended and befriended Thomas Paine; Adams found Edmund Burke's position on the French Revolution more palatable.

Yet, the sages of Quincy and Monticello were both moderate and practical men. Despite the obvious and basic contrasts, both Adams and Jefferson stood side by side on certain essentials: to avoid war, to quiet factionalism, to preserve republican government. Their warm friendship, renewed from 1812 to 1826 in a remarkable and masterful correspondence, was based on frankness, honesty, and respect. "About facts," Jefferson wrote, "you and I cannot differ, because truth is our mutual guide; And if any opinions you may express should be different from mine, I shall receive them with the liberality and indulgence which I ask for my own." Jefferson and Adams represent, respectively, the quintessence of the very best in American liberalism and conservatism. Their indestructible link, then, was "a keen sense of national consciousness," a realization that America's destiny was unique. This is the meaning of Jefferson's words: "We are all republicans—we are all federalists."

NO

Lance Banning

THE REVOLUTION OF 1800 AND THE PRINCIPLES OF NINETY-EIGHT

The final proof of principle is conduct. Accordingly, no study of the origins and nature of Republican convictions can avoid the question whether the persuasion that developed in the years of opposition exercised a central influence when the party came to power....

Were Republicans in power faithful to the principles they urged in opposition? As much so, I will argue, as almost any party we could name. Enough so that historians have made a strong beginning toward an understanding of the Jeffersonian ascendency that has, as one of its essential themes, a recognition of the lasting influence of the principles of 1798. In 1801, if my analysis is right, the "Country" came to power. A party that defined its character in terms derived from eighteenth-century British oppositions was entrusted, for the first time, with the guidance of affairs. Without insisting that Republicans were of a single mind, without suggesting that the most important leaders of the party were the helpless captives of their thought, it still seems possible to argue that the party's triumphs and its failures were the products, in large part, of its attempt to govern in accordance with an ideology that taught that power was a monster and governing was wrong.

If this is so, however, then a second question must be raised. If the party conflict of the 1790s was so largely a derivative of British arguments between the Country and the Court—if, in addition, we can see the history of the United States between 1800 and 1815 as the story of a party's effort to apply its Country principles to the direction of affairs—then when will it be possible to mark and "end of classical politics" and the emergence of a more genuinely indigenous mode of thought? At no point, I would think, before the finish of the War of 1812. Although the years in opposition had already carried the Republicans some distance from the British sources of their thought, there was no point before the months surrounding the conclusion of that war when it is possible to say that the ideas received by revolutionary thinkers from the English eighteenth century had ceased to exercise a guiding influence on American affairs.

* * *

Thomas Jefferson wrote proudly of "the revolution of 1800," calling it "as real a revolution in the principles of our government as that of 1776 was in its form." Many of his followers agreed. Today, however, most historians would probably prefer a different phrase. Too little changed—and that too slowly—to justify the connotations present in that loaded word. There were no radicals among the great triumvirate who guided the Republicans in power, as they had led them through the years of opposition. The President was bent on reconciliation with the body of his former foes. "We are all Republicans, all Federalists," he said. He wanted to detach the mass of Federalists from their former leaders, and he knew that this was incompatible with an abrupt reversal of the policies that had been followed for a dozen years. He had, in any case, no notion that his predecessors' work could be dismantled all at once. The Hamiltonian system might be hateful, but it had bound the nation to a contract it had no alternative except to honor. Madison and Gallatin, who were by instinct more conservative than Jefferson himself, were not disposed to disagree.

From the beginning of the new administration, nonetheless, Republicans insisted that a change of policies, not just of men, was necessary to return the state to its republican foundations. In his inaugural address, Jefferson announced commitment to "a wise and frugal government which shall restrain men from injuring one another, shall leave them otherwise free to regulate their own pursuits of industry and improvement, and shall not take from the mouth of labor the bread it has earned." This kind of government, he hinted, would be guided by a set of principles that could be readily distinguished from the policies of years before. Among them were

Peace, commerce, and honest friendship with all nations; entangling alliances with none.

The support of the state governments in all their rights as the most competent administrations for our domestic concerns and the surest bulwarks against anti-republican tendencies....

A well disciplined militia, our best reliance in peace and for the first moments of war, till regulars may relieve them....

Economy in public expense, that labor may be lightly burdened.

The honest payment of our debts and sacred preservation of the public faith.

Reform began while Jefferson awaited the assembly of the first Republican Congress. Pardons were issued to the few men still affected by sedition prosecutions. The diplomatic corps, a target for its costs and for the influence it was thought to give to the executive, was cut to barest bones. A few of the most active Federalists were purged from office, while the President withheld commissions signed by Adams after his defeat was known. The evolution of a partisan appointments policy was too slow for some members of the party, who argued that "no enemy to democratic government will be provided with the means to sap and destroy any of its principles nor to profit by a government to which they are hostile in theory and practice." But even the most radical were satisfied with the administration's purpose when the President announced his program to the Seventh Congress.

Jefferson's first annual message was "an epitome of republican principles applied to practical purposes." After a review of foreign policy and Indian affairs, the President suggested abolition of all internal taxes. "The remaining sources of revenue will be sufficient," he believed, "to provide for the support of government, to pay the interest on the public debts, and to discharge the principals in shorter periods than the laws or the general expectations had contemplated.... Sound principles will not justify our taxing the industry of our fellow citizens to accumulate treasure for wars to happen we know not when, and which might not perhaps happen but from the temptations offered by that treasure." Burdens, he admitted, could only be reduced if expenditures fell too. But there was room to wonder "whether offices or officers have not been multiplied unnecessarily." The military, for example, was larger than required to garrison the posts, and there was no use for the surplus. "For defence against invasion, their number is as nothing; nor is it conceived needful or safe that a standing army should be kept up in time of peace." The judiciary system, packed and altered by the Federalists at the close of their regime, would naturally "present itself to the contemplation of Congress." And the laws concerning naturalization might again be liberalized.

The Seventh Congress, voting usually on party lines, did everything that Jefferson had recommended. It also gave approval to a plan prepared by Gallatin, the Secretary of the Treasury, for the complete retirement of the public debt before the end of 1817. Along with its repeal of the Judiciary Act of 1800, it reduced the army to three thousand officers and men, while lowering appropriations for the navy in the face of war with Tripoli. Of all its measures, though, the abolition of internal taxes (and four hundred revenue

positions) called forth the most eloquent enunciation of the principles on which the new majority thought it should act:

> The Constitution is as dear to us as to our adversaries.... It is by repairing the breeches that we mean to save it and to set it on a firm and lasting foundation.... We are yet a young nation and must learn wisdom from the experience of others. By avoiding the course which other nations have steered, we shall likewise avoid their catastrophe. Public debts, standing armies, and heavy taxes have converted the English nation into a mere machine to be used at the pleasure of the crown.... We have had no riot act, but we have had a Sedition Act calculated to secure the executive from free and full investigation; we have had an army and still have a small one, securing to the executive an immensity of patronage; and we have a large national debt, for the payment... of which it is necessary to collect 'yearly millions' by means of a cloud of officers spread over the face of the country.... Iniquitous as we deem the manner of its settlement, we mean to discharge; but we mean not to perpetuate it; it is no part of our political creed that 'a public debt is a public blessing.'

Before the session ended, Jefferson could tell a friend that "some things may perhaps be left undone from motives of compromise for a time and not to alarm by too sudden a reformation," but the proceedings of the Congress gave every ground for hope that "we shall be able by degrees to introduce sound principles and make them habitual." Indeed, the session was so good a start that there was little left to recommend in 1802. The effort of the next few years would be to keep the course already set.

"Revolution" may not be the proper word to characterize the changes introduced in 1801 and early 1802. "Apostasy," however, would be worse. Yet every study of the Jeffersonian ascendency must come to terms with the magnificent and multivolumed work of Henry Adams. Though now almost a century old, the scope and literary power of this classic give it influence that has lasted to the present day. And one of Adams' major themes was the abnegation of the principles of 1798 by the Republican regime. Jefferson had hoped to put an end to parties by detaching the great body of Federalists from their irreconcilable leaders. By 1804 he seemed to have approached this end. To Adams, though, his great successes were a consequence of Jefferson's abandonment of principle and single-minded quest for popularity. If party lines were melting, it had been the Jeffersonians who had compromised their principles the most:

> not a Federalist measure, not even the Alien and Sedition laws, had been expressly repudiated;... the national debt was larger than it had ever been before, the navy maintained and energetically employed, the national bank preserved and its operations extended;... the powers of the national government had been increased [in the Louisianna Purchase] to a point that made blank paper of the Constitution.

It was the Federalists, not the Republicans, who now upheld the states' rights principles of 1798.

Every part of Adams' powerful indictment could be contradicted or excused. Thus, Jefferson abandoned scruple in the case of the Louisianna Purchase with reluctance and because there seemed some danger that the Emperor of France might change his mind about a bargain that could guarantee the nation's peace while promising indefinite postponement of the day when overcrowding and development might put an end to its capacity for freedom. Jefferson continued to distrust the national bank, but would not break the public's pledge by moving to revoke its charter. The party *had* repudiated the Sedition Law, explicitly refusing to renew it in the session that had also seen a relaxation of the naturalization law. The national debt *had* been considerably reduced before the purchase of Louisianna raised it once again, and it would fall much further in the years to come.

It is necessary to admit, however, that the list of Adams' charges also could be lengthened. While Jefferson himself was never reconciled, Gallatin and Madison eventually supported the Bank of the United States. While Jefferson preferred to lead by indirection, he was in fact a stronger President than either of his predecessors ever tried to be. His public messages *suggested* measures, but his hints were often taken as commands by party members in the Congress. Informally or through floor leaders in the House, the administration made its wishes known and drafted most of the important legislation. Finally, in 1808, in its progressively more stringent efforts to enforce the embargo, Jefferson's administration wielded powers over the daily life of Americans that far exceeded anything its predecessors' ever sought, even using regulars to help enforce the law.

There were, without a doubt, occasions after 1801 when the warring parties come so close to switching sides that one might doubt that principle meant much to either group. The Federalists stood forth, when they could hope to profit, as defenders of states' rights. They shamelessly employed old opposition rhetoric to criticize the massive force of party loyalty and the influence of the

President on Congress. Nor was Henry Adams first to charge the Jeffersonians with a surrender to the principles of their opponents. Jefferson and his successor faced a swelling discontent from a minority of purists among Republicans themselves.

In October 1801, before the meeting of the Seventh Congress, Edmund Pendleton had published a widely read consideration of the policies that would be necessary to make the revolution of 1800 complete. Jefferson's election, he began, had "arrested a train of measures which were gradually conducting us towards ruin." But the election victory did not permit Republicans to rest content. It merely opened up an opportunity "to erect new barriers against folly, fraud, and ambition and to explain such parts of the Constitution as have been already or may be interpreted contrary to the intention of those who adopted it." Liberty, said Pendleton, is the "chief good" of government, but "if government is so constructed as to enable its administration to assail that liberty with the several weapons heretofore most fatal to it, the structure is defective: of this sort, standing armies—fleets —severe penal laws—war—and a multitude of civil officers are universally admitted to be." Union is a great good, but union can "only be preserved by confining ... the federal government to the exercise of powers clearly required by the general interest ... because the states exhibit such varieties of character and interests that a consolidated general government would ... produce civil war and dissension." A separation of powers is necessary, but the Constitution gives the Senate a part in the exercise of powers that belong to other branches "and tends to create in that body a dangerous aristocracy." Representative government must rest on the will of the people, but the people's will can "never be expressed if their representatives are corrupted or influenced by hopes of office." "Since experience has evinced that much mischief may be done under an unwise administration," it is time to consider several amendments to the Constitution. These should make the President ineligible for a second term and give the appointment of judges and ambassadors to Congress; end the Senate's role in executive functions and shorten the Senators' terms of office; make judges and legislators incapable of accepting any federal office; subject the judges to removal by the legislature; form "some check upon the abuse of public credit;" declare that treaties relating to war or peace or requiring the expenditure of money must be ratified by the whole Congress; and define the powers of the federal government in such a way as to "defy the wiles of construction."

"The Danger Not Over" was a systematic effort to define the fundamental changes that seemed to be implicit in the principles of 1798. And as the years went by without a movement to secure the constitutional amendments it had recommended, without destruction of the national bank, without complete proscription of old Federalists from places of public trust, "there were a number of people who soon thought and said to one another that Mr. Jefferson did many good things, but neglected some better things," who came to "view his policy as very like a compromise with Mr. Hamilton's, ... a compromise between monarchy and democracy." Strongest in Virginia and including several of the most important party writers of the 1790s—George Logan and John Taylor as well as Pendleton himself—this band of "Old Republicans" soon found an eloquent, if vitriolic and eccentric, spokesman in the Congress. In 1806, John Randolph, who had led the party's forces in the Seventh Congress, broke with the administration and commenced a systematic opposition to the moral bankruptcy and "backstairs influence" of the government. As Jefferson and Madison began to face the gravest crisis of their leadership, they were persistently annoyed by a minority of vocal critics from within their former ranks. In 1808, Monroe became the unsuccessful candidate for those expressing this variety of discontent....

Both Adams and the Old Republicans identified the principles of '98 with the Virginia and Kentucky Resolutions that year. To both, the party's creed in years of opposition centered on allegiance to states' rights. But I have tried to show that such an understanding is too narrow. Even in the crisis introduced by the repressive laws, states' rights and strict construction of the Constitution were among the means to more essential ends. The means were taken seriously, indeed, but they were never held among the absolutes. The body of the party and its most important leaders never sought, as their essential end, to hold the federal government within the narrowest of bounds. They sought, instead, a federal government that would preserve the virtues necessary to a special way of life. Their most important goal had been to check a set of policies—among them loose interpretation of the Constitution—that Republicans had seen as fundamentally destructive of the kind of government and social habits without which liberty could not survive. To judge them only on the basis of their loyalty to strict construction and states' rights is to apply a standard they had never held.

Minds changed when party leaders were confronted with responsibility. But they did not change thoroughly enough to justify the charge that they adopted principles of their opponents. The principles of the Republicans had not been Antifederalist. Republicans had traced the evils of the 1790s to the motives of the governors, not to the government itself. With few and brief exceptions, most had thought a change of policy, without a change of structure, would effect a cure. Moreover, in the last years of the decade, the development of party thought had probably persuaded many members to believe that a simple change of men might cure more evils than they once had thought.

The Republican persuasion rose, in the beginning, under circumstances that conjoined to make a reconstruction of an ideology developed in a different time and place seem relevant for the United States. The revolutionary debt to eighteenth-century opposition thought was certainly sufficient, by itself, to have assured loud echoes of the old ideas in the first years of the new republic. But this is not the lesson of this work. Republican convictions were not simply reminiscent of the old ideas. Republicans revived the eighteenth-century ideology as a coherent structure, reconstructed it so thoroughly that the persistence of an English style of argument is easily as striking as the changes we might trace to revolutionary alterations of the American polity. At least three circumstances of the 1790s had to join with expectations prompted by the heritage of revolutionary thought to generate a reconstruction so complete. None of these circumstances persisted to the decade's end. First, popular respect for Washington and ambiguity about the nature of the new executive directed discontent at the first minister. Second, Hamiltonian finance was modeled on an English prototype. And finally, an opposition first appeared in the House of Representatives.

The Republican persuasion, in its early years, attempted to alert the nation to a ministerial conspiracy that was operating through corruption to secure the revival of a British kind of constitution. Ministerial influence would subvert the independence of the Congress, which would acquiesce in constitutional constructions leading to consolidation of the states and thence to monarchy. Meanwhile, a decay of public virtue, spread by the example of the lackeys of administration and encouraged by the shift of wealth resulting from the funding plan, would ease the way for a transition to hereditary forms. With relatively minor changes, this was just the accusation that the eighteenth-century English opposition had traditionally directed at governments in power, and, like its prototype, it was, in the beginning, the weapon of a legislative group that had to reconcile its status as minority with its commitment to majority control. Legislative blocs were fluid, and the minority could understand its own position and appeal for popular support with the assistance of traditional assumptions that the influence of the Treasury, when added to an honest difference of opinion, was sufficient to account for policies with which they disagreed.

Images of conspiracy and accusations of corruption continued to provide the starting point for Republican analyses of Federalist policies, but it was not so many years before events and circumstances pushed Republican opinion away from its original foundations. First, circumstances undermined a logical necessity of neo-opposition arguments by making the Republicans a majority in the House. Then, Hamilton resigned. Concurrently, however, Jay's Treaty and the foreign war became the major issues for dispute. In other words, just when the opposition might have savored the retirement of the archconspirator, just when their logic was endangered by their own success, events conjoined to redirect attention to the powers of the Senate and the actions of the President himself. British influence and affection for the cause of monarchy displaced attachment to the funding system as the leading explanation for administration policies. But the Republicans could see that the financial structure was dependent on the British trade, and thus the Federalists' foreign policy appeared to be a new means to old ends. In this way, the Republicans continued their conspiratorial analysis into the Adams years.

Only in the last years of the decade can we see a clearer movement of Republican concerns away from the inherited foundations of their thought and toward a style of argument that seems more native. The alteration might be traced to 1794, when the Republicans began to count on a majority of Representatives. From that point forward, we have seen, party writers focused somewhat less on the corruption of the lower house and somewhat more on dangers posed by enemies of the Republic in the several branches of the government and in the country as a whole. During the first years under Adams, critics concentrated their denunciations less on the "funding and banking gentry" or the Hamiltonian "phalanx" than on the "anglo-federal," "anglo-monarchical," or simply "tory" party. The crisis of 1798—the popular hysteria, the Quasi-War, and the Sedition Law—strengthened this trend. Such a crisis in a polity that rested on a large electorate made the administration's influence on the legislature seem less important than the efforts of a ruling party to mislead the people and destroy effective checks on Federalist abuses. Finally, the split among the Federalists confirmed the inclination to direct attacks, not at the link between the government and its dependents in the Congress—the characteristic target of the British critics of administration—but at a party that depended on its influence with the voters. During the last two years of the decade, Republican newspapers gave less space to criticism of the Congress or administration than they did to mockery of their Federalist competitors or efforts to assassinate the reputations of the leaders of the other party. The scurrility of party sheets reflected their recognition that the enemy, in the United States, was not a governmental faction of the British type, but a party with its base among the people.

When Jefferson assumed the presidential office, he and the body of his party were prepared to believe that they had wakened a majority of voters and thereby put an end to the most immediate danger to the American Republic. Removal of the enemy from power and from public trust had come to seem sufficient, by itself, to safeguard liberty while friends of freedom worked toward gradual replacement of the Hamiltonian system with one better suited to republican ways. With the conspirators deposed, the country could afford to *ease* toward change—and change would come more certainly that way. Still, change it must—change as rapidly as possible according to a very different vision of the good society. Republicans were still persuaded that the debt must be retired as rapidly as pre-existing contracts would permit, without

internal taxes. It should not be clung to for its broader economic uses. It would not be used as an excuse to push the federal government into revenue resources better left to separate states. Even here, fanaticism was eschewed by a majority. Jefferson's administration did not hesitate to borrow more for the Louisianna Purchase. But the Republicans were willing to subordinate almost all else to the reduction of the debt. Every year the debt existed meant, to them, another year that taxes would inflate the rich, another year of the increasing gap between the rich and poor, which was potentially destructive to free states. By 1812, Republican administrations had reduced the debt from $83 million, where it had climbed under the Federalists, to $27.5 million. They would have retired it completely in a few more years if war had not gotten in the way.

Reform did not go far enough to satisfy the Old Republicans. Change was incomplete enough—and leaders compromised enough—to make it possible for Henry Adams to support his accusation that the Jeffersonians surrendered to the principles of their opponents. Yet even Adams tried to have it several ways. Sometimes he condemned the Jeffersonians for lack of principle. Sometimes he accused them of a change of mind. At other times, however, he switched ground to level his attacks on their adherence to a set of principles that were ill-suited to the country's needs. The effort to retire the debt, he pointed out, committed the first $7.3 million of yearly revenues to payment of principal and interest. The remainder was to small to run the government and meet the costs of national defense. "The army was not large enough to hold the Indians in awe; the navy was not strong enough to watch the coasts.... The country was at the mercy of any Power which might choose to rob it." "Gallatin's economies turned on the question whether the national debt or the risk of foreign aggression were most dangerous to America." The Republicans assumed the former.

If we would choose among the different condemnations Adams made of the Republican regime, it would be better to prefer the last. Adherence to the principles of ninety-eight—a strikingly consistent effort to adopt and maintain policies implicit in the ideology of opposition days—is a better explanation for Republican actions during their years in power than any emphasis upon hypocrisy or change. The Old Republicans were worrisome beyond their numbers for no other reason than that they appealed to principles that still had the allegiance of large portions of the party. And, as Adams saw, it was the party's loyalty to old ideas that brought the country to the edge of ruin in 1812.

POSTSCRIPT

Was President Jefferson a Political Compromiser?

Were there fundamental ideological and policy differences between Thomas Jefferson and his Federalist opponents? Was Jefferson a strict constructionist or a loose constructionist? Did he champion the rights of the states, or was he a nationalist? Was he a hypocrite or a shrewd politician who reversed his policies and outfederalized his opponents when he became president? Most of Jefferson's Federalist opponents, as well as the strict constructionists in his own party, agreed that the president had indeed reversed himself and outfederalized his opponents. Professor Borden, however, sees consistency, not opportunism, in Jefferson's policies. Borden maintains that "Jefferson was ever a national patriot... [who] always conceived of the United States as a unique experiment, destined for greatness so long as a sharp line isolated American civilization from European infection."

Banning, on the other hand, argues that the Jeffersonian Republicans shifted their strategies when they moved from an oppositionist party to a majority party. Like the earlier British oppositionist party in Parliament, Banning asserts, the Jeffersonians employed conspiratorial rhetoric and attacked Alexander Hamilton's "funding and banking gentry" that continued the "anglo-monarchical" pursuit of power through John Adams's quasi-war against the French. Once in power, Banning notes, Jeffersonians could dispense with such rhetoric and pursue their real goals of reducing the debt and the size of government.

Two older works are the starting point for a study of Jefferson. Henry Adams's recently reissued classic *History of the United States During the Administrations of Thomas Jefferson and James Madison (1889–1891)*, and Richard Hofstadter's "Thomas Jefferson: The Aristocrat as Democrat," from his classic book *The American Political Tradition and the Men Who Made It* (1948; reprint, Alfred A. Knopf, 1973).

The three major works on Jefferson of the 1990s are Peter S. Onuf's "The Scholar's Jefferson," *William and Mary Quarterly* (October 1993), which is the most recent and fullest annotated bibliography on topics about Jefferson that are of interest to historians and their students; Onuf's edited *Jeffersonian Legacies* (University Press of Virginia, 1993), a collection of 15 papers given at a conference held at the University of Virginia in honor of Jefferson's 250th birthday; and Douglas L. Wilson's spirited defense of Jefferson, "Thomas Jefferson and the Meanings of Liberty," *The Atlantic Monthly* (November 1992).

ISSUE 9

Did the Bank War Cause the Panic of 1837?

YES: Thomas P. Govan, from "Fundamental Issues of the Bank War," *The Pennsylvania Magazine of History and Biography* (July 1958)

NO: Peter Temin, from *The Jacksonian Economy* (W. W. Norton, 1969)

ISSUE SUMMARY

YES: Professor of history Thomas P. Govan argues that President Andrew Jackson's refusal to recharter the Bank of the United States was politically popular but economically harmful to the long-term growth of the United States.

NO: Professor of history Peter Temin believes that international factors—such as changes in the monetary policies of the Bank of England, the supply of silver from Mexico, and the price of southern cotton—were far more important than Jackson's banking policies in determining fluctuations in the American economy in the 1830s.

On December 12, 1791, the first Bank of the United States opened for business in Philadelphia. Chartered for 20 years as a private institution, the Bank of the United States was capitalized at $10 million, with the government purchasing one-fifth of the stock.

The Bank of the United States more than fulfilled the expectations of its creator, the first secretary of the treasury, Alexander Hamilton. It effectively checked overspeculation by state banks, handled the government's foreign-exchange operations, helped importers pay their duties, and paid respectable dividends to its stockholders.

But from its inception, the bank was controversial. Secretary of State Thomas Jefferson and his congressional colleague James Madison rejected Hamilton's constitutional and economic viewpoints. Jefferson, who believed in strict construction of the Constitution, felt that the bank proposal was unconstitutional because it was not explicitly mentioned in the Constitution. Hamilton, however, argued that the Constitution granted the "implied" powers that were "necessary and proper" to set up a national bank.

More important than constitutional disagreements were the differing world views of the two men. Hamilton was a staunch nationalist who believed that the government should actively promote the economic development of the nation. He believed that America's wealth would depend on the development of trade and manufacturing. Jefferson and, to a lesser extent, Madison were basically southern agrarians who believed in limited government.

The Federalist party died as a nationalist party after 1800, but Hamilton's economic program continued. Presidents Jefferson and Madison allowed the Bank of the United States to run its business until its charter expired in 1811. Five years elapsed before a second Bank of the United States was created. In the interim President Madison discovered to his chagrin the difficulties of running a war without a centralized financial agency to help him to coordinate national policies and rein in reckless expenditures by state banks.

The second Bank of the United States was similar in structure to its predecessor. It was capitalized with $35 million and, again, the government furnished one-fifth of that capital. Although it enabled the country to resume specie payments in 1817 (those made in coin), which had been suspended during the War of 1812, the bank antagonized other state banks by its policies and was blamed somewhat unfairly for the Panic of 1819.

The bank's affairs were straightened out when one if its own directors, Nicholas Biddle, took charge in 1823. Biddle increased the number of branches to 29, checked overexpansion in the Southwest and in New York State, and imposed restraints on the national government's own activities.

Biddle was considered a great banker, but he and Andrew Jackson clashed over the affairs of the bank. The Biddle-Jackson controversy was a replay of the Hamilton-Jefferson struggle of the 1790s, only the result was different. Biddle, whose view was clearly Hamiltonian, believed that the aristocracy of wealth would run the country in the interest of developing a market economy. Jackson adopted Jefferson's agrarian outlook, objecting to the paper notes issued by the banks.

The struggle over the future of the Bank of the United States came to a head in 1832. Biddle tried to circumvent Jackson when he convinced Congress to recharter the bank four years in advance of its expiration date. Knowing that this had become a major campaign issue in his bid for re-election, Jackson successfully vetoed the bank recharter bill; he then won re-election to the presidency by a wide margin. But the struggle between the two men persisted. Biddle created a deflation when he began to contract credit in August 1833. Jackson countered by ordering his secretary of the treasury to withdraw the government's deposits from all the branches of the Bank of the United States.

Was President Jackson responsible for the depression of 1837? In the first of the following selections, Thomas P. Govan argues that the Bank of the United States was the country's main stabilizing economic institution and that Jackson killed it for partisan political reasons. In the second selection, Peter Temin dismisses Jackson's war on the Bank of the United States as irrelevant, arguing instead that international forces determined fluctuations in the American economy in the 1830s.

YES

Thomas P. Govan

FUNDAMENTAL ISSUES OF THE BANK WAR

The Bank of the United States was not an issue in the Presidential campaigns of 1824 and 1828, and Andrew Jackson's opinions about this institution had no part in causing his defeat in the first or his victory in the second. When he was inaugurated on March 4, 1829, the currency supplied by the bank, no matter where made payable, was received in most places at par, sometimes commanded a premium, and was never at a discount of more than a quarter of one per cent. Notes issued by local state banks circulated at par in the immediate vicinity of their issue and were redeemable in specie, and this mixed national currency was elastic, uniform, sound, and completely adequate for the needs of an expanding economy. The developing transportation system, which united the vast geographical regions of the nation and connected them with Europe, was paralleled by a system of domestic and foreign exchange, based upon the movement of agricultural produce and manufactured goods, which facilitated payments and increased the profits of trade.

The United States as a whole was satisfied with its currency and credit systems and with the operations of the national bank. Andrew Jackson himself, in November, 1829, was reported as saying that the bank "was a blessing to the country, administered as it was, diffusing a healthfull circulation, sustaining the general credit without partiallity of political bias," and that he "entertained a high regard for its excellent President... who with the Board of the Parent Bank possessed his entire confidence and indeed his thanks for the readiness and cordiality with which they seemed to meet the views of the government."

The bank performed a useful function for virtually every class and group in the nation by facilitating the exchange of goods and payments in a predominantly commercial society. The market was the aim of all economic activity in the United States from the smallest farm in the remotest cove of the hills of the West to the largest factory in the industrial regions of the East. The provision of a uniform currency and a regular system of exchanges reduced the costs of each transaction and increased the profits of the producers, whether farmer, manufacturer, laborer, artisan, or miner. The merchants, state bankers, and

From Thomas P. Govan, "Fundamental Issues of the Bank War," *The Pennsylvania Magazine of History and Biography* (July 1958). Copyright © 1958 by The Historial Society of Pennsylvania. Reprinted by permission of *The Pennsylvania Magazine of History and Biography*. Notes omitted.

brokers found their compensation in the steadier course of trade and the resulting regularity of their profits.

In Nicholas Biddle's view, the bank which he headed was established for these public purposes and as an auxiliary in some of the highest powers of government. It was not created for the benefit of the private stockholders or for that of any particular group in the society. He came into its management as a government director in January, 1819, having refused an invitation from representatives of the stockholders. In accepting the appointment made by his close personal and political friend, President James Monroe, he wrote: "The truth is that with all its faults the bank is of vital importance to the finances of the govt and an object of great interest to the community." The corruption and mismanagement of its first administrators had aroused the hostility of the people and threatened to cause an annulment of the charter. Such a possible result seemed a national calamity to Biddle. "I think that experience has demonstrated," he said, "the vital importance of such an institution to the fiscal concerns of this country and that the government which is so jealous of the exclusive privilege of stamping its eagles on a few dollars, should be more tenacious of its rights over the more universal currency, and never again abandon its finances to the mercy of four or five hundred banks independent, irresponsible, & precarious."

For three years as a public director, Biddle supported President Langdon Cheves in the arduous task of reorganization, reform, and recuperation, and then, as required by the charter, retired from the board. He was out of the bank for one year and returned as president in January, 1823, being acceptable to the government and the shareholders alike, but still serving as a director by Presidential appointment. Under Cheves the bank had followed a restrictive policy, limiting the issues of its notes, loans, and purchases of exchange. The new president felt that such a course was unwise and prevented the bank from accomplishing the purposes for which it was created. He immediately reversed this policy and during his administration the bank provided a national currency, controlled the rates of exchange, guided and influenced the state banks, and protected the economy from sudden dangers.

The method adopted was essentially simple and safe. The northeastern seaboard cities were the great markets of the nation. The current of exchanges moved from the South and West to the Northeast in payment for the manufactured products of that region and of Europe. Notes issued by the interior branches consequently found their way to Philadelphia, New York, and Baltimore, slowly but certainly, as they passed from hand to hand in the regular settlement of individual transactions. At the same time, the produce of the interior regions, the real means of payment, traveled the same general path to its markets in the East and in Europe, but more directly and rapidly. The southern and western offices of the bank purchased domestic and foreign bills of exchange, based on these shipments of produce, and sent them to the eastern branches where they built up a fund for the redemption of the notes which subsequently appeared.

This control of the domestic exchanges was the key element in Biddle's system. In the producing regions the bank was the great purchaser of bills, and in the East the great seller, preventing too great a fall at one place, and, at the other, too great a rise. As a consequence, there was much less fluctuation, a desirable condition for the merchant, farmer, and manufacturer, and hurtful only to the brokers and speculators, to whose interest it was that exchange be low in the interior where they purchased, and high at the seaboard where they sold.

The bank, a public institution with strictly defined national responsibilities, was under constant restraint. "The State Banks," Biddle wrote to General Samuel Smith, "may make as much money as they can without looking to consequences. But the Bank of the United States, while it makes money must take care always to keep itself in such an attitude that at a moment's warning, it may interpose to preserve the State Banks and the country from sudden dangers."

Great Britain was the financial center of the world, and it was from there that the greatest and most exacting pressures came. The Bank of the United States, by its control of foreign exchange and through its established credits with Baring Brothers and other great financial houses on the Continent, alone had power to guard against these pressures. Whenever the exchanges were adverse to the United States, thus forcing the rate higher than the expense of sending specie, there was an immediate shipment of coin. If this proceeded to a considerable extent, banks, to preserve their solvency, were obliged to diminish their issues and their loans. Such a restriction, if carried out rapidly, was a harsh corrective, because any great and sudden reduction of the circulating medium acted with inconvenient and oppressive force throughout the community. The purpose and function of the national bank were to lessen the force of these results by preparing for them, and by controlling the exchanges so that they would not long remain at a rate which induced large shipments of coin. Where a reduction of issues was necessary, the bank interposed to render it as gradual as possible and not greater than the occasion required.

Biddle's purpose was to preserve a mild and gentle, but effective, control over the other financial institutions of the United States, so as to warn rather than coerce them into a scale of business commensurate with their real means. His aim was not to regulate the domestic industry or the foreign trade of the country, nor was the power of the bank sufficient to accomplish this purpose. The forces of trade were permitted to generate their own effects and their own correctives, while the bank softened and cushioned the financial effects of these necessary adjustments.

Unfortunately for the political welfare of the bank, these services to the national economy were largely hidden from the population as a whole. Its direct loans and dealings in exchange were confined almost exclusively to the mercantile and financial groups. Its decisions to expand or contract credit, the sole instrument of control in its power, were necessarily made privately and without publicity, and the effects were felt only after the passage of time and then indirectly. Very few men understood the role of the Bank of the United States in the complex phenomena of domestic and international trade. As a member of the Pennsylvania legislature in 1810, Biddle had seen that much of the opposition to the first Bank of the United States "was the result of a downright ignorance of its meaning and operation." As president of the second bank, he persuaded the ablest and best informed students and public men to write freely and frankly concerning the financial and banking system, but the results were not what he wished. The people ignored the lengthy, detailed, and profound analyses which explained the operations and functions of the bank, but listened with avidity to the briefer, more exciting charges of corruption and intrigue against the "Philadelphia Monster."

The bank was safe only as long as it did not become an object of political debate. Once it became a party question, its destruction was inevitable. The fear of an oligarchy of wealth was a real and potent force in American thought and could easily be directed against the mammoth corporation. A party attacking it was almost bound to win popular support, while any party unwise enough to defend it was destined to lose. As Thurlow Weed, the New York Whig leader, wrote in November, 1834:

> ... we have gone with our friends through three campaigns, under a strong and settled conviction that, in every issue to be tried by the people to which the bank was a party, we must be beaten. After staggering along from year to year with a doomed bank upon our shoulders, both the bank and our party are finally overwhelmed.

Anticipating this result, the complete exemption of the bank from the influence of, or concern with, political affairs was one of the chief aims of Biddle's administration. "This has been signally seen during the late Presidential contest," he boasted in April, 1826, "when the name even of the Bank was never mentioned during the greatest political excitement."

The bank was completely neutral during the campaign of 1828, though Biddle himself voted for Jackson and desired his election. Any officer engaging actively in political affairs was reprimanded, and every effort was made to include representatives of each political party or faction on the board of directors of the parent bank and of each of the branches. Members of the Jackson party after the election charged that the branches at Portsmouth, Lexington, Louisville, and New Orleans had denied loans for political reasons, but in each instance these accusations were decisively refuted by directors belonging to both political parties. Not once during the long years of controversy between the bank and the Jackson administration did anyone produce evidence to substantiate the oft-repeated charge that the bank had influenced state or national elections, and Biddle, in every way that he could, tried to keep the recharter of the national bank from becoming an issue between the political parties.

The petition for the recharter and the defense of the bank's record were led by congressmen loyal to the President, and it was Jackson himself, not his party or any interested group, who made the recharter of the bank a political issue. He began the attack in his first annual message, but it was not until men read the forceful words of his veto of the recharter that they knew they must make a choice between the President and the Bank of the United States. The decision was easily made. No prominent politician or important political group deserted the cause of Jackson for that of his opponents as a result of his attack upon the bank.

The reason for the President's opposition to the bank is not to be found in any act of commission or omission by the institution itself, or in any widespread discontent with the existing credit structure. As an uncritical Republican in the Jeffersonian tradition, Jackson feared and opposed all banks as the instruments through which a financial oligarchy dominated and exploited the country. On one occasion he wrote, "Every one that knows me, does know that I have been always opposed to the U. States Bank, nay all banks"; and he told Biddle, "I do not dislike your bank any more than all banks. But ever since I read the history of the South Sea bubble I have been afraid of banks." He also thought that Congress had no power under the Constitution to charter a corporation which would operate outside the District of Columbia, even though this argument had been repudiated by James Madison, who had originally advanced it in 1791, and by the three branches of the Federal government, most of the states, and the people.

Despite Jackson's hostility and fear of "all banks," he recommended the creation of a national bank which would be operated as a branch of the Treasury Department and which would provide for its expenses through the sales of bills of exchange. Such a bank, he said, would not be subject to the constitutional objections which were made to the existing bank, and "the States would be strengthened by having in their hands the means of furnishing the local paper currency through their own banks." Many other statements for and against a national bank, state banks, paper money, and specie currency could be quoted from Jackson and his associates to demonstrate the wide fluctuations of their ideas and the different purposes which motivated them, but such a compilation would have little value. The true measure of any political leader—or group—is to be found in his understanding of the problems with which he is confronted, in the remedies which he proposes, and his accomplishments, not in his expressed intentions.

Albert Gallatin, who shared Jackson's preference for specie, realized the practical impossibility of obtaining such a currency in the United States. "Can Congress," he asked in December, 1830, "subvert the whole of the deep-rooted banking system, sustained as it is by almost every State in the Union, and revert at this day to a metallic currency?" He had no doubt as to the constitutional power, but he was equally certain that it would not be exercised. The elimination of paper money in the United States called for the prohibition of issues by the state banks, either through action by the state government, or by the exercise of the taxing power of the national government. Neither was proposed nor sought by the President. He attempted to prevent the circulation of notes of less than five dollars in value, but the coinage act of 1834, one of the most important measures of his second administration, overvalued gold and tended to drive out of circulation the silver which formed the necessary medium of change if small notes were to be eliminated. The actual result of Jackson's financial policies was the replacement of a uniform and sound currency of virtually equal value in all sections of the country by uncontrolled paper, fluctuating in value from place to place and from time to time, and by domestic and foreign exchanges which were subject to speculative manipulation.

Such could hardly have been the purpose which motivated President Jackson in the war upon the bank, but in his paper on the removal of the deposits which was read to the Cabinet on September 18, 1833, he said:

It is the desire of the President that the control of the banks and the currency shall, as far as possible, be entirely separated from the political power of the country.... In his opinion the action of the General Government on this subject ought not to extend beyond the grant in the Constitution, which only authorizes Congress "to coin money and regulate the value thereof;" all else belongs to the States and the people, and must be regulated by public opinion and the interests of trade.

In this statement lies the fundamental issue between Jackson and Biddle. It was not whether a great private monopoly should dominate government, or whether the currency of the country should be paper or specie. It was, stated in its simplest terms, whether the United States should have a controlled or uncontrolled financial and credit system.

No one recognized the dangers and inherent weaknesses of the American credit structure more clearly than the president of the Bank of the United States. But it was not his assigned task to create an ideal currency and banking system. Fundamental changes and reforms were the responsibility of the constitutional authorities, the Executive and the Congress, not of those who directed the affairs of the national bank. Biddle was certain that, in the economy as it existed, the only practicable safeguard against the evils of irresponsible banking and depreciated paper money was a national bank to keep state banks in order. He believed, as he wrote to Albert Gallatin, "that the surrender of the power of controlling the currency & delivering it over to the hands of the State Govts would more effectually weaken the national govt than the relinquishment of the power of making what is called internal improvements and the disbanding of the army & navy."

The public importance of the Bank of the United States as the regulator of the state banks, the currency, and the exchanges was both the cause of its creation and the principal interest of Biddle. The reasons for its destruction were primarily the unchangeable hostility of President Jackson and his determination that it should not be rechartered. The effective charges against it, in addition to the assertion of its unconstitutionality, were that it was a private and irresponsible monopoly, a conspiracy by a financial oligarchy to dominate the political and economic life of the nation, and a device through which the wealth of the rich and the poverty of the poor were both increased. Such indictments, lacking precision, definition, or detail, are incapable of proof or disproof.

If the bank was guilty of these abuses of its admittedly great powers, remedies should have been provided, either by forced reforms of its management, as was done during the Monroe administration, or by the substitution of some other agency for the control of the currency and exchanges. Neither Jackson nor his advisers were interested in such measures or in a real and fundamental examination of the American credit system and its requirements. Acting from hostility to the Bank of the United States, Jackson first prevented its recharter, then placed the public deposits in the state banks, and finally, this experiment proving unsuccessful, talked of a specie currency without either taking or proposing the steps necessary to achieve his avowed purpose.

Jackson was bent upon the destruction of the bank. To gain popular support, he and the small but determined group around him denounced a wealthy aristocracy and paper money, but the people who supported Jackson and his friends were misled and deceived, because no effective attempt was made to limit the powers or profits of the state bankers, the brokers, or the speculators, or to create an adequate and sound substitute currency. Certainly, no one can examine the subsequent history of the United States and find that the influence of wealth was lessened by Jackson's financial policies, or that the opportunity for speculative profits was decreased. The sole accomplishment of this reform movement was the elimination of the public responsibilities and functions of the national bank. The state banks, the currency, and the credit structure were left without controls, guidance, or support, subject to the unrestrained effects of the "laws" of trade, speculative manipulation, and foreign influence. The effects of this policy are to be found not only in the financial crisis of 1837 and 1839 and during the prolonged and costly depression which followed, but also in the disordered and unsatisfactory currency which plagued the United States until once more the solution of a federally chartered banking system with mixed public and private obligations and control was adopted in 1913.

NO

Peter Temin

THE JACKSONIAN ECONOMY

The failure of the Bank of the United States [B. U. S.] has been analyzed in detail, but the reasons why the economy should have been depressed are less clear. "Many factors contributed to the gravity of the slump. Most important undoubtedly was the violence and speculative nature of the boom that had preceded it. Public land sales had reached in 1836 a level which was never again to be equalled. The renewed suspension of the B. U. S. in 1839, following as it did on the widespread bank failures of 1837, caused a profound public mistrust of banks and bank credit generally. The failure on the part of nine of the states to pay the interest due on their debts destroyed American credit in Europe and made it out of the question for any more loans to be obtained in that way. And the state of the cotton market in Britain after 1840 could scarcely have been less hopeful."

This is the traditional story. It is presented with remarkably little variation in any number of places. The precise cause of the crisis of 1837 is the only subject still in dispute, although the actions of President Jackson figure strongly in most explanations. Historians who say that the boom made a crisis inevitable place the responsibility for the crisis on Jackson's actions initiating the boom. Those who say that the Specie Circular [Jackson's 1836 stipulation that public lands must be paid for in hard currency], the distribution of the surplus, or both caused the crisis, also blame Jackson. But a few, who say that the Bank of England produced the crisis, dissent from this view.

A NEW APPROACH

This account is in error at three main points. First, the boom did not have its origins in the Bank War. It resulted from a combination of large capital imports from England and a change in the Chinese desire for silver which together produced a rapid increase in the quantity of silver in the United States. Banks did not expand their operations because they were treating the government deposits as reserves, to finance speculation, or because the Bank of the United States was no longer restraining them; they expanded because their true—that is, specie—reserves had risen. Second, the Panic of 1837 was not caused by President Jackson's actions. The "destruction" of the Bank of the United States did not produce the crisis because it did not produce the boom. The Specie Circular and the distribution of the surplus also did not have the effects attributed to them. And third, the depression of the early 1840's was neither as serious as historians assume nor the fault of Nicholas Biddle. It was primarily a deflation, as opposed to a decline in production, and it was produced by events over which Biddle had little control.

These errors have arisen because of the nature of the sources used to compile the traditional account. The most important source, as is usual in historical investigations, has been the opinion of informed contemporaries. There is no doubt that we must rely on the opinions of informed witnesses for an understanding of some aspects of the 1830's, but there is good reason to doubt that we can discover the whole story from their words. Most of these observers were also participants, and their objectivity may be questioned. Nicholas Biddle could not possibly have given a balanced account of Jackson's involvement with the Panic of 1837. Other contemporary observers held ideas about the operation of the economy that we can no longer accept today. Albert Gallatin, for example, former Secretary of the Treasury and dean of the New York banking community, could assert with great finality: "It has always been the opinion of the writer of this essay that a public debt was always an evil to be avoided whenever practicable; hardly ever justifiable except in time of war." And even if the difficulties of personal subjectivity did not exist, the opinions of illustrious contemporaries would still not

be a good source. They simply were not sufficiently consistent to provide the raw material for a unified account.

The two opinions most often quoted are those of Nicholas Biddle expressed in an open letter to John Quincy Adams, November 11, 1836, and the 1841 essay of Albert Gallatin from which an opinion was just quoted. Biddle supported one line of argument found in the traditional account by saying: "In my judgment, the main cause of it [the current crisis] is the mismanagement of the revenue —mismanagement in two respects: the mode of executing the distribution law, and the order requiring specie for the public lands." And Gallatin supported a different part of the story by announcing: "Overtrading has been the primary cause of the present crisis in America."

Unfortunately, Biddle did not think much of the opinion expressed by Gallatin, and Gallatin did not agree with Biddle. Biddle noted in his letter that "it is said that the country has overtraded —that the banks have overissued, and that the purchasers of public lands have been very extravagant. I am not struck by the truth or propriety of these complaints. The phrase of overtrading is very convenient but not very intelligible. If it means anything, it means that our dealings with other countries have brought us in debt to those countries. In that case the exchange turns against our country, and is rectified by an exportation of specie or stocks in the first instance— and then by reducing [the ratio of] the imports to the exports. Now the fact is, that at this moment [November, 1836], the exchanges are all in favor of this country —that is, you can buy a bill of exchange on a foreign country cheaper than you can send specie to that country."

And as we have already noted, Gallatin said, "[T]he charges against the President for having interfered in the currency resolve themselves into the single fact of having prevented the renewal of the charter of the Bank of the United States." He went on to say, "The direct and immediate effects cannot be correctly ascertained; but they have been greatly exaggerated by party spirit. That he found the currency in a sound and left it in a deplorable state is true; but he cannot certainly be made responsible for the aberrations and misdeeds of the bank [of the United States] under either of its charters. The unforeseen, unexampled accumulation of the public revenue was one of the principal proximate causes of the disasters that ensued. It cannot be ascribed either to the President or to any branch of the government, and its effects might have been the same whether the public deposits were in the State banks, or had been left in the national bank, organized and governed as that was."

These divergent views by well-qualified contemporary observers cannot be reconciled by appeals to opinion alone. Reference must be made to the actual events taking place. Such observations comprise the other main source of data for the traditional account, but they have not been used in any systematic fashion. Each author has chosen a few facts about the monetary system or the banking structure to present, but almost no one has tried to put these data into a systematic framework or tried to make explicit the implications of the cited observations. As Brinley Thomas once said in a different context, the empirical data have been used "as a drunk uses lampposts: more for support than for illumination."

This can be seen clearly in the treatment of the core of the traditional story of the boom: the nature of the "credit expansion." It is stated that banks used government deposits and notes of other banks as reserves, and that they expanded their activities without references to their true reserves, that is, specie. As Schlesinger phrased it in the passage just cited: "The proportion of paper [that is, bank obligations] to specie lengthened." Phrased another way, the reserve ratio of banks—the inverse of the ratio of obligations to specie—declined. But not one of the historians repeating this story cites any evidence on the reserve ratio of the banking system. One occasionally sees references to the behavior of individual banks and states, but never is there documentation of how the system as a whole behaved.

This gap in our knowledge of the 1830's has been extremely costly. The behavior of individual banks does not necessarily parallel the behavior of the banking system as a whole, and the experience of any single state is not always a good index of the progress of the Union. The story of the 1830's constructed from accounts of individual banks and states is seriously in error, and it can be corrected only by the use of data about the economy as a whole. Incorporated systematically into a coherent theoretical framework, the aggregate data on the 1830's enable us to discriminate between alternate hypotheses and schemes of causation. As a result, we can say both that the traditional account is invalid and that the alternate account to be presented here is supported at many points by the available data....

*   *   *

To start, the political importance of Jackson's "destruction" of the Second

Bank of the United States far outweighed the economic. The unsupported bank expansion that the Bank War has been thought to have initiated simply did not take place. Banks did not expand credit without cause, and they do not seem to have regarded government deposits as additions to reserves. They kept more or less constant reserve ratios throughout the boom—excepting 1834, of course—and the supply of money expanded for reasons unconnected with the Bank War.

Unfortunately for Jackson's reputation, the Bank War coincided with two developments, one in England and one in China, that together produced inflation. A series of unusually good harvests in England initiated a boom in that country about 1832, and British eagerness to invest in the United States and to buy American cotton rose and stayed high for several years. For the British to export capital to the United States, the United States had to buy more in Britain than it sold—that is, to run a trade deficit. And in order for the American demand for British goods to rise, prices in the United States had to rise to make imported goods cheaper, and therefore preferable, to domestically produced ones. The British demand for cotton caused prices in America to rise higher than they otherwise would have done; American exports were increasing at the same time as American imports, and a trade deficit was harder to produce.

For prices in America to rise, the supply of money in America had to rise. Since banks were not willing to expand without increased reserves, new reserves—that is, specie—were needed to let the quantity of money rise. This specie could not have come from Britain because the Bank of England was not willing to let its reserves slip across the Atlantic. The Old Lady of

Threadneedle Street showed as much by her actions in 1836 and 1837; she would have acted sooner if need had arisen. Consequently, the English boom by itself could not have caused the American inflation.

Coincidentally, however, changes were taking place in the Far East that had important ramifications for this process. The Chinese were buying opium in increasing quantities, and they no longer desired silver to hoard. They wanted silver to exchange for opium, and any silver the United States sent to them would have been sent to England in payment for Indian opium. This transshipment was avoided by substituting American credit for Mexican silver, and the United States retained the silver imports from Mexico that it had sent to the Orient in earlier years. This silver went into bank reserves in America, allowing prices to rise and the demand for imports to increase. It may be said that the Chinese enabled the British to export capital to the United States by releasing silver to be used as a base for American monetary expansion, or that the capital flow from Britain to the United States allowed the Americans to keep their silver instead of sending it to the East.

The high British demand for cotton acted to increase the inflation by reducing the American trade deficit, but it also acted to retard the inflation by setting off a land boom. As the price of cotton soared upward, speculative fever kept pace. Land sales of the Federal Government rose dramatically in 1835 and 1836, and part of the increase in the money supply went into land purchases. The Federal Government accumulated a surplus, and these funds were removed from circulation. It was thought at the time that these funds were used as the basis for further monetary expansion, but we have shown that this did not happen. The government continued to sell land at a constant price, and funds that otherwise would have been used to raise prices rested in the government's surplus. We have no way of knowing whether the net effect of the cotton price's two offsetting influences was positive or negative.

The inflation had to end, and even be replaced by deflation, if the British stopped exporting capital to the United States. The Bank of England thought it was losing specie to the United States in late 1836 and acted to restrain the capital flow. This produced a commercial crisis in the United States, but the breaking point did not come until the price of cotton fell in early 1837. As this important price fell, the credit structure built with cotton as security collapsed. Banks in the United States refused to preserve the convertibility of their notes and deposits into specie and thus into foreign exchange at a fixed rate; the United States effectively devalued for a short time.

Andrew Jackson has been blamed for the Panic of 1837, but it is clear that he was not the villain. The accumulating surplus had created a political problem, and the distribution of the surplus to the states offered a solution. The distribution would have created some hardship for the banking system, but it was not qualitatively different from previous governmental transactions, and it would not have produced a crisis. The Specie Circular, issued to offset the inflationary effects of the distribution, similarly was not a cause of the panic. The boom had been caused by a tenuous balance of independent forces; when this balance was lost, one or the other of the forces was bound to cause trouble. As it turned out, a diminution in the capital

flow from England to America was the force that led to the crisis.

The effects of the panic were mild, however, and the economy soon recovered from them. The British continued to lend to the United States once the Bank of England had accumulated a satisfactory volume of reserves, the price of cotton revived in early 1839 due to a short harvest and to the effects of Nicholas Biddle's speculations, and the funds distributed to the states were spent by them on a variety of projects. The first and second of these developments restored the financial system to its pre-panic health and allowed American banks to resume specie payments. The restored financial system cooperated with the demand from the states to produce renewed prosperity in 1839.

This prosperity did not last long. A bad wheat harvest in England in 1838 caused the British to export specie in return for imports of wheat in 1839, and the Bank of England tightened credit once again to replenish its reserves. A bumper crop of cotton in 1839 caused the price of cotton to fall in early 1840, and many banks followed the precedent of 1837 by suspending payments. The panic was not as severe in 1839 as it had been in 1837, but it marked the end of the boom.

States ceased their expenditures and defaulted on their bonds. The British replied by ceasing to export capital to the United States. Simultaneously, banks increased their reserve ratios, and people raised the proportion of their funds they wanted to hold in coin. The cessation of British lending meant the end of the opportunity for the United States to finance a trade deficit. The rise in the two monetary ratios lowered the supply of money, reducing the demand for both American and imported goods. The falling demand for imports ended the trade deficit. The effects of the panic thus produced deflation in two ways: Through its effect on the balance of trade and by its effect on the supply of money. As with the inflation, it is not possible to say that the international capital movements or the change in the quantity of money alone produced the deflation; they acted together, and their results are inseparable.

The deflation was as dramatic as the preceding inflation, and its effect on national income appears to have been as small. Many businesses failed, but the resultant change in ownership did not interrupt production. Agricultural production was unaffected by the deflation, and the growing industrial sector of the economy continued to expand. Only the part of the economy servicing trade and commerce suffered, and the overall effects of the decline in trade were small. There is no evidence of widespread unemployment or of distress not produced by the price fall alone during the early 1840's.

Inflation, crisis, deflation: This was the story of the Jacksonian era. The sequence has been known for a long time, but the roles played by historical personages have been confused. Contemporary observers blamed Andrew Jackson, and historians have agreed. Yet analysis shows that Jackson was not the prime mover in the inflation, the crises, or the deflation. His policies did not help the economy to adjust to the harsh requirements of external forces, but they were of little importance beside these far stronger influences.

Andrew Jackson, then, did not pay a high cost for his destruction of the Second Bank. He did not initiate a speculative mania, and he did not plunge the economy into crisis and depression. To the extent that these events have been blamed on his actions, he has been victimized by external events. It would not be appropriate here to defend Jackson's policies, but it must be insisted that they were not tested by the events of the 1830's. We cannot say what would have happened had Jackson not entered into his "war" with Biddle, but it is doubtful that the banking system would have reacted any differently to the shocks it received had the Bank of the United States continued as the government's fiscal agent.

The economy was not as unstable as historians have assumed; there do not appear to have been forces within the banking system leading inevitably toward a crisis unless restrained by superior force. The banking system did not have the ability to adapt to external shocks, but it did not produce sharp inflations like the one culminating in 1837 without external help. The antebellum economy was vulnerable to disturbing influences, but it was not a source of them. The distinction is important.

Finally, the economy possessed a structure of some analytic interest. It functioned to a large extent in the fashion described by what we now call classical economic theory. Prices were flexible, they could vary to facilitate capital transfers, and they could change radically without destroying the ability of the economy to operate near capacity. Yet the price-specie-flow mechanism did not operate according to the textbook rules; without a supply of silver from "outside the system," the mechanism would not have worked. And the price level, while variable, was not "neutral." It mattered what the price level was, or at least what the price of cotton was, because a large part of the antebellum financial system used cotton for security. When its price fell, the system broke down, and a decline in prices was considerably more difficult to effect than a rise.

As Gallatin said, Jackson "found the currency of the country in a sound and left it in a deplorable state," but most of the change was not of Jackson's doing. In destroying the Second Bank of the United States, he had closed off an area of possible future experimentation, but he had not precipitated a "bank-boom-bust sequence." The economic fluctuations of the Jacksonian era may still be deplored, but they cannot any longer be used as an argument against Jacksonianism.

POSTSCRIPT

Did the Bank War Cause the Panic of 1837?

Govan makes a strong case to support his assertion that the second Bank of the United States acted as a stabilizing force for the economy "by facilitating the exchange of goods and payments in a predominantly commercial society." But many would argue that Govan's case in support of bank director Nicholas Biddle has several weaknesses.

Govan's essay, like his biography *Nicholas Biddle* (University of Chicago Press, 1959), has been deemed too uncritical of Biddle. Even Biddle's most ardent defenders would question whether his purpose was (as Govan puts it) "to preserve a mild and gentle, but effective, control over the other financial institutions of the United States, so as to warn rather than coerce them into a scale of business commensurate with their real means." Even though it was the Jacksonians who introduced the rechartering bill, Biddle used his influence to line up Jackson's opponents as supporters of this bill. And even after Jackson vetoed the charter renewal, Biddle kept the bank going himself for several more years. Once the federal deposits were removed, Biddle curtailed loans and demanded regular payments of all imbalances by state banks in hard currency, thus adding to an already recessed economy in 1833.

Govan's views of the Bank War are supported by two earlier works: Ralph C. H. Catterall's *Second Bank of the United States* (University of Chicago Press, 1903) and Bray Hammond's *Banks and Politics in America: From the Revolution to the Civil War* (Princeton University Press, 1957), which is the most widely used synthesis on the subject, and which pushes the outdated entrepreneurial thesis of the Jacksonian man as an expectant capitalist. Hammond's thesis is further explored in two widely reprinted essays: "Jackson, Biddle and the Bank of the United States," *Journal of Economic History* (May 1947), and "Jackson's Fight With the Money Power," *American Heritage* (June 1956).

Additional research on the role of the state banks, however, does not support the views of Govan and Hammond. James Roger Sharp, *The Jacksonians Versus the Banks: Politics in the States After the Panic of 1837* (Columbia University Press, 1970) and William G. Shade, *Banks or No Banks: The Money Question in Western Politics, 1832–1865* (Wayne State University Press, 1972) argue that most Jacksonians were hard-money men who exhibited strong hostility toward state banks. But Larry Schweikart, in "Jacksonian Ideology, Currency Control and Central Banking: A Reappraisal," *The Historian* (November 1988), argues that in spite of their laissez-faire rhetoric, many Jacksonians accepted the need for regulating the state banks. Some wanted a central bank but not Biddle's Bank of the United States.

Temin's work is important for two reasons. First, as a practitioner of the "new" economic history, the author uses the quantitative tools of the economist to build his arguments. His conclusions rely upon statistical analyses over an extended time frame of the following issues: How large or small was the money supply? Was there an excess or a shortage of gold and silver? How widely did loans expand or contract in relation to the balance that existed between the individual bank notes and hard currency? What effect did the price of cotton on the international market have on the economic well-being of the United States?

Temin's *Jacksonian Economy* (W. W. Norton, 1969) is also significant because the author attempts to demolish all of the previous major controversies surrounding the Bank War. The author changes the focus of the argument by shifting from the national to the international arena. In Temin's view, the changes in policies of the Bank of England, the supply of silver from Mexico, and the price of cotton were determining the economic cycle in the United States.

Temin's argument can be criticized on several grounds. His arguments, for example, are not as new as he maintains. The famous nineteenth-century social scientist William Graham Sumner took international factors into account in his biography *Andrew Jackson*, rev. ed. (Houghton Mifflin, 1899), as does Walter Buckingham Smith, in his *Economic Aspects of the Second Bank of the United States* (Harvard University Press, 1953). Some critics also charge that Temin's account underestimates the impact of the constantly shifting domestic economic policies of Biddle, Jackson, and Van Buren upon the American economy. While most accounts focus too narrowly on the Jackson-Biddle controversy as played out in Washington, D.C., and in the states, Temin totally dismisses them as irrelevant.

Two recent guides serve as starting points for any study of this era: *Liberty and Power: The Politics of Jacksonian America* by Harry L. Watson (Hill & Wang, 1990) and *The Market Revolution: Jacksonian America, 1815–1846* by Charles Sellers (Oxford University Press, 1991), which views the era as a clash of Whig and Democratic visions as much as it was a clash of personalities.

Two collections of primary sources—Jackson's veto message and the responses of his opponents—are collected in Frank Otto Gatell, *The Jacksonians and the Money Power, 1829–1840* (Rand McNally, 1967) and in Robert V. Remini, *The Age of Jackson* (University of South Carolina Press, 1972).

PART 3

Antebellum America

*Pressures and trends that began building in the early years
of the American nation continued to gather momentum
until conflict was almost inevitable. Population growth and
territorial expansion brought the country into conflict with
other nations. The United States had to respond to challenges
from Americans who felt alienated from or forgotten by the
new nation because the ideals of human rights and democratic
participation that guided the founding of the nation had been
applied only to selected segments of the population.*

■ Was Antebellum Reform Motivated
   Primarily by Humanitarian Goals?

■ Did Slaves Exercise Religious Autonomy?

■ Was the Mexican War an Exercise in
   American Imperialism?

ISSUE 10

Was Antebellum Reform Motivated Primarily by Humanitarian Goals?

YES: Alice Felt Tyler, from *Freedom's Ferment: Phases of America's Social History from the Colonial Period to the Outbreak of the Civil War* (University of Minnesota Press, 1944)

NO: David J. Rothman, from *The Discovery of the Asylum: Social Order and Disorder in the New Republic* (Little, Brown, 1971)

ISSUE SUMMARY

YES: Professor of history Alice Felt Tyler argues that American reformers in the antebellum period were products of evangelical religion and frontier democracy who accepted the mission of perfecting human institutions.

NO: Professor of history David J. Rothman contends that antebellum reformers established orphan asylums and reformatories primarily to enforce strict discipline and to inculcate respect for authority and order among those seeking refuge in these institutions.

In the era following the War of 1812, several dramatic changes in the United States occurred. Andrew Jackson's military triumph over the British at the Battle of New Orleans generated a wave of nationalistic sentiment in the country, even though the victory had come two weeks *after* the Treaty of Ghent officially ended the conflict with England. The republic experienced important territorial expansion with the addition of new states in each of the half-dozen years following the end of the war. A "transportation revolution" produced a turnpike, canal, and railroad network that brought Americans closer together and enhanced the opportunities for economic growth. In politics, the demise of the nation's first two-party system, following the decline of the Federalists, was succeeded by the rise to prominence of the Democratic and, later, the Whig parties.

Although some historians have characterized this period as the "era of good feelings," it is important to remember that many Americans were aware that the nation was not without its problems. Drawing upon intellectual precepts associated with the Enlightenment, some citizens believed in the necessity of and potential for perfecting American society. Ralph Waldo Emerson captured the sense of mission felt by many nineteenth-century men and women when he wrote: "What is man for but to be a Re-former, a Re-maker of what man has made; a renouncer of lies; a restorer of truth and good, imitating that great Nature which embosoms us all, and which sleeps no moment on an old past, but every hour repairs herself, yielding to us every morning a new day, and with every pulsation a new life?" These ideas were reinforced by the encouragement for moral and spiritual perfection produced by the revivalistic movement known as the Second Great Awakening. Significantly, revivalists like Charles G. Finney combined a desire to promote salvation through faith and spiritual conversion with an active interest in social change.

This "age of reform" was a multifaceted and often interrelated movement. Reformers, most of whom were from the middle and upper classes, hoped to improve the condition of inmates in the country's prisons and asylums or to encourage temperance or even total abstinence from drinking. Some reformers emphasized the necessity of maintaining peace in the world, while others hoped to improve the educational system for the masses. Still others directed their energies into movements emphasizing dietary reform and clothing reform for women. Finally, large numbers of Americans sought to improve society through campaigns to improve the status of women and to eliminate slavery.

Thousands of Americans belonged to one or more of these antebellum reform societies, but some controversy exists as to the motivations of these reformers. Were they driven by humanitarian impulses that surfaced in the reinvigorated American republic after 1815? Or was it merely self-interest that encouraged middle- and upper-class Americans to attempt to order society in such a way as to preserve their positions of power?

Alice Felt Tyler's selection represents the traditional thesis that antebellum reformers were motivated largely by humanitarian ideals and desired primarily to perfect American society. These impulses, Tyler claims, stemmed from America's democratic spirit and the evangelical sentiment produced by the Second Great Awakening.

David J. Rothman, however, focusing upon the various child-care institutions (orphan asylums and reformatories, for example) that began to appear in the 1830s, suggests that the prevailing goal of the reformers involved in those endeavors was to impose a strict disciplinary routine that would ensure absolute respect for authority among the asylum's inmates. In fact, although the superintendents of these institutions frequently employed the metaphor of the family to characterize their operations, they were inclined to exercise over their charges a quasi-military control, which they deemed essential for preserving social and moral order in the United States.

YES
Alice Felt Tyler

FREEDOM'S FERMENT

THE FAITH OF THE YOUNG REPUBLIC

The time has come when the experiment is to be made whether the world is to be emancipated and rendered happy, or whether the whole creation shall groan and travail together in pain.... If it had been the design of Heaven to establish a powerful nation in the full enjoyment of civil and religious liberty, where all the energies of man might find full scope and excitement, on purpose to show the world by one great successful experiment of what man is capable... where should such an experiment have been made but in this country!... The light of such a hemisphere shall go up to Heaven, it will throw its beams beyond the waves; it will shine into the darkness there, and be comprehended—it will awaken desire, and hope, and effort, and produce revolutions and overturnings until the world is free.... Floods have been poured upon the rising flame, but they can no more extinguish it than they can extinguish the flames of Aetna. Still it burns, and still the mountain murmurs; and soon it will explode with voices and thunderings, and great earthquakes.... Then will the trumpet of jubilee sound, and earth's debased millions will leap from the dust, and shake off their chains, and cry, "Hosanna to the Son of David!"

With this vision of the future as a new and glorious epoch Lyman Beecher a hundred years ago voiced the exuberant optimism of the young American republic in which he lived. In that time, if ever in American history, the spirit of man seemed free and the individual could assert his independence of choice in matters of faith and theory. The militant democracy of the period was a declaration of faith in man and in the perfectibility of his institutions. The idea of progress so inherent in the American way of life and so much a part of the philosophy of the age was at the same time a challenge to traditional beliefs and institutions and an impetus to experimentation with new theories and humanitarian reforms.

The period was one of restless ferment. An expanding West was beckoning the hungry and dissatisfied to an endless search for the pot of gold. Growing industrialization and urbanization in the East, new means of communication and transportation, new marvels of invention and science, and advance in the mechanization of industry, all were dislocating influences of mounting importance. And increasing immigration was bringing into the country thousands of Europeans who were dissatisfied with the difficult conditions of life in their native lands. Nor did religion place any restraint on the unrest; recurring revivals, emphasis on individual conversion and personal salvation, and the multiplicity of sects, all made religion responsive to the restlessness of the time rather than a calming influence upon it. The pious editors of the writings of a Shaker seeress asserted in their preface to her revelations:

> Let any candid people, endowed with a common share of discernment seriously examine the signs of the times, and view the many wonderful events and extraordinary changes that are constantly taking place in the moral religious and political world, as well as in the natural elements, through the operations of Providence, and they cannot but consider the present age as commencing the most extraordinary and momentous era that ever took place on earth.

Each in his own way the citizens of the young republic recognized the ferment of the era and made answer to its challenge. Itinerant revivalists and the most orthodox of clergymen alike responded with missionary zeal. For an influential few transcendentalism proved to be a satisfying reconciliation between the rationalism of their training and the romanticism of the age, while among the less intellectual, adventism, spiritualism, Mormonism, and perfectionism each won adherents who founded churches and preached their creeds with fervor. To these sects were added the cults and communities transplanted from abroad. The combination of religious toleration, overflowing optimism, and cheap lands caused Europeans of unorthodox faith or unusual social ideas to seek asylum in America. Each such sect, each isolated religious community, each social utopia, was an evidence of the tolerant, eclectic spirit of the young republic, and each made its contribution to the culture of the land that gave it sanctuary.

The desire to perfect human institutions was the basic cause for each sect and community, and this same desire lay at the roots of all the many social reform movements of the period. The American reformer was the product of evangelical religion, which presented to every person the necessity for positive action to save his own soul, and dynamic frontier democracy, which was rooted deep in a belief in the worth of the individual. Born of this combination, the reformer considered reform at once his duty and his right, and he did not limit his activities to one phase of social betterment. Education, temperance, universal peace, prison reform, the rights of women, the evils of slavery, the dangers of Catholicism, all were legitimate fields for his efforts.

The American reformer knew that he did not work alone. He recognized that each cause he espoused was a part of a world of progress and aspiration, but peculiarly his was the freedom to experiment, for in his homeland there was room and hospitality for adventure. Happy in his privilege, he acknowledged his duty and accepted for his age the sign of his crusade....

DYNAMIC DEMOCRACY

It was a long process of democratization, begun before the signing of the Declaration of Independence, accelerated by the Revolution, and continued through the influence of the frontier, that made American society, in the words of the French traveler, Michel Chevalier, in 1834, "essentially and radically a democracy, not in name merely but in deed." ...

Frederick Jackson Turner, the historian whose name is identified with the frontier, has wisely said that the West is at bottom a form of society, rather than an area. From the beginning each colony had its frontier, its West: areas in which men of courage and vigor won new opportunities, where land was cheap or free and the struggle for existence, although severe, brought rewards commensurate with the effort expended. There the "cake of custom" was broken, old standards were discarded, new ideals and new institutions were set up. The back country was relatively near the Atlantic Coast in the early days, but it was pushed farther west, north, or south decade by decade. In 1790 one hundred thousand had reached the Mississippi Valley. The census of 1810 showed a Western population of a million, that of 1830 gave the West more than three and a half millions, and that of 1840 made the total six millions. ...

From whatever background they came, no matter how diverse their motives or their equipment, the frontier shaped these settlers into its own pattern. And the type of American developed under frontier conditions set his mark upon the life of his nation so unmistakably that the philosophy of the frontier came to color the activities of the entire United States. Equality of condition was a fact, not a theory, on the frontier; station, education, refinement, and even wealth mattered little. All must face the same perils and hardships, the same grueling labor in clearing the land, the same isolation, the same lack of the refinement of civilization. The weaklings move on, dropped back, or died of their failures, while the vigorous and self-

reliant remained to become the leaders and the models of frontier achievement.

The same conditions produced the paradox of the frontier—a belief in equality so profound that the American almost confounded equality of opportunity with equality of ability, together with an intense, militant individualism that resented all restrictions and was restless, buoyant, self-assertive, and optimistic. The frontiersman had the utmost confidence in himself, his region, and his country, and he both craved and resented comparisons and criticisms. Acknowledging no debt to the past, he believed in progress and accepted change as the natural order. Hopeful and idealistic, he yet could not forget the necessity for commons sense and a realistic attitude, for the conquest of the wilderness was an arduous task, exacting, monotonous, and burdensome. ...

The frontier's faith in democracy and freedom soon took on an element of crusading zeal as Americans became convinced of the glorious future ahead of them and came to consider themselves entrusted with the mission of portraying democracy to less favored nations. A magazine article in 1821, perhaps with some sense of humor, illustrated this confidence in the future with the statement:

Other nations boast of what they are or have been, but the true citizen of the United States exalts his head to the skies in the contemplation of what the grandeur of his country is going to be. Others claim respect and honor because of the things done by a long line of ancestors; an American appeals to prophecy, and with Malthus in one hand and a map of the back country in the other he defies us to a comparison with America as she is to be, and chuckles his delight over the splendors the geometrical ratio is to shed over her story. This appeal to the future is his never-failing resource....

Francis Grund, writing in 1836 for an English public, made the same sort of comment in his statement that Americans loved their country not for what it then was, but for what it was to be—not the land of their fathers, but the land their children were destined to inherit. The Scotsman, Alexander Mackay, heard the same idea from a South Carolina farmer in response to a question about genealogy: "We don't vally those things in this country. It's what's above ground, not what's under, that we think on." Whether or not the visiting Europeans approved of American democracy, and many did not, they all were agreed that Americans themselves were content with their institutions and believed them better than those of Europe.

This American solidarity was noted by the most famous foreign visitor of the period, Alexis de Tocqueville, in a letter from the United States in June 1831. After stating that he envied Americans the comfort of their common opinion, he went on to enumerate them: All the people believe that a republic is the best possible government and do not question that the people have a right to govern themselves. This belief is almost a *faith*, which is at basis a faith in the good sense of human beings and in the perfectibility of human institutions. In order that those institutions may constantly improve, education and enlightenment must become as universal as suffrage. De Tocqueville found no evidence of ancient traditions and little effect of old customs or memories. Americans were a new people. He felt that the reason there was so great a respect for law was that the people

made it themselves and could change it themselves. "It is really an incredible thing... to see how this people keeps itself in order through the single conviction that its only safeguard against itself lies in itself." Somewhat reluctantly, apparently, the young Frenchman admitted that on the whole the country presented "an admirable spectacle!" His great work published some years later, *Democracy in America*, reaffirmed this first impression, saying,

> In America, the principle of the sovereignty of the people is not either barren or concealed... it is recognized by the customs and proclaimed by the laws.... If there be a country in the world where the doctrine of the sovereignty of the people can be fairly appreciated, where it can be studied in its application to the affairs of society, and where its dangers and its advantages may be foreseen, that country is assuredly America.

The American's own view of his achievement in democracy was usually optimistic, sometimes complacent, but occasionally tempered by analysis and criticism. The novelist, James Fenimore Cooper, although professing belief in democracy, was a caustic critic of American life, attacking what he thought were its abuses and faults with a vehemence that won him many enemies. In his *America and the Americans: Notions Picked up by a Travelling Bachelor*, published in 1836, he endeavored to explain his country to the outside world and to express his own faith. But in *The American Democrat*, designed for his own countrymen, he warned of the danger of the rise of a "vulgar tyrant" and repeatedly asserted that the leading principle of a republic must be that political power is a trust to be guarded with "ceaseless vigilance." Feeling that imperfect as popular government was, it was less dangerous than any other, Cooper came to the conclusion that men of intelligence and wealth, of education and station, must take their proper place in democratic society and aid in directing national policies.

The self-conscious democracy of the West, in conjunction with the laboring classes of the seaboard states, exercised its newly acquired manhood suffrage in 1828 to bring about the Jacksonian Revolution and install "Old Hickory," the hero of the land-speculating, Indian-fighting West, in the White house....

With the election of Andrew Jackson the creed of the frontier won its victory in the arena of national affairs, and the Western interest in politics became national with the rise of the common man to political importance. While officeholders trembled and Washington official and social circles paled with anticipatory anguish, the President-elect prepared to act in accordance with a creed that summarizes well the essential faith of the young republic:

> I believe man can be elevated; man can become more and more endowed with divinity; and as he does he becomes more God-like in his character and capable of governing himself. Let us go on elevating our people, perfecting our institutions, until democracy shall reach such a point of perfection that we can acclaim with truth that the voice of the people is the voice of God.

EVANGELICAL RELIGION

The religious heritage of the young republic was as important in the development of nineteenth-century ideas as were the liberties won in the struggle with civil authorities. "When the com-mon man has freed himself from political absolutism, he will become dissatisfied with theological absolutism." The cold and repressive doctrines of Calvinism could not win the hearts of those who escaped from its control when its dictatorial governmental power came to an end. Moreover, the rationalism of John Locke and the French philosophes had the same dislocating effect on religious thinking as on political ideas. Calvin's doctrine of total depravity might have sufficed an older generation as an explanation of the presence of evil in human society, but man's reason found other causes, and his common sense rejected the idea that he and his neighbor were utterly depraved. The idea of progress and of the importance of the individual undermined the old doctrines of election and predestination. The consequent dissatisfaction with Genevan dogma, coupled with the aridity and dullness of New England cultural life, caused the people to turn with eagerness to evangelical Protestantism....

The frank and open adoption of emotionalism in religion and the sensational methods of revivalists did not go unnoticed by American and European contemporary commentators. Margaret Bayard Smith in describing a revival in Washington in 1822 stated that the preachers were

> introducing all the habits and hymns of the Methodists into our Presbyterian churches... that they were going through the highways and hedges, to invite guests... into every house exhorting the people, particularly into all the taverns, grog-shops, and other resorts of dissipation and vice. Whether all these excessive efforts will produce a permanent reformation I know not; but there is something very repugnant to my feelings in the public way in which they discuss the conversions and convictions of

people and in which young ladies and children display their feelings and talk of their convictions and experiences. Dr. May calls the peculiar fever, the *night fever*, and he says almost all cases were produced by night meetings, crowded rooms, excited feelings, and exposure to night air.

A somewhat less naíve explanation of revivalistic phenomena was made by Bishop Hopkins of Vermont, who stated that revivalists secured conversions solely because of the terror induced by their exhortations. Disapproval of such tactics seems to have been prevalent among the Episcopalian clergy, one of whom Captain Marryat quoted as saying that revivals were

those startling and astounding shocks which are constantly invented, artfully and habitually applied, under all the power of sympathy, and of a studied and enthusiastic elocution, by a large class of preachers among us. To startle and to shock is their great secret power.

But the American clergy in general probably felt that the revival had come to stay and could be made a valuable part of the religious program of the Protestant churches.

European travelers almost invariably were taken to camp meetings, especially in the West, and reacted to the experience in accord with their own temperaments. Captain Marryat drew back in disgust from the preacher who began his prayer with the words "Almighty and diabolical God," and depreciated all the excesses and extravagances of evangelical religion. Frances Trollope made many caustic comments about both revivals and preachers. Always suspecting the worst, she felt sure that such sessions must turn at times into sex orgies, al-

though the only ocular evidence she had was the sight of a preacher whispering consolation into the ear of a sobbing and distraught young feminine convert.

James Stuart was much impressed by the perfect decorum of the audience, the "faultless" sermons, and the magnificent singing. The revival he attended, however, was on Long Island; he was not exposed to the crudities of a genuine frontier camp meeting. It is more surprising to find the usually censorious Thomas Hamilton commending the camp meeting as an agency of civilization.

In a free community [he wrote] the follies of the fanatic are harmless. The points on which he differs from those around him are rarely of a nature to produce injurious effects on his conduct as a citizen. But the man without religion acknowledges no restraint but human laws; and the dungeon and the gibbet are necessary to secure the rights and interests of his fellow-citizens from violation. There can be no doubt, therefore, that in a newly settled country the strong effect produced by these camp-meetings and revivals is on the whole beneficial. The restraints of public opinion and penal legislation are little felt in the wilderness; and, in such circumstances, the higher principle of action, communicated by religion, is a new and additional security to society.

Two of the most detailed descriptions of camp-meeting revivals are those of Francis Lieber and Fredrika Bremer, written nearly twenty years apart and published in 1835 and 1853. Lieber was repelled by the emotionalism of the camp meeting he attended and was shocked by the "scenes of unrestrained excitement," but the Swedish traveler, Fredrika Bremer, was much impressed by the immense crowd of both white and colored people at the Georgia camp meeting she witnessed in the early 1850's. The grandeur of the night meeting in the forest, the eight fine altars, the campfires of resinous wood, the superb singing of the thousands of Negroes, the wails of the penitent, the thunder and lightning of an approaching storm—all, she said, combined to make the night one never to be forgotten.

The effects of the absence of state control and the consequent multiplicity of sects seemed to interest all foreign observers. Many of them mention the lack of religious intolerance in the United States and the easy "live and let live" philosophy apparent in the attitude of most men. Alexander Mackay, who traveled extensively in America in the 1840's, was so impressed that he wrote:

It is true that the insulting term "toleration" is but seldom heard in America in connexion with the religious system of the country. To say that one tolerates another's creed, implies some right to disallow it, a right that happens to be suspended or in abeyance for the time being. The only mode in which the American manifests any intolerance in reference to religion is that they will not tolerate that the independence of the individual should in any degree, be called in question in connexion with it.

On the more fundamental question of the connection between the American democratic faith and the emotional perfectionistic religion that had swept over the United States the observers seemed in agreement. Again and again missionaries and patriots identified democratic with religious faith and asserted that neither could stand alone, that combined they furnished an invincible bulwark for American freedom. Timothy Flint, writer and missionary preacher of the

first decade of the century, emphasize always that missionary enterprise in the West was for the good of the whole country; the West must not fall into Godless anarchy, for the representative institutions of the East would then also perish. As the Western missionary told De Tocqueville, "It is, therefore, our interest that the New States should be religious, in order that they may permit us to remain free."

In an essay published in 1851, Mark Hopkins, president of Williams College, expressed the same feeling that democracy must be linked with Christianity:

Man himself is the highest product of this lower world, those institutions would seem to be the best which show, not the most imposing results of aggregated labor, but humanity itself, in its most general cultivation and highest forms. This idea finds its origin and support in the value which Christianity places upon the individual, and, fully carried out, must overthrow all systems of darkness and mere authority. Individual liberty and responsibility involve the right of private judgment; this involves the right to all the light necessary to form a correct judgment; and this again must involve the education of the people, and the overthrow of everything, civil and religious, which will not stand the ordeal of the most scrutinizing examination and of the freest discussion.

Regardless of their differences as to details, European and American observers alike were insistent upon the prominence of the part played by religion in the Western World. They saw that the same intensity of faith vivified both the democracy and the religious experience of many Americans, and they realized the potentialities of that combination. The mind and heart quickened by the "lively joy" of a vital religious experience were easily turned toward social reforms, and the spirit of inquiry and soul-searching that animated the revival had a dynamic social significance. The American faith in democratic institutions found its alter ego in the romantic evangelical spirit of American religious life. Together they gave to the Americans of the first half century of the republic their conviction that their institutions could be perfected and their national destiny be fulfilled.

NO

David J. Rothman

THE WELL-ORDERED ASYLUM

No reformers were more confident of the advantage and success of their program than the philanthropists who founded child-saving institutions. For proponents, the movement to incarcerate the orphan, the abandoned child, the youngster living in dire poverty, the juvenile vagrant, and the delinquent promised enormous benefits while entailing few risks. Like their colleagues sponsoring insane asylums and penitentiaries and almshouses, they shared an intense faith in the rehabilitative powers of a carefully designed environment and were certain that properly structured institutions would not only comfort the homeless but reform the delinquent.

Child-care institutions, new to Americans, fundamentally altered traditional practices. In the colonial period, overseers of the poor, in the absence of responsible relatives and friends, typically had apprenticed the orphan to a local householder. In unusual circumstances, when the child suffered from a major disability, they might have recourse in one of the larger towns to the almshouse. The orphan asylum was all but unknown in the eighteenth century. . . .

In the 1830's a basic transformation occurred as child-care institutions spread rapidly through the country. In this decade alone, twenty-three private orphan asylums began operating in various towns and cities, and the movement continued to grow in the 1840's with the founding of thirty more of them. They opened not only in New York, Boston, and Philadelphia—as usual, among the leaders in building institutions—but also in Bangor, Maine; Richmond, Virginia; Mobile, Alabama; Avondale and Cincinnati, Ohio; and Chicago, Illinois. By 1850, New York State alone had twenty-seven public and private child-care institutions. Within two decades they had become common structures, widespread and popular, with their own unique and important attributes, not just a last resort when apprenticeship was impossible. Indeed, their promise seemed so great that trustees quickly spread their nets to catch a wide variety of dependent children. They admitted the abandoned as well as the orphaned child, and those whose widowed or deserted mothers, hard pressed to make ends meet, had little time for supervision. They accepted minors whose parents were quite alive but very poor, and those from

From David J. Rothman, *The Discovery of the Asylum: Social Order and Disorder in the New Republic* (Little, Brown, 1971). Copyright © 1971, 1990 by David J. Rothman. Reprinted by permission of Little, Brown and Company. Notes omitted.

families that seemed to them morally, if not financially, inadequate to their tasks. From an administrator's perspective, there was no reason to penalize the unfortunate child for the fact of his parents' survival.

During these decades another type of caretaker institution became popular—the reformatory for disobedient children, the house of refuge. It took in several types of minors—the juvenile offender, convicted by a court for a petty crime, the wandering street arab, picked up by a town constable, and the willfully disobedient child, turned over by distraught parents. The reformatory, like the orphan asylum, maintained a flexible admissions policy, prepared to accept the commitment decisions of a judicial body, the less formal recommendations of overseers of the poor, or the personal inclinations of the head of a household. Its administrators expressed no fears about a possible miscarriage of justice and were disinclined to bring the protections of due process to these minors. A good dose of institutionalization could only work to the child's benefit.

Once again, the major eastern cities set the trend. New York philanthropists founded a house of refuge in 1825, and colleagues in Boston and Philadelphia followed suit within three years. The idea did not immediately spread to other urban areas, for most municipalities and state legislatures invested their funds first in multifunction orphan asylums. But by the 1840's specialization increased and houses of refuge appeared in Rochester, Cincinnati, and New Orleans; during the 1850's they opened in Providence, Baltimore, Pittsburgh, Chicago, and St. Louis as well. By 1857 the movement was broad enough to hold a national convention of refuge superintendents in New York.

Its first committee on statistics calculated that seventeen reformatories now operated, with a combined inmate population of over 20,000, a value in land and buildings of almost $2,000,000, and total annual expenditures of about $330,000. Here was another sizable investment in institutionalization.

Taken together, the admissions policies of child-care institutions were a catalogue of practically every misfortune that could befall a minor. The abject, the vagrant, the delinquent, the child of poverty-stricken or intemperate parents were all proper candidates for one or another asylum or refuge. Other practices did persist. One could still find minors confined to an almshouse or incarcerated in a local jail; smaller communities continued to rely upon apprenticeship to solve child-care problems. The new structures never won a monopoly. Nevertheless, they did become the model treatment for the homeless and delinquent. Like the mental hospital, penitentiary, and almshouse, they dominated the thinking of interested reformers, competing successfully for city-council, state-legislature, and philanthropic funds. The asylum and the refuge were two more bricks in the wall that Americans built to confine and reform the dangerous classes.

The founders of orphan asylums and houses of refuge shared fully with the proponents of other caretaker institutions a fear that anyone not carefully and diligently trained to cope with the open, free-wheeling, and disordered life of the community would fall victim to vice and crime. The orphan, robbed of his natural guardians, desperately needed protection against these dangers. Many children of the poor were in no better position, since their parents—at best too busy trying to eke out a living and at worst intemperate—provided no defense against corruption. The vagrant, by definition lacking in supervision, would certainly come under the sway of taverns, gambling halls, and theaters, the crowd of drunks, gamblers, thieves, and prostitutes. The nightmare come true, of course, was the juvenile delinquent, his behavior ample testimony to the speed and predictability of moral decline.

To counter these conditions, the asylum was shelter and sanctuary. Supporters pleaded vigorously and passionately for funds in order to snatch the child from the contagion of vice. The directors of the Orphan Society of Philadelphia asked patrons to endow a place where children of misfortune "are sheltered from the perils of want and the contamination of evil example." The Boston Children's Friend Society assumed the task of removing the sons and daughters of intemperate, depraved, and pauper parents as rapidly as possible "from those baleful influences which inevitably tend to make them pests to society, and ultimately the tenants of our prisons." A state reformatory in New Hampshire also defined its function in terms of "the separation of the young convict from society; his seclusion from vicious associates." And the managers of the Philadelphia House of Refuge, appealing for funds, boasted that visitors would find "the orphan, deserted or misguided child, shielded from the temptations of a sinful world."

But the asylum program had another, more important component—to train and rehabilitate its charges. It would not only shelter the orphan and delinquent, but discipline and reform them. Some philanthropic societies, it is true, limited their activities to rescuing the child from his poverty and giving him over to others, to a sea captain going on a lengthy whaling voyage, or to a country farmer needing another hand. For them, removal was a sufficient program. Many organizations, however, assumed a broader function, eager to carry out the tasks of child rearing. Starting afresh, they would organize a model routine, design and administer an upbringing that embodied the highest standards. In a manner clearly reminiscent of the mental hospital and the penitentiary, and to some degree of the almshouse as well, they expected to demonstrate the validity of general principles through the specific treatment of deviants and dependents. The experiment would rehabilitate the particular inmate and by exemplification spark the reform of the whole society.

This perspective dominated the asylum movement. Proponents insisted that the discipline at the Philadelphia House of Refuge would provide delinquents with "a healthy moral constitution, capable of resisting *the assaults of temptations, and strong enough to keep the line of rectitude through the stormy and disturbing influences by which we are continually assailed.*" This siege mentality united those attending the first national convention of house of refuge officials. They quickly formed a consensus around the sentiments expressed by Orlando Hastings, the delegate from the Rochester reformatory. Defining the fundamental purpose of the program, Hastings declared: "The object is not alone to make the boys behave well while in our charge; that is not difficult.... [But] any discipline... which does not enable the boy to *resist temptation* wherever and whenever he finds it, is ineffectual, and the whole object of houses of refuge is a failure." An even more elaborate rationale emerged in the reports of the Boston asylum. "There are," its managers explained, "two ways to aid in the redemption of society—one is to remove the sources of corruption, and the other is to remove the young from the temptations that exist." While some reformers chose to follow the first strategy, they were determined to adopt the second, "to enlighten their [inmates] minds, and aid them in forming virtuous habits, that they may finally go forth, *clothed as in invincible armour.*" Let others try to weaken the force of vice in the society. They would gird the young to withstand temptation.

Once again, the analysis which diagnosed an ostensibly desperate state of things also promised a sure remedy. Since the root of the problem lay in a faulty environment, the means for improvement were ready at hand, and asylum proponents were even more confident than their counterparts in other caretaker institutions of the prospects for success. Although all reformers assumed a plasticity of human nature that gave a logic to their efforts, asylum supporters felt themselves singularly fortunate: their clientele was young, especially impressionable, and not fixed in deviant or dependent behavior. "Youth," happily reported the governors of the Philadelphia House of Refuge, "is particularly susceptible of reform.... It has not yet felt the long continued pressure, which distorts its natural growth.... No habit can then be rooted so firmly as to refuse a cure." In the same spirit, the Boston Children's Friend Society looked forward to rehabilitating those "whose plastic natures may be molded into images of perfect beauty, or as perfect repulsiveness." And managers of the New York House of Refuge assumed that "the minds of children, naturally pliant, can, by early instruction, be formed and molded to our wishes." If the young were highly vulnerable to corruption, they were also eminently teachable.

Asylum proponents were not apprehensive about promoting the very vices they planned to eradicate. Overseers of the poor in this period anxiously wondered whether too comfortable an almshouse might inadvertently attract the lower classes, thereby promoting idleness; wardens also feared that a short sentence in a lax prison which coddled the criminal would increase recidivism. But child-care institutions were free of these concerns. Managers were confident that incarceration would not rob orphans of initiative—they were simply too young for that—or encourage their parents to avoid responsibility through commitment. And an indeterminate sentence to a house of refuge, for a term as long as the young offender's minority, could hardly be considered too lenient. Thus, without hesitation or qualification, they urged the new program.

At the core of the child-reformers' optimism was a faith completely shared by colleagues promoting other caretaker institutions: that a daily routine of strict and steady discipline would transform inmates' character. The asylum's primary task was to teach an absolute respect for authority through the establishment and enforcement of a rigorous and orderly routine. Obedience would bring reform. The function of the orphan asylum, according to Charleston, South Carolina, officials, was to train boys to a proper place in a community where "*systematic labor* of *order* and *regularity* established, and *discipline* enforced, are the social obligations." A strict training in accord with these virtues "disciplines them for... various walks of life," enabling them to become "practical men of business and good citizens, in the middle classes of society." The Boston Asylum and Farm School for destitute and vagrant children was dedicated to the same means and ends. These classes, managers told would-be donors, "have been received within the walls of a Christian asylum, where they have listened to good counsel, and acquired habits of *order, industry* and *usefulness....* We know not how anyone interested in the preservation of order or stability of government... can withhold his sympathy." Its annual reports regularly replayed this theme, noting that "it is almost astonishing how readily boys, hitherto accustomed to have their own way, and to dispute supremacy with inefficient or indulgent parents, are brought into habits of respect and order by a system of *uniformly firm discipline.*" The Boston asylum directors recognized fully the affinity between their program and that of other contemporary caretaker institutions. "A hospital for the insane," they announced, "has hardly greater superiority over the private family in regulating its inmates, in this respect, than the Farm School over the mis-government or no-government of the weak and careless parent."

The primacy of obedience and respect for authority in the process of rehabilitation was even more apparent in the institutions treating delinquents and vagrants. The New York Juvenile Asylum, serving these groups, put the matter aggressively. "We do not believe," announced its superintendent, "in the mawkish, sentimental and infidel philosophy of modern days, which discards the Bible method of disciplining the child into obedience.... It is manifest that but little good can be effected with all our appliances, unless order and obedience to establishment rules are vigilantly maintained.... What is needed for the children whom the law entrusts to us is the government of a well-ordered Christian household." Their neighbors at the New York House of Refuge agreed. Let inmates, officials declared, "be made tractable and obedient... [through] a vigorous course of moral and corporal discipline." With fidelity to this principle, the refuge superintendent argued that "the most benevolent and humane method for the management of children, is, to require prompt and implicit obedience." And to support his point he presented some sample cases. For one typical delinquent, the "discipline of the House was all that was requisite to make him obedient." For another, an especially refractory youngster bent on escaping, "it was found necessary to apply severe and continued punishments, in order to break the obstinacy of his spirit." Ultimately success came: "The discipline enforced had a most happy effect. He became submissive and obedient."

All child-care institutions made this strategy basic to their procedures. In an 1826 prospectus, the founders of the Philadelphia House of Refuge promised to return delinquents to society after "a course of rigid but not cruel or ignominious discipline." There would be "unrelenting supervision, mild but certain punishments for any infraction of the rules, and habits of quiet and good order at all times." They described with obvious pleasure a recent tour through the New York House of Refuge, taking particular delight in one scene: the children silently marching in file into Sunday chapel, sitting attentively and quietly through the service, and then leaving in an orderly line. Here they found an achievement worth emulating. A similar perspective won the general approval of the refuge superintendents meeting in national conference. As Orlando Hastings, the Rochester delegate, expressed it: asylum managers had to secure "the confidence and affection of those committed to their care"; otherwise they were not suitable governors. But this dictum had a very special meaning to Hastings and his audience, and he immediately explained it. "I am prepared further to say," he declared, "that the principle thing to be aimed at, and which must be secured, is obedience." Nothing was quite as pleasant to witness as "cheerful submission," compliance given with affection. However, there was no mistaking priorities; even if one had to resort regularly to punishing the child, obedience had to be won. And there was no need to worry about the possibly detrimental effects of such a policy. "After you establish the proposition in his mind that you are the ruler," Hastings complacently concluded, "he will look to you as his friend and benefactor, and you can cultivate his heart with ten-fold more effect." In this best of systems, authority bred friendship and admiration....

If fidelity to a doctrine could have guaranteed success, the antebellum orphan asylums and houses of refuge would have enjoyed remarkable achievements. Like the other caretaker institutions of the era, they too made isolation and order central to the design. Trustees and managers systematically attempted to remove and protect inmates from the corrupting influences of the community, to impose an exact and demanding schedule, and to enforce rules and regulations with strict and certain discipline. To these ends, they arranged admission policies and visiting rights, established daily activities, and meted out punishments. They translated a good part of prevailing theory into institutional reality.

The first element in the asylum superintendents' program was to abrogate parental authority and substitute their own. To bring the inmate under as absolute a control as possible, trustees characteristically insisted that the parent transfer to them all legal rights upon the child's admission. The requirement was a new one; the occasional colonial benevolent society that had housed dependent children did not attempt to erect legal barriers against parental intervention. Should a family's fortune improve, eighteenth-century officials willingly returned the youngster, at most asking for repayment for past expenses. But nineteenth-century institutions typically would brook no actual or potential interference. The orphan asylum in Philadelphia, for example, compelled destitute parents wishing to institutionalize a child to sign a pledge declaring: "I do hereby surrender to the Orphan Society of Philadelphia, the child A.B. to be provided for.... I will not demand or receive any compensation... or in any way interfere with the views or direction of the said society." The District of Columbia asylum was just as rigid. Under its act of incorporation relatives and friends did not have the right to remove an inmate before he reached the age of twenty-one. Managers insisted upon having the time and the freedom to effect a reformatory program....

The daily routine at the New York House of Refuge represented in slightly exaggerated form the kind of discipline and control that managers everywhere wished to exercise. Officials carefully organized a schedule for the 160 inmates, divided segments of time precisely, and used the house bells to announce each period. The first bells rang at sunrise to wake the youngsters, the second came fifteen minutes later to signal the guards to unlock the individual cells. The inmates stepped into the hallways and then, according to the managers' description, "marched in order to the washroom.... From the washroom they are called to parade in the open air (the weather permitting), where they arranged in ranks, and undergo close and critical inspection as to cleanliness and dress." Inmates next went in formation to chapel for prayer (it was the Sunday variant on this that so impressed the visitors from the Philadelphia refuge), and afterwards spent one hour in school. At seven o'clock the bells announced breakfast and then, a half hour later, the time to begin work. The boys spent till noon in the shops, usually making brass nails or cane seats, while the girls washed, cooked, made and mended the clothes. "At twelve o'clock," officials reported, "a bell rings to call all from work, and one hour is allowed for washing... and dinner.... At one o'clock, a signal is given for recommencing work, which continues till five in the afternoon, when the bell rings for the termination of the labor of the day." There followed thirty minutes to wash and to eat, two and one half hours of evening classes and, finally, to end the day, evening prayers. "The children," concluded the refuge account, "ranged in order, are then marched to the Sleeping Halls, where each takes possession of his separate apartment, and the cells are locked, and silence is enforced for the night." ...

Precision and regularity dominated other aspects of asylum life. Many institutions habitually drilled their inmates, organizing them in parade ranks and marching them up and down the field. "In one place," noted Lydia Child after a visit to the Long Island asylum, "I saw a stack of small wooden guns, and was informed that the boys were daily drilled to military exercises, as a useful means of

forming habits of order." She discovered that this drill-like quality had infected other parts of the institution, the infant school, and even the chapel. "I was informed," wrote Child, "that it was 'beautiful to see them pray; for at the first tip of the whistle, they all dropped on their knees.'" Her verdict on this asylum may well stand for the others: "Everything moves by machinery, as it always must with masses of children never subdivided into families."

The extraordinary emphasis of child-care institutions on obedience and authority was most apparent in their systems of classification and punishment. Houses of refuge in particular went to great lengths to enforce discipline, conceiving and administering elaborate programs. They depended first upon a highly intricate pattern of grading. Some institutions established four classes, others used seven—but the principle was constant. Superintendents assigned a new inmate to the bottom category and then, depending upon his subsequent behavior, promoted him. Every teacher, dormitory guard, and work supervisor had to file reports on each child's performance as a basis for rank, and the inmate wore a numbered badge on his arm to signify his standing. ...

Fundamental to the institutions' discipline was habitual and prompt punishment, so that inmates' infractions not only brought a mark in the grading system, but an immediate penalty as well. Corrections ranged from a deprivation of a usual privilege to corporal punishment, with various alternatives along the way. There was the loss of a play period, increased work load, a diet of bread and water, Coventry—with no one permitted to talk with the offender—solitary confinement in a special prison cell, wearing a ball and chain, the whip—and any one or two of these penalties could be combined with yet another and inflicted for varying lengths of time.

Given their perspective on discipline and order, managers openly admitted and vigorously defended strict punitive tactics. They quoted with predictable regularity Solomon's warnings on spoiling the child, insisting that although the rod should be saved for a last resort, it still had to be used. A resolution of the convention of refuge superintendents set out the creed most succinctly: "The first requisite from all inmates should be a strict obedience to the rules of the institution; and where moral suasion fails to produce the desired result, the more severe punishments of deprivation of meals, in part, and of recreation, and the infliction of corporal punishment should be resorted to: the latter only, however, in extreme cases." The superintendent of the Western House of Refuge at Pittsburgh made the matter a precondition for remaining in his post. "I advocate the judicious use of the rod," he announced. "So well am I convinced of its efficacy ... that I could not think of retaining my connection with such institutions, were the power of using it denied to me.... I never yet have seen the time when I thought the rod could be dispensed with." ...

To follow the metaphors of superintendents of asylums and refuges, the family was the model for institutional organization. Whether serving the poor or the orphan or the delinquent, they repeatedly described their operations in household terms. The Baltimore Home of the Friendless, for example, announced a determination to "see that the order and decorum of a well regulated Christian family be strictly observed." The tougher the clientele, the more elaborate

the family metaphor. The New York Juvenile Asylum insisted that "the government of the Institution has been strictly parental. The prominent object has been to give a home feeling and home interest to the children—to create and cultivate a family feeling ... to clothe the Institution as far as possible with those hallowed associations which usually cluster about home." The manager of the St. Louis Reform School was just as committed to this language. The refuge, he insisted, would succeed "by assimilating the government in Reformatories, as nearly as possible, to that of the *time-honored* institution which guided the infancy of nearly all the truly great and good men and women—that model, and often humble institution—the *family* ... 'God's University' ... the well-ordered Christian family."

But as is readily apparent, rhetoric and reality had little correspondence. Except for these public declarations, one would not have considered the family to be the model for the asylum. Rather, from all appearances, a military tone seems to have pervaded these institutions. Managers imposed on their charges a routine that was to resemble an army camp. They grouped inmates into large companies under a central administration, rather than establishing small familylike units under the individual care of surrogate parents. Inmates slept in separate cells or on cots in large dormitories, all neatly spaced and arranged in ways more reminiscent of orderly military barracks than of households. They ate silently in large refectories, using hand signals to communicate their needs, in a style that was much closer to an army mess than a family meal. They marched about the institution, stood in formation for head counts and public quizzes, and carried wooden guns in parades for recreation. They followed an exact schedule, responding to bells like recruits to a bugler's call. They wore uniforms with badges for insignias and grades for ranks. They learned to drop to one knee at the sound of a whistle, even making prayer into a military exercise. They obeyed rules of silence or suffered punishment. They took the whip like disobedient soldiers being flogged. If anyone escaped, or went AWOL, the ball and chain awaited him upon his return.

As surprising as it may seem, the superintendents saw no contradiction between their language and actions, no opposition between parading children in ranks while paying homage to the family. For they believed that they were offering a critique of the conduct of the antebellum family, and an alternative to it. In their view the family had to emulate the asylum as constituted —that is, put a greater premium on order, discipline, and obedience, not on domesticaffections, pampering the child, or indulging his every whim. The family did not need to march its members from bedroom to kitchen or keep children silent throughout a meal (although the adage did call for children to be seen and not heard), but parents were to exercise a firm and consistent authority and brook no willfulness. Thus, managers found no real divergence between the well-ordered asylum and the well-ordered family. The quasi-military quality of the institution was a rebuke and an example to the lax family. The problem was that parents were too lenient, not that the refuge or asylum were too strict. As long as the desideratum was order and discipline, as long as the virtues most in demand in child rearing were regularity and respect for authority, then the asylum was at least as effective a training center as the home. To the extent that the family neglected or overindulged or corrupted its members, the institution was a distinctly preferable setting.

POSTSCRIPT

Was Antebellum Reform Motivated Primarily by Humanitarian Goals?

The social-control school of thought, into which Rothman's essay could be placed, draws upon the works of Michel Foucault, Erving Goffman, Howard Becker, Thomas Szasz, and others. According to this interpretation, American reformers were more interested in serving their own interests than in providing assistance to mankind. As a result, middle- and upper-class reformers responding to momentous changes within their society imposed their standards of morality and order on the lower classes and, thus, denied the latter group freedom to act as a diverse set of individuals.

Ronald G. Walters, in *American Reformers, 1815–1860* (Hill & Wang, 1978), concludes that although many nineteenth-century reformers expressed sentiments that were self-serving and bigoted, their motivations were not based entirely upon a desire to control the lower classes. Rather, reformers were convinced that improvements could and should be made to help people. In this regard, the essays by Tyler and Rothman are in agreement.

The scholarly literature on the "age of reform" is extensive. Interested students should consult Timothy L. Smith, *Revivalism and Social Reform: American Protestantism on the Eve of the Civil War* (Harper & Row, 1957); Whitney R. Cross, *The Burned-Over District: The Social and Intellectual History of Enthusiastic Religion in Western New York, 1800–1850* (Cornell University Press, 1950); and Clifford S. Griffin, *Their Brothers' Keepers: Moral Stewardship in the United States, 1800–1865* (Rutgers University Press, 1960). David Brion Davis, ed., *Ante-Bellum Reform* (Harper & Row, 1967), is an excellent collection of readings. The social-control thesis can be traced for various reform endeavors in Joseph R. Gusfield, *Symbolic Crusade: Status Politics and the American Temperance Movement* (University of Illinois Press, 1966); Michael B. Katz, *The Irony of Early School Reform: Education and Innovation in Mid-Nineteenth Century Massachusetts* (Beacon Press, 1968); Joseph M. Harris, *Children in Urban Society: Juvenile Delinquency in Nineteenth-Century America* (Oxford University Press, 1971); and Gerald Grob, *Mental Institutions in America: Social Policy to 1875* (Free Press, 1973). For some of the aspects of American reform generally dismissed by Tyler as "fads," see John D. Davies, *Phrenology, Fad and Science: A Nineteenth-Century American Crusade* (Yale University Press, 1955), and Ronald L. Numbers, *Prophetess of Health: A Study of Ellen G. White* (Harper & Row, 1976).

ISSUE 11

Did Slaves Exercise Religious Autonomy?

YES: Albert J. Raboteau, from "Slave Autonomy and Religion," *Journal of Religious Thought* (Fall 1981/Winter 1982)

NO: John B. Boles, from "Introduction," in John B. Boles, ed., *Masters and Slaves in the House of the Lord: Race and Religion in the American South, 1740–1870* (University Press of Kentucky, 1988)

ISSUE SUMMARY

YES: Professor of history Albert J. Raboteau claims that the religious activities of American slaves were characterized by institutional and personal independence, which undermined the ability of the masters to exercise effective control over their chattel property.

NO: Professor of history John B. Boles recognizes that slaves often worshiped apart from their masters, but he asserts that the primary religious experience of southern slaves occurred within a biracial setting in churches dominated by whites.

Since the mid-1950s, few issues in American history have generated more interest among scholars than the institution of slavery. Books and articles analyzing the treatment of slaves, comparative slave systems, the profitability of slavery, slave rebelliousness (or lack thereof), urban slavery, the slave family, and slave religion abound. This proliferation of scholarship, stimulated in part by the civil rights movement, contrasts sharply with the amount of historical literature written on slavery between the two world wars, a time that was monopolized by a single book—Ulrich B. Phillips's apologetic and blatantly racist *American Negro Slavery* (1918).

Phillips, a native Georgian who taught for most of his career at Yale University, based his sweeping view of the southern slave system upon plantation records left by some of the wealthiest slave owners. He concluded that American slavery was a benign institution controlled by paternalistic masters. These owners, Phillips insisted, rarely treated their bond servants cruelly but, instead, provided their childlike, acquiescent human property with food, clothing, housing, and other necessities of life.

Although black historians such as George Washington Williams, W. E. B. Du Bois, Carter G. Woodson, and John Hope Franklin produced scholarly works that emphasized the brutal impact of slavery, their views received almost no consideration from the wider academic community. Consequently, recognition of a "revisionist" interpretation of slavery was delayed until the post–World War II era when, in the wake of the *Brown* desegregation case, Kenneth Stampp, a white northern historian, published *The Peculiar Institution* (1956). Stampp also focused primarily upon antebellum plantation records, but his conclusions were literally a point-by-point rebuttal of the Phillips thesis. The institution of slavery, he said, was a harsh, oppressive system in which slave owners controlled their servants through fear of the lash. Further, in contrast to the image of the passive, happy-go-lucky "Sambo" described by Phillips, Stampp argued that slaves were "a troublesome property" who resisted their enslavement in subtle as well as overt ways.

In 1959, Stanley Elkins synthesized these seemingly contradictory interpretations in his controversial study *Slavery: A Problem in American Institutional and Intellectual Life*. Elkins clearly accepted Stampp's emphasis on the harshness of the slave system by hypothesizing that slavery was a "closed" system in which masters dominated their slaves in the same way that Nazi concentration camp guards in World War II had controlled the lives of their prisoners. Such an environment, he insisted, generated severe psychological dysfunctions that produced the personality traits of Phillips's "Sambo" character type.

As the debate over the nature of slavery moved into the 1960s and 1970s, several scholars, seeking to provide a history of the institution "from the bottom up," began to focus upon the slaves themselves. Interviews with former slaves had been conducted in the 1920s and 1930s under the auspices of Southern University in Louisiana, Fisk University in Tennessee, and the Federal Writers Project of the Works Progress Administration. Drawing upon these interviews and previously ignored slave autobiographies, sociologist George Rawick and historians John Blassingame and Eugene D. Genovese, among others, portrayed a multifaceted community life over which slaves held a significant degree of influence. This community, which operated beyond the view of the "Big House," was, according to Genovese, "the world the slaves made."

These contrasting interpretive currents are reflected in the following essays on the nature of slave religion. In the first selection, Albert J. Raboteau describes the ways in which the acceptance of Christianity produced numerous opportunities for slaves to assume control over their own religious activities, which led to an autonomy that permitted slaves to resist some of the dehumanizing elements of the slave system. John B. Boles admits that slaves in the antebellum South worshiped in a variety of ways (in independent black churches, plantation chapels, or informal, secret gatherings), but he concludes that the typical site for slave religious activities was the church of their masters.

YES
Albert J. Raboteau

SLAVE AUTONOMY AND RELIGION

One of the perennial questions in the historical study of American slavery is the question of the relationship between Christianity and the response of slaves to enslavement. Did the Christian religion serve as a tool in the hands of slaveholders to make slaves docile or did it serve in the hands of slaves as a weapon of resistance and even outright rebellion against the system of slavery? Let us acknowledge from the outset that the role of religion in human motivation and action is very complex; let us recognize also that Christianity played an ambiguous role in the stances which slaves took toward slavery, sometimes supporting resistance, sometimes accommodation. That much admitted, much more remains to be said. Specifically, we need to trace the convoluted ways in which the egalitarian impulse within Christianity overflowed the boundaries of the master-slave hierarchy, creating unexpected channels of slave autonomy on institutional as well as personal levels. To briefly sketch out some of the directions which religious autonomy took among slaves in the antebellum South is the purpose of this essay.

INSTITUTIONAL AUTONOMY

From the beginning of the Atlantic slave trade in the fifteenth century, European Christians claimed that the conversion of slaves to Christianity justified the enslavement of Africans. For more than four centuries Christian apologists for slavery would repeat this religious rationalization for one of history's greatest atrocities. Despite the justification of slavery as a method of spreading the gospel, the conversion of slaves was not a top priority for colonial planters. One of the principal reasons for the refusal of British colonists to allow their slaves religious instruction was the fear that baptism would require the manumission of their slaves, since it was illegal to hold a fellow Christian in bondage. This dilemma was solved quickly by colonial legislation stating that baptism did not alter slave status. However, the most serious obstacle to religious instruction of the slaves could not be legislated away. It was the slaveholder's deep-seated uneasiness at the prospect of a slave laying claim to Christian fellowship with his master. The concept of equality, though only

Excerpted from Albert J. Raboteau, "Slave Autonomy and Religion," *Journal of Religious Thought*, vol. 38 (Fall 1981/Winter 1982), pp. 51–64. Copyright © 1981 by *Journal of Religious Thought*. Reprinted by permission. Notes omitted.

spiritual, between master and slave threatened the stability of the system of slave control. Christianity, complained the masters, would ruin slaves by allowing them to think themselves equal to white Christians. Far worse was the fear, supported by the behavior of some Christian slaves, that religion would make them rebellious. In order to allay this fear, would-be missionaries to the slaves had to prove that Christianity would make better slaves. By arguing that Christian slaves would become obedient to their masters out of duty to God and by stressing the distinction between spiritual equality and worldly equality, the proponents of slave conversion in effect built a religious foundation to support slavery. Wary slaveholders were assured by missionaries that "Scripture, far from making an Alteration in Civil Rights, expressly directs, *that every Man abide in the Condition wherein he is called, with great Indifference of Mind* concerning outward circumstances."

In spite of missionary efforts to convince them that Christianity was no threat to the slave system, slaveowners from the colonial period on down to the Civil War remained suspicious of slave religion as a two-edged sword. Clerical assurances aside, the masters' concern was valid. Religious instruction for slaves had more than spiritual implications. No event would reveal these implications as clearly as the series of religious revivals called the Great Awakenings which preceded and followed the Revolution. The impact of revival fervor would demonstrate how difficult it was to control the egalitarian impulse of Christianity within safe channels.

The first Great Awakening of the 1740s swept the colonies with the tumultuous preaching and emotional conversions of revivalistic, evangelical Protestantism. Accounts by Whitefield, Tennent, Edwards, and other revivalists made special mention of the fact that blacks were flocking to hear the message of salvation in hitherto unseen numbers. Not only were free blacks and slaves attending revivals in significant numbers, they were taking active part in the services as exhorters and preachers. The same pattern of black activism was repeated in the rural camp meetings of the Great Awakening of the early nineteenth century.

The increase in slave conversions which accompanied the awakenings was due to several factors. The evangelical religion spread by the revivalists initiated a religious renaissance in the South where the majority of slaves lived. The revival became a means of church extension, especially for Methodists and Baptists. The mobility of the Methodist circuit rider and the local independence of the Baptist preacher were suited to the needs of the rural South. Among the Southerners swelling the ranks of these denominations, were black as well as white converts.

Moreover, the ethos of the revival meeting, with its strong emphasis upon emotional preaching and congregational response, not only permitted ecstatic religious behavior but encouraged it. Religious exercises, as they were termed, including fainting, jerking, barking, and laughing a "holy laugh," were a common, if spectacular, feature of revivals. In this heated atmosphere slaves found sanction for an outward expression of religious emotion consonant with their tradition of danced religion from Africa. While converting to belief in a "new" God, slaves were able to worship in ways hauntingly similar to those of old.

Extremely important for the development of black participation in revival religion was the intense concentration upon individual inward conversion which fostered an inclusiveness that could become egalitarianism. Evangelicals did not hesitate to preach to racially mixed congregations and had no doubt about the capacity of slaves to share the experience of conversion to Christ. Stressing plain doctrine and emotional preaching, emphasizing the conversion experience instead of religious instruction, made Christianity accessible to illiterate slave and slaveholder alike. The criterion for preachers was not seminary training but evidence of a converted heart and gifted tongue. Therefore, when an awakened slave showed talent for preaching, he preached, and not only to black congregations. The tendency of evangelical Protestantism to level the souls of all men before God reached its logical conclusion when blacks preached to and converted whites.

By the last quarter of the eighteenth century a cadre of black preachers had begun to emerge. Some of these pioneer black ministers were licensed, some not; some were slaves, others free. During the 1780s a black man named Lewis preached to crowds as large as four hundred in Westmoreland County, Virginia. Harry Hosier traveled with Methodist leaders, Asbury, Coke, Garretson, and Whatcoat and was reportedly such an eloquent preacher that he served as a "drawing card" to attract larger crowds of potential converts, white and black. In 1792 the mixed congregation of the Portsmouth, Virginia Baptist Church selected a slave, Josiah Bishop, as pastor, after purchasing his freedom and also his family's. Another black preacher, William Lemon, pastored a white Baptist church in Gloucester County, Virginia, for a time at the turn of the century.

In 1798, Joseph Willis, a freeman, duly licensed as a Baptist preacher, began his ministry in southwest Mississippi and Louisiana. He formed Louisiana's first Baptist church at Bayou Chicot in 1812 and served as its pastor. After developing several other churches in the area, he became the first moderator of the Louisiana Baptist Association in 1818. Uncle Jack, an African-born slave, joined the Baptist church and in 1792 began to preach in Nottoway County, Virginia. White church members purchased his freedom and he continued to preach for over forty years. Henry Evans, a free black licensed as a local preacher by the Methodists, was the first to bring Methodist preaching to Fayetteville, North Carolina. Initially preaching to black people only, he attracted the attention of several prominent whites and eventually the white membership of his congregation increased until the blacks were crowded out of their seats. Evans was eventually replaced by a white minister, but continued to serve as an assistant in the church he had founded until his death.

That black preachers should exhort, convert, and even pastor white Christians in the slave South was certainly antithetical to the premise of slave control. Though such occasions were rare, they were the ineluctable result of the impulse unleashed by revivalistic religion. Of greater importance for the development of autonomy in the religious life of slaves was the fact that black preachers, despite threats of punishment, continued to preach to slaves and in some few cases even founded churches. An early historian of the Baptists applauded the anonymous but effective ministry of these black preachers:

Among the African Baptists in the Southern states there are a multitude of preachers and exhorters whose names do not appear on the minutes of the associations. They preach principally on the plantations to those of their own color, and their preaching though broken and illiterate, is in many cases highly useful.

Several "African" Baptist churches sprang up before 1800. Some of these black congregations were independent to the extent that they called their own pastors and officers, joined local associations with white Baptist churches, and sent their own delegates to associational meetings. Though the separate black church was primarily an urban phenomenon, it drew upon surrounding rural areas for its membership, which consisted of both free blacks and slaves. Sometimes these black churches were founded amidst persecution. Such was the case with the African Baptist Church of Williamsburg, Virginia, whose history was chronicled in 1810:

This church is composed almost, if not altogether of people of colour. Moses, a black man, first preached among them, and was often taken up and whipped, for holding meetings. Afterwards Gowan Pamphlet ... became popular among the blacks, and began to baptize, as well as to preach. It seems, the association had advised that no person of colour should be allowed to preach, on the pain of excommunication; against this regulation, many of the blacks were rebellious, and continued still to hold meetings. Some were excluded, and among this number was Gowan.... Continuing still to preach and many professing faith under his ministry, not being in connexion with any church himself, he formed a kind of church out of some who had been baptized, who, sitting with him, received such as offered

themselves; Gowan baptized them, and was moreover appointed their pastor; some of them knowing how to write, a churchbook was kept; they increased to a large number; so that in the year 1791, the Dover association, stat[ed] their number to be about five hundred. The association received them, so far, as to appoint persons to visit them and set things in order. These making a favourable report, they were received, and have associated ever since.

Several features of this narrative deserve emphasis as significant examples of black religious autonomy. Ignoring the threat of excommunication, not to mention physical punishment, blacks rebelled against white religious control and insisted on holding their own meetings, led by their own ministers. They gathered their own church, apparently according to the norms of Baptist polity, accepted their own members, kept their own minutes, and finally succeeded in joining the local association, all the while growing to a membership of five hundred by 1791!

In Savannah, Georgia, a slave named Andrew Bryan established an African Baptist Church, against white objection and persecution. In 1790, Bryan's church included two hundred and twenty-five full communicants and approximately three hundred and fifty converts, many of whom did not have their masters' permission to be baptized. In 1803, a Second African Church of Savannah was organized from the first, and a few years later a third came into being. Both of the new churches were led by black pastors. After Bryan's death, his nephew, Andrew Marshall, became pastor of the First African Church and by 1830 his congregation had increased in size to two thousand, four hundred and seventeen members.

The labors of these early black preachers and their successors were crucial in the formation of slave religion. In order to adequately understand the development of Christianity among the slaves, we must realize that slaves learned Christianity not only from whites but from other slaves as well. Slave preachers, exhorters, and church-appointed watchmen instructed their fellow slaves, nurtured their religious development, and brought them to conversion in some cases without the active involvement of white missionaries or masters at all. The early independence of black preachers and churches was curtailed as the antebellum period wore on, particularly in periods of reaction to slave conspiracies, when all gatherings of blacks for whatever purpose were viewed with alarm. For slaves to participate in the organization, leadership, and governance of church structures was perceived as dangerous. Surely it was inconsistent, argued the guardians of the system, to allow blacks such authority. As the prominent South Carolinian planter, Charles Cotesworth Pinkney, declared before the Charleston Agricultural Society in 1829, the exercise of religious prerogatives left slaves too free from white control. "We look upon the habit of Negro preaching as a widespreading evil; not because a black man cannot be a good one, but . . . because they acquire an influence independent of the owner, and not subject to his control. . . . When they have possessed this power, they have been known to make an improper use of it." No doubt, Pinkney and his audience had in mind the African Methodist Church of Charleston which had served as a seedbed of rebellion for the Denmark Vesey conspiracy of 1822. (Following discovery of the plot, whites razed the church to the ground.)

Regardless of periodic harassment by civil and ecclesiastical authorities, black preachers continued to preach and separate black churches continued to be organized. Just as Pinkney and others warned, in preaching and in church life some blacks found channels for self-expression and self-governance. To be sure, the exercise of such autonomy was frequently modified by white supervision, but it was nonetheless real. In various sections of the antebellum South, black churches kept gathering members, over the years swelling in size to hundreds and in a few instances thousands of members. Certainly, the vast majority of slaves attended churches under white control. However, even in racially mixed churches some black Christians found opportunities to exercise their spiritual gifts and a measure of control over their religious life. This was so especially in Baptist churches because Baptist polity required that each congregation govern itself. In some churches committees of black members were constituted to oversee their own conduct. These committees listened to black applicants relate their religious experience and heard the replies of members charged with moral laxity. Meeting once a month, committees of "brethren in black" conducted business, reported their recommendations to the general meeting and gave to black church members experience in church governance. This experience laid a foundation upon which freedmen would rapidly build their own independent churches after emancipation.

Hampered though it was, the exercise of religious autonomy among slaves was a fact of antebellum life. It was due to the nature of the revival fervor of the Great Awakenings of the eighteenth and early nineteenth centuries which first brought the slaves to conversion in large numbers and also created a situation in which it became possible for black freemen and slaves to preach and even pastor. (By way of contrast, these avenues to spiritual authority would not open for blacks in either the Church of England or the Roman Catholic Church for a long time to come.) To the extent possible, then, black Christians proved not at all reluctant about deciding their own religious affairs and managing their own religious institutions. For the vast majority of slaves, however, institutional religious autonomy was not possible. This did not stop them from seeking religious independence from whites in more secretive ways.

PERSONAL AUTONOMY

Like their colonial predecessors, antebellum missionaries to the slaves had to face objections from whites that religion for slaves was dangerous. Beginning in the 1820s, a movement led by prominent clerics and laymen attempted to mold southern opinion in support of missions to the slaves. Plantation missionaries created an ideal image of the Christian plantation, built upon the mutual observance of duties by masters and by slaves. One leader of the plantation mission stated the movement's basic premise when he predicted that "religious instruction of the Negroes will *promote our own morality and religion*." For, when "one class rises, so will the other; the two are so associated they are apt to rise or fall together. Therefore, servants do well by your masters and masters do well by your servants." In this premise lay a serious fallacy; for while the interests of master and slave occasionally coincided, they could never cohere. No matter how devoted master

was to the ideal of a Christian plantation, no matter how pious he might be, the slave knew that the master's religion did not countenance the slaves' freedom in this world.

Precisely because the interests of master and slave extended only so far and no further, there was a dimension of the slaves' religious life that was secret. The disparity between the master's ideal of religion on the plantation and that of the slaves led the slaves to gather secretly in the quarters or in brush arbors (aptly named hush harbors) where they could pray, preach, and sing, free from white control. Risking severe punishment, slaves disobeyed their masters and stole off under cover of secrecy to worship as they saw fit. Here it was that Christianity was fitted to their own peculiar experience.

It was the slaveholding gospel preached to them by master's preacher which drove many slaves to seek true Christian preaching at their own meetings. "Church was what they called it," recalled former slave Charlie Van Dyke, "but all that preacher talked about was for us slaves to obey our masters and not to lie and steal." To attend secret meetings was in itself an act of resistance against the will of the master and was punished as such. In the face of the absolute authority of the Divine Master, the authority of the human master shrank. Slaves persisted in their hush harbor meetings because there they found consolation and communal support, tangible relief from the exhaustion and brutality of work stretching from "day clean" to after dark, day in and day out. "Us niggers," remarked Richard Carruthers, describing a scene still vivid in his memory many years later, "used to have a prayin' ground down in the hollow and sometimes we come out of the field... scorchin' and burnin' up with nothin' to eat, and we wants to ask the good Lawd to have mercy.... We takes a pine torch... and goes down in the hollow to pray. Some gits so joyous they starts to holler loud and we has to stop up they mouth. I see niggers git so full of the Lawd and so happy they draps unconscious."

In the hush harbor slaves sought not only substantive preaching and spiritual consolation they also talked about and prayed for an end to their physical bondage. "I've heard them pray for freedom," declared one former slave. "I thought it was foolishness then, but the old time folks always felt they was to be free. It must have been something 'vealed unto 'em. Though some might be skeptical, those slaves who were confident that freedom would come, since God had revealed it, were able to cast their lives in a different light. Hope for a brighter future irradiated the darkness of the present. Their desire for freedom in this world was reaffirmed in the songs, prayers, and sermons of the hush harbor. This was just what the master—those who didn't believe in prayer, as well as those who did —tried to prevent. The external hush harbor symbolized an internal resistance, a private place at the core of the slaves' religious life which they claimed as their own and which, in the midst of bondage, could not be controlled.

For evangelical Christians, black or white, full admission into membership in the church required that the candidate give credible testimony about the inner workings of the Spirit upon his or her heart. The conversion experience, as described by ex-slaves, was typically a visionary one, inaugurated by feelings of sadness and inner turmoil. Frequently the individual "convicted of sin" envisioned Hell and realized that he was destined for damnation. Suddenly, the sinner was rescued from this danger and led to a vision of Heaven by an emissary from God. Ushered into God's presence, the person learned that he was not damned but saved. Awakening, the convert realized that he was now one of the elect and overwhelmed with the joyful feeling of being "made new" shouted out his happiness. For years afterwards, this "peak" experience remained a fixed point of identity and value in the convert's life. He knew that he was saved, and he knew it not just theoretically but experientially. Confident of their election and their value in the eyes of God, slaves who underwent conversion, gained in this radical experience a deeply rooted identity which formed the basis for a sense of purpose and an affirmation of self-worth— valuable psychic barriers to the demeaning and dehumanizing attacks of slavery.

Conversion, as an experience common to white and black Christians, occasionally led to moments of genuine emotional contact, in which the etiquette of racial relationships was forgotten. A dramatic instance of one such occasion was recounted by a former slave named Morte:

One day while in the field plowing I heard a voice... I looked but saw no one... Everything got dark, and I was unable to stand any longer... With this I began to cry, Mercy! Mercy! Mercy! As I prayed an angel came and touched me, and I looked new... and there came a soft voice saying, "My little one, I have loved you with an everlasting love. You are this day made alive and freed from hell. You are a chosen vessel unto the Lord."... I must have been in this trance more than an hour. I went on to the barn and found my master waiting for me.... I began to tell him of my experiences... My master sat watching and listening to me, and then he began to cry. He turned from me and said in a broken voice, "Morte I believe you are a preacher. From now on you can preach to the people here on my place... But tomorrow morning, Sunday, I want to preach to my family and my neighbors."... The next morning at the time appointed I stood up on two planks in front of the porch of the big house and, without a Bible or anything, I began to preach to my master and the people. My thoughts came so fast that I could hardly speak fast enough. My soul caught on fire, and soon I had them all in tears... I told them that they must be born again and that their souls must be freed from the shackles of hell.

The spectacle of a slave reducing his master to tears by preaching to him of his enslavement to sin certainly suggests that religion could bend human relationships into interesting shapes despite the iron rule of slavery. Morte's power over his master was spiritual and (as far as we know) it was temporary. It was also effective.

While commonality of religious belief might lead to moments of religious reciprocity between blacks and whites, by far the more common relationship, from the slaves' side, was one of alienation from the hypocrisy of slaveholding Christians. As Frederick Douglass put it, "Slaves knew enough of the orthodox theology of the time to consign all bad slaveholders to hell." On the same point, Charles Ball commented that in his experience slaves thought that heaven would not be heaven unless slaves could be avenged on their enemies. "A fortunate and kind master or mistress, may now and then be admitted into heaven, but this rather as a matter of favour, to the intercession of some slave, than as a matter of strict justice to the

whites, who will, by no means, be of an equal rank with those who shall be raised from the depths of misery in this world." Ball concluded that "The idea of a revolution in the conditions of the whites and blacks, is the cornerstone of the religion of the latter...."

Slaves had no difficulty distinguishing the gospel of Christianity from the religion of their masters. Ex-slave Douglas Dorsey reported that after the minister on his plantation admonished the slaves to honor their masters whom they could see as they would God whom they could not see, the driver's wife who could read and write a little would say that the minister's sermon "was all lies." Charles Colcock Jones, plantation missionary, found that his slave congregation did not hesitate to reject the doctrine preached in a sermon he gave in 1833:

I was preaching to a large congregation on the *Epistle of Philemon*: and when I insisted upon fidelity and obedience as Christian virtues in servants and upon the authority of Paul, condemned the practice of *running away*, one half of my audience deliberately rose up and walked off with themselves, and those that remained looked any thing but satisfied, either with the preacher or his doctrine. After dismission, there was no small stir among them: some solemnly declared "that there was no such Epistle in the Bible;" others, "that I preached to please the masters;" others, "that it was not the Gospel;" others, "that they did not care if they ever heard me preach again!"... There were some too, who had strong objections against me as a Preacher, because I was a *master*, and said, "his people have to work as well as we."

The slaves' rejection of white man's religion was clearly revealed in their attitudes toward morality. While white preachers repeated the command, "Do not steal," slaves simply denied that this precept allied to them since they themselves were stolen property. Josephine Howard put the argument this way: "Dey allus done tell us it am wrong to lie and steal, but why did de white folks steal my mammy and her mammy... Dat de sinfulles' stealin' dey is." Rachel Fairley demanded, "How could they help but steal when they didn't have nothin'? You didn't eat if you didn't steal." Henry Bibb declared that under slavery "I had a just right to what I took, because it was the labor of my hands." Other slaves concluded that it was not morally possible for one piece of property to steal another since both belonged to the same owner: it was merely a case of taking something out of one tub and putting it in another. This view of stealing referred only to master's goods, however, for a slave to steal from another slave was seriously wrong. As the saying went, "a slave that will steal from a slave is called *mean as master*." Or as one ex-slave remarked, "This is the lowest comparison slaves know how to use: 'just as mean as white folks.' "

Not all slaves, however, were able to distinguish master's religion from authentic Christianity, and were led to reject this religion totally. In 1839, Daniel Alexander Payne explained how this could happen:

The slaves are sensible of the oppression exercised by their masters; and they see these masters on the Lord's day worshipping in his holy Sanctuary. They hear their masters professing Christianity; they see their masters preaching the gospel; they hear these masters praying in their families, and they know that oppression and slavery are inconsistent with the Christian religion; therefore they scoff at religion itself—mock their masters, and distrust both the goodness and justice of God.

Frederick Douglass too remembered being shaken by "doubts arising... from the sham religion which everywhere prevailed" under slavery, doubts which "awakened in my mind a distrust of all religion and the conviction that prayers were unavailing and delusive." Unable to account for the evil of slavery in a world ruled by a just God, some slaves abandoned belief. "I pretended to profess religion one time," recalled one former slave, "I don't hardly know what to think about religion. They say God killed the just and unjust; I don't understand that part of it. It looks hard to think that if you ain't done nothing in the world you be punished just like the wicked. Plenty folks went crazy trying to get that straightened out." There is no way of estimating how many slaves felt these doubts, but they indicate how keenly aware slaves were of the disparity between the gospel of Christ and what they termed "white man's religion."

At the opposite extreme from the agnostic slave was the slave who developed a life of exemplary Christian virtue which placed him in a position of moral superiority over his master. William Grimes, for example, was possessed of a sense of righteousness which led him to take a surprising attitude toward his master when punished for something he had not done:

It grieved me very much to be blamed when I was innocent. I knew I had been faithful to him, perfectly so. At this time I was quite serious, and used constantly to pray to my God. I would not lie nor steal.... When I considered him accusing me of stealing, when I was so innocent, and had endeavored to make him satisfied by every means in my power, that I was so, but he still persisted in disbelieving me, I then said to myself, if this thing is done in a green tree what must be done in a dry? I forgave my master in my own heart for all this, and prayed to God to forgive him and turn his heart.

Grimes is of course alluding to the sacrifice of Christ and identifying himself with the innocent suffering servant who spoke the words concerning green and dry wood on his way to death on Calvary. From this vantage point Grimes is able to forgive his master. Note however the element of threat implied in the question, "if this thing is done in a green tree (to the innocent) what must be done in a dry (to the guilty)?" Those who are guilty of persecuting the innocent, like Grimes's master, will be judged and punished. (The full context of the biblical allusion includes a terrifying prediction of the destruction of Jerusalem.) What did it mean to Grimes's self-image to be able to have moral leverage by which he might elevate his own dignity. A similar impulse lay behind the comment of Mary Younger, a fugitive slave in Canada, "if those slaveholders were to come here, I would treat them well, just to shame them by showing that I had humanity." To asset one's humanity in the face of slavery's power to dehumanize, perhaps explained Grimes's careful adherence to righteousness, a righteousness which might at first glance seem merely servile.

CONCLUSION

In the slave society of the antebellum South, as in most societies, the Christian religion both supported and undermined the status quo. On the one hand, Nat Turner claimed that God's will moved

him to slaughter whites, on the other, "good" slaves protected their masters out of a sense of duty. Slave religion, however was more complex than these alternatives suggest. Institutionally, the egalitarian impulse of evangelical Protestantism, leveling all men before God and lifting some up to declare his word with power and authority, gave slaves and free blacks the opportunity to exercise leadership. Usually this leadership was not revolutionary and from the perspective of political strategy it was overwhelmingly conservative. Yet political action is not the only measure of resistance to oppression. Despite political impotence, the black preacher was still a figure of power as an unmistakable symbol of the talent and ability of black men, a fact which contradicted the doctrine of inherent black inferiority. As white slaveholders occasionally recognized, black preachers were anomalous, if not dangerous, persons under the system of slave control precisely because their authority could not be effectively limited by whites.

Nor were slaveowners able to control the spirit of religious independence once it had been imbibed by their slaves. Continually this spirit sought to break out of the strictures confining slave life. When possible, it sought expression in separate institutions controlled by blacks. When that proved impossible, it found expression in secret religious gatherings "out from under the eye of the master." In both cases, the internal autonomy of the slave's own moral will prove[d] impossible to destroy. Throughout the history of Christianity, earthly rulers (civil and religious) have been troubled by the claim that individuals owed obedience to a higher authority than their own. Antebellum slaveholders and missionaries faced the same problem.

When slaves disobeyed their masters in order to obey God, a long tradition of Christian heroism validated their assertion of human freedom.

The emotional ecstasy of slave religion has been criticized as compensatory and otherworldly, a distraction from the evils of this world. And so it was. But it was much more. Individually, slaves found not only solace in their religion but, particularly in the conversion experience, a source of personal identity and value. Collectively, slaves found in the archetypical symbol of biblical Israel their identity as a community, a new chosen people bound for Divine deliverance from bondage. From this communal identity mutual support, meaning, and hope derived. In the ecstasy of religious performance individual and communal identity and values were dramatically reaffirmed time and time again. In the hand-clapping, footstomping, headshaking fervor of the plantation praisehouse, the slaves, in prayer, sermon, and song, fit Christianity to their own peculiar experience and in the process resisted, even transcended the dehumanizing bonds of slavery.

NO

John B. Boles

MASTERS AND SLAVES IN THE
HOUSE OF THE LORD

Race and religion have probably always been controversial topics in the South, as elsewhere, particularly when their intersection has called into question widely accepted folkways about the place of blacks in southern society. Different interpreters have suggested that the South has been haunted by God and preoccupied with race, so perhaps we should not expect a scholarly consensus on how the two intertwined in the decades from the Great Awakening to Reconstruction. The last generation of our own times has witnessed a remarkable burst of scholarship on blacks and race relations in the region and a similar if not quite as prolific discovery of southern religious history....

Most laypersons today seem completely unaware that a century and a half ago many churches in the Old South had significant numbers of black members: black and white co-worshipers heard the same sermons, were baptized and took communion together, and upon death were buried in the same cemeteries. Such practices seem inconceivable today, when the old cliché that Sunday morning at 11:00 A.M. is the most segregated hour in America still rings true. When I was a boy in the rural South thirty years ago, we all supported the Lottie Moon Christmas offering to send missionaries to convert the "heathen" in Africa and elsewhere, but the church deacons and the congregation would have been scandalized had one of the black converts traveled from Africa expecting to worship with us. Yet a century earlier biracial attendance at Baptist churches like ours was the norm in the rural South.

Blacks worshiped in a variety of ways, and some did not participate in any Christian worship, for, especially in the colonial period, a smattering of blacks practiced Islam and others clung tenaciously to traditional African religions. All non-Christian religious activity was discouraged by most slaveowners, who were as ethnocentric as they were concerned about the potential for unrest and rebellion they sensed in their slaves' participation in what to whites were strange and exotic rites. In addition, many slaveowners in the seventeenth and eighteenth centuries were hesitant to attempt to convert their bondspeople to Christianity—if they themselves were Christians—out

From John B. Boles, "Introduction," in John B. Boles, ed., *Masters and Slaves in the House of the Lord: Race and Religion in the American South, 1740–1870* (University Press of Kentucky, 1988). Copyright © 1988 by University Press of Kentucky. Reprinted by permission. Notes omitted.

of fear that conversion might loosen the ties of their bondage. The English knew of slavery long before they had any New World settlements and had considered it a backward institution that might be promoted by Catholic Spain but not by the England of Elizabeth. Even so, the English believed that certain persons might be held in bondage—convicted felons, war prisoners, in some cases heathens, that is, nonbelievers in Christianity. It took several generations before Englishmen in the North American mainland colonies came to accept the practicality of African slavery, then argue the necessity of it, and finally surpass their Spanish rivals in its applications. To the extent that they needed any noneconomic justification, they assumed that the Africans not being Christians made it morally acceptable to enslave them. But if Africans' "heathenism" justified making them slaves, would not their conversion at the very least call into question the rightness of keeping them in bondage? On at least several occasions in the seventeenth century blacks had won their freedom in court by proving they had been baptized. Hence any moral uneasiness that might have existed among less-than-devout slaveowners for not sharing the gospel with their slaves was entirely overcome by their uneasiness about the stability of their work force should they do so. To clarify this ambiguity obliging laws were passed in the late seventeenth century specifying that a person's "civil state" would not be affected by his conversion to Christianity....

Yet despite the difficulties inherent in converting the slaves—the whites' hesitancy to have their slaves hear Christian doctrines and no doubt a hesitancy on the part of some slaves to give up traditional beliefs, even if those beliefs had been attenuated by a long presence in the New World—in the middle decades of the eighteenth century increasing numbers of bondspeople became members of Christian churches. A dramatic shift was occurring in the history of black Americans, most of whom before 1750 had been outside the Christian church, for within a century the majority of slaves were worshiping in one fashion or another as Christians. After emancipation, freedpersons continued to find in their churches solace from the cares of the world and joy and a purpose for living in a society that continued to oppress black people. Everyone acknowledges the significance of the church in the black community after freedom; less understood is black worship during the antebellum era and earlier. Yet the half-century following 1740 was the critical period during which some whites broke down their fears and inhibitions about sharing their religion with the slaves in their midst, and some blacks—only a few at first—came to find in Christianity a system of ideas and symbols that was genuinely attractive....

Several aspects of African traditional religion bore close enough parallels to Christianity that bondspeople who were initially disinterested in the white man's religion could—once they glimpsed another side to it—see sufficient common ground between the whites' Christianity and their own folk religions to merit closer examination. That willingness, that openness, on the part of blacks to the claims of Christianity was all the entrée white Christian evangelicals needed. Most West African religions assumed a tripartite hierarchy of deities —nature gods, ancestral gods, and an omnipotent creator god who was more remote though more powerful than the others. This conception was roughly transferable to the Christian idea of the trinity. West Africans understood that spirit possession was a sure sign of contact with the divine, an experience not totally dissimilar from the emotional fervor of evangelistic services. Before the mid-eighteenth century slaves had not come into contact with white evangelicals, who were also largely of the lower social order, who worshiped with emotional abandon, and who spoke movingly of being possessed by the Holy Spirit and knowing Jesus as their personal savior. But such evangelical Christians came increasingly to minister to slaves, and they would bridge the chasm between the races and introduce large and growing numbers of slaves to evangelical Christianity.

During the second quarter of the eighteenth century, Evangelicalism and Pietism swept across England and Europe, and the quickening of heartfelt religion soon leapfrogged to the New World in the person of George Whitefield. The resulting Great Awakening occurred primarily north of Maryland, but Whitefield's preaching and the example of his life gained disciples in South Carolina and Georgia. None of Whitefield's followers were more devout than members of the prominent Bryan family in Georgia, and ... the two Bryan brothers sincerely believed Jesus' call for repentance was addressed to all persons, black and white, bond and free. Consequently, they undertook to promote Christianity among their own and neighboring slaves, but they did so in such a way as to support the institution of slavery. From today's perspective, their paternalistic efforts toward the blacks under their control seem a truncated version of Christianity, but they did present the faith to the slaves in a way that was acceptable to the larger society.

A subtle shift in rationales had occurred that would have a far-reaching influence on whites and blacks. At first it had been deemed appropriate to enslave Africans because they were considered heathens; by the mid-eighteenth century some Anglican clergy had begun to argue that it was appropriate to enslave Africans because they might thereby be converted to Christianity. In that sense this development foreshadowed an important tradition of elite white evangelism to blacks, and through such efforts then and in the future thousands of slaves came to know Christianity and, in various ways, to appropriate its message for their own ends.

Another development of the mid-eighteenth century was to be even more important for the growth of Christianity among the slaves than the limited Anglican awakening in the aftermath of Whitefield. In the quarter of a century following 1745 three evangelical Protestant groups planted their seeds in the colonial South—first the Presbyterians, then the Separate Baptists (later the term Separate was dropped as this species came almost completely to swallow all competing versions of believers in adult baptism), and finally the Methodists (first only a subset of the Church of England but after 1784 an independent denomination). These three churches grew at different rates and had different constituencies. The Presbyterians never experienced the extensive growth among rural southerners that the other two did but found increasing support from among those on the upper rungs of society, supplanting the erstwhile Anglican (the postrevolutionary Episcopal) church in influence among the elite. Presbyterian church members, disproportionately wealthy, of course owned disproportionate numbers of slaves, and continuing the elite paternalism pioneered by the Anglican Bryans in colonial Georgia, they tended to minister to blacks by providing them special ministers and separate accommodations. A form of religious noblesse oblige motivated some of them to devise ways to bring the gospel message to their blacks, especially after abolitionists charged that southern whites neglected the spiritual well-being of their slaves. Moreover, the developing argument that slavery was a progressive institution designed by God to effect the Christianization of Africans gave slaveholders a moral obligation to consider the religious needs of their bondspeople. This sentiment, especially strong among Presbyterians and Episcopalians, produced the significant "mission to the slaves" movement of the late antebellum period....

Although the Presbyterian church was to remain relatively small but influential beyond its numbers, the Baptists and Methodists experienced remarkable growth, especially after the Great Revival at the beginning of the nineteenth century. It would be inappropriate in this brief overview to rehearse the reasons for the success these two evangelical denominations had in the rural South; to an extraordinary degree they became the folk churches of the region. Certainly in their youthful decades, the 1750s through 1790s, when their appeal was even more emphatically to those whites who lived at the margins of society—poor, isolated, largely nonslaveholding—the Baptists and Methodists maintained a fairly consistent antislavery stance. Especially south of Maryland, both denominations recognized the political explosiveness of such beliefs if preached incautiously. They tended to criticize slavery in the abstract, delineate its evils both to the slaves and even more to the whites, emphasize that slaves were persons with souls precious in the sight of God, and suggest that slavery be ended "insofar as practicable" —or words to that effect. This is not to argue that they were insincere or hypocritical. Rather, they understood the realities of the economic and social-control imperatives of the institution and occasionally stated explicitly that if they boldly attacked slavery, they would not be allowed to preach to the blacks, thereby —by their lights—causing the unfortunate bondspeople not to hear the gospel. It is easy from today's perspective, and probably incorrect, to see as self-serving such remarks as Methodist Francis Asbury's summation of his position in 1809: "Would not an *amelioration* in the condition and treatment of slaves have produced more practical good to the poor Africans, than any attempt at their *emancipation*? The state of society, unhappily, does not admit of this: besides, the blacks are deprived of the means of instruction; who will take the pains to lead them into the way of salvation, and watch over them that they may not stray, but the Methodists?... What is the personal liberty of the African which he may abuse, to the salvation of his soul; how may it be compared?"

The point is not the limited emancipationist impulse in the evangelical denominations and how it was thwarted over time by political and racial pressures. More appropriate here is the way the lower-class structure of the early Baptist and Methodist churches, most of whose members did not own slaves and felt estranged from the wealthier whites who did, enabled them to see blacks as potential fellow believers in a way that white worshipers in more elite churches seldom could. From the moment of their organization, typical Baptist or Methodist churches included black members, who often signed (or put their "X") on the founding documents of incorporation. Black membership in these two popular denominations was substantial from the last quarter of the eighteenth century through the Civil War. Without claiming too much or failing to recognize the multitude of ways slaves were not accorded genuine equality in these biracial churches, it is still fair to say that nowhere else in southern society were they treated so nearly as equals.

Because church membership statistics for the antebellum period are incomplete, and because churches varied in their definitions of membership, a quantitatively precise portrait of the extent to which blacks and white worshiped together is impossible to obtain. Historian John Blassingame has written that "an overwhelming majority of the slaves throughout the antebellum period attended church with their masters. Then, after the regular services ended, the ministers held special services for the slaves." Such special services were more typical of Episcopal and Presbyterian churches; Methodist and Baptist preachers would usually, sometimes toward the end of the service, call for something like "a special word for our black brothers and sisters" and then turn to them in the back pews or in the balcony and address them with a didactic sermon that often stressed obedience to their earthly masters. Sarah Fitzpatrick, a ninety-year-old former slave interviewed in 1938, recalled that "us 'Niggers' had our meetin' in de white fo'ks Baptist Church in de town o' Tuskegee. Dere's a place up in de loft dere now dat dey built fer de 'Nigger' slaves to 'tend church wid de white fo'ks. White preacher he preach to de white fo'ks an' when he git thu' wid dem he preach some to de 'Niggers.' Tell'em to mind dere Marster an' b'have deyself an' dey'll go to Hebben when dey die."

Slaves saw through these words and felt contempt for the self-serving attention they received. More important to them was the remainder of the service that they heard and participated in with the rest of the congregation. Here the slaves heard a more complete version of the gospel, and despite whatever social-control uses some ministers tried to put religion to in a portion of the Sunday service, most slaves found grounds for hope and a degree of spiritual liberation through their participation in these biracial churches. As Blassingame concluded, "Generally the ministers tried to expose the slaves to the major tenets of Christianity.... [And] only 15 percent of the Georgia slaves who had heard antebellum whites preach recalled admonitions to obedience."

Slaves worshiped apart from whites on some occasions, often with the knowledge of their owners and often without the white supervision the law called for. Some black churches were adjuncts to white churches, and completely independent and autonomous black churches existed in southern cities. Blacks worshiped privately and often secretly in their cabins and in the fields. Sometimes, and especially when their owner was irreligious, slaves had to slip away to hidden "brush arbors" deep in the woods to preach, shout, sing, and worship. But such practices should not lead us to forget that the normative worship experience of blacks in the antebellum South was in a biracial church. "Including black Sunday School scholars and catechumens," Blassingame writes, "there were probably 1,000,000 slaves under the regular tutelage of Southern churches in 1860."

When David T. Bailey examined some 40 autobiographies of blacks and 637 interviews of slaves on the subject of religion, he discovered that 32 percent of the autobiographers who mentioned religion reported that they had gone to white churches, 14 percent said their master led the services for them, and another 14 percent attended worship services at special plantation chapels, whereas 36 percent mentioned that they had attended black prayer meetings. Of the former slaves interviewed, 43.5 percent mentioned attending white churches, 6.5 percent reported master-led services, 6.5 percent described plantation chapels, and only 24 percent discussed attendance at black prayer meetings.

Such substantial black participation in churches normally considered white indicates that white evangelicals, even in the late antebellum period, when they had moved up the social scale, joined the establishment, and come to support the institution of slavery, still felt a Christian responsibility to include slaves in the outreach of the church. Their idea of mission assumed that slaves were persons with souls precious in God's sight. In fact, many white evangelicals came to believe that part of their responsibility to God involved Christianizing the slave work force. It was to that end, they reasoned, that God had sanctioned slavery.... [A]bolitionist charges that the southern church ignored the slaves infuriated southern clergymen and caused them to redouble their efforts to bring slaves into the church. During the Civil War clergy feared that God was chastising the region for not sufficiently supporting the mission effort to the blacks, and religiously inspired attempts to amend slavery by correcting the worst abuses, teaching bondspeople to read (so the Scriptures would be accessible to them), and providing missionaries for them ... almost reformed slavery out of existence in Confederate Georgia.

Devout white clergy often took seriously their responsibilities toward the blacks in their midst, and their paternalistic and racist assumptions should not blind us to their convictions that slaves too were God's children and that white slaveowners stood under God's judgment for the way they treated their bondspeople. It is difficult to understand today how devout whites could define blacks legally as chattel and yet show real concern for the state of their souls. Could genuine Christians so compartmentalize their charity? Apparently so, given their assumptions that blacks were a race of permanent children. A misguided sense of Christian responsibility led well-meaning, decent whites to justify slavery as the white man's duty to Africans, for it was, they argued, through the order and discipline bondage provided that slaves learned—sampled?—Christianity and Western civilization. Almost like whistling in the dark to drive away one's fears, white churchmen sometimes were particularly anxious to Christianize their slaves as though only thus could the institution be justified and their guilt be lessened.

Blacks too must have derived a substantial reward from their participation in the institutional churches or they would not have been involved with them to such an extent for so long. The manuscript records of hundreds of local Baptist churches across the South allow us to see a seldom-studied aspect of white-black interaction that helps explain the attraction biracial churches held for slaves. First,... blacks were accorded a semblance of equality when they joined antebellum Baptist churches. White members often addressed them as brother or sister, just as they did fellow white members. This equality in the terms of address may seem insignificant today, but in an age when only whites were accorded the titles of Mr. and Mrs., and it was taboo for a white to so address a black, any form of address that smacked of equality was notable. Behind it lay the familial idea, accepted by whites in principle if not always in practice, that in the sight of God all were equal and were members of His spiritual family. Incoming or outgoing members of Baptist churches were accepted or dismissed with "letters" attesting to their good standing, and slaves asking to join Baptist churches were expected to "bring their letter" just as prospective white members were. Churches seem to have routinely supplied such letters to their members of both races who moved to other locations. New members, black and white, were usually given the "right hand of fellowship" after their letters were accepted or after they came to the altar following the minister's sermon-ending call for conversion to "confess their sins and accept Christ's mercy." Individual churches often varied in this practice, as in much else in the South, where strict uniformity in anything was the exception.

Blacks usually sat in a separate section of the church, perhaps a balcony or a lean-to. There is evidence, however, that slaves sat scattered throughout Anglican churches in colonial Virginia and that sometimes they sat with or next to the pew of their master. Today, such segregated seating would seem to contradict the idea of spiritual equality, but the contradiction probably did not seem so stark to slaves, who were excluded from most other white-dominated functions.

The white women often sat apart from the white men, too; in that age segregation by gender was almost as common as that by race, and the familiarity of such separation might well have lessened the negative connotation although it accentuated each subgroup's sense of separate identity. That is, the sense of both a separate women's culture and a separate black culture might have been inadvertently strengthened by the prevalent mode of segregated seating under a common roof. In fact, for some blacks who were isolated on farms and small plantations with no or only a few fellow slaves, the gathering together on Sunday at the church house with slaves from other farms may have been the primary occasion for experiencing a sense of black community. For such slaves the forced segregation in seating may have seemed both natural and desirable because they hungered for close interaction with persons of their own kind. The interaction may have been a stronger attraction than the worship itself. No doubt many bondspeople found their marriage partners through such social involvement at church—certainly much white courtship began there. Perhaps, then, for slaves dispersed on farms outside the plantation district, the slave community was largely created and vitalized in the one arena in which slaves belonging to different owners could freely mingle—the biracial church service.

As with church membership practices, there was an important but limited degree of equality in slaves' participation in antebellum church discipline.... [C]ertainly no one would want to argue that whites completely forgot or transcended the racial mores of a slave society in the confines of the church building, but it is significant that slaves were allowed to give testimony—sometimes even conflicting with white testimony—and that on occasion their witness overruled the charges of whites. This occurred in a society that did not allow blacks to testify against whites in civil courts. Moreover, blacks were not disciplined out of proportion to their numbers; on the whole, they were charged with infractions similar to those of whites; and they were held to the same moral expectations as whites with regard to profanity, drunkenness, lying, adultery, failure to attend church, and fighting. There surely were charges against blacks that had no parallel for whites—for example, blacks alone were charged with running away. But nowhere else in southern society were slaves and whites brought together in an arena where both were held responsible to a code of behavior sanctioned by a source outside the society—the Bible. The Scriptures were interpreted in culturally sanctioned ways, but whites as well as blacks were occasionally found wanting.

Blacks discovered in the church and in church discipline a unique sphere wherein to nurture (and be recognized by whites to have) moral responsibility and what Timothy L. Smith has called "moral earnestness." Through the church slaves found a meaning for their lives that could give a touch of moral grandeur to the tragic dimension of their bondage. Images of the children of Israel and the suffering servant provided ways to accept their life predicament without feelings of self-worthlessness. The church offered a spark of joy in the midst of pain, a promise of life-affirming forgiveness to soften the hopelessness of unremitting bondage, an ultimate reward in heaven for unrewarded service in this world. Participation in the biracial churches was one of the ways slaves found the moral and psychological strength to survive their bondage.

It is important to remember that social interaction does not necessarily imply social equality; in a variety of contexts outside the churches slaves and masters mingled closely without narrowing the gap between freedom and bondage. In many ways such interaction could even magnify the sense of enslavement. Yet it would be a mistake so to emphasize the belittling possibilities of white-black interaction that we fail to see the alternative possibilities inherent in the biracial churches. Slaves apparently had their image of being creatures of God strengthened by the sermons they heard —even when that was not the intention of the ministers—and the discipline they accepted. Their evident pleasure in occasionally hearing black preachers speak to biracial congregations no doubt augmented their sense of racial pride. Taking communion together with whites, serving as deacons or Sunday school teachers, being baptized or confirmed in the same ceremonies, even contributing their mite to the temporal upkeep of the church, could surely have been seen as symbolic ways of emphasizing their self-respect and equality before God. Slaves certainly were not dependent on white-controlled institutions to nurture their sense of self-worth, but neither were they adverse to seizing opportunities wherever they found them and using them for that purpose. In a society that offered few opportunities for blacks to practice organizational and leadership skills or hear themselves addressed and see themselves evaluated morally on an equal basis with whites, small matters could have large meanings. Blacks did not discover in the biracial churches an equality of treatment that spiritually transported them out of bondage, but they found in them a theology of hope and a recognition of self-worth that fared them well in their struggle to endure slavery.

As Robert L. Hall documents in his analysis of religion in antebellum Florida, blacks worshiped in a variety of ways in the antebellum South besides in biracial Protestant churches. In most southern cities and large towns there were completely independent black churches, with black ministers, black deacons or elders, and a panoply of self-help associations connected to and supported by the church. Usually such churches, like the St. James African Episcopal Church in Baltimore, were under the control of free blacks, although many if not most of the members were slaves. Although the surrounding white-dominated churches tended to ignore societal ills, emphasize conversion, and minister primarily to individuals, the black churches tended to minister to all the social and religious needs of their parishioners. There was a communal and social thrust in the independent black churches that was notably absent from the mainstream white churches of the South. (That difference even today sets many black churches apart from white.) Often the black churches had very large memberships, and sometimes their meeting places had the largest seating capacity in the city.

Blacks also worshiped in black churches that were adjunct to white churches. Such situations typically arose after the biracial church built a new sanctuary and, with the black members perhaps outnumbering the white, the blacks were allowed ("allowed" seems more accurate than "forced") to conduct separate services in the old structure. The motivation of the whites here is not clear; they often indicated that the blacks preferred their own services, but to what extent whites desired segregated white churches for essentially racist reasons is impossible to determine. In most cases when blacks were split off into separate "African" churches, as they were known, a committee of whites was assigned to oversee their services. The supervision seems to have been honored more in the breach, however. In a variety of other ways black church members were often given some autonomy in regulating portions of their worship life, again apparently more because the blacks desired such separation than because whites required it. These small islands of black autonomy within the biracial church were perhaps the beginning of the complete racial separation that would come after the Civil War.

Not all the organized churches in the South were Protestant, although Protestantism was far more dominant in the South than elsewhere in the nation. There were pockets of Catholic strength in Maryland, Kentucky, and Missouri, and in south Louisiana Catholicism was preponderant. Most southern cities had at least one Catholic church, usually attended primarily by immigrant workers. Louisiana and Maryland had rural Catholic churches as well, with numbers of black Catholic parishioners. Catholic masters sometimes required that their slaves worship as Catholics, though their bondspeople may have preferred the neighboring Baptist or Methodist churches either as a subtle form of rebellion against their masters or because of the appeal of the demonstrative emotionalism of the evangelical churches. In various ways the Catholic church ministered to bondspeople; separate black orders and sisterhoods were established and the sacraments extended. Because it was a minority church in a rabidly Protestant region and was concerned not to attract notoriety, the Catholic church never questioned the morality of slavery. An occasional Catholic institution or order might own slaves, as did the Jesuits in Maryland, though this property in humans was divested for reasons of ethics and economics....

In addition to the various kinds of formal churches—biracial, adjunct, and independent black churches and plantation chapels—to which slaves had access, black worshipers also gathered in more informal, often secret settings. The evidence for this is to be found in black memoirs and slave narratives, although even these sources suggest that most blacks worshiped in one or another of the formal churches. There are many reasons why slaves would choose to worship in a manner less subject to white supervision or control. Some masters sought to prevent slaves from worshiping at all, which forced slaves to develop an underground religion and to meet secretly either in their cabins at night or in the brush arbors. Slaves who were allowed (or required) to attend a biracial church (or any formal service carefully monitored by whites) in which the minister placed too much emphasis on the "slaves-obey-your-master" homily and thereby neglected to preach the gospel in its fullness often sought an alternative worship experience. There must have been other times when slaves felt inhibited in the presence of whites and simply desired a time and a place to preach, sing, and shout without having to suffer the condescending glances of less emotionally involved white churchgoers. Although slaves worshiping apart and secretively may have developed a distinctly black

Christianity significantly different from that which they heard in the more formal institutions, there is no unambiguous evidence that they did so. More probably the services in the brush arbors were simply a longer, more emotionally demonstrative version of those in the biracial churches, with more congregational participation. No precise record exists of the theology implicit in such brush arbor meetings or of special emphases that might have developed, but the similarity in worship practice and ecclesiology of the autonomous black churches that emerged after the Civil War to the earlier biracial churches argues against the evolution of any fundamentally different system in the brush arbors.

A momentous change in the nature of church practice in the South took place at the beginning of Reconstruction. Blacks in significant numbers—eventually all of them—began to move out of the biracial churches and join a variety of independent black denominations. As Katharine Dvorak notes in her insightful essay, the blacks left on their own volition; they were not forced out. At first many white churchmen tried to persuade them to stay, but within several decades the degenerating racial climate of the region led these same churchmen on occasion to applaud the new segregated patterns of worship, so different from the common practice before the Civil War.

Of course, that freedpersons wanted to leave the biracial churches is a commentary on the less-than-complete equality they had enjoyed in them. Blacks had a strong sense of racial identity, reinforced by their having been slaves and, within the confines of the churches, by their segregated seating. The complete sermons they had heard for years, not just the self-serving words the white ministers directed specifically at them, had engendered in blacks a sense of their moral worth and equality in the sight of God. The biracial churches simultaneously nurtured this sense of moral equality and thwarted it by their conformity to the demands of the slave society. Black participation in the biracial churches—as preachers, deacons, stewards, and Sunday school teachers—had given them practical leadership and administrative experience, as had their islands of autonomy within the demographically biracial churches. Theologically and experientially blacks were ready to seize the moment offered by emancipation to withdraw from their old allegiances and create autonomous denominations. No better evidence of the freedom slaves had not enjoyed in the biracial churches exists than the rapidity with which blacks sought to establish separate denominations after the Civil War. And no better evidence exists of the extent to which slaves in the biracial churches accepted evangelical Christianity as their preferred expression of religious faith and molded their lives to its demands than the denominations they created after emancipation.

The worship services and institutional arrangements in the new black churches bore a very close resemblance to the biracial churches from which the blacks withdrew. In fact, black Baptist and Methodist services were closer to the early nineteenth-century post–Great Revival services of the evangelical churches than those of the postbellum all-white churches. Blacks had assimilated the theology and order of service in the biracial churches. Rejecting the modernizing tendencies of the white churches toward less emotion, shorter sermons, an emphasis on choir singing rather than congregational singing, and seminary-trained ministers, they more truly carried on the pioneer evangelical traditions. It should not have been surprising to anyone that when born-again Baptist presidential candidate Jimmy Carter wanted to appeal to blacks in 1976, he spoke to them in their churches. Despite the differences—black services are longer, the music is more expressive, emotions are more freely expressed, there is greater congregational participation—the kinship between the white and black Baptist churches of today is readily apparent, and it points back to a time more than a century ago when the religious culture of the South was fundamentally biracial.

POSTSCRIPT

Did Slaves Exercise Religious Autonomy?

One of the most intriguing issues for students of American slavery is the relationship between religion and resistance. Specifically, did slaves find in Christianity moderation that conditioned them to seek salvation only in God's heavenly kingdom, or did it steel their resolve to seek deliverance from their bondage in the earthly realm? To what extent is Karl Marx's dictum that religion is an "opiate of the masses" applicable to the slave experience?

Actually, there was a certain dualism evident in the slaves' religious life. Some obviously were pacified by a fatalistic attitude that slavery was their permanent status, yet hopeful that salvation would be achieved in the heavenly afterlife. Slave owners, of course, attempted to ensure their bond servants' loyalty and passivity by reminding them of Paul's injunction to Onesimus, the runaway servant, to return to his master. For their own part, slaves much preferred to hear Bible readings related to Moses' deliverance of the Israelites from Egypt. It should be remembered that Gabriel Prosser, Denmark Vesey, and Nat Turner all employed religious symbolism to foster their revolutionary conspiracies.

The nature of slave religion is an important topic in virtually every scholarly treatment of the institution of slavery. Raboteau's conclusions are presented more fully in *Slave Religion: The "Invisible Institution" in the Antebellum South* (Oxford University Press, 1978). Boles's description of the "biracial church" was inspired in part by Kenneth Bailey's seminal article "Protestantism and Afro-Americans in the Old South: Another Look," *Journal of Southern History* (November 1975). Eugene D. Genovese, in *Roll, Jordan, Roll: The World the Slaves Made* (Pantheon Books, 1974), argues that the religion developed in the slave quarters represented a synthesis of African traditions and Protestant Christianity, which fused Moses' promise of deliverance in this world with Jesus' promise of personal redemption. For the "dualism" of slave religion discussed above, see Vincent Harding, "Religion and Resistance Among Antebellum Negroes, 1800–1860," in August Meier and Elliott Rudwick, eds., *The Making of Black America: Volume I* (Atheneum, 1969). Lawrence Levine, in *Black Culture and Black Consciousness* (Oxford University Press, 1977), explores the latent and symbolic elements of protest contained in slave songs.

ISSUE 12

Was the Mexican War an Exercise in American Imperialism?

YES: Ramón Eduardo Ruiz, from "Manifest Destiny and the Mexican War," in Howard H. Quint et al., eds., *Main Problems in American History, vol. 1,* 5th ed. (Dorsey Press, 1988)

NO: Norman A. Graebner, from "The Mexican War: A Study in Causation," *Pacific Historical Review* (August 1980)

ISSUE SUMMARY

YES: Professor of history Ramón Eduardo Ruiz argues that for the purpose of conquering Mexico's northern territories, the United States waged an aggressive war against Mexico from which Mexico never recovered.

NO: Professor of diplomatic history Norman A. Graebner argues that President James Polk pursued an aggressive policy that he believed would force Mexico to sell New Mexico and California to the United States and to recognize the annexation of Texas without starting a war.

The American government in the early 1800s greatly benefited from the fact that European nations generally considered what was going on in North America of secondary importance to what was happening in their own countries. In 1801 President Thomas Jefferson became alarmed when he learned that France had acquired the Louisiana territory from Spain. He realized that western states might revolt if the government did not control the city of New Orleans as a seaport for shipping their goods. Jefferson dispatched negotiators to buy the port. He pulled off the real estate coup of the nineteenth century when his diplomats caught Napoleon in a moment of despair. With a stroke of the pen and $15 million, the Louisiana Purchase of 1803 nearly doubled the size of the country. The exact northern, western, and southeastern boundaries were not clearly defined. "But," as diplomatic historian Thomas Bailey has pointed out, "the American negotiators knew that they had bought the western half of perhaps the most valuable river valley on the face of the globe, stretching between the Rockies and the Mississippi, and bounded somewhere on the north by British North America."

After England fought an indecisive war with the United States from 1812 to 1815, she realized that it was to her advantage to maintain peaceful relations with her former colony. In 1817 the Great Lakes, which border on the United States and Canada, were mutually disarmed. Over the next half century, the principle of demilitarization was extended to the land, resulting in an undefended frontier line that stretched for more than 3,000 miles. The Convention of 1818 clarified the northern boundary of the Louisiana Purchase and ran a line along the 49th parallel from Lake of the Woods in Minnesota to the Rocky Mountains. Beyond that point there was to be a 10-year joint occupancy in the Oregon Territory. In 1819 Spain sold Florida to the United States after Secretary of State John Quincy Adams sent a note telling the Spanish government to keep the Indians on their side of the border or else to get out of Florida. A few years later, the Spanish Empire crumbled in the New World and a series of Latin American republics emerged.

Afraid that the European powers might attack the newly independent Latin American republics and that Russia might expand south into the Oregon Territory, Adams convinced President James Monroe to reject a British suggestion for a joint declaration and to issue instead a unilateral policy statement. The Monroe Doctrine, as it was called by a later generation, had three parts. First, it closed the Western Hemisphere to any future colonization. Second, it forbade "any interposition" by the European monarchs that would "extend their system to any portion of this hemisphere as dangerous to our peace and safety." And third, the United States pledged to abstain from any involvement in the political affairs of Europe. Viewed in the context of 1823, it is clear that Monroe was merely restating the principles of unilateralism and nonintervention. Both of these were at the heart of American isolationism.

While Monroe renounced the possibility of American intervention in European affairs, he made no such disclaimer toward Latin America, as was originally suggested by Great Britain. It would be difficult to colonize in South America, but the transportation revolution, the hunger for land, which created political turmoil in Texas, and the need for ports on the Pacific to increase American trade in Asia encouraged the acquisition of new lands contiguous to the southwestern boundaries. In the 1840s, journalists and politicians furnished an ideological rationale for this expansion and said it was the Manifest Destiny of Americans to spread democracy, freedom, and white American settlers across the entire North American continent, excluding Canada because it was a possession of Great Britain. Blacks and Indians were not a part of this expansion.

In the following selections, Ramón Eduardo Ruiz argues that the United States waged a racist and aggressive war against Mexico for the purpose of conquering what became the American southwest. In his view Manifest Destiny was strictly an ideological rationale to provide noble motives for what were really acts of aggression against a neighboring country. Norman A. Graebner, arguing from a "realistic" perspective, contends that President James Polk pursued the aggressive policy of a stronger nation in order to force Mexico to sell New Mexico and Texas to the United States and to recognize America's annexation of Texas without causing a war.

YES
Ramón Eduardo Ruiz

MANIFEST DESTINY
AND THE MEXICAN WAR

All nations have a sense of destiny. Spaniards braved the perils of unknown seas and the dangers of savage tribes to explore and conquer a New World for Catholicism. Napoleon's armies overran Europe on behalf of equality, liberty, and fraternity. Communism dictates the future of China and the Soviet Union. Arab expansionists speak of Islam. In the United States, Manifest Destiny in the nineteenth century was the equivalent of these ideologies or beliefs. Next-door neighbor Mexico first felt the brunt of its impact and suffered the most from it.

What was Manifest Destiny? The term was coined in December 1845 by John L. O'Sullivan, then editor and cofounder of the *New York Morning News*. Superpatriot, expansionist, war hawk, and propagandist, O'Sullivan lived his doctrine of Manifest Destiny, for that slogan embodied what he believed. O'Sullivan spoke of America's special mission, frequently warned Europe to keep hands off the Western Hemisphere, later joined a filibustering expedition to Cuba, and had an honored place among the followers of President James K. Polk, Manifest Destiny's spokesman in the Mexican War.

Manifest Destiny voiced the expansionist sentiment that had gripped Americans almost from the day their ancestors had landed on the shores of the New World in the seventeenth century. Englishmen and their American offspring had looked westward since Jamestown and Plymouth—confident that time and fate would open the vast West that stretched out before them. Manifest Destiny, then, was first territorial expansion—American pretensions to lands held by Spain, France, and later Mexico; some even spoke of a United States with boundaries from pole to pole. But Manifest Destiny was greater than mere land hunger; much more was involved. A spirit of nationalism was pervasive—the belief that what Americans upheld was right and good, and that providence had designated them the chosen people. In a political framework, Manifest Destiny stood for democracy as Americans conceived it; to spread democracy and freedom was the goal. Also included were ideals of regeneration: the conquest of virgin lands for the sake of their

From Ramón Eduardo Ruiz, "Manifest Destiny and the Mexican War," in Howard H. Quint et al., eds., *Main Problems in American History, vol. 1*, 5th ed. (Dorsey Press, 1988). Copyright © 1972 by Dorsey Press, a division of Wadsworth, Inc. Reprinted by permission.

development, and concepts of Anglo-Saxon superiority. All these slogans and beliefs played a role in the Mexican question that culminated in hostilities in 1846.

Apostles of these slogans pointed out that Mexicans claimed lands from the Pacific to Texas but tilled only a fraction of them, and did so inefficiently. "No nation has the right to hold soil, virgin and rich, yet unproducing," stressed one U.S. representative. "No race but our own can either cultivate or rule the western hemisphere," acknowledged the *United States Magazine and Democratic Review*. The Indian, almost always a poor farmer in North America, was the initial victim of this concept of soil use; expansionists later included nearly everyone in the New World, and in particular, Mexicans. For, Caleb Cushing asked: "Is not the occupation of any portion of the earth by those competent to hold and till it, a providential law of national life?"

Oregon and Texas, and the Democratic Party platform of 1844, kindled the flames of territorial expansion in the roaring forties. Millions of Americans came to believe that God had willed them all of North America. Expansion symbolized the fulfillment of "America's providential mission or destiny"—a mission conceived in terms of the spread of democracy, which its exponents identified with freedom. Historian Albert K. Weinberg has written: "It was because of the association of expansion and freedom in a means-end relationship, that expansion now came to seem most manifestly a destiny."

Americans did not identify freedom with expansion until the forties. Then, fears of European designs on Texas, California, and Oregon, perhaps, prompted an identity of the two. Not only were strategic and economic interests at stake, but also democracy itself. The need to extend the area of freedom, therefore, rose partly from the necessity of keeping absolutistic European monarchs from limiting the area open to American democracy in the New World.

Other factors also impelled Americans to think expansion essential to their national life. Failure to expand imperiled the nation, for as historian William E. Dodd stated, Westerners especially believed "that the Union gained in stability as the number of states multiplied." Meanwhile, Southerners declared the annexation of Texas essential to their prosperity and to the survival of slavery, and for a congressional balance of power between North and South. Other persons insisted that expansion helped the individual states to preserve their liberties, for their numerical strength curtailed the authority of the central government—the enemy of local autonomy and especially autonomy of the South. Moreover, for Southerners extension of the area of freedom meant, by implication, expansion of the limits of slavery. Few planters found the two ideas incompatible. Religious doctrines and natural principles, in their opinion, had ruled the Negro ineligible for political equality. That expansion favored the liberties of the individual, both North and South agreed.

In the forties, the pioneer spirit received recognition as a fundamental tenet of American life. Individualism and expansion, the mark of the pioneer, were joined together in the spirit of Manifest Destiny. Expansion guaranteed not just the political liberty of the person, but the opportunity to improve himself economically as well, an article of faith for the democracy of the age. Furthermore, when antiexpansionists declared that the territorial limits of the United States in 1846 assured all Americans ample room for growth in the future, the expansionists-turned-ecologists replied that some 300 million Americans in 1946 would need more land, a prediction that overstated the case of the population-minded experts. And few Americans saw the extension of freedom in terms other than liberty for themselves —white, Anglo-Saxon, and Protestant. All these concepts, principles, and beliefs entered into the expansionist creed of Manifest Destiny.

None of these was a part of the Mexican heritage, the legacy of three centuries of Spanish rule and countless years of pre-Columbian civilization. Mexico and the United States could not have been more dissimilar in 1846. A comparison of colonial backgrounds helps to bring into focus the reasons that the two countries were destined to meet on the field of battle. One was weak and the other strong; Mexico had abolished slavery and the United States had not; Americans had their Manifest Destiny, but few Mexicans believed in themselves.

Daughter of a Spain whose colonial policy embraced the Indian, Mexico was a mestizo republic, a half-breed nation. Except for a small group of aristocrats, most Mexicans were descendants of both Spaniards and Indians. For Mexico had a colonial master eager and willing to assimilate pre-Columbian man. Since the days of the conqueror Hernán Cortés, Spaniards had mated with Indians, producing a Mexican both European and American in culture and race. Offspring of the Indian as well as the Spaniard, Mexican leaders, and even the society of the time, had come to accept the Indian, if not always as an equal, at least as a member of the republic. To have rejected

him would have been tantamount to the Mexican's self-denial of himself. Doctrines of racial supremacy were, if not impossible, highly unlikely, for few Mexicans could claim racial purity. To be Mexican implied a mongrel status that ruled out European views of race.

Spain bequeathed Mexico not merely a racial attitude but laws, religious beliefs, and practices that banned most forms of segregation and discrimination. For example, reservations for Indians were never a part of the Spanish heritage. Early in the 16th century, the Spaniards had formulated the celebrated Laws of the Indies—legislation that clearly spelled out the place of the Indian in colonial society. Nothing was left to chance, since the Spanish master included every aspect of life—labor, the family, religion, and even the personal relations between Spaniard and Indian. The ultimate aim was full citizenship for the Indian and his descendants. In the meantime, the Church ruled that the Indian possessed a soul; given Christian teachings, he was the equal of his European conqueror. "All of the people of the world are men," the Dominican Bartolomé de las Casas had announced in his justly famous 1550 debate with the scholar Sepúlveda.

Clearly, church and state and the individual Spaniard who arrived in America had more than charity in mind. Dreams of national and personal glory and wealth dominated their outlook. Yet, despite the worldly goals of most secular and clerical conquerors, they built a colonial empire on the principle that men of all colors were equal on earth. Of course, Spain required the labor of the Indian and therefore had to protect him from the avarice of many a conquistador. Spaniards, the English were wont to say, were notorious for their disdain of manual labor of any type. But Spain went beyond merely offering the Indian protection in order to insure his labor. It incorporated him into Hispanic-American society. The modern Mexican is proof that the Indian survived: all Mexicans are Indian to some extent. That the Indian suffered economic exploitation and frequently even social isolation is undoubtedly true, but such was the lot of the poor in the Indies—Indian, half-breed, and even Spaniard.

Spain's empire, as well as the Mexican republic that followed, embraced not just the land but the people who had tilled it for centuries before the European's arrival. From northern California to Central America, the boundaries of colonial New Spain, and later Mexico, the Spaniard had embraced the Indian or allowed him to live out his life. It was this half-breed population that in 1846 confronted and fell victim to the doctrine of Manifest Destiny.

America's historical past could not have been more dissimilar. The English master had no room for the Indian in his scheme of things. Nearly all Englishmen—Puritans, Quakers, or Anglicans—visualized the conquest and settlement of the New World in terms of the exclusive possession of the soil. All new lands conquered were for the immediate benefit of the new arrivals. From the days of the founding of Jamestown and Plymouth, the English had pushed the Indian westward, relentlessly driving him from his homeland. In this activity, the clergy clasped hands with lay authorities, neither offered the red man a haven. Except for a few hardy souls, invariably condemned by their peers, Englishmen of church and state gave little thought to the Indian. Heaven, hell, and the teachings of Christ were the exclusive domain of the conquerors.

Society in the thirteen colonies, and in the Union that followed, reflected English and European customs and ways of life. It was a transplanted society. Where the Indian survived, he found himself isolated from the currents of time. Unlike the Spaniards, whose ties with Africa and darker skinned peoples through seven centuries of Moorish domination had left an indelible imprint on them, most Englishmen had experienced only sporadic contact with people of dissimilar races and customs. Having lived a sheltered and essentially isolated existence, the English developed a fear and distrust of those whose ways were foreign to them. The Americans who walked in their footsteps retained this attitude.

Many American historians will reject this interpretation. They will probably allege that American willingness to accept millions of destitute immigrants in the nineteenth century obviously contradicts the view that the Anglo-Saxon conqueror and settler distrusted what was strange in others. Some truth is present here, but the weight of the evidence lies on the other side. What must be kept firmly in mind is that immigration to the English colonies and later to the United States—in particular, the tidal wave of humanity that engulfed the United States in the post-Civil War era—was European in origin. Whether Italians, Jews, or Greeks from the Mediterranean, Swedes, Scots, or Germans from the North, what they had in common far outweighed conflicting traits and cultural and physical differences. All were European, offspring of one body of traditions and beliefs. Whether Catholics, Protestants, or Jews, they professed adherence to Western religious practices and beliefs. The so-called melting pot was scarcely a melting pot at all; the ingredients were European in origin. All spices that would have given the stew an entirely different flavor were carefully kept out—namely, the Black and the Indian.

It was logical that Manifest Destiny, that American belief in a Providence of special design, should have racial overtones. Having meticulously kept out the infidel, Americans could rightly claim a racial doctrine of purity and supremacy in the world of 1846. Had not the nation of Polk's era developed free of those races not a part of the European heritage? Had the nation not progressed rapidly? Most assuredly, the answer was yes. When American development was compared to that of the former Spanish-American colonies, the reply was even more emphatically in the affirmative. After all, the latin republics to the south had little to boast about. All were backward, illiterate, and badly governed states. Americans had just cause for satisfaction with what they had accomplished.

Unfortunately for Latin America, and especially Mexico, American pride had dire implications for the future. Convinced of the innate racial supremacy which the slogan of Manifest Destiny proclaimed throughout the world, many Americans came to believe that the New World was theirs to develop. Only their industry, their ingenuity, and their intelligence could cope fully with the continental challenge. Why should half-breed Mexico—backward, politically a wasteland, and hopelessly split by nature and man's failures—hold Texas, New Mexico, and California? In Mexico's possession, all those lands would lie virgin, offering a home to a few thousand savage Indians, and here and there a Mexican pueblo of people scarcely different from their heathen neighbors. Manifest Destiny proclaimed what most Americans firmly believed—the right of Anglo-Saxons and others of similar racial origin to develop what Providence had promised them. Weak Mexico, prey of its own cupidity and mistakes, was the victim of this belief.

Manifest Destiny, writes Mexican historian Carlos Bosch García, also contradicts an old American view that means are as important as ends. He stresses that the key to the history of the United States, as the doctrine of Manifest Destiny illustrates, lies in the willingness of Americans to accept as good the ultimate result of whatever they have undertaken. That the red man was driven from his homeland is accepted as inevitable and thus justifiable. American scholars might condemn the maltreatment of the Indian, but few question the final verdict.

Equally ambivalent, says Bosch García, is the American interpretation of the Mexican War. Though some American scholars of the post-Civil War period severely censured the South for what they called its responsibility for the Mexican War, their views reflected a criticism of the slavocracy rather than a heartfelt conviction that Mexico had been wronged. Obviously, there were exceptions. Hubert H. Bancroft, a California scholar and book collector, emphatically denounced Polk and his cohorts in his voluminous *History of Mexico* (1883–88). Among the politicians of the era, Abraham Lincoln won notoriety—and probably lost his seat in the House of Representatives—for his condemnation of Polk's declaration of war against Mexico. There were others, mostly members of the Whig Party, which officially opposed the war; but the majority, to repeat, was more involved with the problem of the South than with the question of war guilt.

Most Americans have discovered ways and means to justify Manifest Destiny's war on Mexico. That country's chronic political instability, its unwillingness to meet international obligations, its false pride in its military establishment—all, say scholars, led Mexican leaders to plunge their people into a hopeless war. Had Mexico been willing to sell California, one historian declares, no conflict would have occurred. To paraphrase Samuel F. Bemis, distinguished Yale University diplomatic scholar, no American today would undo the results of Polk's war. Put differently, to fall back on Bosch García, American writers have justified the means because of the ends. Manifest Destiny has not only been explained but has been vindicated on the grounds of what has been accomplished in California and New Mexico since 1848. Or, to cite Hermann Eduard von Holst, a late nineteenth-century German scholar whose writings on American history won him a professorship at the University of Chicago, the conflict between Mexico and the United States was bound to arise. A virile and ambitious people whose cause advanced that of world civilization could not avoid battle with a decadent, puerile people. Moral judgments that applied to individuals might find Americans guilty of aggression, but the standards by which nations survive and prosper upheld the cause of the United States. Might makes right? Walt Whitman, then editor of the *Brooklyn Daily Eagle*, put down his answer succinctly:

We love to indulge in thoughts of the future extent and power of this Republic—because with its increase is the increase in human happiness and liberty.... What has miserable Mexico —with her superstition, her burlesque upon freedom, her actual tyranny by the few over the many—what has she to do with the great mission of peopling the New World with a noble race? Be it ours, to achieve that mission! Be it ours to roll down all of the upstart leaven of the old despotism, that comes our way.

The conflict with Mexico was an offensive war without moral pretensions, according to Texas scholar Otis A. Singletary. It was no lofty crusade, no noble battle to right the wrongs of the past or to free a subjugated people, but a war of conquest waged by one neighbor against another. President Polk and his allies had to pay conscience money to justify a "greedy land-grab from a neighbor too weak to defend herself." American indifference to the Mexican War, Singletary concludes, "lies rooted in the guilt that we as a nation have come to feel about it."

American racial attitudes, the product of a unique colonial background in the New World, may also have dictated the scope of territorial conquest in 1848 and, ironically, saved Mexico from total annexation. Until the clash with Mexico, the American experience had been limited to the conquest, occupation, and annexation of empty to sparsely settled territories, or lands already colonized by citizens of the United States, such as Oregon and Texas. American pioneers had been reincorporated into the Union with the annexation of Oregon and Texas and even with the purchase of Louisiana in 1803. The alien population proved small and of little importance in all three territories. White planters, farmers, and pioneers mastered the small Mexican population in Texas and easily disposed of the Indians and half-breeds in the Louisiana territory.

Expansionists and their foes had long considered both Indian and Black unfit for regeneration; both were looked on as inferior and doomed races. On this point, most Americans were in agreement. While not entirely in keeping with this view, American opinions of Latin Americans, and of Mexicans in particular, were hardly flattering. Purchase and annexation of Louisiana and Florida, and of Texas and Oregon, had been debated and postponed partly out of fear of what many believed would be the detrimental effect on American democracy resulting from the amalgamation of the half-breed and mongrel peoples of these lands. Driven by a sense of national aggrandizement, the expansionists preferred to conquer lands free of alien populations. Manifest Destiny had no place for the assimilation of strange and exotic peoples. Freedom for Americans—this was the cry, regardless of what befell the conquered natives. The location of sparsely held territory had dictated the course of empire.

James K. Polk's hunger for California reflected national opinion on races as well as desire for land. Both that territory and New Mexico, nearly to the same extent, were almost barren of native populations. Of sparsely settled California, in 1845, the *Hartford Times* eloquently declared that Americans could "redeem from unhallowed hands a land, above all others of heaven, and hold it for the use of a people who know how to obey heaven's behests." Thus, it was that the tide of conquest —the fruits of the conference table at Guadalupe Hidalgo—stopped on the border of Mexico's inhabited lands, where the villages of a people alien in race and culture confronted the invaders. American concepts of race, the belief in the regeneration of virgin lands— these logically ordered annexation of both California and New Mexico, but left Mexico's settled territory alone.

Many Americans, it is true, gave much thought to the conquest and regeneration of all Mexico, but the peace of 1848 came before a sufficiently large number of them had abandoned traditional thoughts on race and color to embrace the new gospel. Apparently, most Americans were not yet willing to accept dark-skinned people as the burden of the white man.

Manifest Destiny, that mid-nineteenth-century slogan, is now merely a historical question for most Americans. Despite the spectacular plums garnered from the conference table, the war is forgotten by political orators, seldom discussed in classrooms, and only infrequently recalled by historians and scholars.

But Mexicans, whether scholars or not, have not forgotten the war; their country suffered most from Manifest Destiny's claims to California. The war of 1846–48 represents one of the supreme tragedies of their history. Mexicans are intimately involved with it, unlike their late adversaries who have forgotten it. Fundamental reasons explain this paradox. The victorious United States went to a post-Civil War success story unequaled in the annals of Western civilization. Mexico emerged from the peace of Guadalupe Hidalgo bereft of half of its territory, a beaten, discouraged, and divided country. Mexico never completely recovered from the debacle.

Mexicans had known tragedy and defeat before, but their conquest by General Zachary Taylor and Winfield Scott represented not only a territorial loss of immense proportions, but also a cataclysmic blow to their morale as a nation and as a people. From the Mexican point of view, pride in what they believed they had mastered best —the science of warfare—was exposed as a myth. Mexicans could not even fight successfully, and they had little else to recall with pride, for their political development had enshrined bitter civil strife and callous betrayal of principle. Plagued by hordes of scheming politicians, hungry military men, and a backward and reactionary clergy, they had watched their economy stagnate. Guadalupe Hidalgo clearly outlined the scope of their defeat. There was no success story to write about, only tragedy. Mexicans of all classes are still engrossed in what might have been *if* General Antonio López de Santa Anna had repelled the invaders from the North.

Polk's war message to Congress and Lincoln's famous reply in the House cover some dimensions of the historical problem. Up for discussion are Polk's role in the affair, the responsibility of the United States and Mexico, and the question of war guilt—a question raised by the victorious Americans and their allies at Nuremberg after World War II. For if Polk felt "the blood of this war, like the blood of Abel, is crying to Heaven against him," as Lincoln charged, then both the war and Manifest Destiny stand condemned.

NO

Norman A. Graebner

THE MEXICAN WAR:
A STUDY IN CAUSATION

On May 11, 1846, President James K. Polk presented his war message to Congress. After reviewing the skirmish between General Zachary Taylor's dragoons and a body of Mexican soldiers along the Rio Grande, the president asserted that Mexico "has passed the boundary of the United States, has invaded our territory and shed American blood upon the American soil.... War exists, and, notwithstanding all our efforts to avoid it, exists by act of Mexico." No country could have had a superior case for war. Democrats in large numbers (for it was largely a partisan matter) responded with the patriotic fervor which Polk expected of them. "Our government has permitted itself to be insulted long enough," wrote one Georgian. "The blood of her citizens has been spilt on her own soil. It appeals to us for vengeance." Still, some members of Congress, recalling more accurately than the president the circumstances of the conflict, soon rendered the Mexican War the most reviled in American history—at least until the Vietnam War of the 1960s. One outraged Whig termed the war "illegal, unrighteous, and damnable," and Whigs questioned both Polk's honesty and his sense of geography. Congressman Joshua R. Giddings of Ohio accused the president of "planting the standard of the United States on foreign soil, and using the military forces of the United States to violate every principle of international law and moral justice." To vote for the war, admitted Senator John C. Calhoun, was "to plunge a dagger into his own heart, and more so." Indeed, some critics in Congress openly wished the Mexicans well.

For over a century such profound differences in perception have pervaded American writings on the Mexican War. Even in the past decade, historians have reached conclusions on the question of war guilt as disparate as those which separated Polk from his wartime conservative and abolitionist critics....

In some measure the diversity of judgment on the Mexican War, as on other wars, is understandable. By basing their analyses on official rationalizations, historians often ignore the more universal causes of war which transcend individual conflicts and which can establish the bases for greater consensus.

From Norman A. Graebner, "The Mexican War: A Study in Causation," *Pacific Historical Review*, vol. 49, no. 3 (August 1980), pp. 405–426. Copyright © 1980 by The Pacific Coast Branch, American Historical Association. Reprinted by permission. Notes omitted.

Neither the officials in Washington nor those in Mexico City ever acknowledged any alternatives to the actions which they took. But governments generally have more choices in any controversy than they are prepared to admit. Circumstances determine their extent. The more powerful a nation, the more remote its dangers, the greater its options between action and inaction. Often for the weak, unfortunately, the alternative is capitulation or war.... Polk and his advisers developed their Mexican policies on the dual assumption that Mexico was weak and that the acquisition of certain Mexican territories would satisfy admirably the long-range interests of the United States. Within that context, Polk's policies were direct, timely, and successful. But the president had choices. Mexico, whatever its internal condition, was no direct threat to the United States. Polk, had he so desired, could have avoided war; indeed, he could have ignored Mexico in 1845 with absolute impunity.

* * *

In explaining the Mexican War historians have dwelled on the causes of friction in American-Mexican relations. In part these lay in the disparate qualities of the two populations, in part in the vast discrepancies between the two countries in energy, efficiency, power, and national wealth. Through two decades of independence Mexico had experienced a continuous rise and fall of governments; by the 1840s survival had become the primary concern of every regime. Conscious of their weakness, the successive governments in Mexico City resented the superior power and effectiveness of the United States and feared American notions of destiny that anticipated the annexation of Mexico's northern provinces.

Having failed to prevent the formation of the Texas Republic, Mexico reacted to Andrew Jackson's recognition of Texan independence in March 1837 with deep indignation. Thereafter the Mexican raids into Texas, such as the one on San Antonio in 1842, aggravated the bitterness of Texans toward Mexico, for such forays had no purpose beyond terrorizing the frontier settlements.

Such mutual animosities, extensive as they were, do not account for the Mexican War. Governments as divided and chaotic as the Mexican regimes of the 1840s usually have difficulty in maintaining positive and profitable relations with their neighbors; their behavior often produces annoyance, but seldom armed conflict. Belligerence toward other countries had flowed through U.S. history like a torrent without, in itself, setting off a war. Nations do not fight over cultural differences or verbal recriminations; they fight over perceived threats to their interests created by the ambitions or demands of others.

What increased the animosity between Mexico City and Washington was a series of specific issues over which the two countries perennially quarreled—claims, boundaries, and the future of Texas. Nations have made claims a pretext for intervention, but never a pretext for war. Every nineteenth-century effort to collect debts through force assumed the absence of effective resistance, for no debt was worth the price of war. To collect its debt from Mexico in 1838, for example, France blockaded Mexico's gulf ports and bombarded Vera Cruz. The U.S. claims against Mexico created special problems which discounted their seriousness as a rationale for war. True, the Mexican government failed to protect the possessions and the safety of Americans in Mexico from robbery, theft, and other illegal actions, but U.S. citizens were under no obligation to do business in Mexico and should have understood the risk of transporting goods and money in that country. Minister Waddy Thompson wrote from Mexico City in 1842 that it would be "with somewhat of bad grace that we should war upon a country because it could not pay its debts when so many of our own states are in the same situation." Even as the United States after 1842 attempted futilely to collect the $2 million awarded its citizens by a claims commission, it was far more deeply in debt to Britain over speculative losses. Minister Wilson Shannon reported in the summer of 1844 that the claims issue defied settlement in Mexico City and recommended that Washington take the needed action to compel Mexico to pay. If Polk would take up the challenge and sacrifice American human and material resources in a war against Mexico, he would do so for reasons other than the enforcement of claims. The president knew well that Mexico could not pay, yet as late as May 9, 1846, he was ready to ask Congress for a declaration of war on the question of unpaid claims alone.

Congress's joint resolution for Texas annexation in February 1845 raised the specter of war among editors and politicians alike. As early as 1843 the Mexican government had warned the American minister in Mexico City that annexation would render war inevitable; Mexican officials in Washington repeated that warning. To Mexico, therefore, the move to annex Texas was an unbearable affront. Within one month after Polk's inauguration on March 4, General Juan Almonte, the Mexican minister in Washington, boarded a packet in New York and sailed for Vera Cruz to sever his country's diplomatic relations with the United States. Even before the Texas Convention could meet on July 4 to vote annexation, rumors of a possible Mexican invasion of Texas prompted Polk to advance Taylor's forces from Fort Jesup in Louisiana down the Texas coast. Polk instructed Taylor to extend his protection to the Rio Grande but to avoid any areas to the north of that river occupied by Mexican troops. Simultaneously the president reinforced the American squadron in the Gulf of Mexico. "The threatened invasion of Texas by a large Mexican army," Polk informed Andrew J. Donelson, the American chargé in Texas, on June 15, "is well calculated to excite great interest here and increases our solicitude concerning the final action by the Congress and the Convention of Texas." Polk assured Donelson that he intended to defend Texas to the limit of his constitutional power. Donelson resisted the pressure of those Texans who wanted Taylor to advance to the Rio Grande; instead, he placed the general at Corpus Christi on the Nueces River. Taylor agreed that the line from the mouth of the Nueces to San Antonio covered the Texas settlements and afforded a favorable base from which to defend the frontier.

Those who took the rumors of Mexican aggressiveness seriously lauded the president's action. With Texas virtually a part of the United States, argued the *Washington Union*, "We owe it to ourselves, to the proud and elevated character which America maintains among the nations of the earth, to guard our own territory from the invasion of the ruthless Mexicans." The *New York Morning News* observed that Polk's policy would, on the whole, "command a general concurrence of the public opinion of his country." Some Democratic leaders, fearful of a Mexican attack, urged the president to strengthen Taylor's forces and order them to take the offensive should Mexican soldiers cross the Rio Grande. Others believed the reports from Mexico exaggerated, for there was no apparent relationship between the country's expressions of belligerence and its capacity to act. Secretary of War William L. Marcy admitted that his information was no better than that of other commentators. "I have at no time," he wrote in July, "felt that war with Mexico was probable—and do not now believe it is, yet it is in the range of possible occurrences. I have officially acted on the hypothesis that our peace may be temporarily disturbed without however believing it will be." Still convinced that the administration had no grounds for alarm, Marcy wrote on August 12: "The presence of a considerable force in Texas will do no hurt and possibly may be of great use." In September William S. Parrott, Polk's special agent in Mexico, assured the president that there would be neither a Mexican declaration of war nor an invasion of Texas.

Polk insisted that the administration's show of force in Texas would prevent rather than provoke war. "I do not anticipate that Mexico will be mad enough to declare war," he wrote in July, but "I think she would have done so but for the appearance of a strong naval force in the Gulf and our army moving in the direction of her frontier on land." Polk restated this judgment on July 28 in a letter to General Robert Armstrong, the U.S. consul at Liverpool: "I think there need be but little apprehension of war with Mexico. If however she shall be mad enough to make war we are prepared to meet her." The president assured Senator William H. Haywood of North Carolina that the American

forces in Texas would never aggress against Mexico; however, they would prevent any Mexican forces from crossing the Rio Grande. In conversation with Senator William S. Archer of Virginia on September 1, the president added confidently that "the appearance of our land and naval forces on the borders of Mexico & in the Gulf would probably deter and prevent Mexico from either declaring war or invading Texas." Polk's continuing conviction that Mexico would not attack suggests that his deployment of U.S. land and naval forces along Mexico's periphery was designed less to protect Texas than to support an aggressive diplomacy which might extract a satisfactory treaty from Mexico without war. For Anson Jones, the last president of the Texas Republic, Polk's deployments had precisely that purpose:

> Texas never actually needed the protection of the United States after I came into office. . . . There was no necessity for it after the 'preliminary Treaty,' as we were at peace with Mexico, and knew perfectly well that that Government, though she might bluster a little, had not the slightest idea of invading Texas either by land or water; and that nothing would provoke her to (active) hostilities, but the presence of troops in the immediate neighborhood of the Rio Grande, threatening her towns and settlements on the southwest side of that river. . . . But Donelson appeared so intent upon 'encumbering us with help,' that finally, to get rid of his annoyance, he was told he might give us as much protection as he pleased. . . . The protection asked for was only *prospective* and contingent; the *protection* he had in view was *immediate* and *aggressive*.

For Polk the exertion of military and diplomatic pressure on a disorganized Mexico was not a prelude to war. Whig critics of annexation had predicted war; this alone compelled the administration to avoid a conflict over Texas. In his memoirs Jones recalled that in 1845 Commodore Robert F. Stockton, with either the approval or the connivance of Polk, attempted to convince him that he should place Texas "in an attitude of active hostility toward Mexico, so that, when Texas was finally brought into the Union, *she might bring war with her.*" If Stockton engaged in such an intrigue, he apparently did so on his own initiative, for no evidence exists to implicate the administration. Polk not only preferred to achieve his purposes by means other than war but also assumed that his military measures in Texas, limited as they were, would convince the Mexican government that it could not escape the necessity of coming to terms with the United States. Washington's policy toward Mexico during 1845 achieved the broad national purpose of Texas annexation. Beyond that it brought U.S. power to bear on Mexico in a manner calculated to further the processes of negotiation. Whether the burgeoning tension would lead to a negotiated boundary settlement or to war hinged on two factors: the nature of Polk's demands and Mexico's response to them. The president announced his objectives to Mexico's troubled officialdom through his instructions to John Slidell, his special emissary who departed for Mexico in November 1845 with the assurance that the government there was prepared to reestablish formal diplomatic relations with the United States and negotiate a territorial settlement....

* * *

Actually, Slidell's presence in Mexico inaugurated a diplomatic crisis not unlike those which precede most wars. Fundamentally the Polk administration, in dispatching Slidell, gave the Mexicans the same two choices that the dominant power in any confrontation gives to the weaker: the acceptance of a body of concrete diplomatic demands or eventual war. Slidell's instructions described U.S. territorial objectives with considerable clarity. If Mexico knew little of Polk's growing acquisitiveness toward California during the autumn of 1845, Slidell proclaimed the president's intentions with his proposals to purchase varying portions of California for as much as $25 million. Other countries such as England and Spain had consigned important areas of the New World through peaceful negotiations, but the United States, except in its Mexican relations, had never asked any country to part with a portion of its own territory. Yet Polk could not understand why Mexico should reveal any special reluctance to part with Texas, the Rio Grande, New Mexico, or California. What made the terms of Slidell's instructions appear fair to him was Mexico's military and financial helplessness. Polk's defenders noted that California was not a sine qua non of any settlement and that the president offered to settle the immediate controversy over the acquisition of the Rio Grande boundary alone in exchange for the cancellation of claims. Unfortunately, amid the passions of December 1845, such distinctions were lost. Furthermore, a settlement of the Texas boundary would not have resolved the California question at all.

Throughout the crisis months of 1845 and 1846, spokesmen of the Polk administration repeatedly warned the Mexican government that its choices were limited. In June 1845, Polk's mouthpiece, the *Washington Union*, had observed characteristically that, if Mexico resisted Washington's demands, "a corps of properly organized volunteers... would invade, overrun, and occupy Mexico. They would enable us not only to take California, but to keep it." American officials, in their contempt for Mexico, spoke privately of the need to chastize that country for its annoyances and insults. Parrott wrote to Secretary of State James Buchanan in October that he wished "to see this people well flogged by Uncle Sam's boys, ere we enter upon negotiations.... I know [the Mexicans] better, perhaps, than any other American citizen and I am fully persuaded, they can never love or respect us, as we should be loved and respected by them, until we shall have given them a positive proof of our superiority." Mexico's pretensions would continue, wrote Slidell in late December, "until the Mexican people shall be convinced by hostile demonstrations, that our differences must be settled promptly, either by negotiation or the sword." In January 1846 the *Union* publicly threatened Mexico with war if it rejected the just demands of the United States: "The result of such a course on her part may compel us to resort to more decisive measures.... to obtain the settlement of our legitimate claims." As Slidell prepared to leave Mexico in March 1846, he again reminded the administration: "Depend upon it, we can never get along well with them, until we have given them a good drubbing." In Washington on May 8, Slidell advised the president "to take the redress of the wrongs and injuries which we had so long borne from Mexico into our own hands, and to act with promptness and energy."

Mexico responded to Polk's challenge with an outward display of belligerence and an inward dread of war. Mexicans feared above all that the United States intended to overrun their country and seize much of their territory. Polk and his advisers assumed that Mexico, to avoid an American invasion, would give up its provinces peacefully. Obviously Mexico faced growing diplomatic and military pressures to negotiate away its territories; it faced no moral obligation to do so. Herrera and Paredes had the sovereign right to protect their regimes by avoiding any formal recognition of Slidell and by rejecting any of the boundary proposals embodied in his instructions, provided that in the process they did not endanger any legitimate interests of the American people. At least to some Mexicans, Slidell's terms demanded nothing less than Mexico's capitulation. By what standard was $2 million a proper payment for the Rio Grande boundary, or $25 million a fair price for California? No government would have accepted such terms. Having rejected negotiation in the face of superior force, Mexico would meet the challenge with a final gesture of defiance. In either case it was destined to lose, but historically nations have preferred to fight than to give away territory under diplomatic pressure alone. Gene M. Brack, in his long study of Mexico's deep-seated fear and resentment of the United States, explained Mexico's ultimate behavior in such terms:

President Polk knew that Mexico could offer but feeble resistance militarily, and he knew that Mexico needed money. No proper American would exchange territory and the national honor for cash, but President Polk mistakenly believed that the application of military pressure would convince Mexicans to do so. They did not respond logically, but patriotically. Left with the choice of war or territorial concessions, the former course, however dim the prospects of success, could be the only one.

* * *

Mexico, in its resistance, gave Polk the three choices which every nation gives another in an uncompromisable confrontation: to withdraw his demands and permit the issues to drift, unresolved; to reduce his goals in the interest of an immediate settlement; or to escalate the pressures in the hope of securing an eventual settlement on his own terms. Normally when the internal conditions of a country undermine its relations with others, a diplomatic corps simply removes itself from the hostile environment and awaits a better day. Mexico, despite its animosity, did not endanger the security interests of the United States; it had not invaded Texas and did not contemplate doing so. Mexico had refused to pay the claims, but those claims were not equal to the price of a one-week war. Whether Mexico negotiated a boundary for Texas in 1846 mattered little; the United States had lived with unsettled boundaries for decades without considering war. Settlers, in time, would have forced a decision, but in 1846 the region between the Nueces and the Rio Grande was a vast, generally unoccupied wilderness. Thus there was nothing, other than Polk's ambitions, to prevent the United States from withdrawing its diplomats from Mexico City and permitting its relations to drift. But Polk, whatever the language of his instructions, did not send Slidell to Mexico to normalize relations with that government. He expected Slidell to negotiate an immediate boundary settlement favorable to the United States, and nothing less.

Recognizing no need to reduce his demands on Mexico, Polk, without hesitation, took the third course which Mexico offered. Congress bound the president to the annexation of Texas; thereafter the Polk administration was free to formulate its own policies toward Mexico. With the Slidell mission Polk embarked upon a program of gradual coercion to achieve a settlement, preferably without war. That program led logically from his dispatching an army to Texas and his denunciation of Mexico in his annual message of December 1845 to his new instructions of January 1846, which ordered General Taylor to the Rio Grande. Colonel Atocha, spokesman for the deposed Mexican leader, Antonio López de Santa Anna, encouraged Polk to pursue his policy of escalation. The president recorded Atocha's advice:

He said our army should be marched at once from Corpus Christi to the Del Norte, and a strong naval force assembled at Vera Cruz, that Mr. Slidell, the U.S. Minister, should withdraw from Jalappa, and go on board one of our ships of War at Vera Cruz, and in that position should demand the payment of [the] amount due our citizens; that it was well known the Mexican Government was unable to pay in money, and that when they saw a strong force ready to strike on their coasts and border, they would, he had no doubt, feel their danger and agree to the boundary suggested. He said that Paredes, Almonte, & Gen'l Santa Anna were all willing for such an arrangement, but that they dare not make it until it was made apparent to the Archbishop of Mexico & the people generally that it was necessary to save their country from a war with the U. States.

Thereafter Polk never questioned the efficacy of coercion. He asserted at a cabinet meeting on February 17 that "it would be necessary to take strong measures towards Mexico before our difficulties with that Government could be settled." Similarly on April 18 Polk told Calhoun that "our relations with Mexico had reached a point where we could not stand still but must treat all nations whether weak or strong alike, and that I saw no alternative but strong measures towards Mexico." A week later the president again brought the Mexican question before the cabinet. "I expressed my opinion," he noted in his diary, "that we must take redress for the injuries done us into our own hands, that we had attempted to conciliate Mexico in vain, and had forborne until forbearance was no longer either a virtue or patriotic." Convinced that Paredes needed money, Polk suggested to leading senators that Congress appropriate $1 million both to encourage Paredes to negotiate and to sustain him in power until the United States could ratify the treaty. The president failed to secure Calhoun's required support.

Polk's persistence led him and the country to war. Like all escalations in the exertion of force, his decision responded less to unwanted and unanticipated resistance than to the requirements of the clearly perceived and inflexible purposes which guided the administration. What perpetuated the president's escalation to the point of war was his determination to pursue goals to the end whose achievement lay outside the possibilities of successful negotiations. Senator Thomas Hart Benton of Missouri saw this situation when he wrote: "It is impossible to conceive of an administration less warlike, or more intriguing, than that of Mr. Polk. They were *men of peace, with objects to be accomplished by means of war;*

so that war was a necessity and an indispensability to their purpose."

Polk understood fully the state of Mexican opinion. In placing General Taylor on the Rio Grande he revealed again his contempt for Mexico. Under no national obligation to expose the country's armed forces, he would not have advanced Taylor in the face of a superior military force. Mexico had been undiplomatic; its denunciations of the United States were insulting and provocative. But if Mexico's behavior antagonized Polk, it did not antagonize the Whigs, the abolitionists, or even much of the Democratic party. Such groups did not regard Mexico as a threat; they warned the administration repeatedly that Taylor's presence on the Rio Grande would provoke war. But in the balance against peace was the pressure of American expansionism. Much of the Democratic and expansionist press, having accepted without restraint both the purposes of the Polk administration and its charges of Mexican perfidy, urged the president on to more vigorous action....

Confronted with the prospect of further decline which they could neither accept nor prevent, [the Mexicans] lashed out with the intention of protecting their self-esteem and compelling the United States, if it was determined to have the Rio Grande, New Mexico, and California, to pay for its prizes with something other than money. On April 23, Paredes issued a proclamation declaring a defensive war against the United States. Predictably, one day later the Mexicans fired on a detachment of U.S. dragoons. Taylor's report of the attack reached Polk on Saturday evening, May 9. On Sunday the president drafted his war message and delivered it to Congress on the following day. Had Polk avoided the crisis, he might have gained the time required to permit the emigrants of 1845 and 1846 to settle the California issue without war.

What clouds the issue of the Mexican War's justification was the acquisition of New Mexico and California, for contemporaries and historians could not logically condemn the war and laud the Polk administration for its territorial achievements. Perhaps it is true that time would have permitted American pioneers to transform California into another Texas. But even then California's acquisition by the United States would have emanated from the use of force, for the elimination of Mexican sovereignty, whether through revolution or war, demanded the successful use of power. If the power employed in revolution would have been less obtrusive than that exerted in war, its role would have been no less essential. There simply was no way that the United States could acquire California peacefully. If the distraught Mexico of 1845 would not sell the distant province, no regime thereafter would have done so. Without forceful destruction of Mexico's sovereign power, California would have entered the twentieth century as an increasingly important region of another country.

Thus the Mexican War poses the dilemma of all international relations. Nations whose geographic and political status fails to coincide with their ambition and power can balance the two sets of factors in only one manner: through the employment of force. They succeed or fail according to circumstances; and for the United States, the conditions for achieving its empire in the Southwest and its desired frontage on the Pacific were so ideal that later generations could refer to the process as the mere fulfillment of destiny. "The Mexican Republic," lamented a Mexican writer in 1848, "... had among other misfortunes of less account, the great one of being in the vicinity of a strong and energetic people." What the Mexican War revealed in equal measure is the simple fact that only those countries which have achieved their destiny, whatever that may be, can afford to extol the virtues of peaceful change.

POSTSCRIPT

Was the Mexican War an Exercise in American Imperialism?

According to Professor Graebner, President James Polk assumed that Mexico was weak and that acquiring certain Mexican territories would satisfy "the long-range interests" of the United States. But when Mexico refused Polk's attempts to purchase New Mexico and California, he was left with three options: withdraw his demands; modify and soften his proposals; or aggressively pursue his original goals. According to Graebner, the president chose the third option.

Graebner is one of the most prominent members of the "realist" school of diplomatic historians. His writings were influenced by the cold war realists, political scientists, diplomats, and journalists of the 1950s who believed that American foreign policy oscillated between heedless isolationism and crusading wars without developing coherent policies that suited the national interests of the United States.

Graebner's views on the Mexican War have not gone unchallenged. See, for example, Professor David M. Pletcher's *The Diplomacy of Annexation* (University of Missouri, 1973), which remains the definitive study of the Polk administration. Charles Sellers's biography *James K. Polk*, 2 vols. (Princeton University Press, 1957–1966) is also a valuable resource.

Professor Ruiz offers a Mexican perspective on the war in chapter 11 of his book *Triumphs and Tragedy: A History of the Mexican People* (W. W. Norton, 1992), in which he argues that while the United States went on to achieve great economic success after the Civil War, Mexico never recovered from losing half of her territories.

Ruiz also takes issue with Graebner, who considers Manifest Destiny to be mere political rhetoric with very limited goals. In Ruiz's view, Manifest Destiny was a reflection of the racist attitudes shown toward the non-white Native Americans, African Americans, and Mexican Americans who stood in the way of white America's desire for new land.

The best two collections of readings from the major writers on the war are old but essential: see Archie McDonald, ed., *The Mexican War: Crisis for American Democracy* (D.C. Heath, 1969) and Ramón Eduardo Ruiz, ed., *The Mexican War: Was It Manifest Destiny?* (Holt, Rinehart & Winston, 1963).

There are several nontraditional books that cover the Mexican War, including John H. Schroeder, *Mr. Polk's War: American Opposition and Dissent, 1846–1848* (Wisconsin, 1973). Finally Robert W. Johannsen summarized the ways in which contemporaries viewed the war in *To the Halls of the Montezuma: The Mexican War In the American Imagination* (Oxford University Press, 1985).

PART 4

Conflict and Resolution

The changing nature of the United States and the demands of its own principles finally erupted into violent conflict. Perhaps it was an inevitable step in the process of building a coherent nation from a number of distinct and diverse groups. The leaders, attitudes, and resources that were available to the North and the South were to determine the course of the war itself, as well as the national healing process that followed.

- Were Southern Slaveholding Women Covert Abolitionists?

- Have Historians Overemphasized the Slavery Issue as a Cause of the Civil War?

- Was the Confederacy Defeated Because of Its "Loss of Will"?

- Was Abraham Lincoln America's Greatest President?

- Was Reconstruction a Success?

ISSUE 13

Were Southern Slaveholding Women Covert Abolitionists?

YES: Suzanne Lebsock, from *The Free Women of Petersburg: Status and Culture in a Southern Town, 1784–1860* (W. W. Norton, 1984)

NO: Elizabeth Fox-Genovese, from *Within the Plantation Household: Black and White Women of the Old South* (University of North Carolina Press, 1988)

ISSUE SUMMARY

YES: Professor of history Suzanne Lebsock believes that slaveholding women subverted the institution of slavery by protecting favored bond servants and even by freeing slaves through their wills.

NO: Professor of southern history Elizabeth Fox-Genovese insists that the privileges associated with owning slaves prevented these women from joining the ranks of the abolitionists.

Opposition to slavery in the American colonies dates back to the seventeenth and eighteenth centuries, when Puritan leaders like Samuel Sewall and Quakers such as John Woolman and Anthony Benezet published a number of pamphlets condemning the existence of the slave system. The connection between religion and antislavery sentiment also is evident in the decision of the Society of Friends in 1688 to prohibit members from owning bond servants because slavery was contrary to Christian principles. These attacks, however, did little to diminish the institution. In fact, efforts to force emancipation gained little headway in the colonies until the outbreak of the American Revolution. Complaints that the English government had instituted a series of measures that "enslaved" the colonies in British North America also raised thorny questions about the presence of *real* slavery in those colonies. How could Americans demand their freedom from King George III, who was cast in the role of oppressive master, and at the same time deny freedom and liberty to black bondsmen in their midst? Such a contradiction inspired a gradual emancipation movement in the North, which often was accompanied by compensation for former slave owners.

In addition, antislavery societies sprang up throughout the nation to continue the crusade against bondage. Interestingly, the majority were located in the South. Prior to the 1830s the most prominent antislavery organization was the American Colonization Society, which offered a twofold program: (1) gradual, compensated emancipation of slaves and (2) exportation of the newly freed former slaves to colonies outside the boundaries of the United States, especially to Africa.

In the 1830s antislavery activity underwent an important transformation. As the colonizationists proved unable to eliminate either slavery or African Americans from the country, a new strain of antislavery sentiment expressed itself in the abolitionist movement. Drawing momentum from both the Second Great Awakening and the example set by England (which prohibited slavery in its imperial holdings in 1833), abolitionists called for an immediate end of slavery without compensation to masters for the loss of their property. Abolitionists viewed slavery not so much as a practical problem to be resolved but as a moral offense incapable of being resolved through traditional channels of political compromise.

The rise of abolitionism produced a vigorous countermovement by white southerners to protect the embattled slave system. Whereas many southern leaders prior to the 1830s had characterized slavery as a necessary evil that would disappear within a generation or two, in response to the abolitionist critique, southern spokesmen such as George Fitzhugh, James Hammond, and John C. Calhoun fashioned a multifaceted proslavery argument. Calhoun, responding to the abolitionists' condemnation of slavery as a moral evil, determined that, in fact, slavery was a positive good.

The following selections address the possible abolitionist tendencies of a group of white southerners who, until recently, have been largely ignored by historians—the plantation mistresses. To what extent did they share their husbands' mostly proslavery views? Is it possible that, as women subordinated within a patriarchal society, female slaveholders identified closely enough with their chattel property so as to desire freedom for their slaves? Clearly, these women were not likely to jeopardize their reputations or invoke judgments of their sanity by being outspoken opponents of slavery. But was this abolitionist sentiment present nevertheless? In her study of antebellum women in Petersburg, Virginia, Suzanne Lebsock reports that female slave owners lacked a firm commitment to the slave system. An analysis of the wills of Petersburg's slaveholders reveals that more women than men used their wills to liberate slaves, to protect their slaves from sale, or to provide cash payments to permit their slaves to maintain themselves. These subversive actions, Lebsock concludes, were the product of a distinct female value system based on personalism. By contrast, Elizabeth Fox-Genovese insists that the only southern women who opposed slavery were female slaves. White women's attitudes toward slaves and the slave system were shaped by their own racism and by the fact that they relished the many privileges associated with slaveholding. These attitudes, concludes Fox-Genovese, prevented slaveholding women from engaging in any concerted attack on the institution of slavery.

YES

Suzanne Lebsock

WOMEN ALONE:
PROPERTY AND PERSONALISM

Much as we have learned recently about particular groups of American women, some stereotypes still stand between us and a clear vision of the past. One thinks of the stereotypical single woman in the nineteenth-century propertied family—dependent on the charity of her brother's household, useful after her fashion, and smelling of lavender and timidity. This is an image in urgent need of revision, because single women, and widows, too, are pivotal characters in the recovery of the female past. For all the limitations on their lives, spinsters and widows did have the same legal options as men. As time went on, the single and widowed women of Petersburg became increasingly active in exercising these options. In the process, they set in place a series of windows on women's consciousness; when women were in a position to make decisions about money, about family, about slaves, and about their own capabilities, their choices were often different from those made by men. From this evidence, it looks very much as though women did indeed operate from a distinct female value system. And at its center, if it can be captured in a phrase, was a persistent personalism....

Families are full of inequalities, inequalities of love and loyalty, inequalities of need. Women recognized this in the terms of their wills, and they were occasionally explicit about it. "I have not given any thing to my son Seth and daughter Susan purposely for reasons which they are apprized of"; "I do not wish for Henry Johnson'[s] child to have any posion of my estate being he is well enough off without my little estate"; "I hope my brother Robert and Sister Mary will not think that there is any want of affection on my part for them, I am only anxious to secure my little property to those of my family who need it most"; "I love all my children alike but my daughters I feel most attached to and think they ought to have what I own at my death, and therefore this disposition."

While men for the most part distributed their property according to formula, women tended to pick and choose. There may have been an element of the power play in this; a propertied woman could keep her heirs on their good behavior for years, as long as she kept them guessing as to the terms of her last will. The women's wills were, in any case, highly personalized. They rewarded special qualities of loyalty and affection. They also funneled property into the hands of the heirs who needed it most, and here again the women's penchant for economic security was revealed.... [W]omen were more likely than were men to protect the legacies they gave their female heirs by making the legacies separate estates. (The desire to exempt bequests to married women from the control of husbands and husbands' creditors was in itself a major incentive for writing a will.) What is more, the women took the lead in a more novel procedure of establishing extra measures of economic security for sons. After 1820, there were ten wills that set up trusts for the benefit of adult sons. Eight of them were written by women.

Thus women had good reason to avoid intestacy: They wanted their property divided on the basis of personal merit and particular need, and they often wanted it conveyed on more protective terms than the ordinary course of probate law would permit. They also wanted, more often than did the men, special treatment for their slaves. "It is my first desire to make some comfortable provision for my servants as a just reward for their affection and fidelity." So began the will that Dorothy Mitchell wrote in 1837, and as more women began to write wills, they left more evidence of a special relationship between southern white women and chattel slavery. It has been proposed by some observers that the white women of the South were covert abolitionists, or, at the least, that they lacked a full-scale commitment to the slave system. The wills of Petersburg's white slaveholders, though their numbers are relatively small, give us

a first opportunity to put this proposition to the test.

The results appear to be positive. First of all, more women than men used their wills to set slaves free. After 1840, twelve white women emancipated slaves by will; only eight white men did the same. (A much larger number of emancipations were performed by deed, and here, too, white women appear to have outdone the men in liberating slaves.) Second, more women than men (again after 1840, eight women and five men) inserted clauses either to prevent their slaves from being moved or sold or to restrict the terms of sale. Lucy Frances Branch, a single woman of fifty, made herself very clear: "It is my express wish and desire to make such a disposition of my woman *Martha Graves* as to prevent her being removed farther from her mother and husband than she now lives." To that end, Branch stipulated that Graves was not to be moved or mortgaged, and that if a sale ever became unavoidable, Graves be permitted to choose her purchaser.

Finally, women more often than men (twelve women, seven men) gave their slaves legacies, single cash payments in some cases, maintenance for life in others. For Mary Lithgow, the central clauses of her will, written more lovingly and in more detail than any of the provisions concerning her son and her grandchildren, were those written for the benefit of William Alexander, a seven-year-old boy whom she had recently freed. Lithgow directed that William be given fifty dollars a year until he turned twenty-one, that he receive five hundred dollars on his majority along with some furniture and traveling trunks, that he be put to a good trade, that he be educated in morals and religion, that he be allowed to stay in Virginia, and that, if this last request were impossible, he be placed with a gentleman of good standing in the North. Lithgow subsequently revised her will twice, and each revision brought a bonus for William Alexander. The first allotted the three hundred dollars Lithgow had stashed in her savings account to William's "plain education, so as to fit him for business." The second authorized him to buy members of his family, and at a fair price.

So far as the wills let us judge, white women were kinder to their slaves than were men, and the women were more likely to set their slaves free. But was this a quiet form of abolitionism? Was it an implicit critique of the slave system?

The best answer seems to be that white women were in fact a subversive influence on chattel slavery, not so much because they opposed slavery as a system (the abstract merits of systems did not concern them much), but because they operated out of an essentially personal frame of reference. The women who wrote special provisions for their slaves into their wills worked from the same mentality that caused women as a group to divide property unevenly among their heirs: Women indulged particular attachments—they were alert to the special case, to the personal exception.

White women's thinking about slavery was almost always grounded in the particulars of day-to-day human interaction. Their letters and diaries, at least those that survive from Petersburg, said next to nothing about slavery as an institution. Instead, they spoke of individual slaves, as personalities and especially as workers. This is not to say they were above condescension and stereotyping. Kate Spaulding missed her family in Petersburg terribly, the more so as the rift between North and South widened. On

Christmas Day 1860, she wrote from her new home in New York, sending holiday greetings to "the dear darkies! If they *have* been the cause of so much fuss, they are dear to me as house-hold things!" Most often, however, women's comments on slaves were reports on the status of the household labor force—who performed which tasks and how well. Mary Cumming described her retinue to her Irish sister in 1811:

And now to give a description of a large family in the kitchen. First there is old Nancy the cook, who is an excellent good one, Jennie the housemaid, who seems to be a very decent woman. She has four fine children, the eldest a girl about twelve years old, who is to be my little attendant, her name is Mary. Then there is Betty, Cora, and Joseph. They can all do something, Mary is a pretty good worker at her needle, she is now sitting beside me making a slip for herself. I think I shall make her very useful to me in some time. The man's name who attends at table is Palermo. This is an account of our family, the servants appear to be all regular and well behaved.

More than forty years later, Anna Campbell outlined the work of fourteen-year-old Lavinia and nine-year-old Solomon:

the former being a mulatto, is quite smart & really does a woman's work, helps me much with the children, occasionally sews a little. The latter runs errands blacks shoes cleans knives & forks, occasionally spills a bucket of water on the stairs, drops a tray full of dishes or a part of the dinner or breakfast as the case may be, but upon the whole is a good boy & rightly named, has only been caught stealing once....

The mistresses were not always so well satisfied, of course. "We have engaged a woman for next year whose *appearance* is not very prepossessing," wrote Eliza K. Myers, "but I dare say she may suit us quite as well & I hope better than the last *incumbent*—or *incumbrance* whichever you please." But the point is, while the mistresses' feelings ran the gamut from an almost comradely affection to extreme exasperation, they remained focused on individual slaves.

Consider by contrast the diary of Edmund Ruffin. Slaves must have been a constant presence in Ruffin's days, yanking off his boots, one imagines, stirring up his woodstove, serving his suppers. But Ruffin never talked about them. And this was not because he was writing an essentially public diary. Ruffin wrote pages on his aches and pains, on his flirtations with little children, on his leisure reading (which included a fair number of sentimental novels). He also wrote about the pamphlets he was composing to try to persuade his countrymen that western civilization owed its greatest achievements to chattel slavery. Ruffin is remembered now as a major proslavery apologist. His refusal to acknowledge the living presence of particular slaves undoubtedly helped him to keep his theory clean.

Of all the Petersburg women who left some record, none gave any indication that she regarded slavery as a positive good. The closest any Petersburg woman came to an endorsement of slavery was a letter written by Ann T. Davis in 1859, after John Brown's raid had made it look as though the abolitionists were prepared to enflame the South in insurrection and war. Davis feared her sons would be marched off to fight; she prayed for the destruction of abolitionism, and, in a uniquely general statement, repeated the rather old-fashioned creed of the colonizationists:

My trust is in God, who knows the great heart of the South, and who sees that they are doing all that they can do, for the comfort, and happiness of the slaves, providentially committed to their care. I, for one, would gladly hail the day, when every son and daughter of degraded Ham, were free and independent, in some country of their own, but until that can be peacefully effected, I believe that they had better remain in bondage under the care of good masters, than be free in the United States.

This was faint praise. It may have been that women's propensity to look at life in personal terms prevented their becoming wholehearted defenders of the slave system; the auction block and the separation of families were too appallingly commonplace. At the same time, the personal approach—thinking about the immediate needs and talents and sins of particular slaves—must have helped white women get along day by day with an institution they believed to be evil in at least some respects. The alternative was not thinking. English immigrant Mary L. Simpson said it in 1821, after witnessing her first Christmas rush of slave hirings and auctions: "Now dont you often wonder how I can live contented and happy in such a quarter of the world? Why I assure you it is only when I leave out of the question or rather forget all these things." Then she added, "But a truce to *treason*."

Mary L. Simpson made some sort of peace with slavery and in so doing became an accomplice to it. So did almost all white women of the slaveholding classes. But theirs was an unsteady complicity, for there was in women's willingness to make the personal exception a quality of sabotage. The will of Mary Lithgow was a case in point. Almost all of Lithgow's property was in her seven slaves, and she had her own family to consider. She had a son, and he had a wife, children, and chronic financial problems. So six of Lithgow's slaves were to remain in bondage. Three of them she had placed in trust, the income to be applied to the support of her son's family. Three of them she ordered sold, though not to slavetraders. The seventh was the boy William Alexander, to whom she granted freedom, property, and education. Mary Lithgow was no abolitionist. On the other hand, it was widely believed that free black people undermined the slave system by their very existence. Mary Lithgow could hardly have been unaware of this.

* * *

It is worth pausing to appreciate the importance of the deeds and wills for the recovery of values. It seems logical enough that a set of distinctive values should have grown out of women's distinctive experiences, out of their experience with nurture, with personal service, and with the maintenance of life day by day. But it is difficult to describe those values with any precision, and it is equally difficult to discern when and how much they informed women's behavior in activities other than marriage and mothering. We know, for example, that in Petersburg and elsewhere, women took the lead in religion and organized charity.... But it is hard to say how much this activity was an expression of female values, and how much it merely reflected the fact that women were allowed to do church and charity work while they were not allowed to enter formal politics, the professions, big business, or the military. There were not many occasions in the nineteenth century when women exercised something approximating free

choice. There were even fewer occasions when women's choices were systematically recorded and rendered comparable to the choices made by men.

This is what makes the deeds and wills so special, and here, in one list, are the documentable components of a women's value system. Women, more than men, noticed and responded to the needs and merits of particular persons. This showed in their tendency to reward favorite slaves and to distribute their property unevenly among their heirs. It also showed in their ability to make independent judgments about their own fitness to administer estates. Women were particularly sensitive to the interests of other women and to their precarious economic position; this was demonstrated in favoritism toward female heirs and in the establishment of separate estates. As their real estate and credit transactions suggest, women wanted financial security for themselves as well as for others. Beyond that they were not as ego-invested as were men in the control of wealth. Our list grows a bit longer if we add the more ambiguous evidence derived from women's vanguard action in providing relief to the poor and in promoting religion. Women as a group were more invested than were men in Christian communities and the life of the spirit. And in their efforts to give assistance to the poor, both personalism and regard for other women surfaced again; the poor were mainly women and children, most of whom cannot have "deserved" their poverty.

The people who wrote the antebellum period's popular literature have been trying to tell us all along that women were different from men, better than men in some respects. Perhaps it is time we took their message more seriously. The Petersburg evidence does help explain why the nineteenth century's theory of gender differences was so long-lived and so powerful: The cult of true womanhood owed its pervasiveness to the fact that it was in some fundamental way plausible. That portion of the cult that addressed spheres of activity always generated a certain amount of controversy and was always subject to additions and corrections, for in the real world the limits of acceptable female activity were in constant flux. But the portion of the cult that dealt with character was obdurately uncontroversial. By the end of the century, even woman suffragists fell into line, insisting along with everyone else that human kindness, moral virtue, and religious devotion were the distinguishing traits of the female character.

And so they were. If Petersburg is any indication, the cult of true womanhood carried the day in part because some of its claims conformed closely to observed female behavior. This is not to say that the women of Petersburg were true women down the line. In the literature of true womanhood, the focus was on relationships between women and their men, and women were told that they owed their husbands, even cruel husbands, uncomplaining obedience. Real-life women of Petersburg, however, were deeply engaged in the lives of other females, as well as males, and as they demonstrated in the granting of separate estates, they were quite willing to undercut male authority when the welfare of a beloved kinswoman was at stake. Otherwise, purveyors of the cult of true womanhood would have found in the behavior of Petersburg's women a lot to like. Women *were* first in piety and benevolence, including, it appears, benevolence toward slaves—a dimension of true womanhood

peculiar to the South—just as the popular literature claimed.

If we take gender differences as seriously as the nineteenth century did, the implications for the way we look at history are enormous. Most existing scholarship implicitly takes men as the measure. That is, events and ideas are evaluated on the basis of how much they helped women achieve what men already had. This is obviously an essential line of inquiry. But it needs to be balanced with the recognition that women had standards of their own. One of the cult of true womanhood's many messages —and this is the one worth saving in our own time—is that there were two standards, two scales of achievement, two sets of values. In the antebellum period, of course, it could not be admitted that the values of women might be subversive; writers brightly insisted that the respective roles of men and women were harmonious and complementary. Whether we are dealing with harmony or subversion, the issue needs to be explored for as many times and as many places as the sources permit. The Petersburg evidence suggests that it is possible to reconstruct female values in considerable detail. This is precisely what we need to take us beyond compensatory women's history, beyond the weary and ultimately impoverishing process of testing how women measured up on a masculine scale. The past, as a result, is going to look different—richer, more complex, probably more embattled.

For the future, emphasis on gender differences has great promise and great strategic risks. The risks derive from the difficulty we have in thinking in genuinely egalitarian terms; "different" is readily translated into "inferior," and thus is discrimination justified. The promise lies farther off. If we find that all along women have managed to create and sustain countercultures, then the chances increase that as women come to power, a more humane social order will indeed come with them. This is a hopeful vision, but not necessarily a utopian one; we may be talking about the realm of the small improvement.

That returns us to Petersburg and to the concrete terms that Petersburg's women found most congenial. The immediate significance of the women's value system was that some slaves were freed, some orphans were fed, and some daughters were protected from economic exploitation. That was not so very little.

NO

Elizabeth Fox-Genovese

AND WOMEN WHO DID NOT

Slaveholding women did not share their slaves' opposition to slavery. Nor did slaveholding women embrace the fledgling cause of women's rights, which was gaining ground among northerners and which they, like others, viewed as intimately linked to abolitionism. They were known to grumble in private about certain aspects of their lives and even, on occasion, to blame slavery for the most disagreeable ones. Women, like men—black and white, northern and southern—will sometimes grumble. But the complaints of slaveholding women never amounted to a concerted attack on the system, the various parts of which, as they knew, stood or fell together. Slavery, with all its abuses, constituted the fabric of their beloved country—the warp and woof of their social position, their personal relations, their very identities....

To view slaveholding women as the opponents of southern social relations is to extrapolate from their depictions of slavery as a personal burden to an assumed opposition to the social system as such. That southern women complained about slavery and sometimes about men does not mean that they opposed slavery as a social system or even the prerogatives with which its class and race relations endowed men. Slaveholding women did not accept bourgeois feminism's claims to universality, did not accept its claims to be an accurate statement about the relations between women and men in all times and places. Nor did they agree that northern women's rights advocates primarily proposed a radical critique of their own bourgeois society. In fact, they assumed that those advocates were advancing a radical critique of someone else's society—namely southern society. Literate southern women responded to this perceived attack in kind, repeatedly denouncing the evils and immorality of free society and comparing it unfavorably to the slave society they overwhelmingly favored, despite its acknowledged failings....

In truth, southern women shared many values with northern women and fashioned their identities in reference to many of the same discourses. But as Frederick Porcher insisted, that conventional language was "drawn from scenes totally at variance with those which lie about us." Slaveholding women's commitments to their own versions of evangelicalism, motherhood, and companionate marriage do not constitute proof that they shared some northern women's commitments to feminism and abolitionism, nor do their complaints about the flaws of the society to which they belonged. Those complaints must be understood within the context that gave them utterance. How, for example, do Mary Boykin Chesnut's pithy and scathing broadsides on slavery and the men who presided over it—"Poor women, poor slaves!"—relate to the beliefs and feelings of other slaveholding women? Mary Chesnut as "feminist-abolitionist" cannot pass muster as a typical slaveholding woman. She cannot even pass muster as representative of a significant minority of southern women, for although quasi abolitionists and quasi feminists existed, they were few and far between. Perhaps she should simply be understood as an anomaly—charming and talented, but no less an anomaly. Or perhaps she did not intend her scathing words in an abolitionist or feminist spirit at all....

Those who wish to see Mary Chesnut as a feminist and abolitionist refer to the celebrated passages in her diary in which she bemoaned the related fates of women and slaves in southern society. For the date of 4 March 1861 she offered, in the published version:

> So I have seen a negro woman sold—up on the block—at auction. I was walking. The woman on the block overtopped the crowd. I felt faint—seasick. The creature looked so like my good little Nancy. She was a bright mulatto with a pleasant face. She was magnificently gotten up in silks and satins. She seemed delighted with it all—sometimes ogling the bidders, sometimes looking quite coy and modest, but her mouth never relaxed from its expanded grin of excitement. I daresay the poor thing knew who would buy her.

> I sat down on a stool in a shop. I disciplined my wild thoughts....
>
> You know how women sell themselves and are sold in marriage, from queens downward, eh?
>
> You know what the Bible says about slavery—and marriage. Poor women. Poor slaves.

This passage bears comparison with the version that Chesnut drafted in her original diary:

> I saw to day a sale of Negroes—Mulatto women in *silk dresses*—one girl was on the stand. Nice looking—like my Nancy—she looked as coy and pleased at [as?] the bidder. South Carolina slaveholder as I am my very soul sickened—it is too dreadful. I tried to reason—this is not worse than the willing sale most women make of themselves in marriage—nor can the consequences be worse. The Bible authorizes marriage & slavery—poor women! poor slaves!

Consider the differences between the original and the published versions. In the original, Chesnut began her entry by noting, "I saw something to day which has quite unsettled me. I was so miserable [several illegible words] that one character in the world is lost—it knocks away the very ground I stand on—but away night mare." Although it might be tempting to identify the unsettling sight with the slave auction, the text discourages that interpretation. Rather, it appears that, as with other southern women, Chesnut's unhappiness about other matters brought slavery to mind as a target for the displacement of other grief. Before she even saw the slave auction, she had "sat at home this morning eating my own heart—but knew that it would never do." So out she rushed to distract herself with shopping and calls.

In the published version, all references to her personal misery have disappeared. In addition to the changes in context, the original and published versions reveal significant differences in the description of the slave auction itself. The published version records the magnificence of the mulatto woman's attire; the original version all but sneers at the generic inappropriateness of mulatto women in *silk dresses* (her italics). South Carolina slaveholder that she was, she might sicken at direct confrontation with slave auctions, but she also scorned a slave woman's espousal of upper-class garb and ladylike wiles. From my reading of the diaries and private papers of the slaveholders, I have sadly concluded that the racism of the women was generally uglier and more meanly expressed than that of the men. The published version of Chesnut's diary reveals a hardening of her own always deep racism: witness her description of the slave woman "ogling the bidders" and her "expanded grin of excitement."

Mary Chesnut's class and racial attitudes recur with a vengeance in her other frequently cited outcry against the oppression of women and slaves. "I wonder," she mused in the entry for 18 March 1861, "if it be a sin to think slavery a curse to any land." Northern opponents of slavery speak true: "Men and women are punished when their masters & mistresses are brutes & not when they do wrong—& then we live surrounded by prostitutes. An abandoned woman is sent out of any decent house elsewhere. Who thinks any worse of a Negro or Mulatto woman for being a thing we can't name. God forgive *us*, but ours is a *monstrous* system & wrong & iniquity." She continued with scathing remarks about every family's mulatto children who resembled the white children

and about women's unwillingness to recognize their husbands' responsibility for the children's conception. Yet she concluded by defending the women of her class and region, who were, she believed, "in conduct the purest women God ever made." The men were another matter: "No worse than men every where, but the lower their mistresses, the more degraded they must be." ...

This personal history imperceptibly merged, as do all personal histories, with her social attitudes, deftly captured in her passing reference to nonslaveholding whites as an armed rabble, and subtly evoked in the manifest racism of her comments on black and mulatto women. In the end, the presumed lasciviousness of slave women merged with the domination of slaveholding men and the blindness and cruelty of slaveholding women in a seamless social web. Under the combined influences of personal misery and the opium she took to alleviate it, Mary Chesnut could momentarily condemn the system as monstrous. But she never mounted a critique of her society's fundamental social relations, which her own social and racial attitudes clearly supported. She offered no hint that she favored equality among individuals. She compared the woman on the auction block with "my Nancy," never suggesting that Nancy should be anything other than her personal possession. She deplored the sight of slave women's sporting the finery of their betters. She worried about her husband's reference to other white men as rabble only because they, being armed, might react violently. "Poor women! Poor slaves!" constituted, not a call for emancipation and equality, but a lament for the human condition.

Mary Chesnut was well schooled in the opinions of abolitionists, notably those of

Harriet Beecher Stowe, whom she mentioned with the same contempt expressed in print by Louisa McCord. Like many other southern women, she bristled at the presumption of northerners in judging southern social relations and regularly insisted that they had no idea what they were talking about. Reading Charles Kingsley's *Two Years Ago,* she admitted to finding the main character, Tom Thurnall, deeply stirring. But Kingsley knew nothing about negroes. "These beastly negroes—if Kingsley had ever lived among them! How different is the truth." She knew a wretched mulatto slave woman "who is kept a mistress—& her son a negro boy—with a black father—beats her white lover for giving her brandy to drink—& white people say well done! to the boy!" And she wondered if there were more impure women, "Negroes & all, North or South." In her revisions, she directly confronted the question of northern attitudes. Northerners' antislavery amounted to little more than the most lucrative hobbyhorse for New Englanders, snug and smug in their "clean, clear, sweet-smelling" homes or shut up in their libraries, "writing books which ease their hearts of their bitterness to us, or editing newspapers—all [of] which pays better than anything else in the world." She condemned them all: Stowe, Greeley, Thoreau, Emerson, Sumner. Even among the politicians, "antislavery is the beast to carry him highest." Did they practice self denial? No, theirs was "the cheapest philanthropy trade in the world—easy. Easy as setting John Brown to come down here and cut our throats in Christ's name. These people's obsession with other decent people's customs reduced to self-serving and sanctimonious nonsense."

Against them she arrayed her mother, her grandmother, and her mother-in-law.

Who were these Yankees, she asked, to lecture pure southern women, many of whom were educated in northern schools and who read "the same books as their Northern contemners, the same daily newspapers, the same Bible—have the same ideas of right and wrong—are highbred, lovely, good, pious, doing their duty as they conceive it." Southern women faced a reality that their northern sisters could not begin to understand. Southern women lived in "negro villages"; rather than preaching insurrection, they attempted to ameliorate the lives of those in their charge. "They set them the example of a perfect life—life of utter self-abnegation." How would these "holy New England women" feel if they were "forced to have a negro village walk through their houses whenever they saw fit—dirty, slatternly, idle, ill-smelling by nature (when otherwise it is the exception)." Southern women could not have done more for negroes if they had been African missionaries. "They have a swarm of blacks about them as children under their care—not as Mrs. Stowe's fancy paints them, but the hard, unpleasant, unromantic, underdeveloped savage Africans."

Slaveholders, Chesnut insisted, were doing their duty as well as possible, and it had crippled them with debt. In the end, only northerners and negroes profited. Her father-in-law's money went to support "a horde of idle dirty Africans —while he is abused and vilified as a cruel slave-owner." Everything he made went back to his laborers, "those here called slaves and elsewhere called operative, tenants &c... peasantry &c." The slaveholders, who were "good men and women, are the martyrs." They were "human beings of the nineteenth century —and slavery has to go, of course."

Mary Chesnut believed, as did southern intellectuals like Thomas Roderick Dew and George Tucker, that history would sooner or later outrun the kind of slavery that existed in the South. But she insisted that northern and European bourgeois, with their sanctimonious platitudes and callous disregard of the laboring classes, had nothing better to put in its place. "I hate slavery," Mary Chesnut wrote. But she immediately added, in a manner designed to draw the teeth of any charge of abolitionism: "I even hate the harsh authority I see parents think it their duty to exercise *toward their children.*" Harriet Beecher Stowe could make one feel "utterly confounded at the atrocity of African slavery." Yet, "at home we see them, the idlest, laziest, fattest, most comfortably contented peasantry that ever cumbered the earth—and we forget there is any wrong in slavery at all." In expressing these sentiments, she did not veer from the view; loudly trumpeted by southern divines as well as by other social theorists during the 1850s, that a more humane slavery or personal servitude would characterize the society of the future. Nor did Mary Chesnut substantively depart from Caroline Lee Hentz's avowed apology for slavery, *The Planter's Northern Bride,* which depicted the frail female worker, dismissed from her job because she was dying of tuberculosis, and thrown back to starve in the arms of the widowed mother she had been supporting; the arrogant and ignorant abolitionist, who was robbed by the fugitive slave whom he had taken into the sanctity of his domestic circle as a matter of principle; the lordly, beneficent slaveholder who brought happiness to his bride, the abolitionist's daughter.

Was slavery wrong in the abstract, as the abolitionists argued and the proslavery theorists denied, or was it wrong only in its abuses? Mary Chesnut did not devote much attention to slavery as a social system. She did insistently call attention to the pain—the martyrdom—it imposed on women. But her pervasive racism suggests that she believed that blacks had to be enslaved. She betrayed scant concern for their rights. "Topsys," she averred, "I have known—but none that were beauties—or ill used. Evas are mostly in the heaven of Mrs. Stowe's imagination. People can't love things dirty, ugly, repulsive, simply because they ought, but they can be good to them —at a distance." And, confirming the personal nature of her own response, she admitted, "You see, I cannot rise very high. I can only judge by what I see."

Mary Chesnut took slavery for granted as the foundation of her world. Time and again she referred to slaves who did one thing or another for her. After emancipation she expected them to stand by her. With dismay she noted that when, in February 1865, the Martins left Columbia, "their mammy, the negro woman who had nursed them, refused to go with them. That daunted me." She might have been borrowing from Caroline Lee Hentz when she noted the death of Burwell Boykin (the son of her uncle), whom her sister called "the very best man I ever knew; the kindest" from the typhoid he contracted by attending to his sick slaves....

Mary Chesnut read *Uncle Tom's Cabin* more than once, as if she were engaged in a private debate with the author. In March 1862, she "read *Uncle Tom's Cabin* again," and again in June, "tried to read *Uncle Tom.* Could not. Too sickening. It is bad as Squeers beating Smike in the hack. Flesh and blood revolts." In May 1864, she met a lovely relative, "the woman who might have sat for Eva's mother in *Uncle Tom's Cabin*." The beautifully dressed, graceful, languid woman made eyes at all comers and "softly and in dulcet accents" regretted the necessity under which she labored, "to send out a sable Topsy who looked shining and happy—quand même—to her sabler parent, to be switched for some misdemeanor—which I declined to hear as I fled in my haste." She wrestled with Stowe's views, and probably with her success as an author as well. She did not embrace Stowe as an authority on the woes of southern women, black or white. Negro women in the South "have a chance here women have nowhere else. They can redeem themselves. The 'impropers.'" In the South, they "can marry decently—and nothing is remembered against them, these colored ladies." The topic was not nice, yet she felt that Stowe reveled in it. "How delightfully pharisaic a feeling it must be, to rise superior and fancy we are so degraded as to defend and like to live with such degraded creatures around us."

However indirectly expressed, Chesnut's resentment of Stowe, like her reservations about Stowe's picture of southern social relations, had much in common with Louisa McCord's frontal attack. She could only have concurred with Louisa McCord's sneering association of *Uncle Tom* with the sensationalist fiction of their day. Nor would she have differed with Louisa McCord's judgment that the "public feeling with us is, we believe, as delicate and as much on the alert upon such points, as in any part of the world." The transgressions and wanton violence that Stowe depicted were not sanctioned by southern laws, which held masters to account in their treatment of their people. Louisa McCord asserted that "the existence of a system of slav-ery rather tends to increase than diminish this feeling, as, leaving a larger portion of society in a state of tutelage, naturally and necessarily greater attention is turned to the subject." What must Mrs. Stowe's social background be, for her to assume that slaveholders admitted slave traders into their houses? "We have lived at the South, in the very heart of a slave country, for thirty years out of forty of our lives, and have never seen a slave-trader set foot in a gentleman's house." Here, Louisa McCord pressed her polemic beyond reasonable limits. No doubt, she did not admit slave traders into her house, but others did, although they distinguished between the "gentlemen slave traders," who owned plantations and married into the high planter class, and the rest. Louisa McCord exaggerated in order to label Harriet Beecher Stowe as hopelessly middle class—lower middle class at that. To Louisa McCord, Stowe's assertions offered a dubious impression of the society "with which madame and her clerk-brother have associated, and prepares us for some singular scenes in the elegant circles to which she introduces us." Stowe, in McCord's belief, did not know what she was talking about. Worse, she lacked the social standing to write authoritatively of gentle folks.

Mrs. Stowe, Louisa McCord continued, knew no more of morals than she knew of manners. How could she believe that slaveholding men and women labored under a cloud of guilt? How could she believe that slaveholders were good to their slaves only to repay them in part for the fraud of owning them at all? "To rob a man and pay him back a moderate percentage on the spoils of his own pocket, is not Southern honour." Neither slaveholders nor other honest people degraded their laborers. Louisa

McCord, who was exceptionally well read in the political economy of her day, insisted that only economic illiterates could think that any laborers, slave or free, earned more than the subsistence they in fact got. Southern men and women, "who do what they think right," did not live "with a constant lie on their lips and in their hearts." They owned slaves because "they believe 'the system' to be the best possible for black and white, for slave and master." They could, on their knees, "gratefully worship the all-gracious providence of an Almighty God, who has seen fit, so beautifully, to suit every being to the place which its nature calls it." There were, McCord asserted,

> pious slaveholders; there are chris-
> tian slaveholders; there are gentlemanly
> slaveholders; there are slaveholders
> whose philosophic research has looked
> into nature and read God in his works,
> as well as in his Bible, and who own
> slaves because they think it, not expe-
> dient only, but right, holy and just so
> to do, for the good of the slave—for the
> good of the master—for the good of the
> world.... There are men, and women
> too, slaveowners and slaveholders, who
> need no teachings to act as closely as hu-
> man weakness can, to such a rule.

With the arrogance of those who claim a monopoly on absolute truth and who have no sense of human nature, Harriet Beecher Stowe had, McCord felt, dismissed an entire people. "If we answer that there is no more moral population in the world than that of our Slave States (few, indeed, equally so) we are answered with a sneer of derision." . . .

Mary Chesnut could envision no alternative to the system she could momentarily describe as monstrous. Piety and piemaking, not to mention scrubbing and bedmaking, did not interest her. She may

have deplored the ways in which slave-holding men abused their prerogatives, but she did not propose stripping them, much less their women, of their privileged social positions. Mary Chesnut criticized her society, in precisely the way the militantly proslavery divines—for example, the Reverend Dr. James Henley Thornwell, whom she much admired—did. She criticized its imperfections and abuses, but not, despite an occasional rhetorical flourish, its social relations. She may have wanted to reform the men of her class, or even to punish them for certain transgressions, but she did not want to dissolve that class into some great mass of human equality.

Other slaveholding women occasionally voiced similar complaints about the baleful effects of slave society on their lives. Anna Matilda Page King, who, like Mary Chesnut, wrote from the marrow of the slaveholding elite, once wrote plaintively to her husband of how bad slavery was for boys—and girls. She wished they could sell their slaves, "get rid of *all* at *their value* and leave this wretched country." The slave South was no place to rear children. "To bring up boys on a plantation makes them tyrannical as well as lazy, and girls too." On the day this letter was written, it had been raining, seemingly forever, on St. Simon's Island. The walls of the house were leaking. Servants and children were sick. Unexpected guests had descended. The mountain of debts was staggering. Poor Anna had been forced to retreat to a closet to nurse her headache and write to her absent husband. How was a woman to preside over a plantation and to rear children without her husband? Small wonder that she found the burdens of life too much to bear. But her heartfelt complaints, rather than developing into a critique of her society, later disappeared from her correspondence. The mood passed, and with it her criticism of the society that gave her an identity. Her protests at her husband's absence recurred but focused on other objects. And in 1861 her devoted daughter, Georgia, attending Georgia's secession convention with her father, wrote home to her brother, Fuddy: "All the women here are 'right' but it is strange to say, there are *many men*, quite willing to be ruled by the Yankee and the nigger." In horror, she added that she supposed he knew "that New York has passed the law for *universal suffrage—all* the niggers!"

Keziah Brevard, who had never married and who managed her own affairs without suffering the immediate burdens of male domination, railed against life among slaves without mentioning women's condition. Brevard bitterly resented her slaves for the troubles they imposed upon her: theft, disrespect, laziness. Her complaints might even be read as an indictment of slavery's subjugation of slaveholding women, but only with the understanding that she feared and mistrusted the slaves much more than she disliked slavery. Her dislike of slavery, like that of other women of her class, could be traced to extreme racism: How was it possible for a decent woman to live among such people? She would solve the social problem by shipping them all back to Africa as soon as possible. Should that prove impossible, then obviously they must remain slaves, whatever the burdens on long-suffering women. Some semblance of social order had to be preserved.

Many slaveholding women may have secretly felt that in everyday life slavery contributed as much to disarray as to order. Some expressed doubts in their diaries and letters, but, like the southern

clergy to whom they readily turned for guidance, they were more likely to stress the need for reform of the system than its abolition. Most of their doubts concerned the effects of slavery on the character and behavior of slaveholders, notably boys and men. Although they might blame slavery for aspects of their lives that they found painful and occasionally intolerable, they rarely opposed it on principle or in the abstract. Writing long after the war, Elizabeth Meriwether claimed to have opposed slavery on principle, but her principles did not prevent her from accepting a slave to relieve her of the unacceptable responsibility for her own housework. Even Mary Minor Blackford, who did oppose slavery on principle, hired a slave nurse for her children and lived to see both of her sons fight for the Confederacy. Many slaveholding women understood that abuses of sexuality and power could be directly linked to slavery but had difficulty understanding that the main victims were the slaves. They were not much concerned with justice to the slaves and not at all concerned with individual freedom and with justice in the abstract.

Before the war Gertrude Thomas, who has been advanced as an example of slaveholding women's "feminism," did not protest slavery, but she did express reservations about prevailing attitudes toward women. After the war she actively supported women's rights; before the war, if we are to credit her journal, she did not. During the 1850s she wrote primarily of her daily activities, her extensive reading, her religious feelings, and her family relations. Her husband, who would subsequently disappoint her, at that time constituted the source of all her stability and happiness, and she thanked God for her good fortune. In her view, Jeff Thomas combined "such moral qualitys, such an affectionate heart, with just such a master will as suits my womans nature, for true to my sex, I delight *in looking up*, and love to feel my womans weakness protected by man's superior strength."

She noted that women did not always remain true to their nature. At a prayer meeting during which the minister invited all to speak their minds, "one lady addressed us with a few words." Presumably, she had been prompted to her boldness by the minister's text on the previous night: "Quench not the spirit." Gertrude Thomas had no doubt that "many felt it their duty to speak but quenched the spirit." Had not Paul said, " 'Let not your women speak in public' "? This admonition, "aside from their natural diffidence would cause a female to remain silent upon such an occasion." She nonetheless thought that there was a case for treating women more equally with men. "*Christine or Womans Trials and Womans Triumphs*" differed dramatically from her normal reading, "being very decided womans rights book advocating women—Their perfect equality with the other sex." Thomas admitted that the author made some very good arguments, although the denouement of the plot disappointed her, because the Christian heroine "*marries* and then confesses that she is glad that the tie of marriage is so strong that it cannot be broken, this too after she has been advocating to the contrary." Gertrude Thomas believed strongly in the indissolubility of marriage but reproached this author for a muddled argument. At the same time, she had been reading a book, *Caste*, by "a decided Abolitionist." In this work, the orphan heroine's proposed marriage to the son of the household to which she had gone as governess was called off when she was discovered to be the child of a mulatto slave and a neighboring planter. Gertrude Thomas had to "confess I was sufficiently *Southern* to think him justifiable in breaking off the engagement."

White women's trials remained closer to Gertrude Thomas's heart than those of slaves. She referred regularly to her own slaves, noting the tasks they accomplished or failed to accomplish, her dependence on them for the care of her children, their nursing of her children, and their thefts. Tamah was caught red-handed. Isabella was incorrigible. A slave preacher won her admiration for his moving rhetoric. But we catch here not a breath of their deserving freedom, not a breath that they complicated the lives of white women beyond taxing their powers of discipline. . . .

To view Mary Chesnut and other slaveholding women as critics of slavery and "patriarchy" is implicitly to challenge McCord's wisdom on the "woman question," and to cast McCord herself as exceptional. In reality, McCord knew as well as any that women had grounds for discontent, just as she knew that Mary Chesnut was not alone in railing against the monstrous system that hedged slaveholding women in. She merely opposed generalizing from individual unhappiness, and she understood that few slaveholding women, least of all Mary Chesnut, would have chosen to mingle in equality with the white—much less with the black—masses. Mary Chesnut's bitterness at the self-indulgence and arrogance of her father-in-law and his kind did not justify a broadside attack on the system simply because it left room for abuse. For that system provided privileges and amenities for its women that they had no intention of surrendering.

POSTSCRIPT

Were Southern Slaveholding Women Covert Abolitionists?

In the past decade, a number of historians have focused their attention on the status and roles of southern women. In addition to the larger works from which the preceding essays have been selected, interested readers should find Catherine Clinton's *The Plantation Mistress: Woman's World in the Old South* (Pantheon Books, 1982) and Sally G. McMillen's *Southern Women: Black and White in the Old South* (Harlan Davidson, 1992) quite informative. In addition, see Elisabeth Muhlenfeld, *Mary Boykin Chesnut: A Biography* (Louisiana State University Press, 1981); Jane Turner Censer, *North Carolina Planters and Their Children, 1800–1860* (Louisiana State University Press, 1984); and Carol Bleser, ed., *In Joy and In Sorrow: Women, Family, and Marriage in the Victorian South* (Oxford University Press, 1990). For a biography of two southern white women who became abolitionists, see Gerda Lerner's *The Grimke Sisters from South Carolina: Pioneers for Woman's Rights and Abolition* (Schocken, 1967).

One of the weaknesses of most studies of abolitionism is that they are generally written from a monochromatic perspective. In other words, historians typically discuss whites within the abolitionist crusade and give little, if any, attention to the roles that African Americans themselves played in the movement. Students should be aware that African Americans, enslaved and free, also rebelled against slavery, both directly and indirectly.

Benjamin Quarles, in *Black Abolitionists* (Oxford University Press, 1969), describes a wide range of roles played by blacks in the abolitionist movement. For example, blacks organized themselves into local antislavery societies, became members of the national abolitionist organizations (especially the American Anti-Slavery Society and the American and Foreign Anti-Slavery Society), contributed funds to the operations of those societies, made black churches available for abolitionist meetings, and promoted abolitionism through pamphleteering and speaking engagements. Between 1830 and 1835 the Negro Convention Movement sponsored annual meetings of blacks, during which protests against slavery were a central feature.

The black challenge to the slave system is also evident in the network known as the Underground Railroad, a system in which fugitive slaves were secretly helped to gain their freedom. Larry Gara, in *The Liberty Line: The Legend of the Underground Railroad* (University of Kentucky Press, 1961), concludes that the real heroes of the Underground Railroad were not white abolitionists who "conducted" runaways to freedom in the northern United States or Canada but the slaves themselves who depended primarily upon their own resources or assistance they received from other blacks.

ISSUE 14

Have Historians Overemphasized the Slavery Issue as a Cause of the Civil War?

YES: Joel H. Silbey, from *The Partisan Imperative: The Dynamics of American Politics Before the Civil War* (Oxford University Press, 1985)

NO: Michael F. Holt, from *The Political Crisis of the 1850s* (John Wiley & Sons, 1978)

ISSUE SUMMARY

YES: Professor of history Joel H. Silbey argues that historians have overemphasized the sectional conflict over slavery and have neglected to analyze local enthnocultural issues among the events leading to the Civil War.

NO: Professor of history Michael F. Holt maintains that both northern Republicans and southern Democrats seized the slavery issue to sharply distinguish party differences and thus reinvigorate the loyalty of party voters.

In the 85 years between the start of the American Revolution and the coming of the Civil War, Americans made the necessary political compromises on the slavery issue in order not to split the nation apart. The Northwest Ordinance of 1787 forbade slavery from spreading into those designated territories under its control, and the new Constitution written in the same year prohibited the slave trade from Africa after 1808.

There was some hope in the early nineteenth century that slavery might die from natural causes. The Revolutionary generation was well aware of the contradiction between the values of an egalitarian society and the practices of a slave-holding aristocracy. Philosophically, slavery was viewed as a necessary evil, not a positive good. Several northern states abolished slavery after 1800, and the erosion of the tobacco lands in Virginia and Maryland contributed to the lessening importance of a slave labor system.

Unfortunately, two factors—territorial expansion and the market economy—made slavery the key to the South's wealth in the 35 years before the Civil War. First, new slave states were created out of a population expanding into lands ceded to the United States as a result of the Treaty of Paris of 1783 and the Louisiana Purchase of 1803. Second, slaves were sold from the upper to the lower regions of the South because the cotton gin (invented by Eli Whitney in 1793) made it possible to harvest large quantities of cotton, ship it to the textile mills of New England and the British Isles, and turn it into wool and finished clothing as part of the new, specialized market economy.

The slavery issue came to the forefront in 1819 when some northern congressmen proposed that slavery be banned from the states being carved out of the Louisiana Purchase. A heated debate ensued, but the Missouri Compromise of 1821 drew a line that preserved the balance between free and slave states and that (with the exception of Missouri) prohibited slavery north of the 36° 30' latitude.

The annexation of Texas in 1845 and the acquisition of New Mexico, Utah, and California three years later reopened the slavery question. The question of whether or not to annex Texas to the union, after she gained her independence from Mexico in 1836, scared politicians from all sections because they were afraid of upsetting the political balance between free and slave states. Attempts at compromises in 1850 and 1854 only accelerated the situation. In 1854 Stephen A. Douglas, a senator from Illinois, hoped to boost Chicago's burgeoning market economy by encouraging the building of a transcontinental railroad. The Kansas-Nebraska Act of 1854, which repealed the Missouri Compromise, allowed the citizens of those territories to decide whether or not they wanted slavery. Abolitionists were furious because Douglas's doctrine of "popular sovereignty" had the potential to allow slavery to spread to territories where it was previously forbidden by the Missouri Compromise. For the next three years, Kansas became a battleground between pro-slavery forces and "Free-Soilers" who voted to keep slavery out of the territory.

The Kansas-Nebraska Act had major political implications. The second party system of Whigs versus Democrats fell apart, and a new realignment took place. The Whig party disappeared. In the South the need to defend slavery caused pro-business and yeoman-farmer Whigs from the back country to join the southern Democrats in a unified alliance against the North. Major and minor parties in the North joined to form the new Republican party whose unifying principle was to confine slavery to states where it already existed but not to allow it to spread to any new territories. Quickly the Republicans mounted a successful challenge against the Democrats.

The 1860 presidential election was won by the Republican Abraham Lincoln. However, the southern states refused to accept the election of Lincoln. Seven states seceded from the Union before he was inaugurated on March 4, 1861. When Lincoln refused to abandon the federal forts off the coast of Charleston in April 1861, the governor of South Carolina fired on Fort Sumter. The Civil War had begun. Four more states then joined the Confederacy.

Have historians overemphasized the sectional conflict over the slavery question as a cause of the Civil War? In the first of the following selections, Joel H. Silbey argues that historians have overemphasized the sectional conflict over slavery and have neglected to analyze local ethnocultural issues among the events leading to the Civil War. In the second selection, Michael F. Holt argues that politicians in the 1850s used the slavery issue to sharply distinguish party differences.

YES
Joel H. Silbey

THE CIVIL WAR SYNTHESIS IN AMERICAN POLITICAL HISTORY

The Civil War has dominated our studies of the period between the Age of Jackson and 1861. Most historians of the era have devoted their principal attention to investigating and analyzing the reasons for differences between the North and South, the resulting sectional conflict, and the degeneration of this strife into a complete breakdown of our political system in war. Because of this focus, most scholars have accepted, without question, that differences between the North and the South were the major political influences at work among the American people in the years between the mid-1840s and the war. Despite occasional warnings about the dangers of overemphasizing sectional influences, the sectional interpretation holds an honored and secure place in the historiography of the antebellum years. We now possess a formidable number of works which, in one way or another, center attention on the politics of sectionalism and clearly demonstrate how much the Civil War dominates our study of American political history before 1861.

Obviously nothing is wrong in such emphasis if sectionalism was indeed the dominant political influence in the antebellum era. However, there is the danger in such emphasis of claiming too much, that in centering attention on the war and its causes we may ignore or play down other contemporary political influences and fail to weigh adequately the importance of nonsectional forces in antebellum politics. And, in fact, several recent studies of American political behavior have raised serious doubts about the importance of sectional differences as far as most Americans were concerned. These have even suggested that the sectional emphasis has created a false synthesis in our study of history which increases the importance of one factor, ignores the significance of other factors, and ultimately distorts the reality of American political life between 1844 and 1861.

*   *   *

Scholars long have used the presidential election of 1844 as one of their major starting points for the sectional analysis of American political history. In a general sense they have considered American expansion into Texas to be the

From Joel H. Silbey, *The Partisan Imperative: The Dynamics of American Politics Before the Civil War* (Oxford University Press, 1985). Adapted from Joel H. Silbey, "The Civil War Synthesis in American Political History," *Civil War History* (1964). Copyright © 1964 by Kent State University Press. Reprinted by permission. Notes omitted.

most important issue of that campaign. The issue into Texas to be the most important issue of that campaign. The issue stemmed from the fact that Texas was a slave area and many articulate Northerners attacked the movement to annex Texas as a slave plot designed to enhance Southern influence within the Union. Allegedly because of these attacks, and the Southerners' defending themselves, many people in both North and South found themselves caught up in such sectional bitterness that the United States took a major step toward civil war. Part of this bitterness can be seen, it is pointed out, in the popular vote in New York State where the Whig candidate for the presidency, Henry Clay, lost votes to the abolitionist Liberty party because he was a slaveholder. The loss of these votes cost him New York and ultimately the election. As a result of Clay's defeat, historians have concluded that as early as 1844 the problem of slavery extension was important enough to arouse people to act primarily in sectional terms and thus for this episode to be a milestone on the road to war.

Recently Professor Lee Benson published a study of New York State politics in the Jacksonian era. Although Benson mainly concerned himself with other problems, some of his findings directly challenge the conception that slavery and sectional matters were of major importance in New York in 1844. In his analysis Benson utilized a more systematic statistical compilation of data than have previous workers in the field of political history. Observing that scholars traditionally have looked at what people said they did rather than at what they actually did, Benson compiled a great number of election returns for New York State in this period. His purpose was to see who ac-

tually voted for whom and to place the election in historical perspective by pinpointing changes in voting over time and thus identifying the basic trends of political behavior. Through such analysis Benson arrived at a major revision of the nature of New York State voting in 1844.

Benson pointed out, first of all, that the abolitionist, anti-Texas Liberty party whose vote total should have increased if the New York population wanted to strike against a slave plot in Texas, actually lost votes over what it had received in the most immediate previous election, that of 1843. Further analysis indicated that there was no widespread reaction to the Texas issue in New York State on the part of any large group of voters, although a high degree of anti-Texas feeling indeed existed among certain limited groups in the population. Such sentiment, however, did not affect voting margins in New York State. Finally, Benson concluded that mass voting in New York in 1844 pivoted not on the sectional issue but rather on more traditional divisions between ethnic and religious groups whose voting was a reaction to matters closer to home. These proved of a more personal and psychological nature than that of Texas and its related issue of slavery extension. Sectional bitterness, contrary to previous historical conceptions, neither dominated nor seriously influenced the 1844 vote in New York. Although Benson confined his study to one state, his conclusions introduce doubts about the influence of sectionalism in other supposedly less pivotal states.

* * *

Another aspect of the sectional interpretation of American politics in the pre–Civil War era involves Congress. Political historians have considered that body to be both a forum wherein leaders personally expressed attitudes that intensified sectional bitterness, as well as an arena which reflected the general pattern of influences operative in the country at large. Therefore, writers on the period have considered the behavior of congressmen to have been more and more dominated by sectionalism, particularly after David Wilmot introduced his antislavery extension proviso into the House of Representatives in 1846. Although there may have been other issues and influences present, it is accepted that these were almost completely overborne in the late 1840s and 1850s in favor of a widespread reaction to sectional differences.

In a recently completed study, I have analyzed congressional voting in the allegedly crucial pivotal decade 1841–52, the period which historians identify as embodying the transition from nationalism to sectionalism in congressional behavior. This examination indicates that a picture of the decade as one in which sectional influences steadily grew stronger, overwhelmed all other bases of divisions, and became a permanent feature of the voting behavior of a majority of congressmen, is grossly oversimplified and a distortion of reality. In brief, although sectional influences, issues, and voting did exist, particularly between 1846 and 1850, sectional matters were not the only problems confronting congressmen. In the period before the introduction of the Wilmot Proviso in 1846, national issues such as the tariff, financial policy, foreign affairs, and land policy divided congressmen along political, not sectional, lines. Furthermore, in this earlier period issues which many believed to have shown a high degree of sectional content, such as admittance of Texas and Oregon, reveal highly partisan national divisions and little sectional voting.

Even after the rise of the slavery-extension issue, other questions of a national character remained important. Slavery was but one of several issues before Congress and it was quite possible for congressmen to vote against one another as Northern and Southern sectionalists on an issue and then to join together, regardless of section, against other Northerners and Southerners on another matter. Certainly some men from both geographic areas were primarily influenced by sectional considerations at all times on all issues, but they were a minority of all congressmen in the period. The majority of congressmen were not so overwhelmingly influenced by their being Northerners or Southerners, but continued to think and act in national terms, and even resisted attempts by several sectionally minded congressmen to forge coalitions, regardless of party, against the other section.

A careful study of congressional voting in these years also demonstrates that another assumption of historians about the nature of politics is oversimplified: the period around 1846 did *not* begin the steady forward movement of congressional politics toward sectionalism and war. Rather, it was quite possible in the period between 1846 and 1852 for congressmen to assail one another bitterly in sectional terms, physically attack one another, and even threaten secession, and still for the majority of them to return in the following session to a different approach—that of nonsectional political differences with a concomitant restoration of nonsectional coalitions. For example, it was possible in 1850, after several years of sectional fighting, for a national coalition of Senators and Representatives to join together and settle in compromise terms the differences between North and South over expansion. And they were able to do this despite the simultaneous existence of a great deal of sectional maneuvering by some congressmen in an attempt to prevent any such compromise. Furthermore, during this same session Congress also dealt with matters of railroad land grants in a way that eschewed sectional biases. Obviously the usual picture of an inexorable growth of sectional partisanship after 1846 is quite overdone. And lest these examples appeared to be isolated phenomena, preliminary research both by Gerald Wolff and by myself demonstrates that as late as 1854 there was still no complete or overwhelming sectional voting even on such an issue as the Kansas-Nebraska Act.

Such analyses of congressional behavior in an alleged transition period reinforce what Lee Benson's work on New York politics demonstrated: many varieties and many complexities existed with respect to political behavior in the antebellum period, so that even slavery failed to be a dominating influence among all people at all times—or even among most people at most times—during the 1840s and early 1850s. Again, our previous image of American politics in this period must be reconsidered in light of this fact and despite the emergence of a Civil War in 1861.

* * *

Perhaps no aspect of antebellum politics should demonstrate more fully the overpowering importance of sectional influences than the presidential election of 1860. In the preliminaries to that contest the Democratic party split on the rock of slavery, the Republican party emerged as a power in the Northern states with a

good chance of winning the presidency, and loud voices in the Southern states called for secession because of Northern attacks on their institutions. In dealing with these events, historians, as in their treatment of other aspects of antebellum politics, have devoted their primary attention to sectional bickering and maneuvering among party leaders, because they considered this activity to be the most important facet of the campaign and the key to explaining the election. Although such a focus obviously has merit if one is thinking in terms of the armed conflict which broke out only five months after the election, once again, as in the earlier cases considered here, recent research has raised pertinent questions about the political realities of the situation. We may indeed ask what were the issues of the campaign as seen by the majority of voters.

Earlier studies of the 1860 election, in concerning themselves primarily with the responses and activities of political leaders, have taken popular voting behavior for granted. This aspect has either been ignored or else characterized as reflecting the same influences and attitudes as that of the leadership. Therefore, the mass of men, it is alleged, voted in response to sectional influences in 1860. For instance, several scholars concerned with the Germans in the Middle West in this period have characterized the attitudes of that group as overwhelmingly antislavery. Thus the Republican party attracted the mass of the German vote because the liberal "Forty-Eighters" saw casting a Lincoln vote as a way to strike a blow against slavery in the United States. Going beyond this, some historians have reached similar conclusions about other Middle Western immigrant groups. As a result, according to most historians, although narrowly divided, the area went for Lincoln thanks in large part to its newest citizens, who were Northern sectionalists in their political behavior. Such conclusions obviously reinforce the apparent importance of geographic partisanship in 1860.

Testing this hypothesis, two recent scholars systematically studied and analyzed election returns in Iowa during 1860. Such examinations are important because they should reveal, if the sectional theory is correct, preoccupation among Iowa voters—especially immigrants—with the slavery question and the increasingly bitter differences between North and South. Only one of these studies, that of Professor George H. Daniels of Northwestern University, has appeared in print. But Daniels's findings shatter earlier interpretations which pinpointed sectional concerns as the central theme of the 1860 election.

Briefly stated, Daniels isolated the predominantly German townships in Iowa and, following Lee Benson's methodological lead, analyzed their vote. He found that, far from being solidly Republican voters, or moved primarily by the slavery question, the Germans of Iowa voted overwhelmingly in favor of the Democratic party. And Daniels discovered that the primary issue motivating the Germans in 1860 was an ethnic one. They were conscious of the antialien Know-Nothing movement which had been so strong in the United States during the 1850s and they identified the Republican party as the heir and last refuge of Know-Nothingism. If the Germans of Iowa were attracted to the Republicans by the latter's antislavery attitudes, such attraction was more than overcome by the Republicans' aura of antiforeignism. Furthermore, the Republicans were also identified in the minds of

the Iowa Germans as the party of prohibitionism, a social view strongly opposed by most Germans. Thus, as Daniels concludes, "... The rank and file Germans who did the bulk of the voting considered their own liberty to be of paramount importance. Apparently ignoring the advice of their leaders, they cast their ballots for the party which consistently promised them liberty from prohibition and native-American legislation." As a result, the Germans of Iowa voted Democratic, not Republican, in 1860.

Lest this appear to be an isolated case, the research of Robert Swierenga on Dutch voting behavior in Iowa in 1860 confirms Daniels's findings. Swierenga demonstrated that the Dutch also voted Democratic despite their vaunted antislavery attitudes; again, revulsion from certain Republican ideals overpowered any attraction toward that party on the slavery issue.

Such research into the election of 1860, as in the earlier cases of the election of 1844 and congressional voting behavior in the 1840s and early 1850s, suggests how far the sectional and slavery preconceptions of American historians have distorted reality. Many nonsectional issues were apparently more immediately important to the groups involved than any imminent concern with Northern-Southern differences. Once again, the Civil War synthesis appears to be historically inaccurate and in need of serious revision.

* * *

Several other provocative studies recently have appeared which, while dealing with nonpolitical subjects, support the conclusion that sectional problems, the slavery issue, and increasing bitterness between North and South were not always uppermost concerns to most Americans in the fifteen years before the outbreak of the war. Building upon the work of Leon Litwack, which emphasizes the general Northern antagonism toward the Negro before 1860, and that of Larry Gara demonstrating the fallacy of the idea that a well-organized and widespread underground railroad existed in the North, Professor C. Vann Woodward has cautioned students against an easy acceptance of a "North-Star" image—a picture of a universally militant Northern population determined to ease the burden of the slave in America. Rather, as Woodward points out, a great many Northerners remained indifferent to the plight of the slave and hostile to the would-be antislavery reformer in their midst.

In this same tenor, Milton Powell of Michigan State University has challenged long-held assumptions that the Northern Methodist church was a bulwark of antislavery sentiment after splitting with its Southern branch in 1844. As Powell makes clear, Northern Methodists were concerned about many other problems in which slavery played no part, as well as being beset by conditions which served to tone down any antislavery attitudes they may have held. More importantly, this led many of them to ignore slavery as an issue because of its latent tendency to divide the organization to which they belonged. Thus, even in areas outside of the political realm, the actual conditions of antebellum society challenge the validity of the sectional concept in its most general and far-reaching form.

* * *

This review of recent research indicates that much of our previous work on the prewar period should be reexamined free from the bias caused by looking first at the fact of the Civil War and then turning back to view the events of the previous decade in relation only to that fact. Although it is true that the studies discussed here are few in number and by no means include the entire realm of American politics in the antebellum era, their diversity in time and their revisionist conclusions do strongly suggest the fallacy of many previous assumptions. No longer should any historian blithely accept the traditional concept of a universal preoccupation with the sectional issue.

But a larger matter is also pointed up by this recent research and the destruction of this particular myth about political sectionalism. For a question immediately arises as to how historians generally could have accepted so readily and for so long such oversimplifications and inaccuracies. Fortunately for future research, answers to this question have been implicitly given by the scholars under review, and involve methodological problems concerning evidence and a certain naïveté about the political process.

Historians generally have utilized as evidence the writings and commentaries of contemporary observers of, and participants in, the events being examined. But, as both Benson and Daniels emphasize, this can endanger our understanding of reality. For instance, not enough attention has been paid to who actually said what, or of the motives of a given reporter or the position he was in to know and understand what was going on around him. Most particularly, scholars have not always been properly skeptical about whether the observer's comments truly reflected actuality. As Daniels pointed out in his article on German voting behavior, "contemporary opinion, including that of newspapers, is a poor guide."

If such is true, and the evidence presented by these studies indicates that it is, a question is raised as to how a historian is to discover contemporary opinion if newspapers are not always reliable as sources. The work of Benson, Daniels, and myself suggests an answer: the wider use of statistics. When we talk of public opinion (that is, how the mass of men acted or thought) we are talking in terms of aggregate numbers, of majorities. One way of determining what the public thought is by measuring majority opinion in certain circumstances—elections, for example, or the voting of congressmen —and then analyzing the content and breakdown of the figures derived. If, for example, 80 percent of the Germans in Iowa voted Democratic in 1860, this tells us more about German public opinion in 1860 than does a sprightly quote from one of the Germans in the other 20 percent who voted Republican "to uphold freedom." Historians are making much more use of statistics than formerly and are utilizing more sophisticated techniques of quantitative analysis. And such usage seems to be prelude to, judging by the works discussed here, a fuller and more accurate understanding of our past.

There are also other ways of approaching the problems posed by the 1850s. Not enough attention has been paid, it seems to me, to the fact that there are many different levels of political behavior —mass voting, legislative activity, leadership manipulation, for example—and that what is influential and important on one level of politics may not be on another. Certainly the Germans and Dutch of Iowa in 1860 were not paying much attention to the desires of their leaders. They were responding to influences

deemed more important than those influences shaping the responses of their leaders. As Swierenga pointed out in his analysis of Dutch voting:

> While Scholte [a leader of the Dutch community] fulminated against Democrats as slave mongers, as opponents of the Pacific Railroad and Homestead Bills, and as destroyers of the Constitution, the Dutch citizens blithely ignored him and the national issues he propounded and voted their personal prejudices against Republican nativists and prohibitionists.

Obviously, when historians generalize about the nature of political behavior they must also be sure which group and level of political activity they mean, and so identify it, and not confuse different levels or assume positive correlations between the actions of people on one level with those on another level. Such precision will contribute greatly to accuracy and overcome tendencies toward distortion.

Finally, based on the work under discussion here, it is clear that historians must become more aware of the complexities of human behavior. All people, even of the same stratum of society or living in the same geographic area, do not respond with the same intensity to the same social or political stimuli. Not everyone perceives his best interests in the same way, or considers the same things to be the most important problems confronting him. Depending upon time and circumstances, one man may respond primarily to economic influences; another one, at the same time and place, to religious influences; and so on. Sometimes most people in a given community will respond to the same influences equally, but we must be careful to observe *when* this is true and not generalize from it that this is *always* true. Single-factor explanations for human behavior do not seem to work, and we must remain aware of that fact.

With improved methodological tools and concepts historians may begin to engage in more systematic and complete analyses of popular voting, legislative voting, and the motivations and actions of political leaders. They will be able to weigh the relative influence of sectional problems against other items of interest and concern on all levels of political behavior. Until this is done, however, we do know on the basis of what already has been suggested that we cannot really accept glib explanations about the antebellum period. The Civil War has had a pernicious influence on the study of American political development that preceded it—pernicious because it has distorted the reality of political behavior in the era and has caused an overemphasis on sectionalism. It has led us to look not for what was occurring in American politics in those years, but rather for what was occurring in American politics that tended toward sectional breakdown and civil war—a quite different matter.

NO

Michael F. Holt

THE POLITICAL CRISIS OF THE 1850s

Historians have long looked to politics for the origins of the Civil War, and they have offered two major interpretations of political developments between 1845 and 1860. Both are primarily concerned with the breakdown of the old party system and the rise of the Republicans and not with the second aspect of the crisis—the loss of faith in politicians, the desire for reform, and their relationship to republican ideology. By spelling out my reservations about and disagreements with these interpretations, the assumptions behind and, I hope, the logic of my own approach to the political crisis of the 1850s will become clearer.

The standard interpretation maintains that intensifying sectional disagreements over slavery inevitably burst into the political arena, smashed the old national parties, and forced the formation of new, sectionally oriented ones. The Second Party System was artificial, some historians contend, since it could survive only by avoiding divisive sectional issues and by confining political debate to sectionally neutral economic questions on which the national parties had coherent stands. Once sectional pressure was reaggravated by the events of the late 1840s and early 1850s, those fragile structures shattered and were replaced. "On the level of politics," writes Eric Foner, "the coming of the Civil War is the intrusion of sectional ideology into the political system, despite the efforts of political leaders of both parties [Whigs and Democrats] to keep it out. Once this happened, political competition worked to exacerbate, rather than to solve, social and sectional conflicts."

There is much to be said for this interpretation. The Republican party did rise to dominance in the North largely because of an increase of Northern hostility toward the South, and its ascendance worsened relations between the sections. Attributing the political developments prior to its rise to the same sectional force that caused the rise has the virtue of simplicity. But that argument distorts a rapidly changing and very complex political situation between 1845 and 1860. There were three discrete, sequential political developments in those years that shaped the political crisis that led to war—the disappearance of the Whig party and with it of the old framework of two-party competition, a realignment of voters as they switched party affiliation, and a shift from a nationally balanced party system where both major parties competed on fairly even terms in all parts of the nation to a sectionally polarized one with Republicans dominant in the North and Democrats in the South. Although related, these were distinct phases, occurring with some exceptions in that order, and they were caused by different things. Although the inflammation of sectional antagonism between 1855 and 1860 helped to account for the new sectional alignment of parties, sectional conflict by itself caused neither the voter realignment of middecade nor the most crucial event of the period— the death of the Whig party, especially its death at the state level. It bears repeating that the demise of the Whig party, and with it of the traditional framework of two-party competition at the local, state, and national levels, was the most critical development in this sequence. Its disappearance helped foster popular doubts about the legitimacy of politics as usual, raised fears that powerful conspiracies were undermining republicanism, allowed the rise of the Republican party in the North, and created the situation in the lower South that produced secession there and not elsewhere.

The theory that the Second Party System was artificial and was shattered once the slavery issue arose, like the larger theory of the war's causation it reflects, founders on the problem of timing. There is considerable evidence that sectional conflict over slavery characterized the Second Party System throughout its history. Slavery was not swept under the rug; it was often the stuff of political debate. Proponents of the traditional interpretation, indeed, have often confused internal divisions within the national parties with their demise. Although they

point to different dates when the rupture was fatal, they have assumed that once the national parties were split into Northern and Southern wings over slavery, the parties were finished. Yet the Whig and Jacksonian parties, like almost all political organizations at any time, had frequently been divided—over slavery as well as other issues. They functioned for years in that condition. To establish the existence of sectional splits within the national parties is not to answer the vexed question of why those divisions were fatal in the 1850s and not in the 1830s and 1840s. If it was the sectional conflict that destroyed the old party system, the crucial question is why the parties were able to manage that conflict at some times and not at others. For a number of reasons, the easy reply that the volatile slavery issue simply became more explosive in the 1850s than earlier is not an adequate answer to this question.

The second major interpretation of the politics of the 1850s also has its merits and liabilities. Arguing that traditional historians have viewed events in the 1850s with the hindsight knowledge that the Civil War occurred, a new group of political historians insist that the extent to which sectionalism affected political behavior, especially popular voting behavior at the grass-roots level, has been exaggerated. Local social tensions, especially ethnic and religious tensions, motivated voters in the 1850s, they contend, not national issues like slavery, which was of so much concern to national political elites. What applies to Congress and national leaders, these new political historians say in effect, does not apply to the local level of politics. Prohibitionism, nativism, and anti-Catholicism produced the voter realignment in which the Whigs disappeared and new parties emerged in the North.

By focusing on voting behavior, this ethnocultural interpretation presents a compelling analysis of why an anti-Democratic majority was created in many parts of the North. Explaining why Northern voters realigned between 1853 and 1856, however, does not answer why the Republican party appeared or why party politics were sectionally polarized at the end of the decade. Prophets of the ethnocultural thesis, moreover, have done little to explain Southern politics, yet developments in Dixie where Catholics and immigrants were few were just as important as events in the North in leading to war. Nor do voting studies really explain the crucial first phase —the death of the Whig party. Party reorganization accompanied voter realignment in the 1850s, and ethnocultural tensions alone do not explain why new parties were necessary. Why didn't anti-Democratic voters simply become Whigs? This question has a particular urgency when one realizes that in the 1840s ethnocultural issues had also been present and that the Whigs and Democrats had aligned on opposite sides of them. The problem with stressing ethnocultural issues, as with stressing sectionalism, is why those issues could be contained within, indeed could invigorate, old party lines at one time yet could help to destroy them at another.

The fundamental weakness of previous interpretations of why the old two-party system broke down is their misunderstanding of how and why it worked. They have not adequately explored either the relationship between political parties and issues or the impact of the federal system with its divided responsibilities among local, state, and national governments on the parties and the party system. Whether historians stress sectionalism or ethnocultural issues, their central assumption seems to be that issues arising from the society at large caused political events. The Second Party System functioned because it dealt with "safe" economic questions, but once those issues were replaced or displaced by new disruptive matters the parties broke down and realignment followed. Yet what made the Second Party System work in the end was not issues *per se* or the presence of safe issues and absence of dangerous ones. In the end what made the two-party system operate was its ability to allow political competition on a broad range of issues that varied from time to time and place to place. If the genius of the American political system has been the peaceful resolution of conflict, what has supported two-party systems has been the conflict itself, not its resolution. As long as parties fought with each other over issues or took opposing stands even when they failed to promote opposing programs, as long as they defined alternative ways to secure republican ideals, voters perceived them as different and maintained their loyalty to them. Party health and popular faith in the political process depended on the perception of party difference, which in turn depended on the reality—or at least the appearance—of interparty conflict. As long as parties seemed different from each other, voters viewed them as viable vehicles through which to influence government.

Politicians had long recognized that group conflict was endemic to American society and that the vitality of individual parties depended on the intensity of their competition with opposing parties. Thomas Jefferson had perceived in

1798 that "in every free and deliberating society, there must, from the nature of man, be opposite parties, and violent dissensions and discords." "Seeing that we must have somebody to quarrel with," he wrote John Taylor, "I had rather keep our New England associates for that purpose, than to see our bickerings transferred to others." Even more explicit in their recognition of what made parties work were the founders of New York's Albany Regency in the 1820s. They deplored the lack of internal discipline and cohesion in the Jeffersonian Republican party once the Federalists disappeared, and they moved quickly to remedy it. Although any party might suffer defeats, they realized, "it is certain to acquire additional strength... by the attacks of adverse parties." A political party, indeed, was "most in jeopardy when an opposition is not sufficiently defined." During "the contest between the great rival parties [Federalists and Jeffersonians] each found in the strength of the other a powerful motive of union and vigor." Significantly, those like Daniel Webster who deplored the emergence of mass parties in the 1820s and 1830s also recognized that strife was necessary to perpetuate party organization and that the best way to break it down was to cease opposition and work for consensus. Politicians in the 1840s and 1850s continued to believe that interparty conflict was needed to unify their own party and maintain their voting support. Thus an Alabama Democrat confessed that his party pushed a certain measure at the beginning of the 1840 legislative session explicitly as "the best means for drawing the party lines as soon as possible" while by 1852, when opposition to that state's Democracy appeared to disintegrate, another warned perceptively, "I think the only danger

to the Democratic party is that it will become too much an omnibus in this State. We have nothing to fear from either the Union, or Whig party or both combined. From their friendship and adherence much." Many of the important decisions in the 1840s and 1850s reflected the search by political leaders for issues that would sharply define the lines between parties and thus reinvigorate the loyalty of party voters.

If conflict sustained the old two-party system, what destroyed it was the loss of the ability to provide interparty competition on *any* important issue at *any* level of the federal system. Because the political system's vitality and legitimacy with the voters depended on the clarity of the definition of the parties as opponents, the blurring of that definition undid the system. What destroyed the Second Party System was consensus, not conflict. The growing congruence between the parties on almost all issues by the early 1850s dulled the sense of party difference and thereby eroded voters' loyalty to the old parties. Once competing groups in society decided that the party system no longer provided them viable alternatives in which they could carry on conflict with each other, they repudiated the old system by dropping out, seeking third parties that would meet their needs, or turning to nonpartisan or extrapolitical action to achieve their goals. Because the collapse of the Second Party System was such a vital link in the war's causation, therefore, one arrives at a paradox. While the Civil War is normally viewed as the one time when conflict prevailed over consensus in American politics, the prevalence of consensus over conflict in crucial parts of the political system contributed in a very real way to the outbreak of war in the first place....

The sectionalization of American politics was emphatically *not* simply a reflection or product of basic popular disagreements over black slavery. Those had long existed without such a complete polarization developing. Even though a series of events beginning with the Kansas-Nebraska Act greatly increased sectional consciousness, it is a mistake to think of sectional antagonism as a spontaneous and self-perpetuating force that imposed itself on the political arena against the will of politicians and coerced parties to conform to the lines of sectional conflict. Popular grievances, no matter how intense, do not dictate party strategies. Political leaders do. Some one has to politicize events, to define their political relevance in terms of a choice between or among parties, before popular grievances can have political impact. It was not events alone that caused Northerners and Southerners to view each other as enemies of the basic rights they both cherished. Politicians who pursued very traditional partisan strategies were largely responsible for the ultimate breakdown of the political process. Much of the story of the coming of the Civil War is the story of the successful efforts of Democratic politicians in the South and Republican politicians in the North to keep the sectional conflict at the center of political debate and to defeat political rivals who hoped to exploit other issues to achieve election.

For at least thirty years political leaders had recognized that the way to build political parties, to create voter loyalty and mobilize support, and to win elections was to find issues or positions on issues that distinguished them from their opponents and that therefore could appeal to various groups who disliked their opponents by offering them an alternative for political action—in sociological terms, to make their party a vehicle for negative reference group behavior. Because of the American ethos, the most successful tactic had been to pose as a champion of republican values and to portray the opponent as antirepublican, as unlawful, tyrannical, or aristocratic. Jackson, Van Buren, and Polk, Antimasons and Whigs, had all followed this dynamic of the political system. Stephen A. Douglas and William H. Seward had pursued the same strategy in their unsuccessful attempt to rebuild the disintegrating Second Party System with the Kansas-Nebraska Act in 1854. After faith in the old parties had collapsed irreparably, when the shape of future political alignments was uncertain, Republican politicians quite consciously seized on the slavery and sectional issue in order to build a new party. Claiming to be the exclusive Northern Party that was necessary to halt slavery extension and defeat the Slave Power conspiracy was the way they chose to distinguish themselves from Democrats, whom they denounced as pro-Southern, and from the Know Nothings, who had chosen a different organizing principle—anti-Catholicism and nativism—to construct their new party.

To say that Republican politicians agitated and exploited sectional grievances in order to build a winning party is a simple description of fact. It is not meant to imply that winning was their only objective or to be a value judgment about the sincerity or insincerity of their personal hatred of black slavery. Some undoubtedly found slavery morally intolerable and hoped to use the national government to weaken it by preventing its expansion, abolishing it in federal enclaves like the District of Columbia, and undermining it within Southern states by whatever means were constitutionally possible, such as opening the mails to abolitionist literature and prohibiting the interstate slave trade. The antislavery pedigree of Republican leaders, however, was in a sense irrelevant to the triumph of the Republican party. The leaders were divided over the policies they might pursue if they won control of the national government, and leadership views were often far in advance of those held by their electorate. Much more important was the campaign they ran to obtain power, their skill in politicizing the issues at hand in such a way as to convince Northern voters that control of the national government by an exclusive Northern party was necessary to resist Slave Power aggressions. The Republicans won more because of what they were against than because of what they were for, because of what they wanted to stop, not what they hoped to do....

The key to unraveling the paradoxes in Republican rhetoric, the juxtaposition of egalitarianism and racism, of pledges not to interfere with slavery in the South alongside calls to end slavery and join a great crusade for freedom, is to remember that the word "slavery" had long had a definite meaning aside from the institution of black slavery in the South. It was in this sense that many Republicans used the word. Slavery implied subordination to tyranny, the loss of liberty and equality, the absence of republicanism. Slavery resulted when republican government was overthrown or usurped, and that, charged Republicans, was exactly what the Slave Power was trying to do. Hence the slavery that many Republicans objected to most was not the bondage of blacks in the South but the subjugation of Northern whites to the despotism of a tiny oligarchy of slaveholders bent on destroying their rights, a minority who controlled the Democratic party and through it the machinery of the federal government. Thus one Republican complained privately in 1857, "The Slave power will not submit. The tyrants of the lash will not withhold until they have put padlocks on the lives of freemen. The Union which our fathers formed seventy years ago is not the Union today... the sons of the Revolutionary fathers are becoming *slaves* or *masters*." Thus a Chicago Republican congressman, after reciting a litany of supposed Slave Power aggressions against the North, later recalled, "All these things followed the taking possession of the Government and lands by the slave power, until we [in the North] were the slaves of slaves, being chained to the car of this Slave Juggernaut." Thus the black abolitionist Frederick Douglass perceptively observed, "The cry of Free Men was raised, not for the extension of liberty to the black man, but for the protection of the liberty of the white."

The basic objective of Republican campaigns from 1856 to 1860, therefore, was to persuade Northerners that slaveholders meant to enslave them through their control of the national government and to enlist Northern voters behind the Republican party in a defensive phalanx to ward off *that* slavery, and not in an offensive crusade to end black slavery, by driving the Slave Power from its control of the national government. For such a tactic to succeed, the Republicans required two things. First, to make an asset and not a liability of their existence as an exclusive Northern party, they needed events to increase Northern antagonism toward the South so that men believed the South, and not foreigners and Catholics or the Republicans themselves, posed the chief threat to the republic. More important, they had successfully to identify the Democratic party as an agent or lackey of the South. Because the Republicans campaigned only in the North, because Northern voters chose among Northern candidates instead of between Northerners and Southerners, only by making Northern Democrats surrogates for the Slave Power could they make their case that Republicans alone, and not simply any Northern politicians, were needed to resist and overthrow the slavocracy. Because they dared not promise overt action against slaveholders except for stopping slavery expansion, in other words, Republicans could not exploit Northern anger, no matter how intense it was, unless they could convince Northern voters that supporting the Republicans and defeating Northern Democrats was an efficacious and constitutional way to defeat the Slave Power itself.

By the summer of 1856 it was much easier to identify the Democracy with the South than it had been earlier. For one thing, the results of the congressional elections of 1854 and 1855 had dramatically shifted the balance of sectional power within the Democratic party, a result that was plainly evident when the 34th Congress met during 1856. From 1834 to 1854 the Democratic congressional delegation had usually been reasonably balanced between North and South. In the 33rd Congress, Northern Democrats had even outnumbered Southern Democrats in the House by a margin of 91 to 67. But in 1856 there were only 25 Northerners as compared to 63 Southerners, and even though Northern Democratic representation would increase after the 1856 elections, the sectional balance would never be restored before the Civil War. The South seemed to dominate the Democracy, and that fact was especially difficult to hide during a presidential election year. Because the Democrats, unlike the Republicans, met in a common national convention with Southerners and campaigned in both sections, Democrats could not deny their Southern connection. The democratic platform endorsing the Kansas-Nebraska Act strengthened that identification, thereby flushing out regular Northern Democrats who had tried to evade the Nebraska issue in 1854 and 1855 and infuriating anti-Nebraska Democrats who had clung to the party in hopes of reversing its policy but who now bolted to the Republicans....

The Democratic party within the Deep South had, in fact, changed in significant ways. During the 1830s and 1840s, it had normally been controlled by and represented the interests of nonslaveholders from the hill country and piney woods regions. Even at that time slaveholders and their lawyer allies from the normally Whig black belt areas had contested for leadership of the Democracy. Sharing the same economic concerns as their Whig neighbors in those plantation regions, concerns that nonslaveholding Democrats generally opposed, Democrats from the black belt had bid for control of the party by trying to shift attention to national issues and asserting that the threat to Southern equality posed the greatest menace to the liberties of all Southern voters. During the 1850s, for a variety of reasons, those slaveholding elements took over the Democracy, and in state after state it became much less receptive at the state level to the wishes of the nonslaveholding majority who nonetheless remained Democrats because of traditional Jacksonian loyalties. For one thing, Franklin Pierce favored Southern Rights Democrats in the distribution of federal patronage. Second, as the Whig party dissolved, Democratic politicians from the slaveholding regions won over some of its former adherents by stressing the menace to slaveholders' interests, thereby increasing their own power within the Democratic party. Finally, during the 1850s, the cotton culture spread away from the old black belt to staunchly Democratic regions, thus enlarging the constituency that would respond to politicians riding the slavery issue.

As a result of this transformation, the economic priorities of the Democratic party changed. Democratic newspapers openly advised Democratic legislators not to offend their new Whig allies, and the new Democratic leaders wanted positive economic programs in any case. Occasionally the nonslaveholders found individual champions of the old Jacksonian orthodoxy like Governor George Winston of Alabama and Governor Joe Brown of Georgia who vetoed probusiness legislation, but Democratic legislatures invariably overrode those vetoes. To nonslaveholders, the Democratic party, as a party, and the political process as a whole no longer seemed as responsive as they once had been.

The shift of power within the dominant Democracy hastened the almost exclusive concentration of political rhetoric on the slavery and sectional issues. For one thing, slaveholders were more genuinely concerned about potential threats to black slavery than nonslaveholders. For another, the Democrats attributed their rise to dominance by 1852 to their ability to appear more pro-Southern than the Whigs, and they saw no reason to change a winning strategy. Third, the new leaders of the party continued to feel the need of holding the loyalty of the nonslaveholding backbone of the Democratic electorate. That support had always been won by identifying and crusading against antirepublican monsters. Because the new leaders did not want to attack the economic programs they were themselves promoting and because internal opposition was so weak from former Whigs who approved of those programs, they more and more portrayed the external Republican party as the chief danger to the liberty, equality, and self-esteem of all Southerners, slaveholders and nonslaveholders alike. Like the Republicans in the North, they translated the sectional conflict into the republican idiom in order to win the votes of men who were not primarily concerned with black slavery.

POSTSCRIPT

Have Historians Overemphasized the Slavery Issue as a Cause of the Civil War?

Professor Silbey's article represents the first sustained attack on the sectional interpretation of the events leading to the Civil War. Historians, he claims, have created a false "Civil War synthesis" that positioned slavery as the major issue that divided America, thereby distorting "the reality of American political life between 1844 and 1861."

Silbey is one of the "new political historians" who have applied the techniques of modern-day political scientists in analyzing the election returns and voting patterns of Americans' nineteenth- and early-twentieth-century predecessors. These historians use computers and regression analysis of voting patterns, they favor a quantitative analysis of past behavior, and they reject the traditional sources of quotes from partisan newspapers and major politicians because these sources provide anecdotal and often misleading portraits of our past. Silbey and other new political historians maintain that all politics are local. Therefore, the primary issues in the 1860 election for voters and their politicians were ethnic and cultural, and party loyalty was more important than sectional considerations.

Professor Holt is also interested in analyzing the struggles for power at the state and local levels by the major political parties, but he is critical of the ethnocultural school that Silbey represents. In Holt's view, Silbey's emphasis on voter analysis explains why an anti-Democratic bloc of voters developed in the North. But it does not explain why the Whig party disappeared nor why the Republican party became the majority party in the northern and western states by 1850. More important, since Silbey and other ethnoculturalists have little to say about southern politics, reasons why secession and the subsequent Civil War took place are left unanswered.

Holt also rejects the more traditional view that the Civil War resulted from the "intensifying sectional disagreements over slavery." Instead, he promotes a more complicated picture of the events leading to the Civil War. Between 1845 and 1860, he maintains, three important things happened: the breakdown of the Whig party; the realignment of voters; and "a shift from a nationally balanced party system where both major parties competed on fairly even terms in all parts of the nation to a sectionally polarized one with Republicans dominant in the North and Democrats in the South."

Holt builds his argument on the assumption that two-party competition at the state and local levels is healthy in resolving conflicts. With the demise of the Whig party in the middle 1850s, the two-party system of competition broke down at the state and local levels. A national realignment was completed by 1860: Republicans controlled northern states while Democrats dominated the southern ones. Holt maintains that the Whig and Democratic parties had argued over the slavery issue in the 1830s and 1840s but that they did not fragment into state and local parties. He implies that if the second-party system continued through the 1850s, the slavery issue might have been resolved in a more peaceful manner.

One criticism of both Silbey and Holt is that neither author interprets the political events leading up to the Civil War within the context of the socio-economic changes taking place in the country. Both authors explain how many Americans manifested their hostility to the Irish Catholics who came here in the 1840s and 1850s by joining the Know-Nothing party, which in turn caused a realignment of the political parties. But they make no mention of the reasons why the Irish and other immigrants came here: the market revolution and the need for workers to build and staff the canals, railroads, and factories.

The list of books about the Civil War is extensive. Two good starting points are John Niven, *The Coming of the Civil War, 1837–1861* (Harlan Davidson, 1990) and Bruce Levine, *Half Slave and Half Free* (Hill & Wang, 1992). An older, extensive work with a compelling narrative and sound interpretations is David Potter, *The Impending Crisis, 1848–1861* (Harper & Row, 1976). Michael Perman has updated the well-worn problems of American civilization in *The Coming of the American Civil War,* 3rd ed. (D.C. Heath, 1993).

Both Silbey and Holt have published numerous articles in scholarly journals. Silbey, who has extensive knowledge of the nineteenth-century Democratic party, has collected his articles in *The American Political Nation 1838–1893* (Stanford University Press, 1991). A collection of Holt's articles can be found in *Political Parties and American Political Development from the Age of Jackson to the Age of Lincoln* (Louisiana State University Press, 1992).

Historians who reject the ethnocultural school, which minimizes the slavery issue as the cause of the Civil War, include Eric Foner and Kenneth M. Stampp. Foner's *Free Soil, Free Labor, Free Men* (Oxford University Press, 1970) is an excellent study of the bourgeois capitalism and conservative idealism that formed the ideological basis of the Republican party before the Civil War. In *America in 1857: A Nation on the Brink* (Oxford University Press, 1990), Stampp argues that conflict became inevitable after the election of James Buchanan to the presidency, the firestorm in Kansas, and the Supreme Court's decision in *Dred Scott v. Sandford.* A shorter version of this thesis is contained in Stampp's *The Imperiled Union: Essays on the Background of the Civil War* (Oxford University Press, 1980). A recent summary of the traditional view is found in Richard H. Sewell's, *House Divided: Sectionalism and Civil War, 1848–1865* (Johns Hopkins University Press, 1988).

ISSUE 15

Was the Confederacy Defeated Because of Its "Loss of Will"?

YES: Richard E. Beringer et al., from *Why the South Lost the Civil War* (University of Georgia Press, 1986)

NO: James M. McPherson, from *Battle Cry of Freedom: The Civil War Era* (Oxford University Press, 1988)

ISSUE SUMMARY

YES: Professor of history Richard E. Beringer and his colleagues believe that the Confederacy lacked the will to win the Civil War because of an inability to fashion a viable Southern nationalism, increasing religious doubts about the Confederate cause, and guilt over slavery.

NO: Pulitzer Prize–winning historian James M. McPherson maintains that either side might have emerged victorious in the Civil War but that the Union success was contingent upon winning three major campaigns between 1862 and 1864.

Over the past 125 years contemporaries and historians have advanced dozens of explanations for the defeat of the Confederacy in the Civil War. Most of these can be divided into two categories: external and internal.

There are two external reasons for the Confederacy's failure: the Union's overwhelming numbers and resources and the uneven quality of leadership between the two sides. The North possessed two-and-one-half times the South's population, three times its railroad capacity, and nine times its industrial production. Given the statistical imbalance between the North and the South, it seems that the South lost the war even before the fighting had begun.

The Unionists also appear to have had better leadership. Lincoln is ranked as America's greatest president because he united his political objectives of saving the Union and freeing the slaves with a military strategy designed to defeat the Confederacy. Lincoln's generals—Ulysses S. Grant, William T. Sherman, and Philip H. Sheridan—outsmarted the Confederate leadership. In 1864, for example, massive frontal attacks were made against the Confederates in the eastern and western theater. At the same time, Sherman destroyed much of the agricultural base of the Southerners as he marched his troops through South Carolina and Georgia.

Internal conflicts also spelled doom for the Confederacy, according to a number of historians. In his book *State Rights in the Confederacy* (1925), Frank Owsley maintained that the centrifugal forces of state rights killed the Confederacy. Owsley, a long-time Vanderbilt scholar, believed that governors in North Carolina and Georgia withheld men and equipment from the Confederate armies in order to build up their own state militias. On the Confederate tombstone, he said, should be inscribed: "Died of State Rights."

A second version of the internal conflict argument appeared in a 1960 essay in a symposium on *Why the North Won the Civil War*. In it, the editor, Pulitzer Prize–winning historian David Donald, argued that the resistance of Southerners to conscription, taxes, and limitations on speeches critical of the war effort fatally crippled the Confederacy's war effort. Instead of state rights, says Donald, the tombstone should read: "Died of Democracy."

A third variant of the internal conflict argument has recently been promoted by four Southern scholars: Richard E. Beringer, Herman Hattaway, Archer Jones, and William N. Still, Jr. Their main thesis is that the Confederacy lacked the will to win because of its inability to fashion a viable Southern nationalism, increasing religious doubts that God was on the Confederacy's side, and guilt over slavery. The first selection of this issue succinctly summarizes the "loss of will" thesis.

In a recent Gettysburg symposium, edited by Gabor S. Borritt, on *Why the Confederacy Lost* (Oxford University Press, 1992), James M. McPherson dismisses all the external and internal explanations for the South's defeat listed above. In his critique, McPherson applies the theory of reversibility. Briefly stated, the hindsight provided by knowing the outcome of the war allows the writer to attribute causes that explain the Northern victory.

But what if the South won the Civil War? Could the same external explanations that are attributed to the Union victory also be used to explain a Confederate win? Would Jefferson Davis's leadership emerge as superior to Abraham Lincoln's? Would the great military leaders be Robert E. Lee, Thomas "Stonewall" Jackson, and Braxton Bragg instead of Grant, Sherman, and Sheridan? Would one Confederate soldier be considered equal to four Union soldiers? Would a triumvirate of yeoman farmers, slaveholding planters, and small industrialists have proven the superiority of agrarian values over industrial ones?

McPherson rejects the traditional internal and external explanations as well as the theory of reversibility. In the second selection, McPherson advances the theory of contingency as an explanation for the Union victory. Of the four turning points in the war from the Union campaigns of 1862 through the Atlanta and western campaigns in 1864, the North won the latter three. In McPherson's view, chance or luck and not loss of will determined the outcome of the Civil War in favor of the Union.

YES

Richard E. Beringer et al.

WHY THE SOUTH LOST

The immediate popular response to the question posed by this... chapter is usually that the North overwhelmed the South with its great numbers and resources. The Union possessed more than twice the population of the Confederacy, and the South endured an even greater disadvantage in military population, for the South included four million slaves, excluded from direct military participation on the Confederate side. But though numbers were certainly important, the inherent advantages of defense, illustrated by the virtual impossibility of destroying an enemy army unless it had an incompetent commander, required a greater disparity before the size and resources of the Union could explain Confederate defeat.

Many Confederates agreed that numbers or resources did not provide the margin, although they disagreed on what did. General Beauregard, for example, claimed that "no people ever warred for independence with more relative advantages than the Confederates; and if, as a military question, they must have failed, then no country must aim at freedom by means of war." "The South," Beauregard asserted, "would be open to discredit as a people if its failure could not be explained otherwise than by mere material conquest." To Beauregard, the Confederates did not owe their defeat to numbers but to faulty strategy and the poor leadership of Jefferson Davis, who attempted to defend all Confederate territory, thus dispersing Confederate strength and forbidding adequate concentration.

Some historians of our own generation agree with the thrust of Beauregard's remarks, though finding different flaws in Confederate military leadership. Clement Eaton, for example, aligned himself with T. Harry Williams, both of them maintaining that despite northern superiority in men and resources, the South had a good chance of success until Gettysburg and Vicksburg. "The chance was lost," says Eaton, because Davis "made the dubious decision of allowing [Lee]... to invade Pennsylvania instead of sending strong reinforcements from his army to defeat Grant at Vicksburg." But the ultimate cause of Confederate defeat, according to Eaton—and in agreement with a number of other historians... —was a loss of the will to fight. Both sides suffered from this problem, but after July 1863 it was worse for the

South. Southerners' "morale rose and fell with victory and defeat, and also with their estimation of the northern will to persevere." At this point we should recall the biting comment of Confederate Senator Williamson S. Oldham, who maintained that the argument of numbers flattered one's vanity but that the Confederacy had everything it needed to fight in 1865, "morale alone excepted."

But the Confederates did lack morale, and their morale was sapped by uncertainty about their war aims. To fight to be left alone, as Davis and others put it, did not prove very inspiring. Most Confederates thought the war was fought to attain security of slave property and autonomous government, with independence as merely the means by which they would achieve the desired end. But the growth of power of the central government compromised autonomous government, and the exigencies of manpower policy and foreign policy jeopardized slave property. The authorization for enlistment of slaves in the army and the proposal to grant them freedom as a result of their service reflected a Confederate alteration in war aims whereby the means became an end. Secession to protect slavery had, ironically, led to a war by the end of which the Confederacy would arm slaves and even offer them their freedom. But in denying the original motive for the establishment of a separate country, the Confederacy undermined the fundamental basis of its tentative nationalism and deprived many of its citizens of their motive for continuing the conflict.

Lincoln's Emancipation Proclamation made it difficult for Confederates to feel entirely at ease with their assertion that they were fighting for liberty. It aggravated the misgivings of those who long had harbored quiet doubts about slavery and made many others even more uneasy about their isolation in a world in which the great powers of Europe, now joined by the United States, sought to extirpate slavery. Many southerners felt guilt over the institution or at least unease about their position. Thus, as the struggle drew to a close, the commitment to slavery of many southerners withered in the face of the contradiction it created and under the weight of world moral disapproval, which some Confederates felt acutely.

The change in the Confederacy's explanation for secession and war shows the seriousness of the cognitive dissonance created by the problem of slavery. To consider it merely a contest for the proper interpretation of the Constitution was to deny recent historical fact, but the constitutional question offered a far more comfortable explanation for the sacrifice of so much blood and treasure than the protection of slavery had. But to reject slavery as the cause for secession eliminated the characteristic that most distinguished the North from the South. Common history and language united the sections and so, too, in a lesser and more complex sense, did religion; only slavery truly separated them. By the end of the conflict many southerners had denied the basis of their distinctiveness and of their nationalism. Without a sufficiently distinctive history to undergird their weak sense of nationality, Confederates created their own mythic past to support the notion that the war was the logical outcome of a controversy over state rights, not slavery.

In any case, slavery had provided a very slender foundation for a distinguishing nationalism. When southerners' allegiance to slavery faltered, no ground for distinctiveness would remain. This lack of significant difference from the

Union even applied to the emerging constitutional explanation of secession and war. Those who came to see state rights and a decentralized government as the cause for which they fought were very often the same people who denounced the centralized despotism of the Davis administration. Why, many asked, fight against one centralized government only to preserve another?

Thus the course of the conflict quickly exacerbated the weakness in the southern sense of separate identity and in the original cause of secession. Frank Owsley remarked that "the up-country people could easily fight a ninety-day war ... but not a war that lasted over several years. Anger and enthusiasm are too transient to serve as a basis of war." What he said of the up-country people could reasonably have been said of the low-country people also, even though they, in fact, displayed much greater allegiance to the cause. But neither, as it turned out, had enough deep and enduring support for the struggle.

In fact, considering their fragile and insecure nationalism one could almost ask what induced southerners to make such a powerful and prolonged resistance? Certainly the climate of opinion, which for two decades had reflected a consciousness of divergence between the sections and a hostility to Yankees, had much to do with magnifying grievances and strengthening the feeling of separateness. The churches contributed powerfully to fostering this climate of opinion, but they, too, like slavery and limited government, failed as the conflict wore on. In the same way that slavery was removed as a motive for continuing the struggle by the understanding that it was doomed regardless of who won, and development of centralized Confederate government mitigated state rights as a source

of motivation, so, too, religion ceased to sustain Confederate morale and confidence in victory. Defeat in battle and loss of territory cast doubt on whether God truly favored the Confederacy and, for those who concluded that God did not, the cause seemed hopeless. The devout had no motive to keep struggling against God's will. A powerful prop initially, religion thus became a source of weakness in adversity.

As Confederates pondered the religious meaning of the Civil War, especially in the last dark months, they questioned why God had failed them. Southerners answered that question in various ways, most of which related to sin and punishment. But in identifying God's will with their own affairs on earth, Confederates unconsciously had been expanding their faith to the point that they created—in effect—a civil religion.

It is beyond the scope of this [chapter] to apply the concept of civil religion to the events of the Civil War. It is sufficient to our thesis to note that an American civil religion existed and that it was profoundly related to American nationalism. We suspect that it was also related to vague notions of Confederate nationalism....

And what of the South's civil religion, however embryonic: did it not exist? Yes, but only in embryo; it was aborted before birth. The reason is because its mother could not carry it to term: the philosophical and religious underpinnings of the Confederacy were not spawned in an atmosphere of nationalism but in one of racism and fear. And when at last it became obvious that even Confederate victory could not have resulted in a satisfactory continuation of white supremacy through the maintenance of slavery, white supremacy had to be nurtured in other ways. In a secular sense, this was done by salvaging the extant social structure in the nationalism of the lost cause, but the process also had its religious history because much of it occurred within the churches. Within those potent and significant institutions, a virile response to the Confederacy's change in war aims was forged.

Owsley's thesis "that the Confederacy collapsed more from internal than from external causes" certainly could find strong support in the embryonic nature of Confederate nationalism and the debilitating effects of southern civil religion in the face of God's apparent disfavor. But Owsley's original hypothesis, the crippling effect of state rights, does not, upon closer examination, suffice.

The tangible effects of state rights, as distinguished from the rhetoric, had little negative effect on the Confederate war effort. Even the total number of exempted men was small in relation to the Confederate armies, and most of them made significant economic contributions, served in local defense forces, or both. The protection of ports and the production of such important items as salt had an importance that military authorities and President Davis both recognized, and state local defense forces therefore contributed materially to this effort. Further, state endeavors to supply and equip local defense forces and to meet the needs of their own men in the Confederate service provided a major supplement to the national war effort. State uniforms and blankets did not come from stocks accessible to the Confederate government; rather, they constituted an addition to the total available. If Governor Vance in truth had ninety-two thousand uniforms at the end of the war, as he claimed, they did not belong to the Confederate government but

were an addition to the total stock of uniforms in the Confederacy, a supply made ready by the state's funds, enterprise, and concern for its fighting men. On balance, state contributions to the war effort far outweighed any unnecessary diversion of resources to local defense.

State-rights attempts to obstruct the Confederate government by resisting conscription or the suspension of habeas corpus, for example, also had a negligible effect. State rights in writing and oratory provided a rallying cry for opposition that already existed in any case. Just as in England under the early Hanoverians the association of the Prince of Wales with the group out of power showed the opposition's loyalty to the king and dynasty, so an appeal to the universally accepted notion of state rights provided a legitimacy to the opposition and protected it from accusations of disloyalty during a struggle for national existence. Thus state rights made a political contribution, one probably necessary in the absence of organized political parties.

In view of the rhetoric of state rights and the long, disputatious correspondence between Governor Brown and the Richmond government, Frank L. Owsley made a natural mistake in choosing state rights as the internal cause of Confederate collapse. But in placing the blame on disunity caused by state rights, he did not show that military causes inadequately explained defeat. Considering the still continuing flow of books and articles about Civil War military operations, he displayed wisdom in avoiding a topic on which he would have had difficulty securing agreement. But in view of the harmony of [Carl von] Clausewitz and [Henri] Jomini [both prominent nineteenth-century European military strategists] on the relevant strategic variables, it is possible to use them effectively as authorities to provide a fairly firm basis for settling the military questions about the Confederacy. Their essential consensus says that an invader needs more force than the North possessed to conquer such a large country as the South, even one so limited in logistical resources....

So Confederate military competence that capably managed its armies and consciously, and skillfully, used cavalry raids to aid guerrillas in destroying Union supply lines provided the means of validating Clausewitz's and Jomini's judgment about the impossibility of the Union attaining its strategic objective by military means if faced with a determined, unremitting national resistance. If, then, the Confederacy had the means to resist military conquest, one must find the cause of defeat within. If state rights was not this cause, what alternatives are there to the thesis of insufficient nationalism as the internal cause of defeat?

In spite of the blockade and the steady decline of the railways, Confederate supply did not fail. After each apparently catastrophic shock, such as the closure of communication with the trans-Mississippi or the loss of key railroad lines, the ramshackle Confederate logistic organization, displaying an amazing resilience, continued to make adequate provision for the armies. The accumulation in Richmond during the winter of 1865 of a week's reserve of rations for Lee's army illustrates the South's capability. Lee still had this reserve available in early April, in spite of the earlier closure of Wilmington, the presence of Sherman's army in North Carolina, and Sheridan's devastating raid against supply and communications northwest of Richmond. The Confederacy provided its armies with food

and clothing, albeit often in barely adequate and sometimes inadequate quantities, and with a sufficiency of weapons and ammunition. And all the while it kept a higher proportion of the population under arms than did the Union.

As Stanley Lebergott has shown, the Confederate Congress did not prohibit the export of cotton, a measure many believed would bring intervention on the South's behalf by France and the United Kingdom in an effort to save their cotton textile industries. This failure, like the failure to restrict cotton planting during the war, reflects a lack of appreciation of the nature of total economic mobilization and a concern for the pecuniary interests of the growers of cotton. But the production of so much cotton between 1861 and 1865 (the 1864 inventory equaled twice the exports during the war) also indicates a debilitating confidence in a short conflict and an early return to unimpeded cotton exports. Significantly, the 1862 cotton crop was the second largest on record.

But the production of too much cotton and not enough food crops, like the decline in railway service and the constraints of the blockade, severely affected the home front, already heavily taxed through inflation and diminished in manpower because of the needs of the army and of war production. These costs and hardships, like the casualties in battle and the gloom occasioned by defeats, depressed civilian morale. Many of the deficiencies of Confederate supply affected civilians more than the armies and aggravated hardships inseparable from such a bloody and costly war. And the depressed morale of the home front communicated itself to the soldiers through newspapers and the Confederate postal service, which continued to function throughout the war in spite of numerous obstacles, including a constitutionally mandated requirement that postal expenses not exceed postal income.

The defeats, shortages, reduced standard of living, and change of war goals, as well as the war's length, obviously placed a severe strain on the Confederates' dedication to their cause. The high degree of dependence of Confederate morale on military events meant that setbacks on the battle front usually had a significance far beyond the military importance of the loss of a battle or a fragment of territory. A succession of defeats and territorial losses, though not representing militarily consequential conquests of the South's vast land area, worked steadily to depress morale and confidence in victory. With fewer such military disappointments and less hardship for civilians, or with a shorter war, Confederate nationalism, weak though it was, would have equaled the demands placed upon it and might well have developed real strength after the war; in any case, a greater measure of nationalism during the conflict certainly would have enabled the Confederates to resist longer.

In addition, planters felt alienated from a government that seemed to threaten their privileges and property and, in spite of the exemplary relief efforts of Georgia and North Carolina, and the similar, if not so extensive, measures in other states, the yeomen, too, felt disaffection with the Confederacy. Both planter and yeoman paid economically for the immense war effort, but too many yeomen lived too close to the margin of existence not to feel the hardships acutely; the costs of the war deprived them of the means to meet their basic needs, or threatened to do so. At the same time they felt that, with such perquisites as the exemption

of the overseers of twenty slaves and the right to purchase substitutes for military service, the rich did not bear their fair share of the burdens. Paul Escott stressed that throughout the struggle the planters gave primacy to their own rather than national interests. He points out that "a selfish and short-sighted ruling class had led its region into secession and then proven unwilling to makes sacrifices or to surrender its privileges for independence." These class differences in the demands of the war effort created another drain on the limited supply of Confederate nationalism.

But the resulting decline in commitment to the struggle did not begin to affect the war effort very seriously until after the middle of 1864. Then soldiers began to leave the army in increasing numbers. The fall of Atlanta in early September and Sheridan's victories over Early in the Shenandoah Valley, victories that significantly improved Lincoln's chances of reelection, also signaled the beginning of a marked rise in desertion from the Confederate army. Soldiers left not only from discouragement at these defeats but also from a realization that Union victories increased the likelihood of Lincoln's continuation in office and his policy of prosecuting the war to victory. As the fall elections confirmed this apprehension, the augmented stream of deserters continued unabated. The soldiers were voting for peace with their feet, and the few disaffected conscripts sent to the Confederate army probably hurt morale and effectiveness more than their small numbers could have added to its strength. By the early spring of 1865 the Confederate armies east of the Mississippi had shrunk to barely half their size the previous August.

Adventitiously, Grant's strategy began to play some part in this Confederate decline soon after the Union presidential contest of 1864, when Sherman marched from Atlanta to Savannah, breaking railways, destroying factories, stripping the countryside of slaves, and subsisting an army of sixty thousand men on the country. Sherman perceived the effect of this devastation on southerners when he wrote that his march would show the falsity of Davis's "promise of protection. If we can march a well-appointed army right through his territory, it is a demonstration to the world, foreign and domestic, that we have a power which Davis cannot resist." He believed that there were "thousands of people abroad and in the South who will reason thus: If the North can march an army right through the South, it is proof positive that the North can prevail in this struggle." But Sherman's raid occurred well after the exodus from the army began. His raids through Georgia and later into the Carolinas only reinforced a discouragement that already had begun to manifest itself in a dramatic rise in the desertion rate.

Since Lee's army and the other main armies remained sufficiently supplied until the end of the war, one reasonably can conclude that Grant's military strategy influenced the outcome of the conflict but did not determine it. The Confederacy's forces dwindled and surrendered before Grant's raids could deprive them of supplies. The strategy of raids had, of course, considerable political and psychological significance, reinforcing the effect on southern will of the defeats of September and October and the return of Lincoln to the Executive Mansion.

In any event, Grant's strategy alone could not have won a war against a people sufficiently determined to maintain their independence. Grant aimed only to break up the Confederacy's main armies by severing the railroads that connected them to their supplies of food, shoes, uniforms, weapons, and ammunition. He provided no means of dealing with these armies should they disperse and thereafter continue offering organized resistance as units ranging in size from a division of several brigades down to independent companies. These units would have dominated the country, reducing Federal control to the immediate vicinity of the Union armies, as Jomini had learned in Spain. Such forces, aided by guerrilla activity, could have found some food and other supplies in the country they controlled and secured more from the invader's always vulnerable supply columns.

But Confederate armies surrendered rather than dispersing into small but formidable groups, and the soldiers went home for the same reason that many had already deserted—they did not want an independent Confederacy badly enough to continue the struggle, and they placed the welfare of their loved ones ahead of the creation of a new nation. But even if they had wished to continue, slavery would have inhibited the usual war waged by small units and guerrillas against invading armies. Indeed, many slaves already had become sympathizers and recruits for the Union. The same bitter experience of Santo Domingo might have come to the South, just as southerners always had feared.

As old Confederates resolved their dissonance in one way or another, they indicated directly or indirectly that what Ulrich B. Phillips called the central theme of southern history inevitably had dictated their actions. Whether pro-Union or prosecession, in favor of the war or opposed, pushing for peace or desiring to fight to the bitter end, willing to accept Radical Reconstruction or challenging it, white southerners had "a common resolve indomitably maintained—that it [the South] shall be and remain a white man's country." The South could give up slavery with more relief than regret, as events proved. But it could not surrender white supremacy, "especially," notes Carl Degler, "when it was imposed by a North whose hands in this respect were far from clean." To be sure, slavery supplied an instrument of racial adjustment, and independence constituted a long-shot effort to ensure freedom of action on racial as well as other issues; but state rights and honor remained, state rights to provide a political ideology that permitted local control of racial relations, and honor to require that southerners shape their own institutions without outside pressure. Thus today's historian, like Henry James on his southern tour early in the twentieth century, must come to the realization that "the negro had always been, and could absolutely not fail to be, intensely 'on the nerves' of the South, and that as, in the other time [before the war], the observer from without had always, as a tribute to this truth, to tread the scene on tiptoe, so even yet, in the presence of the immitigable fact, a like discretion is imposed on him."

In the antebellum era and throughout most of the war, the desire to preserve slavery exemplified this constant concern. And slavery turned out to have a far-reaching effect on the strategy of the Civil War, for it made unlikely a Confederate resort to its most promising means of resistance, "general insurrection." Clausewitz and Jomini made a strong case that a resort to guerrilla warfare constituted an inefficient means of defense because the results of such a total effort were "not commensurate with the energies" expended. More relevant, such a strategy incurred high nonmilitary costs. Clausewitz noted one of these costs when he pointed out that guerrilla warfare could be considered "a state of legalized anarchy that is as much a threat to the social order at home as it is to the enemy." When that social order included race relations, it would have been dangerous for the Confederacy to have resorted to it, as some Confederate Unionists had realized in 1861.

Further, by 1863 the black population had proved itself willing to enlist in the Union army and had surprised skeptics by its military effectiveness when adequately trained. In any guerrilla resistance the black population in the Confederacy would constitute a resource for an enormously powerful indigenous counterinsurgency force. The turmoil introduced into the countryside would have made slavery more precarious, not less, and would have provided slaves with even more opportunity to subvert the Confederate war effort, perhaps by sabotage and espionage, but more likely by escape and enlistment in the Union army. The Union would certainly have used this formidable weapon, and its use would have changed race relations well beyond the point that the actual events did change them, even beyond the possibility of recognition or restoration.

By surrendering without resort to wholesale use of guerrillas, southerners had, as John Shy has pointed out, "saved the basic elements—with the exception of slavery itself—of the Southern social, that is to say racial, order. The social order could not possibly have survived the guerrilla warfare which a continued resistance movement would have required."

Thus slavery brought on the conflict, but, with the underlying problem of race relations, it paradoxically ended it as well, by making fainthearted southerners too fearful to employ their one, otherwise invincible, military weapon. Under such circumstances, it is unreasonable to expect that a people not fully committed to the war would run the risk of creating another Santo Domingo, or at least breaking down remaining social controls. Doubtless, the reasoning of many southerners did not reach that far. The wholesale desertion that took away 40 percent of the Confederate armies east of the Mississippi in the fall and early winter of 1864–65 showed that, before a full-scale resort to guerrilla warfare loomed as the alternative, a critical number of Confederates had given to the cause all that their commitment warranted.

Clausewitz excoriated such behavior. Although he did not use the word "honor," he demanded that a people fight to preserve it. "No matter how small and weak a state may be in comparison with its enemy," he wrote, "it must not forego these last efforts, or one would conclude that its soul is dead." "There will always be time enough to die," he continued. "Like a drowning man who will clutch instinctively at a straw, it is a natural law of the moral world that a nation that finds itself on the brink of an abyss will try to save itself by any means." Clausewitz felt that a failure to fight to the last shows that the nation "did not deserve to win, and, possibly for that very reason was unable to." But Clausewitz did not take into sufficient account moral and religious factors, such as those that made some Confederates more than willing to surrender slavery. For, when the institution faced severe pressure, a multitude of Confederates were willing to see it go, having "discovered" that they were not fighting for slavery at all, or even for state rights, but for white supremacy, independence, and honor.

But Clausewitz's caustic criticism has relevance only if one assumes that the Confederacy was a nation—that it was sufficiently separated from the Union and the glory of their common history to make it a distinct nationality. Analyzing conflict "between *states of very unequal strength*," Clausewitz noted that "inability to carry on the struggle can, in practice, be replaced by two other grounds for making peace: the first is the improbability of victory; the second is its unacceptable cost." Powerful Union armed forces and sophisticated and innovative strategy supplied the first ground; the insufficiency of a nationalism based on slavery, state rights, and honor meant that the cost of continuing the struggle ran too high. Perhaps no white southerners could contemplate such a war. Slavery, the cause of secession and four years of military conflict, would thus have limited the extent and persistence of the Confederacy's resistance even had it wished to carry on beyond the defeat of the principal armies; but desertion and surrender showed that few Confederates had any such desire.

So the Confederacy succumbed to internal rather than external causes. An insufficient nationalism failed to survive the strains imposed by the lengthy hostilities. Necessary measures alienated planters, who, by planting cotton and husbanding their slaves, already had limited the national effort. Privation affected many yeomen, soldiers, and their families as the costs and shortages of the contest reduced their already meager standards of living. These hardships and the perception of inequitable and unwise actions placed an added strain on a nationalism already taxed by the duration and bloodshed of the conflict. Slavery, in a sense the keystone of secession, became a liability as the Union's fight against slavery and the South's own religious beliefs induced more guilt among more southerners. After three years of essentially successful defense against powerful invading forces, these prolonged strains proved more than Confederate nationalism could bear and, frequently encouraged by a sense that defeat must be the Lord's work, Confederates, by thousands of individual decisions, abandoned the struggle for and allegiance to the Confederate States of America.

The transformation southerners made in identifying the causes of the struggle well illustrates the South's essentially ephemeral allegiance to slavery and devotion to independence, and the rapid development of a powerful central government indicated the slender cord that bound some state-righters to the concept of state rights until they appealed to state rights once again after the war was over. Only the determination to hold fast to honor, and the concomitant desire to dictate the terms of racial adjustment, proved constant.

And yet, . . . in some respects the South did not lose the Civil War. Southerners eventually resolved the dissonance between the world as it was and the world as they had wanted it to be by securing enough of their war aims—state rights, white supremacy, and honor—to permit them to claim their share of the victory.

NO

James M. McPherson

TO THE SHOALS OF VICTORY

The weeks after Booth fulfilled his vow on Good Friday passed in a dizzying sequence of events. Jarring images dissolved and reformed in kaleidoscopic patterns that left the senses traumatized or elated: Lincoln lying in state at the White House on April 19 as General Grant wept unabashedly at his catafalque; Confederate armies surrendering one after another as Jefferson Davis fled southward hoping to re-establish his government in Texas and carry on the war to victory; Booth killed in a burning barn in Virginia; seven million somber men, women, and children lining the tracks to view Lincoln's funeral train on its way back home to Springfield; the steamboat *Sultana* returning northward on the Mississippi with liberated Union prisoners of war blowing up on April 27 with a loss of life equal to that of the *Titanic* a half-century later; Jefferson Davis captured in Georgia on May 10, accused (falsely) of complicity in Lincoln's assassination, imprisoned and temporarily shackled at Fortress Monroe, Virginia, where he remained for two years until released without trial to live on until his eighty-first year and become part of the ex-Confederate literary corps who wrote weighty tomes to justify their Cause; the Army of the Potomac and Sherman's Army of Georgia marching 200,000 strong in a Grand Review down Pennsylvania Avenue on May 23–24 in a pageantry of power and catharsis before being demobilized from more than one million soldiers to fewer than 80,000 a year later and an eventual peacetime total of 27,000; weary, ragged Confederate soldiers straggling homeward begging or stealing food from dispirited civilians who often did not know where their own next meal was coming from; joyous black people celebrating the jubilee of a freedom whose boundaries they did not yet discern; gangs of southern deserters, guerrillas, and outlaws ravaging a region that would not know real peace for many years to come.

The terms of that peace and the dimensions of black freedom would preoccupy the country for a decade or more. Meanwhile the process of chronicling the war and reckoning its consequences began immediately and has never ceased. More than 620,000 soldiers lost their lives in four years of conflict— 360,000 Yankees and at least 260,000 rebels. The number of southern civilians who died as a direct or indirect result of the war cannot be known; what *can* be said is that the Civil War's cost in American lives was as great as in all of the nation's other wars combined through Vietnam. Was the liberation of four million slaves and the preservation of the Union worth the cost? That question too will probably never cease to be debated —but in 1865 few black people and not many northerners doubted the answer.

In time even a good many southerners came to agree with the sentiments of Woodrow Wilson (a native of Virginia who lived four years of his childhood in wartime Georgia) expressed in 1880 when he was a law student at the University of Virginia: "*Because* I love the South, I rejoice in the failure of the Confederacy.... Conceive of this Union divided into two separate and independent sovereignties!... Slavery was enervating our Southern society.... [Nevertheless] I recognize and pay loving tribute to the virtues of the leaders of secession... the righteousness of the cause which they thought they were promoting—and to the immortal courage of the soldiers of the Confederacy." Wilson's words embodied themes that would help reconcile generations of southerners to defeat: their glorious forebears had fought courageously for what they believed was right; perhaps they deserved to win; but in the long run it was a good thing they lost. This Lost Cause mentality took on the proportions of a heroic legend, a southern *Götterdämmerung* with Robert E. Lee as a latter-day Siegfried.

But a persistent question has nagged historians and mythologists alike: if Marse Robert was such a genius and his legions so invincible, why did they lose? The answers, though almost as legion as Lee's soldiers, tend to group themselves into a few main categories. One popular answer has been phrased, from the northern perspective, by quoting Napoleon's aphorism that God was on the side of the heaviest battalions. For southerners this explanation usually took some such form as these words of a Virginian: "They never whipped us, Sir, unless they were four to one. If we had had anything like a fair chance, or less disparity of numbers, we should have won our cause and established our independence." The North had a potential manpower superiority of more than three to one (counting only white men) and Union armed forces had an actual superiority of two to one during most of the war. In economic resources and logistical capacity the northern advantage was even greater. Thus, in this explanation, the Confederacy fought against overwhelming odds; its defeat was inevitable.

But this explanation has not satisfied a good many analysts. History is replete with examples of peoples who have won or defended their independence against greater odds: the Netherlands against the Spain of Philip II; Switzerland against the Hapsburg Empire; the American rebels of 1776 against mighty Britain; North Vietnam against the United States of 1970. Given the advantages of fighting on the defensive in its own territory with interior lines in which stalemate would be victory against a foe who must invade conquer, occupy, and destroy the capacity to resist, the odds faced by the South were not formidable. Rather, as another category of interpretations has it, internal divisions fatally weakened the Confederacy: the state-rights conflict between certain governors and the Richmond government; the disaffection of non-slaveholders from a rich man's war and poor man's fight; libertarian opposition to necessary measures such as conscription and the suspension of habeas corpus; the lukewarm commitment to the Confederacy by quondam Whigs and unionists; the disloyalty of slaves who defected to the enemy whenever they had a chance; growing doubts among slaveowners themselves about the justice of their peculiar institution and their cause. "So the Confederacy succumbed to internal rather than external causes," according to numerous historians. The South suffered from a "weakness in morale," a "loss of the will to fight." The Confederacy did not lack "the means to continue the struggle," but "the will to do so."

To illustrate their argument that the South could have kept fighting for years longer if it had tried harder, four historians have cited the instructive example of Paraguay. That tiny country carried on a war for six years (1865–71) against an alliance of Brazil, Argentina, and Uruguay whose combined population outnumbered Paraguay's by nearly thirty to one. Almost every male from twelve to sixty fought in the Paraguayan army; the country lost 56 percent of its total population and 80 percent of its men of military age in the war. Indeed, "the Confederate war effort seems feeble by comparison," for a mere 5 percent of the South's white people and 25 percent of the white males of military age were killed. To be sure, Paraguay lost the war, but its "tenacity... does exhibit how a people can fight when possessed of total conviction."

It is not quite clear whether these four historians think the South should have emulated Paraguay's example. In any case the "internal division" and "lack of will" explanations for Confederate defeat, while not implausible, are not very convincing either. The problem is that the North experienced similar internal divi-

sions, and if the war had come out differently the Yankees' lack of unity and will to win could be cited with equal plausibility to explain that outcome. The North had its large minority alienated by the rich man's war/poor man's fight theme; its outspoken opposition to conscription, taxation, suspension of habeas corpus, and other war measures; its state governors and legislatures and congressmen who tried to thwart administration policies. If important elements of the southern population, white as well as black, grew disaffected with a war to preserve slavery, equally significant groups in the North dissented from a war to abolish slavery. One critical distinction between Union and Confederacy was the institutionalization of obstruction in the Democratic party in the North, compelling the Republicans to close ranks in support of war policies to overcome and ultimately to discredit the opposition, while the South had no such institutionalized political structure to mobilize support and vanquish resistance.

Nevertheless, the existence of internal divisions on both sides seemed to neutralize this factor as an explanation for Union victory, so a number of historians have looked instead at the quality of leadership both military and civilian. There are several variants of an interpretation that emphasizes a gradual development of superior northern leadership. In Beauregard, Lee, the two Johnstons, and Jackson the South enjoyed abler military commanders during the first year or two of the war, while Jefferson Davis was better qualified by training and experience than Lincoln to lead a nation at war. But Lee's strategic vision was limited to the Virginia theater, and the Confederate government neglected the West, where Union armies developed a strategic design and the generals to carry it out, while southern forces floundered under incompetent commanders who lost the war in the West. By 1863, Lincoln's remarkable abilities gave him a wide edge over Davis as a war leader, while in Grant and Sherman the North acquired commanders with a concept of total war and the necessary determination to make it succeed. At the same time, in Edwin M. Stanton and Montgomery Meigs, aided by the entrepreneurial talent of northern businessmen, the Union developed superior managerial talent to mobilize and organize the North's greater resources for victory in the modern industrialized conflict that the Civil War became.

This interpretation comes closer than others to credibility. Yet it also commits the fallacy of reversibility—that is, if the outcome had been reversed some of the same factors could be cited to explain Confederate victory. If the South had its bumblers like Bragg and Pemberton and Hood who lost the West, and Joseph Johnston who fought too little and too late, the North had its McClellan and Meade who threw away chances in the East and its Pope and Burnside and Hooker who nearly lost the war in that theater where the genius of Lee and his lieutenants nearly won it, despite all the South's disadvantages. If the Union had its Stanton and Meigs, the Confederacy had its Josiah Gorgas and other unsung heroes who performed miracles of organization and improvisation. If Lincoln had been defeated for re-election in 1864, as he anticipated in August, history might record Davis as the great war leader and Lincoln as an also-ran.

Most attempts to explain southern defeat or northern victory lack the dimension of *contingency*—the recognition that at numerous critical points during the war things might have gone altogether differently. Four major turning points defined the eventual outcome. The first came in the summer of 1862, when the counter-offensives of Jackson and Lee in Virginia and Bragg and Kirby Smith in the West arrested the momentum of a seemingly imminent Union victory. This assured a prolongation and intensification of the conflict and created the potential for Confederate success, which appeared imminent before each of the next three turning points.

The first of these occurred in the fall of 1862, when battles at Antietam and Perryville threw back Confederate invasions, forestalled European mediation and recognition of the Confederacy, perhaps prevented a Democratic victory in the northern elections of 1862 that might have inhibited the government's ability to carry on the war, and set the stage for the Emancipation Proclamation which enlarged the scope and purpose of the conflict. The third critical point came in the summer and fall of 1863 when Gettysburg, Vicksburg, and Chattanooga turned the tide toward ultimate northern victory.

One more reversal of that tide seemed possible in the summer of 1864 when appalling Union casualties and apparent lack of progress especially in Virginia brought the North to the brink of peace negotiations and the election of a Democratic president. But the capture of Atlanta and Sheridan's destruction of Early's army in the Shenandoah Valley clinched matters for the North. Only then did it become possible to speak of the inevitability of Union victory. Only then did the South experience an irretrievable "loss of the will to fight."

Of all the explanations for Confederate defeat, the loss of will thesis suffers most from its own particular fallacy of reversibility—that of putting the cart before the horse. Defeat causes demoralization and loss of will; victory pumps up morale and the will to win. Nothing illustrates this better than the radical transformation of *northern* will from defeatism in August 1864 to a "depth of determination... to fight to the last" that "astonished" a British journalist a month later. The southern loss of will was a mirror image of this northern determination. These changes of mood were caused mainly by events on the battlefield. Northern victory and southern defeat in the war cannot be understood apart from the contingency that hung over every campaign, every battle, every election, every decision during the war. This phenomenon of contingency can best be presented in a narrative format—a format this book has tried to provide.

Arguments about the causes and consequences of the Civil War, as well as the reasons for northern victory, will continue as long as there are historians to wield the pen—which is, perhaps even for this bloody conflict, mightier than the sword. But certain large consequences of the war seem clear. Secession and slavery were killed, never to be revived during the century and a quarter since Appomattox. These results signified a broader transformation of American society and polity punctuated if not alone achieved by the war. Before 1861 the two words "United States" were generally rendered as a plural noun: "the United States *are* a republic." The war marked a transition of the United States to a singular noun. The "Union" also became the nation, and Americans now rarely speak of their Union except in an historical sense. Lincoln's wartime speeches betokened this transition. In his

first inaugural address he used the word "Union" twenty times and the word "nation" not once. In his first message to Congress, on July 4, 1861, he used "Union" thirty-two times and "nation" three times. In his letter to Horace Greeley of August 22, 1862, on the relationship of slavery to the war, Lincoln spoke of the Union eight times and of the nation not at all. Little more than a year later, in his address at Gettysburg, the president did not refer to the "Union" at all but used the word "nation" five times to invoke a new birth of freedom and nationalism for the United States. And in his second inaugural address, looking back over the events of the past four years, Lincoln spoke of one side seeking to dissolve the *Union* in 1861 and the other accepting the challenge of war to preserve the *nation*.

The old federal republic in which the national government had rarely touched the average citizen except through the post-office gave way to a more centralized polity that taxed the people directly and created an internal revenue bureau to collect these taxes, drafted men into the army, expanded the jurisdiction of federal courts, created a national currency and a national banking system, and established the first national agency for social welfare—the Freedman's Bureau. Eleven of the first twelve amendments to the Constitution had limited the powers of the national government; six of the next seven, beginning with the Thirteenth Amendment in 1865, vastly expanded those powers at the expense of the states.

This change in the federal balance paralleled a radical shift of political power from South to North. During the first seventy-two years of the republic down to 1861 a slaveholding resident of one of the states that joined the

Confederacy had been President of the United States for forty-nine of those years —more than two-thirds of the time. In Congress, twenty-three of the thirty-six speakers of the House and twenty-four of the presidents pro tem of the Senate had been southerners. The Supreme Court always had a southern majority; twenty of the thirty-five justices to 1861 had been appointed from slave states. After the war a century passed before a resident of an ex-Confederate state was elected president. For half a century *none* of the speakers of the House or presidents pro tem of the Senate came from the South, and only five of the twenty-six Supreme Court justices appointed during that half-century were southerners.

These figures symbolize a sharp and permanent change in the direction of American development. Through most of American history the South has seemed different from the rest of the United States, with "a separate and unique identity... which appeared to be out of the mainstream of American experience." But when did the northern stream become the mainstream? From a broader perspective it may have been the *North* that was exceptional and unique before the Civil War. The South more closely resembled a majority of the societies in the world than did the rapidly changing North during the antebellum generation. Despite the abolition of legal slavery or serfdom throughout much of the western hemisphere and western Europe, most of the world —like the South—had an unfree or quasi-free labor force. Most societies in the world remained predominantly rural, agricultural, and labor-intensive; most, including even several European countries, had illiteracy rates as high or higher than the South's 45 percent;

most like the South remained bound by traditional values and networks of family, kinship, hierarchy, and patriarchy. The North—along with a few countries of northwestern Europe—hurtled forward eagerly toward a future of industrial capitalism that many southerners found distasteful if not frightening; the South remained proudly and even defiantly rooted in the past before 1861.

Thus when secessionists protested that they were acting to preserve traditional rights and values, they were correct. They fought to protect their constitutional liberties against the perceived northern threat to overthrow them. The South's concept of republicanism had not changed in three-quarters of a century; the North's had. With complete sincerity the South fought to preserve its version of the republic of the founding fathers— a government of limited powers that protected the rights of property and whose constituency comprised an independent gentry and yeomanry of the white race undisturbed by large cities, heartless factories, restless free workers, and class conflict. The accession to power of the Republican party, with its ideology of competitive, egalitarian, free-labor capitalism was a signal to the South that the northern majority had turned irrevocably toward this frightening, revolutionary future. Indeed, the Black Republican party appeared to the eyes of many southerners as "essentially a revolutionary party" composed of "a motley throng of Sans culottes... Infidels and freelovers, interspersed by Bloomer women, fugitive slaves, and amalgamationists." Therefore secession was a pre-emptive counterrevolution to prevent the Black Republican revolution from engulfing the South. "*We are not revolutionists*," insisted James B. D. DeBow and Jefferson Davis during the

Civil War, "We are resisting revolution.... We are conservative."

Union victory in the war destroyed the southern vision of America and ensured that the northern vision would become the American vision. Until 1861, however, it was the North that was out of the mainstream, not the South. Of course the northern states, along with Britain and a few countries in northwestern Europe, were cutting a new channel in world history that would doubtless have become the mainstream even if the American Civil War had not happened. Russia had abolished serfdom in 1861 to complete the dissolution of this ancient institution of bound labor in Europe. But for Americans the Civil War marked the turning point. A Louisiana planter who returned home sadly after the war wrote in 1865: "Society has been completely changed by the war. The revolution of '89 did not produce a greater change in the 'Ancien Régime' than this has in our social life." And four years later George Ticknor, a retired Harvard professor, concluded that the Civil War had created a "great gulf between what happened before in our century and what has happened since, or what is likely to happen hereafter. It does not seem to me as if I were living in the country in which I was born." From the war sprang the great flood that caused the stream of American history to surge into a new channel and transferred the burden of exceptionalism from North to South.

What would be the place of freed slaves and their descendants in this new order? In 1865 a black soldier who recognized his former master among a group of Confederate prisoners he was guarding called out a greeting: "Hello, massa; bottom rail on top dis time!" Would this new arrangement of rails last?

POSTSCRIPT

Was the Confederacy Defeated Because of Its "Loss of Will"?

Beringer et al. give a new twist to the old argument that the Confederacy lost because it lacked the will to win. Rather than blaming Jefferson Davis's political failures or General Robert E. Lee's strategy of attacking Gettysburg, the authors argue that Southern guilt over slavery and the inability of Southern political and religious leaders to fashion a viable nationalism caused the Confederacy to lapse.

Beringer et al. also believe that internal dissension among the Confederate states and their central government was not an important factor in the South's defeat. The authors maintain that the states made positive contributions to the Confederate war effort through the organization of state militias and provisions for the coastal defenses. The economies of the states, say the authors, also provided enough uniforms and equipment for the military, even though the planters continued to overproduce cotton.

The Civil War was fought between two sections that had been united under the same government for 85 years. Southerners controlled the presidency, the Supreme Court, and the major offices in Congress during much of this time. Could it be that the South left the Union, as McPherson and others have pointed out, because the northern and western states, with their free labor ideology of an industrial-based economy, were to dominate nationally once Lincoln was elected president in 1860?

McPherson, now the acknowledged dean of the Civil War scholars, rejects all prior internal and external arguments for the defeat of the Confederacy as hindsight arguments. In his view, historians could have cited economic power, military brilliance, political leadership, internal dissension, and loss of will to explain a Confederate victory had the South emerged victorious.

McPherson argues that chance or contingency best explains why the North won. He points out that victories at Antietam in 1862, Gettysburg in 1863, and the total war campaigns of Grant and Sherman in 1864 led to political victories for the Republicans in Congress in 1862 and for Lincoln's reelection in 1864. Victories at Antietam and Gettysburg in particular were not foregone conclusions. If the South had won these battles, the outcome of the war might have been different.

Students who wish to pursue the causation question should compare the essays in David Donald, ed., *Why the North Won the Civil War* (Louisiana State University Press, 1960) with a more recent collection edited by Gabor S. Boritt on *Why the Confederacy Lost* (Oxford University Press, 1992).

ISSUE 16

Was Abraham Lincoln America's Greatest President?

YES: Phillip Shaw Paludan, from *The Presidency of Abraham Lincoln* (University Press of Kansas, 1994)

NO: M. E. Bradford, from *Remembering Who We Are: Observations of a Southern Conservative* (University of Georgia Press, 1985)

ISSUE SUMMARY

YES: Professor of history Phillip Shaw Paludan believes that Abraham Lincoln's greatness exceeds that of all other American presidents because Lincoln, in the face of unparalleled challenges associated with the Civil War, succeeded in preserving the Union and freeing the slaves.

NO: Professor of English literature M. E. Bradford characterizes Lincoln as a cynical politician whose abuse of authority as president and commander in chief during the Civil War marked a serious departure from the republican goals of the Founding Fathers.

The American Civil War (1861–1865) produced what historian Arthur M. Schlesinger, Jr., has called "our greatest national trauma." To be sure, the War Between the States was a searing event that etched itself on the collective memory of the American people and inspired an interest that has made it the most thoroughly studied episode in American history. During the last century and a quarter, scholars have identified a variety of factors (including slavery, economic sectionalism, cultural distinctions between the North and South, the doctrine of states' rights, and the irresponsibility of abolitionists and proslavery advocates) that contributed to sectional tensions and that ultimately led to war. Although often presented as "sole causes," these factors are complicated, interconnected, and controversial. Consequently, historians must consider as many of them as possible in their evaluations of the war, even if they choose to spotlight one or another as the main explanation.

Most historians, however, agree that the war would not have occurred had 11 Southern states not seceded from the Union to form the Confederate States of America following Abraham Lincoln's election to the presidency in 1860. Why was Lincoln viewed as a threat to the South? A Southerner by birth, Lincoln's career in national politics (as a congressman representing his adopted state of Illinois) apparently had been short-circuited by his unpopular opposition to the Mexican War. His attempt to emerge from political obscurity a decade later failed when he was defeated by Stephen Douglas in a bid for an Illinois Senate seat. This campaign, however, gained for Lincoln a reputation as a powerful orator, and in 1860 Republican party managers passed over some of their more well known leaders, such as William Henry Seward, and nominated the moderate Mr. Lincoln for the presidency. His victory was guaranteed by factionalism within Democratic ranks, but the election results revealed that the new president received only 39 percent of the popular vote. This fact, however, provided little solace for Southerners, who mistook the new president's opposition to the extension of slavery into the territories for evidence that he supported the abolitionist wing of the Republican party. Despite assurances during the campaign that he would not tamper with slavery where it already existed, Lincoln could not prevent the splintering of the Union.

Given such an inauspicious beginning, few observers at the time could have predicted that future generations would view Lincoln as America's greatest president. What factors have contributed to this assessment? The answer would appear to lie in his role as commander in chief during the Civil War. Is this reputation deserved? The selections that follow assess Lincoln's presidency from dramatically different perspectives.

Phillip Shaw Paludan, who has recently published a biography of Lincoln, sees unparalleled greatness in the leadership of America's 16th chief executive. Lincoln's greatness, Paludan concludes, derived from his ability to mobilize public opinion in the North behind his goal of saving the Union and freeing the slaves. Significantly, Paludan does not separate these accomplishments. Rather, he argues that they were inextricably connected; one could not be realized without the other.

M. E. Bradford offers a sharp critique of the conclusions reached by Paludan. By pursuing an anti-Southern strategy, Bradford argues, President Lincoln perverted the republican goals advanced by the Founding Fathers and destroyed the Democratic majority that was essential to the preservation of the Union. Furthermore, Bradford asserts, Lincoln abused his executive authority by cynically expanding the scope of presidential powers to an unhealthy extent. Finally, Bradford charges that Lincoln was uncommitted to the cause of black Americans.

YES

Phillip Shaw Paludan

THE PRESIDENCY OF ABRAHAM LINCOLN

The oath is a simple one, made all the more austere because there is no coronation, no anointing by priest or predecessor. The office has passed from one person to another months before, first by popular election and then by a ritualistic casting of votes by presidential electors, whose names are forgotten if anyone knew them in the first place. The only requirement on the day the president takes office is an oath or affirmation: "I do solemnly swear that I will faithfully execute the Office of President of the United States, and will to the best of my ability preserve, protect and defend the Constitution of the United States."

Each president in the history of the nation has tried to protect and defend the Constitution—some with more dedication than others. Each responded to the challenges and the opportunity that his time gave him. No president had larger challenges than Abraham Lincoln, and the testimony to his greatness rests in his keeping of that oath, which led him to be responsible for two enormous accomplishments that are part of folk legend as well as fact. He saved the Union and he freed the slaves.

He preserved the unity of the nation both in size and in structure. There were still thirty-six states at the end of his presidency; there might have been twenty-five. The population of the nation when he died was 30 million; it might have been 20 million. The constitutional instrument for changing governments was still in 1865 what it had been in 1861—win a free election and gain the majority of the electoral votes. Another option might have existed—secede from the country and make war if necessary after losing the election. A divided nation might have been more easily divided again— perhaps when angry westerners felt exploited by eastern capitalists, perhaps when urban minorities felt oppressed by powerful majorities. And there were lasting international consequences from Lincoln's achievement: Foreign oppressors of the twentieth century were not allowed to run free, disregarding the two or perhaps three or four countries that might have existed between Canada and Mexico.

From Phillip Shaw Paludan, *The Presidency of Abraham Lincoln* (University Press of Kansas, 1994). Copyright © 1994 by University Press of Kansas. Reprinted by permission. Notes omitted.

Because of Lincoln, 4 million black Americans gained options beyond a life of slavery for themselves and their children. Men, women, and children were no longer bought and sold, denied their humanity—because of Lincoln, but certainly not because of Lincoln alone. Perhaps 2 million Union soldiers fought to achieve these goals. Women behind the lines and near the battlefields did jobs that men would not or could not do. Workers on farms and in factories supplied the huge army and the society that sustained it. Managers and entrepreneurs organized the resources that helped gain the victory. But Lincoln's was the voice that inspired and explained and guided soldiers and civilians to continue the fight.

Black soldiers, too, preserved the Union and freed slaves. And these black soldiers were in the army because Lincoln wanted them there, accepted the demands of black and white abolitionists and growing numbers of soldiers and sailors that they be there. Hundreds of thousands, perhaps millions, of slaves, given the chance, walked away from slavery and thus "stole" from their masters the labor needed to sustain the Confederacy and the ability of those masters to enslave them. No one would ever again sell their children, their husbands, their wives; no one would rape and murder and mutilate them, control their work and much of their leisure.

Lincoln kept his oath by leading the nation, guiding it, insisting that it keep on with the task of saving the Union and freeing the slaves.

Too often historians and the general populace (which cares very much, and may define itself in vital ways by what Lincoln did and means) have divided his two great achievements. They have made

saving the Union, at least for the first half of his presidency, a different task from freeing the slaves. They have noted that Lincoln explained to Horace Greeley that he could not answer Greeley's "Prayer of Twenty Million" and simply free the slaves. His prime goal, he told Greeley, was to save the Union, and he would free none, some, or all the slaves to save that Union. But before Lincoln wrote those words he had already decided that to save the Union he would have to free the slaves.

... Freeing the slaves and saving the Union were linked as one goal, not two optional goals. The Union that Lincoln wanted to save was not a union where slavery was safe. He wanted to outlaw slavery in the territories and thus begin a process that would end it in the states. Slave states understood this; that is why they seceded and why the Union needed saving.

Freeing the slaves, more precisely ending slavery, was the indispensable means to saving the Union. In an immediate practical sense, those 180,000 black soldiers were an essential part of the Union army in the last two years of the war. They made up almost 12 percent of the total Union land forces by 1865, adding not only to Union numbers but subtracting from the Confederate labor force. Moreover, those black soldiers liberated even where they did not march. Their example was noted throughout the South so that slaves far from Union occupation knew that blacks could be soldiers, not just property, and they began to march toward freedom.

Ending slavery also meant saving the Union in a larger sense. Slavery had endangered the Union, hurting black people but also hurting white people, and not only by allowing them to be brutes, as Jefferson had lamented. Slavery had divided the nation, threatening the processes of government by making debate over the most crucial issue of the age intolerable in the South and, for decades, dangerous in the Congress of the United States. To protect slavery the Confederate States of America would challenge the peaceful, lawful, orderly means of changing governments in the United States, even by resorting to war. Lincoln led the successful effort to stop them and thus simultaneously saved the Union and freed the slaves.

Why does it matter that Lincoln linked saving the Union and the emancipation of the nation from slavery? First, it is necessary to get the historical record straight. It matters also because in understanding our history Americans gain access to the kind of faith that Lincoln held that our means, our legal processes, our political-constitutional system work to achieve our best ideals. Too many people, among them the first black justice of the United States Supreme Court, Thurgood Marshall, have doubted that respect for the law and the Constitution can lead to greater equality. "The system" too often has been the villain, "institutional racism" the disease that obstructs the struggle for equality. The underlying premise of this [essay] is that the political-constitutional system, conceived of and operated at its best, inescapably leads to equality. Lincoln operated on that premise and through his presidency tried to achieve that goal.

But how did he do that? One of his accomplishments, the one that took most of his time, was fighting and winning a war. He chose the generals, gathered the armies, set the overall strategy; he restrained the dissenters and the opponents of the war; he helped to gather the resources that would maintain the Union economy and that would enable the Union military to remain strong and unrelenting. He kept himself and his party in office, the only party that was dedicated to saving the Union and ending slavery. And he kept an eye on foreign affairs, seeing to it that Great Britain remained willing to negotiate and to watch the conflict rather than joining or trying to stop it....

I am particularly interested in what Lincoln said, for the most important power of a president, as Richard Neustadt has argued, is the power to persuade. Thus it is vital for a president to inform and to inspire, to warn and to empower the polity, to bring out the "better angels of our nature"—better in the sense of allowing the nation to achieve its best aspirations. "Events have controlled me," Lincoln said, but what he did most effectively was to define those events and to shape the public opinion that, he noted, was "everything in this country." In the 1840s a Whig newspaper came close to the mark I am admiring in assessing Lincoln:

> Put the case that the same multitude were addressed by two orators, and on the same question and occasion; that the first of these orators considered in his mind that the people he addressed were to be controlled by several passions... the orator may be fairly said to have no faith in the people; he rather believes that they are creatures of passion, and subject to none but base and selfish impulses. But now a second orator arises, a Chatham, a Webster, a Pericles, a Clay; his generous spirit expands itself through the vast auditory, and he believes that he is addressing a company of high spirited men, citizens.... When he says "fellow citizens," they believe him, and at once, from a tumultuous

herd they are converted into men . . . their thoughts and feeling rise to an heroical heights, beyond that of common men or common times. The second orator "had faith in the people"; he addressed the better part of each man's nature, supposing it to be in him—and it *was* in him.

At their best American presidents recognize that their duty as the chief opinion maker is to shape a public understanding that opens options and tells the truth about what the people can be and what their problems are. Appealing to the fears we have, manipulating them to win office or pass a law or achieve another goal, does not so much *reflect* who we are as it in fact *creates* who we are. It affirms us as legitimately fearful—afraid of something that our leaders confirm to be frightening—and as being citizens whose fears properly define us.

Appealing to better angels is more complicated—it requires calling on history for original aspirations—reminding Americans for example that the basic ideal of the nation is that "all men are created equal." Equally vital, such an appeal also requires reminding Americans that they have in fact established institutions that work to that end—not only reminding them of their aspirations but also reassuring them that their history, their lived experience, reveals legitimate paths to achieving those goals. History thus acts to recall the nation's best dreams, but it also restores faith that the means to approach the dream live, abide in the institutions as well as in the values that shape the nation.

I believe that a history of the presidency of Abraham Lincoln can show how Lincoln managed to shape a public understanding, how at times he failed, but how he usually succeeded. Thus he

set a standard that makes it legitimate that we, when the better angels of our nature prevail, define ourselves in important ways by who Lincoln was, by what he did, and by what he said. . . .

* * *

The Lincoln presidency did not end through the operation of the political-constitutional system. There was no joyous ritual, no abiding process that had gone on for generations. It was the first assassination of a president in history. A single bullet erased the decision by the people of the Union that Abraham Lincoln should be their president. It was stunning, an awful repudiation of the system that helped define them as a people, that they had been fighting for over the last four years, that had cost them such blood and treasure.

Yet the process endured. Reacting to the murder of the president newspapers throughout the country spoke of the need to "let law and order resume their sway," as the *San Francisco Chronicle* noted. "The law must reign supreme," the *Philadelphia Evening Bulletin* declared, "or in this great crisis chaos will overwhelm us, and our own maddening feeling bring upon us national wreck and ruin which traitor arms have failed to accomplish." More specifically there was admiration and recognition for a system that could overcome even assassination. "When Andrew Johnson was sworn in as President," the Reverend Joseph Thompson told a New York audience, "the Statue of Liberty that surmounts the dome of the Capitol and was put there by Lincoln, looked down on the city and on the nation and said 'Our Government is unchanged—it has merely passed from the hands of one man into those of another.' "

The words reflected part of a larger legacy. The Union was saved, and thus the political-constitutional process endured—the nation would change governments, settle controversies, and debate alternatives at the polls, in legislative halls, and in courtrooms, not on bloody battlefields. It would be a nation whose size and diversity gave it wealth and opportunities for its citizens and huge potential influence in the world. Future autocrats would have reason to fear that influence, just as future immigrants would be drawn to it. Its power would not always be used well. Native Americans who "obstructed" national mission, foreign governments deemed "un-American" had reason to fear and to protest against invasions of their rights and the destruction of their people. But within the nation itself, because of what it stood for and fought for and preserved, there remained a conscience that could be appealed to in the name of the ideals it symbolized and had demonstrated in its greatest war. Saving the Union had meant killing slavery.

Slavery was dead. Its power to divide the Union, to erode and destroy constitutional and political debate was over. No longer was the highest court in the land able to rule that under the Constitution black people had no rights that white people had to respect and that no political party legally could say otherwise. No longer could men, women, and children be bought and sold: treated as things without ties to each other, without the capacity to fulfill their own dreams. The Thirteenth Amendment, ending slavery throughout the nation and moving through the states toward ratification, ensured that. And in the van of that amendment came protection for civil rights and suffrage. Blacks were promised that they would enter the political arena and the constitutional system—this time as participants, not as objects.

This more perfect Union was achieved chiefly through an extraordinary outreach of national authority. Certainly Lincoln extended presidential power beyond any limits seen before his time—the war demanded that; Congress agreed, the Supreme Court acquiesced, and the people sustained his power. If one compares Lincoln's use of power with executive actions before 1861, popular and even scholarly use of a word such as "dictatorship" makes limited sense. Lincoln had produced, as Edwin S. Corwin observes, "a complete transformation in the President's role as Commander in Chief." Yet war was about the expansion of power, and Congress also stepped forward, expanding national power, extending its authority. Even state governments reached further than precedent admitted, increasing expenditures, strengthening their police powers over health, morals, and safety, and establishing new regulatory agencies to shape the economy.

After the war public pressures demanded a return to peacetime boundaries. Executive authority in most areas, once the fight between Johnson and Congress was settled, rapidly contracted. A few outbursts of presidential influence showed that the White House was still occupied. Grant fought senators bitterly over the Santo Domingo Treaty and presided over an effective Treaty of Washington, which resolved claims against the British for building rebel raiders. Hayes sent federal troops to settle labor protests and worked for civil service reforms. Garfield, Arthur, and Harrison also kept busy; Cleveland's vetoes showed signs of vigor. Generally, however, the presidency declined in power. With the exception of Grant a series of one-term presidents did little to inspire demands that they stay in office. For the rest of the century no president came within miles of Lincoln's power or even close to Polk or Jackson, for that matter. By 1886 Woodrow Wilson was able to write that national government in the United States was "congressional government." M. Ostrogorsky, telling foreign audiences about America, described a lawmaking environment in which "after the [civil] war the eclipse of the executive was complete and definitive"; Lord Bryce told British and American audiences in 1894 that "the domestic authority of the President is in time of peace small." These late-nineteenth-century images may have inspired Theodore Lowi to assert in 1992 that "by 1875 you would not know there had been a war or a Lincoln."

But Lord Bryce had added a caveat about the president's domestic authority: In time of war, "especially in a civil war, it expands with portentous speed." Clearly it had been thus with Lincoln. Despite calls to retreat from the vast domains of Civil War there is a sense in which Lincoln's legacy of power in the presidency survived the retreat. Certainly presidential authority, like the national authority with which it was connected, diminished when the war was over. But national power was still available after Appomattox and for the fundamental purpose that had called it forth originally: to destroy slavery and its vestiges. The fight between Congress and Lincoln's successor has obscured the fact that congressional Republicans were acting in the same cause for which Lincoln had acted. They were not recapturing power lost to the president; they were claiming power that they had shared increasingly with Lincoln.

Before Lincoln died many of the more radical Republicans had been attacking him for moving too slowly toward emancipation and then for yielding too much to military necessity and Southern loyalists. After early statements of satisfaction with Johnson they quickly came to their senses as Johnson proved not only to be slower than Lincoln to march to their goals but also to be a bitter racist obstructionist. Thus they fought against Johnson and for goals that Lincoln had espoused and had used his power to try to achieve: civil rights, education, suffrage for the freedmen. The army, which had been the major instrument of Lincoln's expanding egalitarianism and which looked to its commander in chief for direction, shifted its allegiance to Congress. Soldiers such as Grant, whom Lincoln had charged with leading the army to save the Union, did not think it incongruous to support Congress in its battle to preserve the gains of war. And when legislators moved to weaken executive power over the army with the Tenure of Office and the Command of the Army acts, they were trying to save Lincoln's legacy by weakening Johnson.

Although President Grant retreated on other issues, he tried to protect former slaves from white Southerners' efforts to restore as much of the prewar South as they could. Grant sent troops into Louisiana, Mississippi, North Carolina, and South Carolina to effect the Force Acts and to destroy the Ku Klux Klan. A vocal element in the Republican party continued to push for federal intervention in the South in the form of national civil rights and suffrage-enforcement laws well into the 1890s. Despite retreating from the broadest definitions of federal power when it interpreted the Civil War amendments, the Supreme Court struck down laws that kept blacks off juries, and that denied Chinese Americans equal chances to work, and it upheld federal power to protect blacks from political violence. The Justice Department prosecuted thousands of election officers under this power. Local juries usually acquitted their white neighbors, but the national prohibition remained. Because of the Lincoln presidency the constitutional system carried promises of equality, and the processes to bring those promises to life endured. One hundred years after Lincoln had been awakened by the Kansas Nebraska Act to the dangers of slavery to the constitutional system, blacks and whites would see the United States Supreme Court strike down inequality in that system (that case would, interestingly enough, also involve Kansas).

Not every element, even in that reformed constitutional system, promised equal justice. The Union that Lincoln and his forces had saved remained a Union of states. Lincoln's respect for those states, demonstrated in his commitment to reconstruct them rather than to allow Congress to govern territories and in his insistence that only a constitutional amendment, ratified by states, would secure slavery's death, strengthened later arguments that states should control the fate of their citizens, old and new. Lincoln's abiding insistence that the Constitution guided his actions meant that black equality could be hindered or denied by constitutional claims of states' rights and local self-government. Brutal racism could find shelter in such legal arguments.

Yet the triumph and the irony of his administration resided in Lincoln's commitment to the Constitution; without that there would have been no promises to keep to 4 million black Americans. Because so many Americans cherished the Union that the Constitution forged, they made war on slave masters and their friends, on a government that Alexander Stephens claimed rested "on the great truth that the negro is not the equal of the white man; that slavery ... is his natural and normal condition."

Without the president's devotion to and mastery of the political-constitutional institutions of his time, in all probability the Union would have lacked the capacity to focus its will and its resources on defeating that Confederacy. Without Lincoln's unmatched ability to integrate egalitarian ends and constitutional means he could not have enlisted the range of supporters and soldiers necessary for victory. His great accomplishment was to energize and mobilize the nation by affirming its better angels, by showing the nation at its best: engaged in the imperative, life-preserving conversation between structure and purpose, ideal and institution, means and ends.

NO

M. E. Bradford

THE LINCOLN LEGACY: A LONG VIEW

With the time and manner of his death Abraham Lincoln, as leader of a Puritan people who had just won a great victory over "the forces of evil," was placed beyond the reach of ordinary historical inquiry and assessment. Through Booth's bullet he became the one who had "died to make men free," who had perished that his country's "new birth" might occur: a "second founder" who, in Ford's theater, had been transformed into an American version of the "dying god." Our common life, according to this construction, owes its continuation to the shedding of the sacred blood. Now after over a century of devotion to the myth of the "political messiah," it is still impossible for most Americans to see through and beyond the magical events of April 1865. However, Lincoln's daily purchase upon the ongoing business of the nation requires that we devise a way of setting aside the martyrdom to look behind it at Lincoln's place in the total context of American history and discover in him a major source of our present confusion, our distance from the republicanism of the Fathers, the models of political conduct which we profess most to admire....

Of course, nothing that we can identify as part of Lincoln's legacy belongs to him alone. In some respects the Emancipator was carried along with the tides. Yet a measure of his importance is that he was at the heart of the major political events of his era. Therefore what signifies in a final evaluation of this melancholy man is that many of these changes in the country would never have come to pass had Lincoln not pushed them forward. Or at least not come so quickly, or with such dreadful violence. I will emphasize only the events that he most certainly shaped according to his relentless will, alterations in the character of our country for which he was clearly responsible. For related developments touched by Lincoln's wand, I can have only a passing word. The major charges advanced here, if proved, are sufficient to impeach the most famous and respected of public men. More would only overdo.

The first and most obvious item in my bill of particulars for indictment concerns Lincoln's dishonesty and obfuscation with respect to the nation's future obligations to the Negro, slave and free. It was of course an essential ingredient of Lincoln's position that he make a success at being anti-Southern

From M. E. Bradford, *Remembering Who We Are: Observations of a Southern Conservative* (University of Georgia Press, 1985). Copyright © 1985 by University of Georgia Press. Reprinted by permission.

or antislavery without at the same time appearing to be significantly impious about the beginnings of the Republic (which was neither anti-Southern nor antislavery)—or significantly pro-Negro. He was the first Northern politician of any rank to combine these attitudes into a viable platform persona, the first to make his moral position on slavery in the South into a part of his national politics. It was a posture that enabled him to unite elements of the Northern electorate not ordinarily willing to cooperate in any political undertaking. And thus enabled him to destroy the old Democratic majority—a coalition necessary to preserving the union of the states. Then came the explosion. But this calculated posturing has had more durable consequences than secession and the Federal confiscation of property in slaves....

In the nation as a whole what moves toward fruition is a train of events set in motion by the duplicitous rhetoric concerning the Negro that helped make Abraham Lincoln into our first "sectional" president. Central to this appeal is a claim to a kind of moral superiority that costs absolutely nothing in the way of conduct. Lincoln, in insisting that the Negro was included in the promise of the Declaration of Independence and that the Declaration bound his countrymen to fulfill a pledge hidden in that document, seemed clearly to point toward a radical transformation of American society. Carried within his rejection of Negro slavery as a continuing feature of the American regime, his assertion that the equality clause of the Declaration of Independence was "the father of all moral principle among us," were certain muted corollaries. By promising that the peculiar institution would be made to disappear if candidates for national office adopted the proper "moral attitude" on that subject, Lincoln recited as a litany the general terms of his regard for universal human rights. But at the same time he added certain modifications to this high doctrine: modifications required by those of his countrymen to whom he hoped to appeal, by the rigid racism of the Northern electorate, and by "what his own feelings would admit." The most important of these reservations was that none of his doctrine should apply significantly to the Negro in the North. Or, after freedom, to what he could expect in the South. It was a very broad, very general, and very abstract principle to which he made reference. By it he could divide the sheep from the goats, the wheat from the chaff, the patriot from the conspirator. But for the Negro it provided nothing more than a technical freedom, best to be enjoyed far away. Or the valuable opportunity to "root, hog, or die." For the sake of such vapid distinctions he urged his countrymen to wade through seas of blood.

To be sure, this position does not push the "feelings" of that moralist who was our sixteenth president too far from what was comfortable for him. And it goes without saying that a commitment to "natural rights" which will not challenge the Black Codes of Illinois, which promises something like them for the freedman in the South, or else offers him as alternative the proverbial "one-way-ticket to nowhere" is a commitment of empty words. It is only an accident of political history that the final Reconstruction settlement provided a bit more for the former slave—principally, the chance to vote Republican; and even that "right" didn't last, once a better deal was made available to his erstwhile protectors. But the point is that Lincoln's commitment was precisely of the sort that the North was ready to make—while passing legislation to restrict the flow of Negroes into its own territories, elaborating its own system of segregation by race, and exploiting black labor through its representatives in a conquered South. Lincoln's double talk left his part of the country with a durable heritage of pious self-congratulation....

The second heading in this "case against Lincoln" involves no complicated pleading. Neither will it confuse any reader who examines his record with care. For it has to do with Lincoln's political economy, his management of the commercial and business life of the part of the Republic under his authority. This material is obvious, even though it is not always connected with the presidency of Abraham Lincoln. Nevertheless, it must be developed at this point. For it leads directly into the more serious charges upon which this argument depends. It is customary to deplore the Gilded Age, the era of the Great Barbecue. It is true that many of the corruptions of the Republican Era came to a head after Lincoln lay at rest in Springfield. But it is a matter of fact that they began either under his direction or with his sponsorship. Military necessity, the "War for the Union," provided an excuse, an umbrella of sanction, under which the essential nature of the changes being made in the relation of government to commerce could be concealed. Of his total policy the Northern historian Robert Sharkey has written, "Human ingenuity would have had difficulty in contriving a more perfect engine for class and sectional exploration: creditors finally obtaining the upper hand as opposed to debtors, and the developed East holding the whip over the underdeveloped West

and South." Until the South left the Union, until a High Whig sat in the White House, none of this return to the "energetic government" of Hamilton's design was possible. Indeed, even in the heyday of the Federalists it had never been so simple a matter to translate power into wealth. Now Lincoln could try again the internal improvements of the early days in Illinois. The difference was that this time the funding would not be restrained by political reversal or a failure of credit. For if anything fell short, Mr. Salmon P. Chase, "the foreman" of his "green printing office," could be instructed "to give his paper mill another turn." And the inflationary policy of rewarding the friends of the government sustained. The euphemism of our time calls this "income redistribution." But it was theft in 1864, and is theft today.

A great increase in the tariff and the formation of a national banking network were, of course, the cornerstones of this great alteration in the posture of the Federal government toward the sponsorship of business. From the beginning of the Republican Party Lincoln warned his associates not to talk about their views on these subjects. Their alliance, he knew, was a negative thing: a league against the Slave Power and its Northern friends. But in private he made it clear that the hidden agenda of the Republicans would have its turn, once the stick was in their hand. In this he promised well. Between 1861 and 1865, the tariff rose from 18.84 percent to 47.56 percent. And it stayed above 40 percent in all but two years of the period concluded with the election of Woodrow Wilson. Writes the Virginia historian Ludwell H. Johnson, it would "facilitate a massive transfer of wealth, satisfying the dreariest predictions of John C. Calhoun." The new Republican system of banking (for which we should note Lincoln was directly accountable) was part of the same large design of "refounding." The National Banking Acts of 1863 and 1864, with the earlier Legal Tender Act, flooded the country with $480 million of fiat money that was soon depreciated by about two-thirds in relation to specie. Then all notes but the greenback dollar were taxed out of existence, excepting only United States Treasury bonds that all banks were required to purchase if they were to have a share in the war boom. The support for these special bonds was thus the debt itself—Hamilton's old standby. Specie disappeared. Moreover, the bank laws controlled the money supply, credit, and the balance of power. New banks and credit for farms, small businesses, or small town operations were discouraged. And the Federalist model, after four score and seven years, finally achieved.

As chief executive, Lincoln naturally supported heavy taxes. Plus a scheme of tax graduation. The war was a legitimate explanation for these measures. Lincoln's participation in huge subsidies or bounties for railroads and in other legislation granting economic favors is not so readily linked to "saving the Union." All of his life Lincoln was a friend of the big corporations. He had no moral problem in signing a bill which gifted the Union Pacific Railway with a huge strip of land running across the West and an almost unsecured loan of $16,000 to $48,000 per mile of track. The final result of this bill was the Credit Mobilier scandal. With other laws favoring land speculation it helped to negate the seemingly noble promise of the Homestead Act of 1862—under which less than 19 percent of the open lands settled between 1860 and 1900 went to legitimate homesteaders. The Northern policy of importing immigrants with the promise of this land, only to force them into the ranks of General Grant's meatgrinder or into near slavery in the cities of the East, requires little comment. Nor need we belabor the rotten army contracts given to politically faithful crooks. Nor the massive thefts by law performed during the war in the South. More significant is Lincoln's openly disgraceful policy of allowing special cronies and favorites of his friends to trade in Southern cotton—even with "the enemy" across the line—and his calculated use of the patronage and the pork barrel. Between 1860 and 1880, the Republicans spent almost $10 million breathing life into state and local Republican organizations. Lincoln pointed them down that road. There can be no doubt of his responsibility for the depressing spectacle of greed and peculation concerning which so many loyal Northern men of the day spoke with sorrow, disappointment, and outrage....

A large part of the complaint against Lincoln as a political precedent for later declensions from the example of the Fathers has to do with his expansion of the powers of the presidency and his alteration of the basis for the Federal Union. With reference to his role in changing the office of chief magistrate from what it had been under his predecessors, it is important to remember that he defined himself through the war powers that belonged to his post. In this way Lincoln could profess allegiance to the Whig ideal of the modest, self-effacing leader, the antitype of Andrew Jackson, and, in his capacity as Commander-in-Chief, do whatever he wished. That is, if he could do it in the name of preserving the Union. As Clinton Rossiter has stated, Lincoln believed there were "no limits" to his powers if he exercised them in that "holy cause "

Gottfried Dietze compares Lincoln in this role to the Committee of Public Safety as it operated in the French Revolution. Except for the absence of mass executions, the results were similar. War is of course the occasion for concentration of power and the limitation of liberties within any nation. But an internal war, a war between states in a union of states, is not like a war to repel invasion or to acquire territory. For it is an extension into violence of a domestic political difference. And it is thus subject to extraordinary abuses of authority—confusions or conflations of purpose which convert the effort to win the war into an effort to effect even larger, essentially political changes in the structure of government. War, in these terms, is not only an engine for preserving the Union; it is also an instrument for transforming its nature. But without overdeveloping this structure of theory, let us shore it up with specific instances of presidential misconduct by Lincoln: abuses that mark him as our first imperial president. Lincoln began his tenure as a dictator when between April 12 and July 4 of 1861, without interference from Congress, he summoned militia, spent millions, suspended law, authorized recruiting, decreed a blockade, defied the Supreme Court, and pledged the nation's credit. In the following months and years he created units of government not known to the Constitution and officers to rule over them in "conquered" sections of the South, seized property throughout both sections, arrested upwards of twenty thousand of his political enemies and confined them without trial in a Northern "Gulag," closed over three hundred newspapers critical of his policy, imported an army of foreign mercenaries (of perhaps five hundred thousand men), interrupted the assembly of duly elected legislatures and employed the Federal hosts to secure his own re-election—in a contest where about thirty-eight thousand votes, if shifted, might have produced an armistice and a negotiated peace under a President McClellan. To the same end he created a state in West Virginia, arguing of this blatant violation of the explicit provisions of the Constitution that it was "expedient." But the worst of this bold and ruthless dealing (and I have given but a very selective list of Lincoln's "high crimes") has to do with his role as military leader per se: as the commander and selector of Northern generals, chief commissary of the Federal forces, and head of government in dealing with the leaders of an opposing power. In this role the image of Lincoln grows to be very dark—indeed, almost sinister.

The worst that we may say of Lincoln is that he led the North in war so as to put the domestic political priorities of his political machine ahead of the lives and the well-being of his soldiers in the field. The appointment of the venal Simon Cameron of Pennsylvania as his secretary of war, and of lesser hacks and rascals to direct the victualing of Federal armies, was part of this malfeasance. By breaking up their bodies, the locust hoard of contractors even found a profit in the Union dead. And better money still in the living. They made of Lincoln (who winked at their activities) an accessory to lost horses, rotten meat, and worthless guns. But all such mendacity was nothing in comparison to the price in blood paid for Lincoln's attempts to give the nation a genuine Republican hero. He had a problem with this project throughout the entire course of the war. That is, until Grant and Sherman "converted" to radicalism. Prior to their emergence all of Lincoln's "loyal" generals disapproved of either his politics or of his character. These, as with McClellan, he could use and discharge at will. Or demote to minor tasks. One thinks immediately of George G. Meade —who defeated Lee at Gettysburg, and yet made the mistake of defining himself as the defender of a separate Northern nation from whose soil he would drive a foreign Southern "invader." Or of Fitz John Porter, William B. Franklin, and Don Carlos Buell—all scapegoats thrown by Lincoln to the radical wolves. In place of these heterodox professionals, Lincoln assigned such champions of the "new freedom" as Nathaniel P. ("Commissary") Banks, Benjamin F. ("Beast") Butler, John C. Fremont, and John A. McClernand. Speaking in summary despair of these appointments (and adding to my list, Franz Sigel and Lew Wallace), General Henry Halleck, Lincoln's chief-of-staff, declared that they were "little better than murder." Yet in the East, with the Army of the Potomac, Lincoln make promotions even more difficult to defend, placing not special projects, divisions, and brigades but entire commands under the authority of such "right thinking" incompetents as John Pope (son of an old crony in Illinois) and "Fighting Joe" Hooker. Or with that "tame" Democrat and late favorite of the radicals, Ambrose E. Burnside. Thousands of Northern boys lost their lives in order that the Republican Party might experience rejuvenation, to serve its partisan goals. And those were "party supremacy within a Northern dominated Union." A Democratic "man-on-horseback" could not serve those ends, however faithful to "the Constitution as it is, and the Union as it was" (the motto of the Democrats) they might be. For neither of these commitments promised a Republican hege-

mony. To provide for his faction both security and continuity in office, Lincoln sounded out his commanders in correspondence (much of which still survives), suborned their military integrity, and employed their focus in purely political operation. Writes Johnson:

> Although extreme measures were most common in the border states, they were often used elsewhere too. By extreme measures is meant the arrest of anti-Republican candidates and voters, driving anti-Republican voters from the polls or forcing them to vote the Republican ticket, preventing opposition parties from holding meetings, removing names from ballots, and so forth. These methods were employed in national, state and local elections. Not only did the army interfere by force, it was used to supply votes. Soldiers whose states did not allow absentee voting were sent home by order of the President to swell the Republican totals. When voting in the field was used, Democratic commissioners carrying ballots to soldiers from their state were... unceremoniously thrown into prison, while Republican agents were offered every assistance. Votes of Democratic soldiers were sometimes discarded as defective, replaced by Republican ballots, or simply not counted.

All Lincoln asked of the ordinary Billy Yank was that he be prepared to give himself up to no real purpose—at least until Father Abraham found a general with the proper moral and political credentials to lead him on to Richmond. How this part of Lincoln's career can be reconciled to the myth of the "suffering savior" I cannot imagine.

We might dwell for some time on what injury Lincoln did to the dignity of his office through the methods he employed in prosecuting the war. It was no small thing to disavow the ancient

Christian code of "limited war," as did his minions, acting in his name. However, it is enough in this connection to remember his policy of denying medicines to the South, even for the sake of Northern prisoners held behind the lines. We can imagine what a modern "war crimes" tribunal would do with that decision. There may have been practicality in such inhumane decisions. *Practicality* indeed! As Charles Francis Adams, Lincoln's ambassador to the Court of St. James and the scion of the most notable family in the North, wrote in his diary of his leader, the "President and his chief advisers are not without the spirit of the serpent mixed in with their wisdom." And he knew whereof he spoke. For practical politics, the necessities of the campaign of 1864 had led Lincoln and Seward to a decision far more serious than unethical practices against prisoners and civilians in the South. I speak of the rejection by the Lincoln administration of peace feelers authorized by the Confederate government in Richmond: feelers that met Lincoln's announced terms for an end to the Federal invasion of the South. The emissary in this negotiation was sponsored by Charles Francis Adams. He was a Tennessean living in France, one Thomas Yeatman. After arriving in the United States, he was swiftly deported by direct order of the government before he could properly explore the possibility of an armistice on the conditions of reunion and an end to slavery. Lincoln sought these goals, but only on his terms. And in his own time. He wanted total victory. And he needed a still-resisting, impenitent Confederacy to justify his re-election. We can only speculate as to why President Davis allowed the Yeatman mission. We know that he expected little of such peace feelers. (There were many

in the last stages of the conflict.) He knew his enemy too well to expect anything but subjection, however benign the rhetoric used to disguise its rigor. Adam's peace plan was perhaps impossible, even if his superiors in Washington had behaved in good faith. The point is that none of the peace moves of 1864 was given any chance of success. Over one hundred thousand Americans may have died because of the Rail-Splitter's rejection of an inexpedient peace. Yet we have still not touched upon the most serious of Lincoln's violations of the Presidential responsibility. I speak, finally, of his role in bringing on the War Between the States.

There is, we should recall, a great body of scholarly argument concerning Lincoln's intentions in 1860 and early 1861. A respectable portion of this work comes to the conclusion that the first Republican president expected a "tug," a "crisis," to follow his election. And then, once secession had occurred, also expected to put it down swiftly with a combination of persuasion, force, and Southern loyalty to the Union. The last of these, it is agreed, he completely overestimated. In a similar fashion he exaggerated the force of Southern "realism," the region's capacity to act in its own pecuniary interest. The authority on Lincoln's political economy has remarked that the Illinois lawyer-politician and old line Whig always made the mistake of explaining in simple economic terms the South's hostile reaction to anti-slavery proposals. To that blunder he added the related mistake of attempting to end the "rebellion" with the same sort of simplistic appeals to the prospect of riches. Or with fear of a servile insurrection brought on by his greatest "war measure," the emancipation of slaves behind Southern lines, beyond his control. A full-scale Southern revolution, a revolution of all classes of men against the way he and some of his supporters thought, was beyond his imagination. There was no "policy" in such extravagant behavior, no human nature as he perceived it. Therefore, on the basis of my understanding of his overall career, I am compelled to agree with Charles W. Ramsdell concerning Lincoln and his war. Though he was no sadist and no war-monger, and though he got for his pains much more of a conflict than he had in mind, Lincoln hoped for an "insurrection" of some sort—an "uprising" he could use.

The "rational" transformation of our form of government which he had first predicted in the "Springfield Lyceum Speech" required some kind of passionate disorder to justify the enforcement of a new Federalism. And needed also for the voting representatives of the South to be out of their seats in the Congress. It is out of keeping with his total performance as a public man and in contradiction of his campaigning after 1854 not to believe that Lincoln hoped for a Southern attack on Fort Sumter. As he told his old friend Senator Orville H. Browning of Illinois: "The plan succeeded. They attacked Sumter—it fell, and thus did more service than it otherwise could." And to others he wrote or spoke to the same effect. If the Confederacy's offer of money for Federal property were made known in the North and business relations of the sections remained unaffected, if the Mississippi remained open to Northern shipping, there would be no support for "restoring" the Union on a basis of force. Americans were in the habit of thinking of the unity of the nation as a reflex of their agreement in the Constitution, of law as limit on government and on the authority of temporary

majorities, and of revisions in law as the product of the ordinary course of push and pull within a pluralistic society, not as a response to the extralegal authority of some admirable abstraction like equality. In other words, they thought of the country as being defined by the way in which we conducted our political business, not by where we were trying to go in body. Though once a disciple of Henry Clay, Lincoln changed the basis of our common bond away from the doctrine of his mentor, away from the patterns of compromise and dialectic of interests and values under a limited, Federal sovereignty with which we as a people began our adventure with the Great Compromise of 1787-1788. The nature of the Union left to us by Lincoln is thus always at stake in every major election, in every refinement in our civil theology; the Constitution is still to be defined by the latest wave of big ideas, the most recent mass emotion. Writes Dietze:

> Concentrations of power in the national and executive branches of government, brought about by Lincoln in the name of the people, were processes that conceivably complemented each other to the detriment of free government. Lincoln's administration thus opened the way for the development of an omnipotent national executive who as a spokesman for the people might consider himself entitled to do whatever he felt was good for the Nation, irrespective of the interests and rights of states, Congress, the judiciary, and the individual....

But in my opinion the capstone of this case against Lincoln... is what he had done to the language of American political discourse that makes it so difficult for us to reverse the ill effects of trends he set in motion with his executive fiat. When I say that Lincoln was our first

Puritan president, I am chiefly referring to a distinction of style, to his habit of wrapping up his policy in the idiom of Holy Scripture, concealing within the Trojan horse of his gasconade and moral superiority an agenda that would never have been approved if presented in any other form. It is this rhetoric in particular, a rhetoric confirmed in its authority by his martyrdom, that is enshrined in the iconography of the Lincoln myth preserved against examination by monuments such as the Lincoln Memorial, where his oversized likeness is elevated above us like that of a deified Roman emperor.

POSTSCRIPT

Was Abraham Lincoln America's Greatest President?

Biographer Stephen B. Oates, in *Abraham Lincoln: The Man Behind the Myths* (Harper & Row, 1984), suggests that Lincoln, at the time of his assassination, was perhaps the most hated president in history. Still, virtually no scholars in recent times have launched the type of assault exhibited by Bradford. Instead, since Arthur M. Schlesinger, Jr., first polled experts on the subject in 1948, historians consistently have rated Lincoln the nation's best chief executive. George Washington, Thomas Jefferson, Theodore Roosevelt, Franklin D. Roosevelt, and, Woodrow Wilson have all done well in the presidential popularity polls conducted by Gary Maranell (1970), Steve Neal (1982), and Robert K. Murray (1983), but none as well as Abraham Lincoln. Another president, Harry Truman, also ranked Lincoln in the category of "great" chief executives. In words that are echoed by Paludan, Truman wrote of Lincoln: "He was a strong executive who saved the government, saved the United States. He was a President who understood people, and, when it came time to make decisions, he was willing to take the responsibility and make those decisions, no matter how difficult they were. He knew how to treat people and how to make a decision stick, and that's why his is regarded as such a great Administration."

Lincoln also is the most written-about president. Students should consult Carl Sandburg, *Abraham Lincoln*, 6 vols. (Harcourt, Brace & World, 1926–1939), a poetic panorama that focuses upon the mythic Lincoln. Benjamin Thomas, *Abraham Lincoln: A Biography* (Alfred A. Knopf, 1952) and Stephen B. Oates, *With Malice Toward None: The Life of Abraham Lincoln* (Harper & Row, 1977) are both excellent one-volume biographies. David Donald, *Lincoln Reconsidered: Essays on the Civil War Era* (Alfred A. Knopf, 1956) and Richard N. Current, *The Lincoln Nobody Knows* (McGraw-Hill, 1958) offer incisive interpretations of many aspects of Lincoln's political career and philosophy. Psychoanalytical approaches to Lincoln are offered by George B. Forgie, *Patricide in the House Divided: A Psychological Interpretation* (W. W. Norton, 1979) and Dwight G. Anderson, *Abraham Lincoln: The Quest for Immortality* (Alfred A. Knopf, 1982). The events leading up to the Civil War are presented best in David M. Potter, *The Impending Crisis, 1848–1861* (Harper & Row, 1976). Lincoln's responsibility for the precipitating event of the war is explored in Richard N. Current, *Lincoln and the First Shot* (Lippincott, 1963). T. Harry Williams, *Lincoln and His Generals* (Alfred A. Knopf, 1952) looks at Lincoln as commander in chief and remains one of the best Lincoln studies. Peyton McCrary, *Abraham Lincoln and Reconstruction: The Louisiana Experiment* (Princeton University Press, 1978) examines Lincoln's plan for restoring the Southern states to the Union. For his role as "the Great Emancipator" and his attitudes toward race and slavery, see Benjamin Quarles, *Lincoln and the Negro* (Oxford University Press, 1962) and LaWanda Cox, *A Study in Presidential Leadership* (University of South Carolina Press, 1981). Gabor S. Boritt, ed., *The Historian's Lincoln: Pseudohistory, Psychohistory, and History* (University of Illinois Press, 1988) is a valuable collection.

ISSUE 17

Was Reconstruction a Success?

YES: Kenneth M. Stampp, from *The Era of Reconstruction, 1865–1877* (Alfred A. Knopf, 1965)

NO: Eric Foner, from *Reconstruction: America's Unfinished Revolution, ¯863–1877* (Harper & Row, 1988)

ISSUE SUMMARY

YES: Kenneth M. Stampp, a professor emeritus of history, argues that the period of Reconstruction after the Civil War succeeded economically, by consolidating the position of industrial capitalism; politically, by producing the most democratic governments the South had ever seen; and socially, by promoting ratification of the Fourteen and Fifteenth Amendments, which gave African Americans the promise of equal rights.

NO: Professor of history Eric Foner admits that radical rule produced a number of accomplishments, but he maintains that it failed to secure civil, political, and economic rights for southern blacks or to establish the Republican party as a permanent force in the South.

Given the complex political, economic, and social issues that America's leaders were forced to address in the post–Civil War years, it is not surprising that the era of Reconstruction (1865–1877) is shrouded in controversy. For the better part of the century following the war, historians typically characterized Reconstruction as a total failure that had proved detrimental to all Americans—northerners and southerners, whites and blacks. According to this traditional interpretation, a vengeful Congress, dominated by radical Republicans, imposed military rule upon the southern states. Carpetbaggers from the North, along with traitorous white scalawags and their black accomplices in the South, established coalition governments that rewrote state constitutions, raised taxes, looted state treasuries, and disenfranchised former Confederates while extending the ballot to the freedmen. This era finally ended in 1877, when courageous southern white Democrats successfully "redeemed" their region from "Negro rule" by toppling the Republican state governments.

This portrait of Reconstruction dominated the historical profession until the 1960s. One reason for this is that white historians (both northerners and southerners) who wrote about this period operated from two basic assumptions: (1) the South was perfectly capable of solving its own problems without federal government interference; and (2) the former slaves were intellectually inferior to whites and incapable of running a government (much less one in which some whites would be their subordinates). African American historians, such as W. E. B. Du Bois, wrote several essays and books that challenged this negative portrayal of Reconstruction, but their works were seldom taken seriously in the academic world and were rarely read by the general public. Still, these black historians foreshadowed the acceptance of revisionist interpretations of Reconstruction, which coincided with the successes of the civil rights movement (or "Second Reconstruction") in the 1960s.

Revisionist historians identified a number of accomplishments of the Republican state governments in the South and their supporters in Washington, D.C. For example, revisionists argued that the state constitutions written during Reconstruction were the most democratic documents that the South had seen up to that time. While taxes increased in the southern states, the revenues generated by these levies financed the rebuilding and expansion of the South's railroad network, the creation of a number of social service institutions, and the establishment of a public school system that benefited African Americans as well as whites. At the federal level, Reconstruction achieved the ratification of the Fourteenth and Fifteenth Amendments, which extended significant privileges of citizenship to African Americans, both North and South. Revisionists also placed the charges of corruption that were leveled by traditionalists against the Republican regimes in the South in a more appropriate context by insisting that political corruption was a *national* malady in the second half of the nineteenth century. Finally, revisionist historians sharply attacked the notion that African Americans dominated the reconstructed governments of the South. They pointed out that there were no black governors, only 2 black senators, and 15 black congressmen during this period. In no southern state did blacks control both houses of the legislature.

Kenneth M. Stampp's 1965 book *The Era of Reconstruction, 1865–1877*, is a classic statement of the revisionist viewpoint. Published a century after the end of the Civil War, this work offered a more balanced appraisal of Reconstruction and, in fact, emphasized the successes of the period of Republican rule in the South. In the excerpt that follows, Stampp admits the shortcomings of radical rule but insists that the Republican state governments chalked up a number of positive accomplishments during Reconstruction.

More recently, a third group of historians, the postrevisionists, have challenged the validity of the term *radical* as applied to the Reconstruction era by both traditional and revisionist historians. Eric Foner's essay represents an example of this postrevisionist approach. Although he recognizes a number of positive accomplishments, Foner concludes that Reconstruction must be judged a failure, part of an "unfinished revolution" initiated at the close of the Civil War. A number of forces, says Foner, conspired to eradicate the idealistic goal of full freedom for African Americans and the more pragmatic desire to establish an effective presence in the South for the Republican party.

YES

Kenneth M. Stampp

THE ERA OF RECONSTRUCTION, 1865–1877

RADICAL RULE IN THE SOUTH

When Lord Bryce, in the 1880's, wrote *The American Commonwealth*, he commented at length on the southern state governments created under the radical plan of reconstruction. What he had to say about them was not remarkable for its originality, but a few passages are worth quoting to give the flavor of the approaching historical consensus. "Such a Saturnalia of robbery and jobbery has seldom been seen in any civilized country.... The position of these [radical] adventurers was like that of a Roman provincial governor in the latter days of the Republic.... [All] voting power lay with those who were wholly unfit for citizenship, and had no interest as taxpayers, in good government.... [Since] the legislatures were reckless and corrupt, the judges for the most part subservient, the Federal military officers bound to support what purported to be the constitutional authorities of the State, Congress distant and little inclined to listen to the complaints of those whom it distrusted as rebels, greed was unchecked and roguery unabashed." In drawing this unpleasant picture Lord Bryce anticipated the generalizations of the Dunningites, as did many others.

Each of the eleven states of the former Confederacy, during all or part of the decade between 1867 and 1877, fell under the control of the radical Republicans. Tennessee was the first to be captured by them—indeed, it never had a Johnson government—but it was also the first to be lost. Tennessee was "redeemed," as southern white Democrats liked to call their return to power, as early as 1869. The last three states to be redeemed were South Carolina, Florida, and Louisiana, where the radical regimes lasted until the spring of 1877....

The first step in the organization of new southern state governments, as required by the reconstruction acts, was the election of delegates to conventions to frame new state constitutions. Since these conventions were controlled by the radicals, since they were the first political bodies in the South to contain Negroes, white conservatives subjected them to violent denunciation. They contemptuously called them "black and tan conventions"; they described the delegates as "baboons, monkeys, mules," or "ragamuffins and jailbirds." The South Carolina convention, according to a local newspaper, was the "maddest, most infamous revolution in history."

Yet, the invectives notwithstanding, there was nothing mad and little revolutionary about the work of these conventions. In fact, one of the most significant observations to be made about them is that the delegates showed little interest in experimentation. For the most part the radicals wrote orthodox state constitutions, borrowing heavily from the previous constitutions and from those of other states. To find fault with the way these southern constitutions were drawn is to find fault with the way most new state constitutions have been drawn; to criticize their basic political structure is to criticize the basic political structure of all the states. They were neither original nor unique. There was no inclination to test, say, the unicameral legislature, or novel executive or judicial systems.

Nor did the conventions attempt radical experiments in the field of social or economic policy. Since land reform had been defeated in Congress, a few delegates tried to achieve it through state action. The South Carolina convention provided for the creation of a commission to purchase land for sale to Negroes. In Louisiana, some Negro delegates proposed that when planters sold their estates purchases of more than 150 acres be prohibited. One white scalawag suggested a double tax on uncultivated land. A few delegates in other states advocated various policies designed to force the breakup of large estates. But these and all other attacks upon landed property were easily defeated.

As for the freedmen, the new constitutions proclaimed the equality of all men by quoting or paraphrasing the Declaration of Independence. Negroes were given the same civil and political rights as white men. "The equality of all persons before the law," proclaimed the Arkansas constitution, "is recognized and shall ever remain inviolate; nor shall any citizen ever be deprived of any right, privilege, or immunity, nor exempted from any burden or duty, on account of race, color, or previous condition." But on the subject of the social relations of Negroes and whites, most of the radical constitutions were evasive. South Carolina provided that its public schools were to be open to all "without regard to race or color," but only the state university actually made an attempt at integration. The Louisiana constitution declared: "There shall be no separate schools or institutions of learning established exclusively for any race by the State of Louisiana." In New Orleans from 1871 to 1877 about one third of the public schools were integrated, and white resistance was remarkably mild; but elsewhere in Louisiana segregation was the rule. Outside of South Carolina and Louisiana the radicals made no explicit constitutional provision for social integration. The Mississippi convention first defeated a proposal that segregated schools be required, then defeated a proposal that they be prohibited; the result was that the new constitution ignored the issue altogether. The only reference to segregation in it was a vague statement that "the rights of all citizens to travel upon public conveyances shall not be infringed upon, nor in any manner abridged in this state." But whether or not this clause prohibited segregation in public transportation is far from clear.

Yet, though the new constitutions were essentially conservative documents, they did accomplish some modest reforms, most of which were long overdue. In general, they eliminated certain undemocratic features of the old constitutions, for example, the inequitable systems of legislative apportionment that had discriminated against the interior regions of Virginia, North Carolina, and South Carolina. In the states of the Southeast, many offices that had previously been appointive were now made elective, and county government was taken out of the hands of local oligarchies. The rights of women were enlarged, tax systems were made more equitable, penal codes were reformed, and the number of crimes punishable by death was reduced. Most of the constitutions provided for substantial improvements in the state systems of public education and in the facilities for the care of the physically and mentally handicapped and of the poor.

In South Carolina, according to the historians of reconstruction in that state, the radical convention was an orderly body which accomplished its work with reasonable dispatch. It produced a constitution "as good as any other constitution that state has ever had"—good enough to remain in force for nearly two decades after the white Democrats regained control. This was, in fact, the state's first really democratic constitution; for, in addition to removing distinctions based on race, it provided for manhood suffrage, abolished property qualifications for office-holding, gave the voters the power for the first time to select the governor and other state officers, and transferred the election of presidential electors from the legislature to the voters. Another important provision related to public education: unlike the previous constitution, "the fundamental law of the state carried the obligation of universal education" and aimed at "the creation of a school system like that of Northern states." Other reforms included an extension of women's rights, adoption of the state's first divorce law, strengthening of the state's fiscal power, revision of the tax system, and modernization of the judiciary and of county government.

The responsible behavior of South Carolina's radical constitutional convention was in striking contrast to the angry and irresponsible criticism of the Democrats. Chiefly because of its provisions for racial equality, they ridiculed the new constitution as "the work of sixty-odd negroes, many of them ignorant and depraved, together with fifty white men, outcasts of Northern society, and Southern renegades, betrayers of their race and country." Specifically, the Democrats charged that manhood suffrage was designed to further the ambitions of "mean whites"; that Negro suffrage would bring ruin to the state; that the judicial reforms were "repugnant to our customs and habits of thought"; and that the public school requirements were "a fruitful source of peculant corruption." In spite of this fanciful criticism by a party whose chief appeal was to racial bigotry, the work of the radical convention was ratified by a majority of nearly three to one.

At the time that the new constitutions were ratified, elections were held for state officers and legislators. After the elections, when Congress approved of the constitutions, political power was transferred from the military to the new civil governments. Thus began the era of radical government in the South—an era which, according to tradition, produced some of the worst state administrations in American history. Some of the southern radical regimes earned their evil reputations, others did not; but viewed collectively, there was much in the record they made to justify severe criticism. To say that they were not always models of efficiency and integrity would be something of an understatement. "The great impediment of the Republican party in this state," wrote a Tennessee radical, "is the incompetence of its leaders.... After the war the loyal people in many counties had no competent men to be judges, lawyers or political leaders." Indeed, all of the radical governments suffered more or less from the incompetence of some, the dishonesty of a few, and above all the inexperience of most of the officeholders....

Meanwhile, the credit of some of the southern states was impaired as public debts mounted. In Florida the state debt increased from $524,000 in 1868 to $5,621,000 in 1874. In South Carolina a legislative committee reported that between 1868 and 1871 the state debt had increased from $5,403,000 to $15,768,000, but another committee insisted that it had increased to $29,159,000. By 1872 the debts of the eleven states of the former Confederacy had increased by approximately $132,000,000. The burden on taxpayers grew apace. Between 1860 and 1870 South Carolina's tax rate more than doubled, while property values declined by more than fifty per cent. In Tennessee a radical reported that during the first three years after the war taxes had increased sevenfold, though property had declined in value by one third. Throughout the South the tax burden was four times as great in 1870 as it had been in 1860. Such rates, complained many southern landholders, were confiscatory; and, indeed, taxes and other adversities of the postwar

years forced some of them to sell all or part of their lands. Sympathy for South Carolina's planter aristocracy caused a northern conservative to ask: "When before did mankind behold the spectacle of a rich, high-spirited, cultivated, self-governed people suddenly cast down, bereft of their possessions, and put under the feet of the slaves they had held in bondage for centuries?"

High taxes, mounting debts, corruption, extravagance, and waste, however, do not constitute the complete record of the radical regimes. Moreover, to stop with a mere description of their misdeeds would be to leave all the crucial questions unanswered—to distort the picture and to view it without perspective. For example, if some of these governments contained an uncommonly large number of inexperienced or incompetent officeholders, if much of their support came from an untutored electorate, there was an obvious reason for this. Howard K. Beale, in a critique of various reconstruction legends, observed that the political rulers of the ante-bellum South "had fastened ignorance or inexperience on millions of whites as well as Negroes and that it was this ignorance and inexperience that caused trouble when Radicals were in power.... Wealthy Southerners... seldom recognized the need for general education of even the *white* masses." Even in 1865 the men who won control of the Johnson governments showed little disposition to adopt the needed reforms. In South Carolina the Johnsonians did almost nothing to establish a system of public education, and at the time that the radicals came to power only one eighth of the white children of school age were attending school. The Negroes, of course, had been ignored entirely. It was probably no coincidence that the radicals made their poorest record in South Carolina, the state which had done the least for education and whose prewar government had been the least democratic.

As for the corruption of the radical governments, this phenomenon can be understood only when it is related to the times and to conditions throughout the country. One must remember that the administrations of President Grant set the moral tone for American government at all levels, national, state, and local. The best-remembered episodes of the Grant era are its numerous scandals—the Crédit Mobilier and the Whiskey Ring being the most spectacular of them—involving members of Congress as well as men in high administration circles. There were, moreover, singularly corrupt Republican machines in control of various northern states, including Massachusetts, New York, and Pennsylvania. But corruption was not a phenomenon peculiar to Republicans of the Gilded Age, as the incredible operations of the so-called Tweed Ring in New York City will testify. Indeed, the thefts of public funds by this organization of white Tammany Democrats surpassed the total thefts in all the southern states combined....

Most of the debt increases in the southern states resulted not from the thefts and extravagance of radical legislators but from the grants and guarantees they gave to railroad promoters, among whom were always some native white Democrats. In Florida more than sixty per cent of the debt incurred by the radical regime was in the form of railroad guarantee bonds. In North Carolina the radical government, prodded by the carpetbagger Milton S. Littlefield, a skilled lobbyist, issued millions of dollars of railroad bonds. Among those who benefited were many of the state's "best

citizens," including George W. Swepson, a local business promoter and Democrat. Most of Alabama's reconstruction debt —$18,000,000 out of $20,500,000—was in the form of state bonds issued to subsidize railroad construction, for which the state obtained liens upon railroad property. When one measure for state aid was before the Alabama legislature, many Democrats were among the lobbyists working for its passage. Yet, complained a radical, the Democrats who expect to profit from the bill "will use the argument that the Republican party had a majority in the Legislature, and will falsely, but hopefully, charge it upon Republicans as a partisan crime against the state."

Indeed, all of the southern states, except Mississippi, used state credit to finance the rebuilding and expansion of their railroads, for private sources of credit were inadequate. This policy had been developed before the war; it was continued under the Johnsonians; and in some cases when the Democrats overthrew the radicals there was no decline in the state's generosity to the railroads. While the radicals controlled the southern legislatures, not only they but many members of the Democratic minority as well voted for railroad bond issues. According to an historian of reconstruction in Louisiana, "Such measures were supported by members of both parties, often introduced by Democrats, in every case supported by a large majority of Democrats in both houses." The subservience of many postwar southern legislatures to the demands of railroad and other business promoters is in some respects less shocking than pathetic. For it expressed a kind of blind faith shared by many Southerners of both parties that railroad building and industrialization would swiftly solve all of their section's problems. No price seemed too high for such a miracle.

In several states, for obviously partisan reasons, the actual increase in the size of the public debt was grossly exaggerated. In Mississippi, for example, there was a durable legend among white Democrats that the radicals had added $20,000,000 to the state debt, when, in fact, they added only $500,000. Mississippi radicals had guarded against extravagance by inserting a clause in the constitution of 1868 prohibiting the pledging of state funds to aid private corporations —a clause which the conservatives, incidentally, had opposed. In Alabama, apart from railroad bonds secured by railroad property, the radicals added only $2,500,000 to the state debt. They did not leave a debt of $30,000,000 as conservatives claimed. In most other states, when loans to the railroads are subtracted, the increases in state debts for which the radicals were responsible appear far less staggering.

As for taxes, one of the positive achievements of many of the radical governments was the adoption of more equitable tax systems which put a heavier burden upon the planters. Before the war the southern state governments had performed few public services and the tax burden on the landed class had been negligible; hence the vehement protests of the landholders were sometimes as much against radical tax policies as against the alleged waste of taxpayers' money. The restoration governments often brought with them a return to the old inequitable fiscal systems. In Mississippi the subsequent claim of the conservatives that they had reduced the tax burden the radicals had placed upon property holders was quite misleading. The conservatives did

lower the state property tax, but, as a consequence, they found it necessary to shift various services and administrative burdens from the state to the counties. This led to an increase in the cost of county government, an increase in the rate of county taxes, and a net increase in total taxes, state and county, that Mississippi property holders had to pay.

As a matter of fact, taxes, government expenditures, and public debts were bound to increase in the southern states during the postwar years no matter who controlled them. For there was no way to escape the staggering job of physical reconstruction—the repair of public buildings, bridges, and roads— and costs had started to go up under the Johnson governments before the radicals came to power. So far from the expenditures of the reconstruction era being totally lost in waste and fraud, much of this physical reconstruction was accomplished while the radicals were in office. They expanded the state railroad systems, increased public services, and provided public school systems—in some states for the first time. Since schools and other public services were now provided for Negroes as well as for whites, a considerable increase in the cost of state government could hardly have been avoided. In Florida between 1869 and 1873 the number of children enrolled in the public schools trebled; in South Carolina between 1868 and 1876 the number increased from 30,000 to 123,000. The economies achieved by some of the restoration governments came at the expense of the schools and various state institutions such as hospitals for the insane. The southern propertied classes had always been reluctant to tax themselves to support education or state hospitals, and in many cases the budget-cutting of the conservatives simply strangled them.

Thus radical rule, in spite of its shortcomings, was by no means synonymous with incompetence and corruption; far too many carpetbagger, scalawag, and Negro politicians made creditable records to warrant such a generalization. Moreover, conditions were improving in the final years of reconstruction. In South Carolina the last radical administration, that of the carpetbagger Governor Daniel H. Chamberlain, was dedicated to reform; in Florida "the financial steadiness of the state government increased toward the end of Republican rule." In Mississippi the radicals made a remarkably good record. The first radical governor, James L. Alcorn, a scalawag, was a man of complete integrity; the second, Adelbert Ames, a carpetbagger, was honest, able, and sincerely devoted to protecting the rights of the Negroes. Mississippi radicals, according to Vernon L. Wharton, established a system of public education far better than any the state had known before; reorganized the state judiciary and adopted a new code of laws; renovated public buildings and constructed new ones, including state hospitals at Natchez and Vicksburg; and provided better state asylums for the blind, deaf, and dumb. The radicals, Wharton concludes, gave Mississippi "a government of greatly expanded functions at a cost that was low in comparison with that of almost any other state." No major political scandal occurred in Mississippi during the years of radical rule—indeed, it was the best governed state in the postwar South. Yet white conservatives attacked the radical regime in Mississippi as violently as they did in South Carolina, which suggests that their basic grievance was not corruption but race policy.

Finally, granting all their mistakes, the radical governments were by far the most democratic the South had ever known. They were the only governments in southern history to extend to Negroes complete civil and political equality, and to try to protect them in the enjoyment of the rights they were granted. The overthrow of these governments was hardly a victory for political democracy, for the conservatives who "redeemed" the South tried to relegate poor men, Negro and white, once more to political obscurity. Near the end of the nineteenth century another battle for political democracy would have to be waged; but this time it would be, for the most part, a more limited version—for whites only. As for the Negroes, they would have to struggle for another century to regain what they had won—and then lost—in the years of radical reconstruction. . . .

TRIUMPH OF THE CONSERVATIVES

During the state and presidential elections of 1876, when violence broke out in South Carolina, Florida, and Louisiana, President Grant would do nothing more than issue a sanctimonious proclamation. Indeed, when the outcome of that election was in dispute, Republicans had to bargain hard with southern Democrats in order to secure the peaceful inauguration of Rutherford B. Hayes. In one last sectional compromise, that of 1877, the Republicans promised to remove the remaining federal troops in the South, to be fair to Southerners in the distribution of federal patronage, and to vote funds for a number of southern internal improvements. In return, southern Democrats agreed to acquiesce in the inauguration of Hayes and to deal fairly with the Negroes.

The Compromise of 1877 signified the final end of radical reconstruction, for with the removal of federal troops, the last of the radical regimes collapsed. Soon after his inauguration President Hayes made a goodwill tour of the South. Conservative Democratic leaders, such as Governor Wade Hampton of South Carolina, greeted him cordially and assured him that peace and racial harmony now reigned in the South. Hayes tried hard to believe it, because he hoped so much that it was true.

"What is the President's Southern policy?" asked ex-Governor Chamberlain of South Carolina. Judged by its results, "it consists in the abandonment of Southern Republicans, and especially the colored race, to the control and rule not only of the Democratic party, but of that class at the South which regarded slavery as a Divine Institution, which waged four years of destructive war for its perpetuation, which steadily opposed citizenship and suffrage for the negro—in a word, a class whose traditions, principles, and history are opposed to every step and feature of what Republicans call our national progress since 1860."

It was in the 1870's, then, and not in 1865, that the idealism of the antislavery crusade finally died. Along with the loss of the idealism that had been one of the prime motivating forces behind radical reconstruction, the practical considerations also lost their relevance. Whereas in 1865 the urban middle classes still regarded the agrarian South and West as a serious threat, by the 1870's their position was consolidated and their power supreme. By then the leaders of business enterprise had so far penetrated the Democratic party and had so much influence among the so-called "redeemers" of the South that they no longer equated Re-

publican political defeat with economic disaster. Samuel J. Tilden, the Democratic presidential candidate in 1876, was a wealthy, conservative New York corporation lawyer, thoroughly "sound" on monetary, banking, and fiscal policy, in no respect unfriendly to business interests. Whichever way the presidential election of 1876 had gone, these interests could hardly have lost. Grover Cleveland, the only Democrat elected President between James Buchanan before the Civil War and Woodrow Wilson in the twentieth century, was also "sound" and conservative on all the economic issues of his day.

As for the Republican party, it too felt more secure than it had before. In 1865 it was still uncertain whether this party, born of crisis, could survive in a reunited, peaceful Union in which the slavery issue was resolved. But by the 1870's the party was firmly established, had an efficient, powerful, amply endowed organization, and had the unswerving support of a mass of loyal voters. True, the Republicans lost the congressional elections of 1874 and almost lost the presidency in 1876, but this could be attributed to the depression and abnormal conditions. Normally, in order to exist as a major national party, Republicans no longer needed the votes of southern Negroes. The reason for this was that during and since the war they had won control of the Old Northwest, once a stronghold of agrarianism and copperheadism. Indeed, a significant chapter in the history of reconstruction is the political and economic reconstruction of this flourishing region. The Civil War, the identification of the Republican party with nationalism and patriotism, the veteran vote, the Homestead Act, and federal appropriations for internal improvements all helped to make the states of the Old Northwest Republican strongholds. Moreover, the westward advance of the industrial revolution —the growth of urban centers such as Cleveland, Detroit, and Chicago— identified powerful economic groups in the Old Northwest with the industrial interests of the Northeast.

How these western states voted in the eleven presidential elections between 1868 and 1908 is significant when it is remembered that they had consistently gone Democratic before the Civil War. In eight elections the Old Northwest went Republican unanimously. Of the seven states in this region, Indiana voted Democratic three times, Illinois and Wisconsin once, the rest never. Thus, with the Old Northwest made safe for the Republican party, the political motive for radical reconstruction vanished, and practical Republicans could afford to abandon the southern Negro. With the decline of the idealism and the disappearance of the realistic political and economic considerations that had supported it, radical reconstruction came to an end.

* * *

Viewing radical reconstruction with its three chief motivating forces in mind, are we to call it a success or a failure? Insofar as its purpose was to consolidate the position of American industrial capitalism, it was doubtless a striking success. During the last three decades of the nineteenth century, social and economic reformers subjected irresponsible business entrepreneurs to constant attack, but they won no significant victories. In fact, they met constant defeat, climaxed by the failure of the Populists in the 1890's. With William McKinley, the conservative son of an Ohio industrialist, installed in power in 1897, American capitalism rode

to the end of the nineteenth century with its power uncurbed and its supremacy not yet effectively challenged. Above all, the conservative Democratic leaders of the New South were no longer enemies but allies.

Politically, radical reconstruction was also a success. Even though Republicans failed in their effort to establish an effective and durable organization in the South, they nevertheless emerged from the era of reconstruction in a powerful position. Most of their subsequent political victories were narrow; sometimes they lost a congressional campaign. But until Wilson's election in 1912, only once, in 1892, did the Democrats win control of the presidency and both houses of Congress simultaneously. And if conservative Republican Congressmen counted almost no Southerners in their caucus, they found a large number of southern Democrats remarkably easy to work with. The coalition of northern Republicans and southern Dixiecrats, so powerful in recent Congresses, was an important fact of American political life as early as the 1880's. The coalition had to be an informal one and had to endure a great deal of partisan rhetoric, but it was real nonetheless.

Finally, we come to the idealistic aim of the radicals to make southern society more democratic, especially to make the emancipation of the Negroes something more than an empty gesture. In the short run this was their greatest failure. In the rural South the basic socioeconomic pattern was not destroyed, for share-cropping replaced the antebellum slave-plantation system. Most of the upper-class large landowners survived the ordeal of war and reconstruction, and the mass of Negroes remained a dependent, propertyless peasantry. After reconstruction, in spite of the Fourteenth and Fifteenth Amendments, the Negroes were denied equal civil and political rights. In 1883 the Supreme Court invalidated the Civil Rights Act of 1875; in 1894 Congress repealed the Force Acts; and in 1896 the Supreme Court sanctioned social segregation if Negroes were provided "equal" accommodations. Thus Negroes were denied federal protection, and by the end of the nineteenth century the Republican party had nearly forgotten them. In place of slavery a caste system reduced Negroes to an inferior type of citizenship; social segregation gave them inferior educational and recreational facilities; and a pattern of so-called "race etiquette" forced them to pay deference to all white men. Negroes, in short, were only half emancipated.

Still, no one could quite forget that the Fourteenth and Fifteenth Amendments were now part of the federal Constitution. As a result, Negroes could no longer be deprived of the right to vote, except by extralegal coercion or by some devious subterfuge. They could not be deprived of equal civil rights, except by deceit. They could not be segregated in public places, except by the spurious argument that this did not in fact deprive them of the equal protection of the laws. Thus Negroes were no longer denied equality by the plain language of the law, as they had been before radical reconstruction, but only by coercion, by subterfuge, by deceit, and by spurious legalisms. For a time, of course, the denial of equality was as effective one way as the other; but when it was sanctioned by the laws of the Johnson governments and approved by the federal government, there was no hope. When, however, state-imposed discrimination was, in effect, an evasion of the supreme law of the land, the odds, in the long run, were on the side of the Negro.

The Fourteenth and Fifteenth Amendments, which could have been adopted only under the conditions of radical reconstruction, make the blunders of that era, tragic though they were, dwindle into insignificance. For if it was worth four years of civil war to save the Union, it was worth a few years of radical reconstruction to give the American Negro the ultimate promise of equal civil and political rights.

NO

Eric Foner

THE RIVER HAS ITS BEND

Thus, in the words of W. E. B. Du Bois, "the slave went free; stood a brief moment in the sun; then moved back again toward slavery." The magnitude of the Redeemer counterrevolution underscored both the scope of the transformation Reconstruction had assayed and the consequences of its failure. To be sure, the era of emancipation and Republican rule did not lack enduring accomplishments. The tide of change rose and then receded, but it left behind an altered landscape. The freedmen's political and civil equality proved transitory, but the autonomous black family and a network of religious and social institutions survived the end of Reconstruction. Nor could the seeds of educational progress planted then be entirely uprooted. While wholly inadequate for pupils of both races, schooling under the Redeemers represented a distinct advance over the days when blacks were excluded altogether from a share in public services.

If blacks failed to achieve the economic independence envisioned in the aftermath of the Civil War, Reconstruction closed off even more oppressive alternatives than the Redeemers' New South. The post-Reconstruction labor system embodied neither a return to the closely supervised gang labor of antebellum days, nor the complete dispossession and immobilization of the black labor force and coercive apprenticeship systems envisioned by white Southerners in 1865 and 1866. Nor were blacks, as in twentieth-century South Africa, barred from citizenship, herded into labor reserves, or prohibited by law from moving from one part of the country to another. As illustrated by the small but growing number of black landowners, businessmen, and professionals, the doors of economic opportunity that had opened could never be completely closed. Without Reconstruction, moreover, it is difficult to imagine the establishment of a framework of legal rights enshrined in the Constitution that, while flagrantly violated after 1877, created a vehicle for future federal intervention in Southern affairs. As a result of this unprecedented redefinition of the American body politic, the South's racial system remained regional rather than national, an outcome of great importance when economic opportunities at last opened in the North.

Nonetheless, whether measured by the dreams inspired by emancipation or the more limited goals of securing blacks' rights as citizens and free laborers, and establishing an enduring Republican presence in the South, Reconstruction can only be judged a failure. Among the host of explanations for this outcome, a few seem especially significant. Events far beyond the control of Southern Republicans—the nature of the national credit and banking systems, the depression of the 1870s, the stagnation of world demand for cotton—severely limited the prospects for far-reaching economic change. The early rejection of federally sponsored land reform left in place a planter class far weaker and less affluent than before the war, but still able to bring its prestige and experience to bear against Reconstruction. Factionalism and corruption, although hardly confined to Southern Republicans, undermined their claim to legitimacy and made it difficult for them to respond effectively to attacks by resolute opponents. The failure to develop an effective long-term appeal to white voters made it increasingly difficult for Republicans to combat the racial politics of the Redeemers. None of these factors, however, would have proved decisive without the campaign of violence that turned the electoral tide in many parts of the South, and the weakening of Northern resolve, itself a consequence of social and political changes that undermined the free labor and egalitarian precepts at the heart of Reconstruction policy.

For historians, hindsight can be a treacherous ally. Enabling us to trace the hidden patterns of past events, it beguiles us with the mirage of inevitability, the assumption that different outcomes lay beyond the limits of the possible. Certainly, the history of other plantation societies offers little reason for optimism that emancipation could have given rise to a prosperous, egalitarian South, or even one that escaped a pattern of colonial underdevelopment. Nor do the prospects for the expansion of scalawag support —essential for Southern Republicanism's long-term survival—appear in retrospect to have been anything but bleak. Outside the mountains and other enclaves of wartime Unionism, the Civil War generation of white Southerners was always likely to view the Republican party as an alien embodiment of wartime defeat and black equality. And the nation lacked not simply the will but the modern bureaucratic machinery to oversee Southern affairs in any permanent way. Perhaps the remarkable thing about Reconstruction was not that it failed, but that it was attempted at all and survived as long as it did. Yet one can, I think, imagine alternative scenarios and modest successes: the Republican party establishing itself as a permanent fixture on the Southern landscape, the North summoning the resolve to insist that the Constitution must be respected. As the experiences of Readjuster Virginia and Populist-Republican North Carolina suggest, even Redemption did not entirely foreclose the possibility of biracial politics, thus raising the question of how Southern life might have been affected had Deep South blacks enjoyed genuine political freedoms when the Populist movement swept the white counties in the 1890s.

Here, however, we enter the realm of the purely speculative. What remains certain is that Reconstruction failed, and that for blacks its failure was a disaster whose magnitude cannot be obscured by the genuine accomplishments that did endure. For the nation as a whole, the collapse of Reconstruction was a tragedy that deeply affected the course of its future development. If racism contributed to the undoing of Reconstruction, by the same token Reconstruction's demise and the emergence of blacks as a disenfranchised class of dependent laborers greatly facilitated racism's further spread, until by the early twentieth century it had become more deeply embedded in the nation's culture and politics than at any time since the beginning of the antislavery crusade and perhaps in our entire history. The removal of a significant portion of the nation's laboring population from public life shifted the center of gravity of American politics to the right, complicating the tasks of reformers for generations to come. Long into the twentieth century, the South remained a one-party region under the control of a reactionary ruling elite who used the same violence and fraud that had helped defeat Reconstruction to stifle internal dissent. An enduring consequence of Reconstruction's failure, the Solid South helped define the contours of American politics and weaken the prospects not simply of change in racial matters but of progressive legislation in many other realms.

The men and women who had spearheaded the effort to remake Southern society scattered down innumerable byways after the end of Reconstruction. Some relied on federal patronage to earn a livelihood. The unfortunate Marshall Twitchell, armless after his near-murder in 1876, was appointed U.S. consul at Kingston, Ontario, where he died in 1905. Some fifty relatives and friends of the Louisiana Returning Board that had helped make Hayes President received positions at the New Orleans Custom House, and Stephen Packard was awarded the consulship at Liverpool—

compensation for surrendering his claim to the governorship. John Eaton, who coordinated freedmen's affairs for General Grant during the war and subsequently took an active role in Tennessee Reconstruction, served as federal commissioner of education from 1870 to 1886, and organized a public school system in Puerto Rico after the island's conquest in the Spanish-American War. Most carpetbaggers returned to the North, often finding there the financial success that had eluded them in the South. Davis Tillson, head of Georgia's Freedman's Bureau immediately after the war, earned a fortune in the Maine granite business. Former South Carolina Gov. Robert K. Scott returned to Napoleon, Ohio, where he became a successful real estate agent—"a most fitting occupation" in view of his involvement in land commission speculations. Less happy was the fate of his scalawag successor, Franklin J. Moses, Jr., who drifted north, served prison terms for petty crimes, and died in a Massachusetts rooming house in 1906.

Republican governors who had won reputations as moderates by courting white Democratic support and seeking to limit blacks' political influence found the Redeemer South remarkably forgiving. Henry C. Warmoth became a successful sugar planter and remained in Louisiana until his death in 1931. James L. Alcorn retired to his Mississippi plantation, "presiding over a Delta domain in a style befitting a prince" and holding various local offices. He remained a Republican, but told one Northern visitor that Democratic rule had produced "good fellowship" between the races. Even Rufus Bullock, who fled Georgia accused of every kind of venality, soon reentered Atlanta society, serving, among other things, as president of the city's chamber of commerce. Daniel H. Chamberlain left South Carolina in 1877 to launch a successful New York City law practice, but was well received on his numerous visits to the state. In retrospect, Chamberlain altered his opinion of Reconstruction: a "frightful experiment" that sought to "lift a backward or inferior race" to political equality, it had inevitably produced "shocking and unbearable misgovernment." "Governor Chamberlain," commented a Charleston newspaper, "has lived and learned."

Not all white Republicans, however, abandoned Reconstruction ideals. In 1890, a group of reformers, philanthropists, and religious leaders gathered at the Lake Mohonk Conference on the Negro Question, chaired by former President Hayes. Amid a chorus of advice that blacks eschew political involvement and concentrate on educational and economic progress and remedying their own character deficiencies, former North Carolina Judge Albion W. Tourgée, again living in the North, voiced the one discordant note. There was no "Negro problem," Tourgée observed, but rather a "white" one, since "the hate, the oppression, the injustice, are all on our side." The following year, Tourgée established the National Citizens' Rights Association, a short-lived forerunner of the National Association for the Advancement of Colored People, devoted to challenging the numerous injustices afflicting Southern blacks. Adelbert Ames, who left Mississippi in 1875 to join his father's Minnesota flour-milling business and who later settled in Massachusetts, continued to defend his Reconstruction record. In 1894 he chided Brown University President E. Benjamin Andrews for writing that Mississippi during his governorship had incurred a debt of $20 million. The actual figure, Ames pointed out, was less

than 3 percent of that amount, and he found it difficult to understand how Andrews had made "a $19,500,000 error in a $20,000,000 statement." Ames lived to his ninety-eighth year, never abandoning the conviction that "caste is the curse of the world." Another Mississippi carpetbagger, Massachusetts-born teacher and legislator Henry Warren, published his autobiography in 1914, still hoping that one day, "possibly in the present century," America would live up to the ideal of "equal political rights for all without regard to race."

For some, the Reconstruction experience became a springboard to lifetimes of social reform. The white voters of Winn Parish in Louisiana's hill country expressed their enduring radicalism by supporting the Populists in the 1890s, Socialism in 1912, and later their native son Huey Long. Among the female veterans of freedmen's education, Cornelia Hancock founded Philadelphia's Children's Aid Society, Abby May became prominent in the Massachusetts women's suffrage movement, Ellen Collins turned her attention to New York City housing reform, and Josephine Shaw Lowell became a supporter of the labor movement and principal founder of New York's Consumer League. Louis F. Post, a New Jersey-born carpetbagger who took stenographic notes for South Carolina's legislature in the early 1870s, became a follower of Henry George, attended the founding meeting of the NAACP, and as Woodrow Wilson's Assistant Secretary of Labor, sought to mitigate the 1919 Red Scare and prevent the deportation of foreign-born radicals. And Texas scalawag editor Albert Parsons became a nationally known Chicago labor reformer and anarchist, whose speeches drew comparisons between the plight of Southern blacks and Northern industrial workers, and between the aristocracy resting on slavery the Civil War had destroyed and the new oligarchy based on the exploitation of industrial labor it had helped to create. Having survived the perils of Texas Reconstruction, Parsons met his death on the Illinois gallows after being wrongfully convicted of complicity in the Haymarket bombing of 1886.

Like their white counterparts, many black veterans of Reconstruction survived on federal patronage after the coming of "home rule." P. B. S. Pinchback and Blanche K. Bruce held a series of such posts and later moved to Washington, D.C., where they entered the city's privileged black society. Richard T. Greener, during Reconstruction a professor at the University of South Carolina, combined a career in law, journalism, and education with various government appointments, including a stint as American commercial agent at Vladivostok. Long after the destruction of his low country political machine by disenfranchisement, Robert Smalls served as customs collector for the port of Beaufort, dying there in 1915. Mifflin Gibbs held positions ranging from register of Little Rock's land office to American consul at Madagascar. Other black leaders left the political arena entirely to devote themselves to religious and educational work, emigration projects, or personal advancement. Robert G. Fitzgerald continued to teach in North Carolina until his death in 1919; Edward Shaw of Memphis concentrated on activities among black Masons and the AME Church; Richard H. Cain served as president of a black college in Waco, Texas; and Francis L. Cardozo went on to become principal of a Washington, D.C., high school. Aaron A. Bradley, the mili-

tant spokesman for Georgia's lowcountry freedmen, helped publicize the Kansas Exodus and died in St. Louis in 1881, while Henry M. Turner, ordained an AME bishop in 1880, emerged as the late nineteenth century's most prominent advocate of black emigration to Africa. Former Atlanta councilman William Finch prospered as a tailor. Alabama Congressman Jeremiah Haralson engaged in coal mining in Colorado, where he was reported "killed by wild beasts."

Other Reconstruction leaders found, in the words of a black lawyer, that "the tallest tree... suffers most in a storm." Former South Carolina Congressman and Lieut. Gov. Alonzo J. Ransier died in poverty in 1882, having been employed during his last years as a night watchman at the Charleston Custom House and as a city street sweeper. Robert B. Elliott, the state's most brilliant political organizer, found himself "utterly unable to earn a living owing to the severe ostracism and mean prejudice of my political opponents." He died in 1884 after moving to New Orleans and struggling to survive as a lawyer. James T. Rapier died penniless in 1883, having dispersed his considerable wealth among black schools, churches, and emigration organizations. Most local leaders sank into obscurity, disappearing entirely from the historical record. Although some of their children achieved distinction, none of Reconstruction's black officials created a family political dynasty—one indication of how Redemption aborted the development of the South's black political leadership. If their descendants moved ahead, it was through business, the arts, or the professions. T. Thomas Fortune, editor of the New York *Age,* was the son of Florida officeholder Emanuel Fortune; Harlem Renaissance writer Jean Toomer, the grandson of Pinchback; renowned jazz pianist Fletcher Henderson, the grandson of an official who had served in South Carolina's constitutional convention and legislature.

By the turn of the century, as soldiers from North and South joined to take up the "white man's burden" in the Spanish-American War, Reconstruction was widely viewed as little more than a regrettable detour on the road to reunion. To the bulk of the white South, it had become axiomatic that Reconstruction had been a time of "savage tyranny" that "accomplished not one useful result, and left behind it, not one pleasant recollection." Black suffrage, wrote Joseph Le Conte, who had fled South Carolina for a professorship at the University of California to avoid teaching black students, was now seen by "all thoughtful men" as "the greatest political crime ever perpetrated by any people." In more sober language, many Northerners, including surviving architects of Congressional policy, concurred in these judgments. "Years of thinking and observation" had convinced O. O. Howard "that the restoration of their lands to the planters provided for [a] future better for the negroes." John Sherman's recollections recorded a similar change of heart: "After this long lapse of time I am convinced that Mr. Johnson's scheme of reorganization was wise and judicious. . . . It is unfortunate that it had not the sanction of Congress."

This rewriting of Reconstruction's history was accorded scholarly legitimacy —to its everlasting shame—by the nation's fraternity of professional historians. Early in the twentieth century a group of young Southern scholars gathered at Columbia University to study the Reconstruction era under the guidance of Professors John W. Burgess and William A. Dunning. Blacks, their mentors taught, were "children" utterly incapable of appreciating the freedom that had been thrust upon them. The North did "a monstrous thing" in granting them suffrage, for "a black skin means membership in a race of men which has never of itself succeeded in subjecting passion to reason, has never, therefore, created any civilization of any kind." No political order could survive in the South unless founded on the principle of racial inequality. The students' works on individual Southern states echoed these sentiments. Reconstruction, concluded the study of North Carolina, was an attempt by "selfish politicians, backed by the federal government . . . to Africanize the State and deprive the people through misrule and oppression of most that life held dear." The views of the Dunning School shaped historical writing for generations, and achieved wide popularity through D. W. Griffith's film *Birth of a Nation* (which glorified the Ku Klux Klan and had its premiere at the White House during Woodrow Wilson's Presidency), James Ford Rhodes's popular multivolume chronicle of the Civil War era, and the national best-seller *The Tragic Era* by Claude G. Bowers. Southern whites, wrote Bowers, "literally were put to the torture" by "emissaries of hate" who inflamed "the negroes' egotism" and even inspired "lustful assaults" by blacks upon white womanhood.

Few interpretations of history have had such far-reaching consequences as this image of Reconstruction. As Francis B. Simkins, a South Carolina-born historian, noted during the 1930s, "the alleged horrors of Reconstruction" did much to freeze the mind of the white South in unalterable opposition to outside pressures for social change and to any thought of breaching Democratic ascendancy, eliminating segregation, or restoring suffrage to disenfranchised blacks. They also justified Northern indifference to the nullification of the Fourteenth and Fifteenth Amendments. Apart from a few white dissenters like Simkins, it was left to black writers to challenge the prevailing orthodoxy. In the early years of this century, none did so more tirelessly than former Mississippi Congressman John R. Lynch, then living in Chicago, who published a series of devastating critiques of the racial biases and historical errors of Rhodes and Bowers. "I do not hesitate to assert," he wrote, "that the Southern Reconstruction Governments were the best governments those States ever had." In 1917, Lynch voiced the hope that "a fair, just, and impartial historian will, some day, write a history covering the Reconstruction period, [giving] the actual facts of what took place."

Only in the family traditions and collective folk memories of the black community did a different version of Reconstruction survive. Growing up in the 1920s, Pauli Murray was "never allowed to forget" that she walked in "proud shoes" because her grandfather, Robert G. Fitzgerald, had "fought for freedom" in the Union Army and then enlisted as a teacher in the "second war" against the powerlessness and ignorance inherited from slavery. When the Works Progress Administration sent agents into the black belt during the Great Depression to interview former slaves, they found Reconstruction remembered for its disappointments and betrayals, but also as a time of hope, possibility, and accomplishment. Bitterness still lingered over the federal government's failure to distribute land or protect blacks' civil and political rights. "The Yankees helped free us, so they say," declared eighty-one-year old former slave Thomas Hall, "but they let us be put back in slavery again." Yet coupled with this disillusionment were proud, vivid recollections of a time when "the colored used to hold office." Some pulled from their shelves dusty scrapbooks of clippings from Reconstruction newspapers; others could still recount the names of local black leaders. "They made pretty fair officers," remarked one elderly freedman; "I thought them was good times in the country," said another. Younger blacks spoke of being taught by their parents "about the old times, mostly about the Reconstruction, and the Ku Klux." "I know folks think the books tell the truth, but they shore don't," one eighty-eight-year old former slave told the WPA.

For some blacks, such memories helped to keep alive the aspirations of the Reconstruction era. "This here used to be a good county," said Arkansas freedman Boston Blackwell, "but I tell you it sure is tough now. I think it's wrong— exactly wrong that we can't vote now." "I does believe that the negro ought to be given more privileges in voting," echoed Taby Jones, born a slave in South Carolina in 1850, "because they went through the reconstruction period with banners flying." For others, Reconstruction inspired optimism that better times lay ahead. "The Bible says, 'What has been will be again'," said Alabama sharecropper Ned Cobb. Born in 1885, Cobb never cast a vote in his entire life, yet he never forgot that outsiders had once taken up the black cause—an indispensable source of hope for one conscious of his own weakness in the face of overwhelming and hostile local power. When radical Northerners ventured South in the 1930s to help organize black agricultural workers, Cobb seemed almost to have been waiting for them: "The whites came down to bring emancipation, and left before it was over.... Now they've come to finish the job." The legacy of Reconstruction affected the 1930s revival of black militancy in other ways as well. Two leaders of the Alabama Share Croppers Union, Ralph and Thomas Gray, claimed to be descended from a Reconstruction legislator. (Like many nineteenth-century predecessors, Ralph Gray paid with his life for challenging the South's social order— he was killed in a shootout with a posse while guarding a union meeting.)

Twenty more years elapsed before another generation of black Southerners launched the final challenge to the racial system of the New South. A few participants in the civil rights movement thought of themselves as following a path blazed after the Civil War. Discussing the reasons for his involvement, one black Mississippian spoke of the time when "a few Negroes was admitted into the government of the State of Mississippi and to the United States." Reconstruction's legacy was also evident in the actions of federal judge Frank Johnson, who fought a twelve-year battle for racial justice with Alabama Gov. George Wallace. Johnson hailed from Winston County, a center of Civil War Unionism, and his great-grandfather had served as a Republican sheriff during Reconstruction. By this time, however, the Reconstruction generation had passed from the scene and even within the black community, memories of the period had all but disappeared. Yet the institutions created or consolidated after the Civil War—the black family, school, and church—provided the base from which the modern civil rights revolution sprang. And for its legal strategy, the movement returned to the laws and amendments of Reconstruction.

"The river has its bend, and the longest road must terminate." Rev. Peter Randolph, a former slave, wrote these words as the dark night of injustice settled over the South. Nearly a century elapsed before the nation again attempted to come to terms with the implications of emancipation and the political and social agenda of Reconstruction. In many ways, it has yet to do so.

POSTSCRIPT

Was Reconstruction a Success?

In *Nothing But Freedom: Emancipation and Its Legacy* (Louisiana State University Press, 1984), Foner compares the treatment of American freedmen with those who were newly emancipated in Haiti and the British West Indies. Only in the United States, he claims, were the former slaves given voting and economic rights. Although these rights had been stripped away from the majority of black southerners by 1900, Reconstruction had, nevertheless, created a legacy of freedom that inspired succeeding generations of African Americans.

C. Vann Woodward, the dean of southern historians, is less sanguine about the potential for success presented by the Reconstruction proposals. Despite all the successes enumerated by the revisionists, Woodward concludes that the experiment failed. In "Reconstruction: A Counterfactual Playback," an essay in his thought-provoking *The Future of the Past* (Oxford University Press, 1988), Woodward argues that former slaves were as poorly treated in the United States as they were in other countries. He also believes that the confiscation of former plantations and the redistribution of land to the former slaves would have failed in the same way that the Homestead Act of 1862 failed to generate equal distribution of government lands to poor white settlers. Finally, Woodward claims that reformers who worked with African Americans during Reconstruction failed because their goals were out of touch with the realities of the late nineteenth century.

Thomas Holt's *Black Over White: Negro Political Leadership in South Carolina During Reconstruction* (University of Illinois Press, 1977) is representative of state and local studies that employ modern social science methodology to yield new perspectives. While critical of white Republican leaders, Holt (who is African American) also blames the failure of Reconstruction in South Carolina on freeborn mulatto politicians, whose background distanced them economically, socially, and culturally from the masses of freedmen. Consequently, these political leaders failed to develop a clear and unifying ideology to challenge white South Carolinians who wanted to restore white supremacy.

The study of the Reconstruction period benefits from an extensive bibliography. Traditional accounts of Reconstruction include William Archibald Dunning's *Reconstruction, Political and Economic, 1865–1877* (Harper & Brothers, 1907); Claude Bowers's *The Tragic Era: The Revolution After Lincoln* (Riverside Press, 1929); and E. Merton Coulter's *The South During Reconstruction, 1865–1877* (Louisiana State University Press, 1947), which is considered by many to be the last major work written from the Dunning (or traditional) point of view. Early revisionist views are presented in W. E. B. Du Bois, *Black Reconstruction in America: An Essay Toward a History of the Part Which*

Black Folk Played in the Attempt to Reconstruct Democracy in America, 1860–1880 (Harcourt, Brace, 1935), which is a Marxist analysis of Reconstruction, and John Hope Franklin, *Reconstruction: After the Civil War* (University of Chicago Press, 1961). Foner's *Reconstruction: America's Unfinished Revolution, 1863–1877* (Harper & Row, 1988) includes a complete bibliography on the subject. Briefer overviews are available in Forrest G. Wood, *The Era of Reconstruction, 1863–1877* (Harlan Davidson, 1975) and Michael Perman, *Emancipation and Reconstruction, 1862–1879* (Harlan Davidson, 1987). One well-written study of a specific episode from the Reconstruction years is Willie Lee Rose's *Rehearsal for Reconstruction: The Port Royal Experiment* (Bobbs-Merrill, 1964), which describes the failed effort at land reform in the sea islands of South Carolina. Richard Nelson Current's *Those Terrible Carpetbaggers: A Reinterpretation* (Oxford University Press, 1988) is a superb challenge to the traditional view of those much-maligned Reconstruction participants. Finally, for collections of interpretive essays on various aspects of the Reconstruction experience, see Staughton Lynd, ed., *Reconstruction* (Harper & Row, 1967); Seth M. Scheiner, ed., *Reconstruction: A Tragic Era?* (Holt, Rinehart & Winston, 1968); and Edwin C. Rozwenc, ed., *Reconstruction in the South*, 2d ed. (D. C. Heath, 1972).

CONTRIBUTORS
TO THIS VOLUME

EDITORS

LARRY MADARAS is a professor of history and political science at Howard Community College in Columbia, Maryland. He received a B.A. from the College of the Holy Cross in 1959 and an M.A. and a Ph.D. from New York University in 1961 and 1964, respectively. He has also taught at Spring Hill College, the University of South Alabama, and the University of Maryland at College Park. He has been a Fulbright Fellow and has held two fellowships from the National Endowment for the Humanities. He is the author of dozens of journal articles and book reviews.

JAMES M. SoRELLE is an associate professor of history at Baylor University in Waco, Texas. He received a B.A. and an M.A. from the University of Houston in 1972 and 1974, respectively, and a Ph.D. from Kent State University in 1980. He has also taught at Ball State University, and, in addition to introductory courses in American history, he teaches upper-level sections in African American, urban, and late nineteenth- and twentieth-century U.S. history. His scholarly articles have appeared in *Houston Review, Southwestern Historical Quarterly,* and *Black Dixie: Essays in Afro-Texan History and Culture in Houston* (Texas A&M University Press, 1992), edited by Howard Beeth and Cary D. Wintz. He also has contributed entries to *The Handbook of Texas, The Oxford Companion to Politics of the World,* and *Encyclopedia of the Confederacy.*

STAFF

Mimi Egan   Publisher
Brenda S. Filley   Production Manager
Libra Ann Cusack   Typesetting Supervisor
Juliana Arbo   Typesetter
Lara Johnson   Graphics
Diane Barker   Proofreader
David Brackley   Copy Editor
David Dean   Administrative Editor
Richard Tietjen   Systems Manager

AUTHORS

LANCE BANNING is a professor of history and the author of numerous books and articles on the early republican period. His latest book is *Jefferson and Madison: Three Conversations from the Founding* (Madison House, 1995).

RICHARD E. BERINGER is a professor in the Department of History at the University of North Dakota in Grand Forkes, North Dakota. His publications include *The Elements of Confederate Defeat: Nationalism, War Aims, and Religion* (University of Georgia Press, 1989).

JOHN B. BOLES is the Allyn and Gladys Cline Professor of History at Rice University in Houston, Texas, and the managing editor of *The Journal of Southern History*. His publications include *The Great Revival, 1797–1805: Origins of the Southern Evangelical Mind* (University of Kentucky Press, 1972) and *Black Southerners, 1619–1869* (University of Kentucky Press, 1983).

PATRICIA U. BONOMI is a professor in the Department of History at New York University in New York City. She is the author of *Colonial Dutch Studies: An Interdisciplinary Approach* (New York University Press, 1988).

MORTON BORDEN is a professor emeritus of history at the University of California, Santa Barbara. He has also held academic appointments at the City College of the City University of New York, Ohio State University, the University of Montana, and the University of Madrid. He has written and edited numerous books on the American Revolution and on Federalism, and he is the author of *Jews, Turks, and Infidels* (University of North Carolina Press, 1984).

M. E. BRADFORD is a professor of English at the University of Dallas in Irving, Texas, where he has been teaching since 1967. He received a B.A. and an M.A. at the University of Oklahoma and a Ph.D. at Vanderbilt University. His publications include *Against the Barbarians and Other Reflections on Familiar Themes* (University of Missouri Press, 1992) and *Original Intentions: On the Making and Ratification of the United States Constitution* (University of Georgia Press, 1993).

JON BUTLER is the William Robertson Coe Professor of American History at Yale University in New Haven, Connecticut. He is the author of *Awash in a Sea of Faith: Christianizing the American People* (Harvard University Press, 1990).

CARL N. DEGLER is the Margaret Byrne Professor Emeritus of American History at Stanford University in Stanford, California. He is a member of the editorial board for the Plantation Society, and he is a member and a former president of both the American History Society and the Organization of American Historians. His book *Neither Black Nor White: Slavery and Race Relations in Brazil and the United States* (University of Wisconsin Press, 1972) won the 1972 Pulitzer Prize for history.

KAI T. ERIKSON is a professor of sociology and American studies at Yale University in New Haven, Connecticut. He has also taught at the University of Pittsburgh in Pennsylvania and at Emery University in Georgia. He is a fellow of the American Sociological Association and a member and a former president of the Eastern Sociological Society.

DAVID HACKETT FISCHER, considered one of the most imaginative historians in contemporary America, is the Earl Warren Professor of History at Brandeis University in Waltham, Massachusetts, where he has been teaching since 1962. He is also the chair of the Crown Program in American Cultural History. He received an A.B. from Princeton University in 1958 and a Ph.D. from Johns Hopkins University in 1962. His publications include *Historians' Fallacies: Toward a Logic of Historical Thought* (Harper & Row, 1970) and *Growing Old in America: The Bland-Lee Lectures Delivered at Clark University* (Oxford University Press, 1978).

ERIC FONER is the DeWitt Clinton Professor of History at Columbia University in New York City. He is the author of several books and articles on the Civil War and Reconstruction eras, including *Free Soil, Free Labor, Free Men: The Ideology of the Republican Party Before the Civil War* (Oxford University Press, 1970) and *Nothing But Freedom: Emancipation and Its Legacy* (Lousiana State University Press, 1983). He is also the author of *Tom Paine and Revolutionary America* (Oxford University Press, 1976). He received a Ph.D. in history from Columbia University in 1969.

ELIZABETH FOX-GENOVESE is a professor of southern history and literature at Emory University in Atlanta, Georgia. Her publications include *Feminism Without Illusions: A Critique of Individualism* (University of North Carolina Press, 1991).

THOMAS P. GOVAN (1907–1979) was a professor in the Department of History at the University of Oregon in Eugene, Oregon. He also held academic appointments at the University of the South and at New York University. His publications include *The Last Best Hope: A History of the United States* (Addison-Wesley, 1972).

NORMAN A. GRAEBNER is the Randolph P. Compton Professor Emeritus of History at the University of Virginia in Charlottesville, Virginia. He has held a number of other academic appointments, and he has received distinguished teacher awards at every campus at which he has taught. He has edited and written numerous books, articles, and texts on American history, including *Foundations of American Foreign Policy: A Realist Appraisal from Franklin to McKinley* (Scholarly Resources Press, 1985) and *Empire on the Pacific: A Study in American Continental Expansion*, 2d ed. (Regina Books, 1983).

MICHAEL F. HOLT is a professor of history at the University of Virginia in Charlottesville, Virginia. He has written a textbook called *The Political Crisis of the 1850s* (John Wiley & Sons, 1978), and he has collected his many journal articles in *Political Parties and American Political Development from the Age of Jackson to the Age of Lincoln* (Lousiana State University Press, 1992).

CAROL F. KARLSEN is an associate professor of history at the University of Michigan in Ann Arbor, Michigan.

STEVEN T. KATZ is a professor of Near Eastern studies at Cornell University in Ithaca, New York. He is the editor or author of a number of publications, including *Mysticism and Language* (Oxford University Press, 1992) and *The Holocaust in Historical Context: Ancient and Medieval Cases* (Oxford University Press, 1993).

ALLAN KULIKOFF is a professor of history at Northern Illinois University in DeKalb, Illinois.

SUZANNE LEBSOCK is a professor of history at Rutgers–The State University in New Brunswick, New Jersey. She is the coauthor, with Anne F. Scott, of *Virginia Women: The First Two Hundred Years* (Colonial Williamsburg Foundation, 1989).

JEAN BUTENHOFF LEE is a professor in the Department of History and a specialist on the Revolutionary War period at the University of Wisconsin–Madison. She is working on a book on revolution, war, and nationhood in Charles County, Maryland.

JAMES M. McPHERSON is the Edwards Professor of American History at Princeton University in Princeton, New Jersey. His publications include *Ordeal by Fire: The Civil War and Reconstruction* (McGraw-Hill, 1981) and *Abraham Lincoln and the Second American Revolution* (Oxford University Press, 1990).

GARY B. NASH is a professor of history and the dean of undergraduate curriculum development at the University of California, Los Angeles, where he has been teaching since 1966. He is also a member of the editorial board for *American Indian Culture and Research Journal*, and his publications include *Forging Freedom: The Formation of Philadelphia's Black Community, 1720–1840* (Harvard University Press, 1988).

PHILLIP SHAW PALUDAN is a professor of history at the University of Kansas in Lawrence, Kansas. In addition to his biography of Lincoln, he is the author of *A Covenant With Death: The Constitution, Law, and Equality in the Civil War Era* (University of Illinois Press, 1975); *Victims: A True Story of the Civil War* (University of Tennessee Press, 1988); and *A People's Contest: The Union and Civil War, 1861–1865* (Harper & Row, 1988).

MICHAEL PARENTI is a political scientist, lecturer, and social commentator. His publications include *Inventing Reality: Politics and the Mass Media* (St. Martin's Press, 1985) and *The Sword and the Dollar: Imperialism, Revolution, and the Arms Race* (St. Martin's Press, 1988).

ALBERT J. RABOTEAU is the Henry W. Putnam Professor of Religion at Princeton University in Princeton, New Jersey. His publications include *Slave Religion: The Invisible Institution in the Antebellum South* (Oxford University Press, 1978).

JOHN P. ROCHE (1923–1993) was the Olin Distinguished Professor of American Civilization and Foreign Affairs at the Fletcher School of Law and Diplomacy in Medford, Massachusetts, and the director of the Fletcher Media Institute.

DAVID J. ROTHMAN is a professor of history at Columbia University in New York City. He is the author, coauthor, or editor of numerous books, including *Low Wages and Great Sins: Two Antebellum American Views on Prostitution and the Working Girl* (Garland, 1987), coauthored with Sheila M. Rothman.

RAMÓN EDUARDO RUIZ is a professor at the Universidad Nacional Autonoma de Mexico in Mexico and a former professor of Latin American history at the University of California, San Diego. He is the author of *The Great Rebellion: Mexico, 1905–1924* (W. W. Norton, 1980), which won the Herbert C. Herring Prize, and *Triumphs and Tragedy: A History of the Mexican People* (W. W. Norton, 1992).

JOEL H. SILBEY is the President White Professor of History at Cornell University in Ithaca, New York. He has written several books and many important articles on the political parties during the

Civil War. He has published two major collections of articles, *The Partisan Imperative* (Oxford University Press, 1985) and *The American Political Nation, 1838–1893* (Stanford University Press, 1991).

KENNETH M. STAMPP is the Morrison Professor Emeritus of History at the University of California, Berkeley. He has written numerous books on southern history, slavery, and the Civil War, including *Slavery in the Ante-Bellum South* (Alfred A. Knopf, 1956); *And the War Came: The North and the Secession Crisis, 1860–1861* (Lousiana University Press, 1970); and *America in 1857: A Nation on the Brink* (Oxford University Press, 1990). He is also the general editor of *Records of Ante-Bellum Southern Plantations from the Revolution Through the Civil War* (University Publications of America, 1985).

DAVID E. STANNARD is a professor in the Department of American Studies at the University of Hawaii in Honolulu, Hawaii.

PETER TEMIN is a professor of industrial history in the Sloan School of Management at the Massachusetts Institute of Technology in Cambridge, Massachusetts. His publications include *Lessons from the Great Depression* (MIT Press, 1991).

The late **ALICE FELT TYLER** was a professor of history at the University of Minnesota in Minneapolis, Minnesota. Her publications include *The Foreign Policy of James G. Blaine* (University of Minnesota Press, 1927).

GORDON S. WOOD is the University Professor and a professor of history at Brown University in Providence, Rhode Island, where he has been teaching since 1969. He has also held academic appointments at Harvard University, the University of Michigan, and Cambridge University. His publications include *The Creation of the American Republic, 1776–1787* (North Carolina Press, 1969) and *The Radicalism of the American Revolution* (Alfred A. Knopf, 1991). He received his Ph.D. in history from Harvard University in 1964.

INDEX